American Experimental Fighters of WWII

The Pursuit of Excellence

Dedication

To Ashley B, Tim F and Peter H – greatest friends for so many years!

American Experimental Fighters of WWII

The Pursuit of Excellence

Tony Buttler MA FRAeS

First published 2024 by Crécy Publishing Ltd

ISBN 978 180035 3107

A CIP record for this book is available from the British Library

Publisher's Note: Every effort has been made to identify and correctly attribute photographic credits. Any error that may have occurred is entirely unintentional.

Printed in Turkey by Ozlem Print

Crécy Publishing Limited
1a Ringway Trading Estate
Shadowmoss Road
Manchester M22 5LH

www.crecy.co.uk

MIX
Paper | Supporting responsible forestry
FSC® C176481

FRONT COVER TOP The Convair XP-81. The I-40 jet was housed in the rear fuselage with the exhaust exiting beneath the rudder. *Convair via Alan Griffith*

FRONT COVER BOTTOM Very rare photograph of the Curtiss XF14C in flight. *Curtiss via Gerald H. Blazer*

FRONT COVER FLAP Perfect side view of the completed Northrop XP-79 prototype, with a close up of the wing tip rudder bellows which operated instead of conventional rudders, one of numerous advanced features employed on this aircraft. *Northrop via Alan Griffith*

BACK COVER TOP Excellent view of the Curtiss XP-60C in flight. *Curtiss via Dave Ostrowski/Alan Griffith*

BACK COVER LEFT The sole Grumman XP-50 to be built was given the military serial 40-3057. None of the available photographs show this painted on. *Grumman via Mark Aldrich*

BACK COVER MIDDLE In many ways the McDonnell XP-67 was pretty orthodox but it was the heavy fairing to wings and body that made it appear so unusual. *Gerald H. Balzer*

BACK COVER RIGHT Lovely view of the Curtiss 24-B in flight late in its career. Note the fixed undercarriage. *Curtiss via Gerald H. Balzer*

BACK COVER BOTTOM Black and white photos rarely show the different colours of the Grumman Skyrocket's fuselage and wing. Apart from the wing upper surface painted bright Navy Yellow and extending over the leading edges and wingtips, the exterior was silver lacquer over aluminium skin; Navy serial 1442 was then added in black on each fin. *Grumman*

HALF-TITLE PAGE View of the Lockheed XP-58 with undercarriage down, possibly while on the approach to land. *US National Archives RG-342 via Tony Landis*

TITLE PAGE TOP The Northrop XP-56 photographed on 22 March 1943 painted olive drab on top with gray undersides – standard Air Force colours. *Northrop via Gerald H. Balzer*

TITLE PAGE BOTTOM On 30 January 1945 test pilot Bob Lamson flew the Boeing XF8F-1 with engineer Bud Zerega squashed into the seat behind him. *National Archives RG-72 via Ryan Crierie*

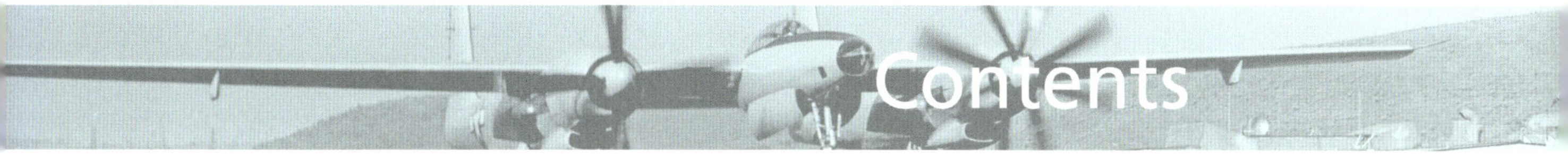

Contents

Acknowledgements

My sincere thanks go to the following for their help in contributing to the research for this book. It would have been far from complete without their help and I apologise if I have left anyone out.

The late John Aldaz; Mark Aldrich; Brooklands Museum Archive; Thomas Culbert (for research at NARA); Rich Dann; Tom Fey; Norman Friedman; George Cully (for research at Maxwell); Craig Kaston; Tony Landis (AFMC Historical Archives); Mike Machat; Kim McCutcheon (Aircraft Engine Historical Society/ AEHS); Kevin Morrow (for research at NARA); Dave Ostrowski; Terry Panopalis; William Pearce; Bill Spidle (Vought Archive); Josh Stoff and Julia Blum (Cradle of Aviation Museum); the staff of the Air Force Historical Research Agency (AFHRA) at Maxwell Air Force Base, and the staff of the US National Archives (NARA II) at College Park.

I must mention in particular the late Gerry Balzer for making his massive photo collection fully available to the author, Ryan Crierie, Tommy H. Thomason and Jared A. Zichek for kindly supplying the results of their substantial original research when it has been impossible for me to visit NARA during the last few years, and Alan Griffith and Mark Nankivil who have helped in so many ways. If I asked any of these gentlemen for help with photos or information on a specific aircraft, their replies usually brought forth droves of scans and images. One of the joys, and privileges, of doing historical work in the field of aviation is that one makes contact with or meets these great people and pretty soon one can consider them as friends! We are so lucky!!

Finally a huge thank you once again to Jeremy and all of the team at Crécy Publishing. You know how much I appreciate your efforts!

Glossary

AAC	Army Air Corps
AAF	Army Air Force (the Air Corps was renamed Army Air Force on 20 June 1941).
ACAS	Assistant Chief Air Staff
ADC	Air Defense Command
AFB	Air Force Base
AFFTC	Air Force Flight Test Center
AMC	Air Materiel Command
Anhedral	Downward slope of wing from root to tip.
Angle of Attack	The angle at which the wing is inclined relative to the airflow
Angle of Incidence	Angle between the chord line of the wing and the fore and aft datum line of the fuselage.
Aspect Ratio	Ratio of wingspan to mean chord, calculated by dividing the square of the span by the wing area.
ATSC	Air Technical Service Command. On 1 September 1944 the AAF's Materiel Command and Air Service Command were consolidated to form the ATSC.
BuAer	Bureau of Aeronautics (US Navy). Organisation responsible for the development and procurement of Navy aircraft between 1921 and 1960.
Capt	Captain
Cdr	Commander
Chord	Distance between centres of curvature of wing leading and trailing edges when measured parallel to the longitudinal axis.
CofG	Centre of gravity

Compressibility The property in air that permits it to change its density and pressure when subjected to a force or an alteration in speed. If the velocity of the air around an aircraft is greater than the speed of sound, the air cannot adjust smoothly to the shape of the aircraft, and so shock waves are formed. An aircraft's controllability can be affected when these shock waves first appear.

CP Circular Proposal

Critical Altitude The maximum attitude at which in standard atmosphere it was possible for a piston engine to maintain a specified power rating.

Dihedral Upward slope of wing from root to tip.

DoD Department of Defense

Gen General.

Gross Weight Usually signifies maximum weight with internal fuel plus all weapons aboard, but not external drop tanks.

HVAR High Velocity Aircraft Rocket

IAS Indicated Airspeed

Lt Lieutenant

mg Machine guns

NACA National Advisory Committee for Aeronautics (became NASA in 1958)

NAMC Naval Air Material Center in Philadelphia. Formed in July 1943 through the expansion of the Naval Aircraft Factory or NAF. This was a separate organisation within the Philadelphia Naval Shipyard and, besides building flying boats, during the war it operated as an experimental base for the development and testing of new naval equipment and technology.

NATC Naval Air Test Center at Patuxent River.

NAS Naval Air Station

nm Nautical mile

ONR Office of Naval Research (in Washington)

OPNAV Office of the Chief of Naval Operations

P & W Pratt & Whitney

RFP Request for Proposals

rpm Revolutions per minute

s.l Sea level

t/c Thickness/chord ratio

USAAC United States Army Air Corps

USAAF United States Army Air Force

USAF United States Air Force

USN United States Navy.

VBT Navy bomber-torpedo, carrier-based.

VF Navy fighter, carrier-based.

A note on US piston aeroengine designations. The type prefix related to the engine/cylinder arrangement or disposition. The letter 'R' prefix related to radial engines, 'L' for inline engines, 'H' for H-shaped, 'O' for Opposed, 'V' for V-shaped, 'W' for W-shaped, and 'X' for X-shaped.

Bibliography and source notes

Considerable primary source material has been consulted during the preparation of this work, in particular flight test reports, USAAF Case Histories and Final Reports, and original accounts from the BuAer Engineering Division's VF Design Branch. Drawings and photographs are credited individually unless taken from the author's collection and supplementary information was forthcoming from many secondary (published) sources, to fill gaps and to link parts of the story together. (Note: A Case History for the Grumman XP-50 has never been found.)

The Airplane Designs of Hughes Aircraft Company: Gerry R. Pape; American Aviation Historical Society Journal, Fall 2010.

The American Fighter: Enzo Angelucci with Peter Bowers; Haynes, 1987.

American Aircraft Development of the Second World War: Research, Experimentation and Modification 1939-1945: Bill Norton; Fonthill, 2019.

American Aircraft Development: World War Two Legacy: 1945-1953 and The Korean War: Bill= Norton; Fonthill, 2021.

American Secret Projects: Fighters, Bombers and Attack Aircraft 1937-1945: Tony Buttler and Alan Griffith; Crécy Publishing, 2015.

American Secret Pusher Fighters of World War II: Gerald H. Balzer; Specialty Press, 2008.

Ascent Tail-First: Francis Allen; Air Enthusiast 51, 1993.

Boeing Aircraft since 1916: Peter M. Bowers; Putnam, 1989.

The Boeing XF8B-1 Fighter: Last of the Line: Jared A. Zichek; Schiffer, 2007.

Boeing XF8B-1 Five-in-One Fighter: Rick Koehnen; Naval Fighters Number 65, Steve Ginter Books, 2005.

Case History of the Hughes D-2, D-5, F-11 Project: AAF Air Material Command, Wright Field, August 1946.

Case History of XP-49 Airplane: Historical Office Air Technical Service Command, Wright Field, December 1944.

Case History of XP-54 Airplane: Historical Office Air= Technical Service Command, Wright Field, November 1944.

Case History of XP-56 Airplane: Historical Division Intelligence, AAF Air Material Command, Wright Field, January 1946.

Case History of XP-58 Airplane: Historical Division Intelligence, Air Technical Service Command, Wright Field, December 1945.

Case History of XP-60 Series Airplane Projects: Historical Office, AAF Air Material Command, Wright Field, February 1945.

Case History of XP-62 Airplane Project: Historical Office, AAF Air Technical Service Command, Wright Field, August 1944.

Case History of XP-75, P-75 Airplane: Historical Office, Air Material Command, November 1944.

Case History of XP-77 Airplane Project: Historical Office, AAF Air Technical Service Command, Wright Field, December 1944.

Consolidated XP-81: Steve Ginter; Air Force Legends Number 214, Steve Ginter Books, 2006.

Convair Advanced Designs II: Secret Fighters, Attack Aircraft and Unique Concepts 1929-1973: Robert E. Bradley; Crécy Publishing, 2013.

Curtiss Aircraft 1907-1947: Peter M. Bowers; Putnam, 1979.

Curtiss Fighter Aircraft: A Photographic History 1917-1948: Francis H. Dean and Dan Hagedorn; Schiffer, 2007.

Effect of Single- and Dual-Rotation Propellers on Longitudinal Stability Characteristics of a 1/9th Scale Model of XP-62 Airplane with Flaps Retracted: I. G. Recant & A. R. Wallace; NACA Advance Confidential Report, October 1943.

Experimental & Prototype U.S. Air Force Jet Fighters: Dennis R. Jenkins & Tony R. Landis; Specialty Press, 2008.

Fighters over the Fleet: Naval Air Defence from Biplanes to the Cold War: Norman Friedman; Seaforth 2016.

Final Report of Development, Procurement, Performance and Acceptance of the XP-55 Airplane: Army Air Forces Technical Report No. 5306; Major C.R. Able, 22 October 1945.

Final Report of Development, Procurement and Acceptance of the XP-56 Airplane: Army Air Forces Technical Report No. 5714; Capt O. B. Thornton, 30 July 1948.

Final Report of Development, Procurement and Acceptance of the XP-47H Airplane: Army Air Forces Technical Report No. 5061; A. K. Dillon, 7 January 1947.

Final Report of the Development, Testing and Acceptance of the Republic XP-47J Airplane: Army Air Forces Technical Report No. 5504; Capt George D. Colchagoff, 20 June 1946.

Final Report of Inspection, Performance and Acceptance of Curtiss Wright Airplane Model XP-46: Army Corps Technical Report No. 4832; W. G. Logan, 17 October 1942.

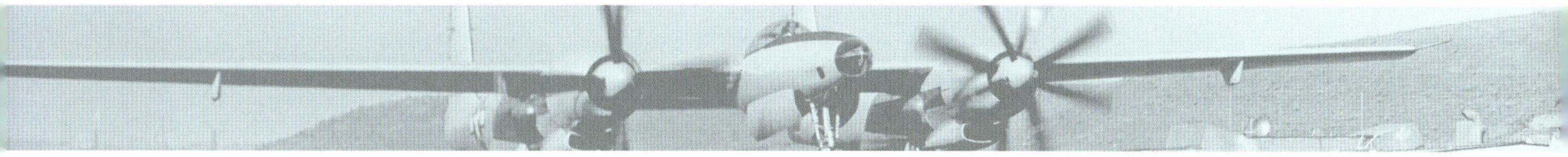

Final Report of the Procurement, Inspection, Testing and Acceptance of the General Motors Fisher Body Division XP-75 Airplane: Air Corps Report No. 5505; Major John F. Aldridge Jnr, 26 June 1946.

Final Report of the Procurement, Inspection, Testing and Acceptance of Lockheed XP-49 Airplane: Air Corps Report No. 5271; Major Charles R. Able, 22 August 1945.

Final Report of the XP-77 Airplane: Army Air Forces Technical Services Command Report No. 5399; Capt George D. Colchagoff, 15 November 1945.

Final Report on the Development of the Northrop XP-79B Airplane: Official Army Air Forces Air Material Command Report No. 5509; Capt. D. T. Tuttle, 11 July 1946.

Final Report on the Development, Procurement and Acceptance of the XP-83 Airplane: Army Air Forces Technical Report No. 5536; Major W.G. Logan and O.B. Thornton, 6 January 1947.

Final Report on the Procurement, Inspection, Testing and Acceptance of North American Model XP-51F, G & J Airplanes: Official Army Air Forces Air Material Command Report No. 5653; Werner R. Rankin, 4 December 1947.

Final Report on the XP-67 Airplane: Official Army Air Forces Air Material Command Report No. 5412; Major John F. Aldridge Jnr, 31 January 1946.

Final Report on the XP-68 Airplane: Army Air Forces Engineering Division Memorandum; Paul M.B. Smith, 17 April 1943.

Flight Tests of Internally Balanced, Sealed Ailerons on the Curtiss XP-60 Airplane: R.R. Gilruth; NACA Confidential Memorandum Report, July 1942.

Flying Wings and Radical Things: Northrop's Secret Aerospace Projects & Concepts 1939-1994: Tony Chong; Specialty Press, 2016.

General Motors Corporation: Fisher Body Division: Operating Report for the Six-Month Period to 1 November 1943.

Grumman Aircraft since 1929: Rene J Francillon; Putnam Aeronautical, 1989.

Grumman Preliminary Performance Demonstration Report No. 1551: XF5F-1 Airplane: March 1941.

Grumman XF5F-1 & XP-50 Skyrocket: David Lucabaugh and Bob Martin; Naval Fighter Number 31, Steve Ginter Books, 1995.

History of the VF Design Branch of the Engineering Division, Bureau of Aeronautics 1932-1945: Lt Patricia L. Offield; VF Design Branch, 1 February 1946.

Hughes' Twin Boomer: Lin Hendrix; Aeroplane, October 1984.

Last of the Line: Boeing's XF8B-1 Multi-purpose Fighter: Francis Allen; Air Enthusiast 55, Autumn 1994.

Lockheed Aircraft since 1913: René J. Francillon; Putnam, 1987.

McDonnell XP-67 "Moonbat": Steve Richardson and Peggy Mason; Osprey Publishing X-Planes No. 17, 2022.

North American P-51 Mustang: Malcolm V. Lowe; Crowood Press, 2009.

Preliminary Drag Tests in Flight of Low-Drag Wing on the Curtiss XP-60 Airplane: Eastman N. Jacobs; NACA Confidential Memorandum Report, 27 May 1942.

Problems of Gas-Turbine Propeller Combinations: Frank W. Davis; Aeronautical Engineering Review, April 1948.

Prop-Nosed Dual-Jet XP-81 Put Through AAF Trials: Aviation, March 1946.

Report of Joint Fighter Conference NAS Patuxent River, MD 16-23 October 1944: Technical Editor Francis H. Dean; Schiffer Military History, 2004.

Ryan FR-1 Fireball and XF2R-1 Dark Shark: Steve Ginter; Naval Fighter Number 28, Steve Ginter Books, 1995.

Summary of Model XP-81 Flight Test Results 7 February 1945 to 7 April 1945; Consolidated-Vultee Aircraft Corporation Report DEVF-1469, 4 June 1945.

The Secret Years: Flight Testing at Boscombe Down: Tim Mason; Hikoki/Crécy, 2010.

US Experimental & Prototype Aircraft Projects: Fighters 1939-1945: Bill Norton; Specialty Press, 2008.

Three websites were also consulted:

Ryan Crierie has posted an excellent selection of Standard Aircraft Characteristics Sheets on www.alternatewars.com.

Paul Martel-Mead has created the splendid web-based 'Secret Projects' forum which can be found on www.secretprojects.co.uk.

And the late Joseph F. Baugher's site www.joebaugher.com is a good source for all manner of additional snippets of information.

Introduction

During World War II America's air arms fielded some excellent fighter types – the Lockheed P-38 Lightning, Republic P-47 Thunderbolt and North American P-51 Mustang, plus the Navy's Grumman F6F Wildcat and Vought F4U Corsair. But, like all of the major 'aviation' countries around the world, US manufacturers also produced plenty of prototypes which, for whatever reason, did not progress as far as entering service. This book brings together the fighter prototypes produced and flown between 1940 and 1946, their descriptions being compiled in the main using original documents such as case histories and flight test reports.

The twenty-four chapters embrace incredible diversity of design and layout, showing in particular the creative flair that was present in the US aircraft industry during the war. Although essentially 'failures' in that they did not enter production, it should never be forgotten that the design and development of any new aircraft is a learning process and the types examined here contributed much to the industry's knowledge. Each prototype is given its own chapter while one appendix looks at a report which summarises the Army Air Forces' various ongoing fighter development programmes as they stood in November 1942, thus presenting a picture for a single point in time. A second appendix briefly reviews a selection of production fighter types that were kitted out a trials and testbed aircraft.

Those prototypes ordered by the Army Air Corps (Army Air Force from June 1941) are covered first, the 'P-' system of designations making the process of listing them here quite straightforward. However, listing the Navy aircraft in the second section was more difficult because of the very different system used by this Service at that time. The best approach seemed to be to put these aircraft in alphabetical order of manufacturer, and not for example by date of first flight.

For a British author there is a problem with a title for a US subject containing the phrase '...of World War II' because America entered the conflict (officially) in December 1941 when war had broken out in Europe in September 1939 (the US had of course been contributing to the Allied cause in many ways well before December 1941). The difference between the two dates raises the question of when to start? In the end I decided, as a sort of half-way point, to include any new prototypes which had made their maiden flights in 1940. I hope readers are happy with this decision, which in part was guided by the completion of my recent book for Hikoki called *Propeller Twilight: The Last Generation of British Piston Engine Fighters* – I really wanted this volume to discuss primarily the last generation of American propeller-driven fighters, but here there is space for prototypes only.

The chapters include two early jet prototypes which flew before the end of the war, plus a reconnaissance type, the Hughes XF-11, because at one brief point this was given an 'XP-' pursuit designation. A weak excuse perhaps, but the XF-11 was a great looker and had the 'build' of a night fighter. And there is the Ryan XF2R-1 Dark Shark which made its maiden flight well after the end of the war. However, this one is gets in because it was a development of Ryan's earlier FR Fireball and documents show that it was under consideration by the time the Pacific conflict came to an end. The XF2R-1 does rather get missed by books covering World War II and those looking at post-war developments – it seems to fall in between the two. Here it gets its chance. Finally, a few unbuilt projects and studies and unrealised ideas are included after new information has come to light since the publication of *American Secret Projects: Fighters, Bombers and Attack Aircraft 1937-1945* (written in company with Alan Griffith).

The diversity of design and layout between the aircraft covered here is quite astonishing, with lightweight fighters, heavy fighters, streamlined aircraft, pusher powerplants, swept wings, flying wings, mixed powerplants and then the first jets. And it is extraordinary how many of the programmes were 'sabotaged' by their powerplants – their choice of engine. In several cases the engine itself was discontinued, or said engine would not provide the projected degree of power to give the fighter the necessary performance. A nightmare for the design teams concerned, but so interesting to write about!

As with my previous titles covering American subjects, there is the question of spelling and phraseology. British spellings ('programme' rather than 'program') are in general used throughout, but not when quoting original documents which refer to items such as these in American form. All data figures are presented both in imperial and metric units.

Readers familiar with my earlier work will know my passion for fighter-type aeroplanes, and so can imagine how putting a volume like this together is always a great joy. I hope those of you who take a look at it will also enjoy the contents, and hopefully find at least some information and illustrations that will be new to you. Thank you to everyone for your support over many years.

Tony Buttler MA AMRAeS
Bretforton, May 2024

1 Curtiss XP-46

The Curtiss XP-46 was one of the new types that came out of a design competition held in 1939 to find a new modern lightweight fighter for the US Army Air Force. This followed the issuing of Army Circular Proposal 39-770 and Specification XC-616 and resulted in a number of prototypes and unbuilt projects being allocated a pursuit 'P-' number, Curtiss having been declared the third place winner of the design competition. The original Curtiss submission had been a redesigned and partially stripped-down version of the same manufacturer's P-40 Warhawk, which was now on order, and it was to be fitted with a newly-developed engine from Allison called the V1710. This aircraft would also draw on recent experience and advances in Europe – for example automatic leading-edge slots were to be fitted to the outer part of the XP-46's wing to improve the effectiveness of the ailerons at lower speeds. The XP-46 was designed by Curtiss chief designer Donovan R. Berlin.

Go-ahead for the development of the Curtiss design was first recommended in a letter, dated 1 September 1939, sent by the Chief of the AAF's Material Division to the Chief of the Air Corps. This was authorised later that month, two prototypes, serial numbers 40-3053 and 40-3054, were subsequently ordered, it was initially planned to procure 195 examples for Fiscal Year 1941, and it was hoped that speeds of the order of 425mph (684km/h) at 15,000ft (4,572m) would be obtained. However, in October, as a result of the experience of the French Air Force with the Curtiss P-36 on the

The first XP-46 prototype to fly was the second example, 40-3054, which, because certain equipment had been left out, was redesignated XP-46A. This picture of this aircraft was taken on 12 September 1941. ***Dave Ostrowski/ Alan Griffith***

Another view of 40-3054 taken on 12 September 1941. To the author's eyes the XP-46 presents an appearance which looks quite advanced for 1939 when it was first designed, but which then looks strangely out of date for say 1942, when it might have been in production. *Dave Ostrowski/Alan Griffith*

ABOVE AND CENTRE The photographer completed a set of walk around views of 40-3054 on 12 September. These shots confirm that the aircraft has no armament installed. *Dave Ostrowski/Alan Griffith*

Western front, the original Curtiss design's fire power was increased and other necessary changes incorporated into the design. These were as follows:

a. The addition of provisions for four 0.30in (7.62mm) calibre wing guns as an alternate load.

b. Another 65lb (29.5kg) of armour plate to protect the pilot from rear gunfire.

c. The addition of external wrapping of the fuel tanks as a means of leak proofing (this idea of wrapping the outside of the fuel tanks was an early attempt to make them self-sealing).

Fitted now with ten guns the XP-46 had become the most heavily-armed American fighter up to this point in time. Unfortunately, however, in order to carry this additional armament and protective armour it was found necessary to add 30sq.ft (2.79sq.m) to the existing wing area. Consequently, these changes brought a reduction in the estimated maximum speed from 425mph down to 403mph (684km/h to 648km/h) at 15,000ft (4,572m). Then in February 1940 it was decided to further alter the armament installation by making provisions for replacing two of the 0.30in (7.62mm) calibre free firing guns in each wing with a single 0.50in (12.70mm) calibre gun. A Change Order to cover the decrease in performance, and various other incidental changes, was prepared and approved on 3 May 1941.

The XP-46 mock-up was inspected at the Contractor's plant at Buffalo, New York State, on 4 March 1940. Then in June 1940 Curtiss was given permission to hold back the XP-46 project for one month so that the Contractor's full effort could be devoted to the P-40D development of its current production fighter, which in fact offered clearer production possibilities than did the XP-46. Next, in September 1940 permission was granted for Curtiss to further delay completion of the two XP-46 prototypes, partly because their engines were still to be delivered, and partly because the load on the shop and engineering force at the Contractor's factory was still excessive in connection with the P-40D programme.

Flight test

In order to expedite delivery of the first aircraft, to gather flight test data reasonably quickly, and to get the project back up to speed, it was decided to make space provisions only, and not fit, the armament installation in the second XP-46 prototype, along with other equipment such as the radio. Consequently this aircraft was redesignated XP-46A and the complete armament installation was then to be introduced in the first XP-46 prototype. As a result the 'stripped' second prototype became the first to fly, on 15 February 1941.

This and succeeding flights quickly revealed the need for a larger oil cooler, because the heat rejection values of the Allison engine had proved to be higher

than originally anticipated, which caused overheating of the power unit. This alteration resulted in a further decrease in maximum speed of 9mph (14km/h), but the enlarged cooler installation was flight tested for the first time on 10 May 1941. Several other minor problems also had to be overcome – for example, prior to the installation of the new oil coolers, some trouble had been experienced with the landing gear fairing not closing properly when the wheels were retracted.

Then, with the arrival of warmer weather in June, the problem of cooling trouble raised its head again. This time Curtiss looked at solving the problem by modifying the design of the air duct, but little advantage was gained from this alteration. Another problem, not solved until July, was engine roughness and it was only after a new propeller had been fitted that no further trouble of this sort was encountered. At last, with these problems now sorted, the Contractor's Demonstration flight tests on the XP-46 were conducted at Buffalo by its own test pilots between 9 and 16 September 1941, though AAF representatives observed these flights and declared that they were satisfactory.

Both the XP-46A and XP-46 were delivered to Wright Field on 11 and 22 September respectively to begin their official performance trials. However, as soon as the XP-46A had arrived some additional backfire screens were installed to prevent any backfire of the V1710, and thus any consequent damage to the airframe. Following this installation work, and also a 50-hour check, the XP-46A 40-3054 was passed to Final Assembly to have flight test instruments installed and its ammunition doors reinforced. Considerable delay was now experienced in getting this aircraft weighed, due to other aeroplanes currently having priority on the scales, and during this period the new fighter's leading edge slots were wired closed.

Unfortunately, in the air, in its 'lightweight' form, the XP-46A 40-3054 could only just manage the officially desired maximum speed of 410mph (660km/h) at 15,000ft (4,572m). What was even more disappointing was that the fully equipped XP-46 prototype, with all of its extra weight, could reach a maximum of only 355mph (571km/h)!

When the project had first come under discussion, and when it was on order, this new Curtiss aircraft had appeared to offer considerable potential but, as its development progressed, interest in the XP-46

ABOVE Some excellent and very rare colour images were taken of the XP-46. This shows the pilot's instrument panel. *Dave Ostrowski/Alan Griffith*

ABOVE LEFT Starting the engine. *Dave Ostrowski/Alan Griffith*

BELOW XP-46 engine installation. *Dave Ostrowski/Alan Griffith*

Engine run up. Apart from the rudder, both aircraft appear to have retained their natural metal finish. These are also early views when only a few national markings have been applied, and as yet no serial numbers. *Dave Ostrowski/Alan Griffith*

fell away. This was in part due to the inaccessibility of its internal equipment and accessories that made maintenance of the aircraft difficult, and that did bring some criticism on to the manufacturer. On top of this, with such a shortfall in performance Curtiss had to pay a financial penalty for not achieving the required limits. However, prior to the disappointing performance becoming apparent, any plans to put the type into production had been abandoned anyway during 1940, to be replaced by the P-40D version of the current Curtiss fighter. There had also apparently been plans for an export P-46A version for France.

Port side three-quarter angle front view of the XP-46 40-3063 taken on 16 October 1941. *Dave Ostrowski/ Alan Griffith*

XP-46 structure

The Curtiss XP-46 was a single-place single-engine all-metal low wing monoplane which had both wing and tail surfaces of full cantilever construction. Its wing had a multi-cellular aluminium light alloy struture which was internally braced and joined at the aircraft's centreline, and the wing was given split trailing edge flaps and wing tip slats which would operate simultaneously with the flaps by the flap operating mechanism; the wing tips could be removed. Both the horizontal tail and the fin also employed flush riveted multi-cellular aluminium alloy construction, both were made in one piece and were internally braced. The Frise-type ailerons, elevators, and rudder were made in aluminium alloy but had fabric covering.

XP-46's fuselage had a flush riveted monocoque structure employing aluminium alloy sheet covering, formed bulkheads and extruded stringers. The engine mount had a welded steel tubular structure and the V1710-39 drove a Curtiss three-blade 10ft 6in (3.20m) diameter constant speed electrically controlled propeller; the radiator was positioned beneath the fuselage and featured a hot air exit ramp to create some forward thrust. The wide-track, inwardly-retracting undercarriage was of a single-strut pneumatic oleo type and the standard armament consisted of two synchronized 0.50in (12.7mm) calibre machine guns in the nose and four 0.30in (7.62mm) calibre free firing guns in each wing. Maximum fuel load was 156galUS (591lit).

Further walk-around views of 40-3063 from 16 October 1941. Again no armament has been fitted but the positions of the wing guns are marked faintly, and are just visible on the front angle view. *Dave Ostrowski/Alan Griffith*

Superb view of the unarmed XP-46A 40-3064 conducting a high speed run. *Dave Ostrowski/Alan Griffith*

Although slightly out of focus this very rare air-to-air shot of an XP-46, in colour, just has to be included. *Dave Ostrowski/Alan Griffith*

Finally, 40-3063 is at last carrying its serial number. It appears that the aircraft may now have some of its guns in place, with ports in the wing and lower nose. *Dave Ostrowski/Alan Griffith*

XP-46 data

Length:	30ft 2in (9.20m)
Wing span:	34ft 3.75in (10.46m)
Wing area:	208sq.ft (19.34sq.m)
j165:	5,625lb (2,552kg)
Gross weight:	7,081lb (3,212kg)
Maximum take-off weight:	7,665lb (3,477kg)
Powerplant:	1 x 1,150hp (858kW) Allison V1710-39 liquid-cooled engine
Maximum speed (at 7,081lb/3,212kg weight):	355mph (571km/h) at 12,200ft (3,719m) **XP-46A:** 410mph (660km/h) at 15,000ft (4,572m)
Maximum rate of climb:	2,600ft/min (792m/min) at 10,000ft (3,048m)
Service ceiling:	29,500ft (8,992m)
Absolute ceiling:	30,500ft (9,296m)
Maximum range:	717 miles (1,154km)
Armament:	2 x 0.50in (12.70mm) machine guns in nose, 8 x 0.30in (7.62mm) machines guns – 4 in each wing panel

2 Lockheed XP-49

The Lockheed XP-49 prototype was in layout, appearance and structure near identical to the manufacturer's highly successful P-38 Lightning production series of fighters, with the exception of the engine installation plus the introduction of a pressurised cabin. Initially the XP-49 appears to have offered some promise, but severe delays in particular with the delivery of its Continental IV1430 engines meant that, when it finally became airborne, the prototype's chance had passed.

Design competition

The design to which the designation XP-49 was allocated had been submitted to a design competition prompted by Circular Proposal 39-775 of 11 March 1939, which had requested proposals for a new twin-engined, high performance high altitude interceptor for the Army Air Force. It was also specified that the submitted designs should use as many features and structure as possible from current existing fighter types, though this was not possible for some of the manufacturers who submitted proposals. The armament requirement had initially comprised two 0.30in (7.62mm) machine guns, two 0.50in (12.7mm) machine guns and one 37mm cannon, but this would change.

The appraisal report for this competition, compiled during July and early August 1939, reviewed designs submitted by Bellanca (Models 33-220 and 33-230), Burnelli (Model XPB-1), Grumman (Model G-41) and Lockheed (Model 222). It placed Lockheed first with the greatest number of points for figure of merit, Grumman runner up, Bellanca third and Burnelli fourth. Prototypes were ordered from Lockheed and Grumman and the resulting aircraft are covered in this and the next chapters.

The original Lockheed Model 222 submission was to be powered by Allison V1710 engines, as per the firm's P-38 Lightning fighter on which the proposal was based; there was also a Model 222A (drawing dated 15 June 1939) to be fitted with Pratt & Whitney R1830 radial units. The 222 had an estimated maximum speed of 420mph (676km/h) at 20,000ft (6,096m) and a design gross weight of 13,500lb (6,124kg), and as proposed it had a span of 52ft (15.85m) and length 37ft 10in (11.53m). Powered by turbo-supercharged Wright R1820

The sole Lockheed XP-49 prototype. *Lockheed/Gerald H. Balzer via Mark Nankivil, Greater St Louis Air & Space Museum*

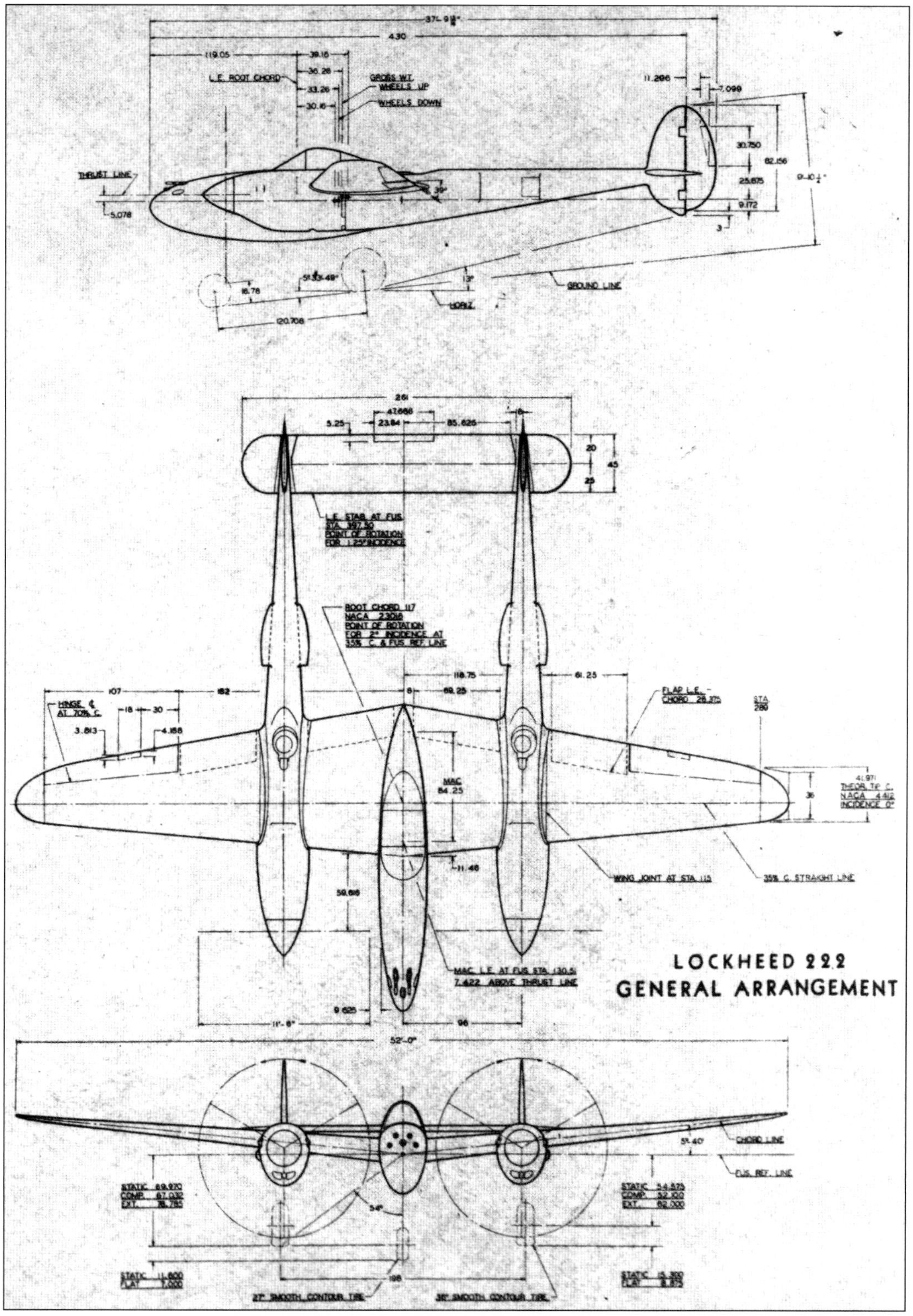

The original Lockheed Model 222 proposal which became the XP-49. *US National Archives RG341 via Jared Zichek*

engines the Grumman project offered the same maximum speed with a gross weight of 9,787lb (4,439kg); span as proposed was 42ft (12.80m) and length 28ft 8.5in (8.75m).

The Burnelli (16 and 17 June 1939) also came in two forms – both had an estimated maximum speed of 421mph (677km/h) at 20,000ft (6,096m) and their gross weights were 11,860lb (5,380kg) when fitted with a tricycle undercarriage and 11,660lb (5,289kg) with a four-wheel version (here there was a tail wheel in the rear of each boom). Bellanca's Model 33-220 (4 July 1939) offered 400mph (644km/h) at 20,000ft (6,096m) with a gross weight of 9,709lb (4,404kg), whilst the larger Model 33-230 was quoted as giving 408mph (656km/h) at 20,000ft (6,096m) with a gross weight of 11,277lb (5,115kg).

In July 1939 Major-General H. H. Arnold, Chief of the Air Corps, noted in a memo that "it is believed

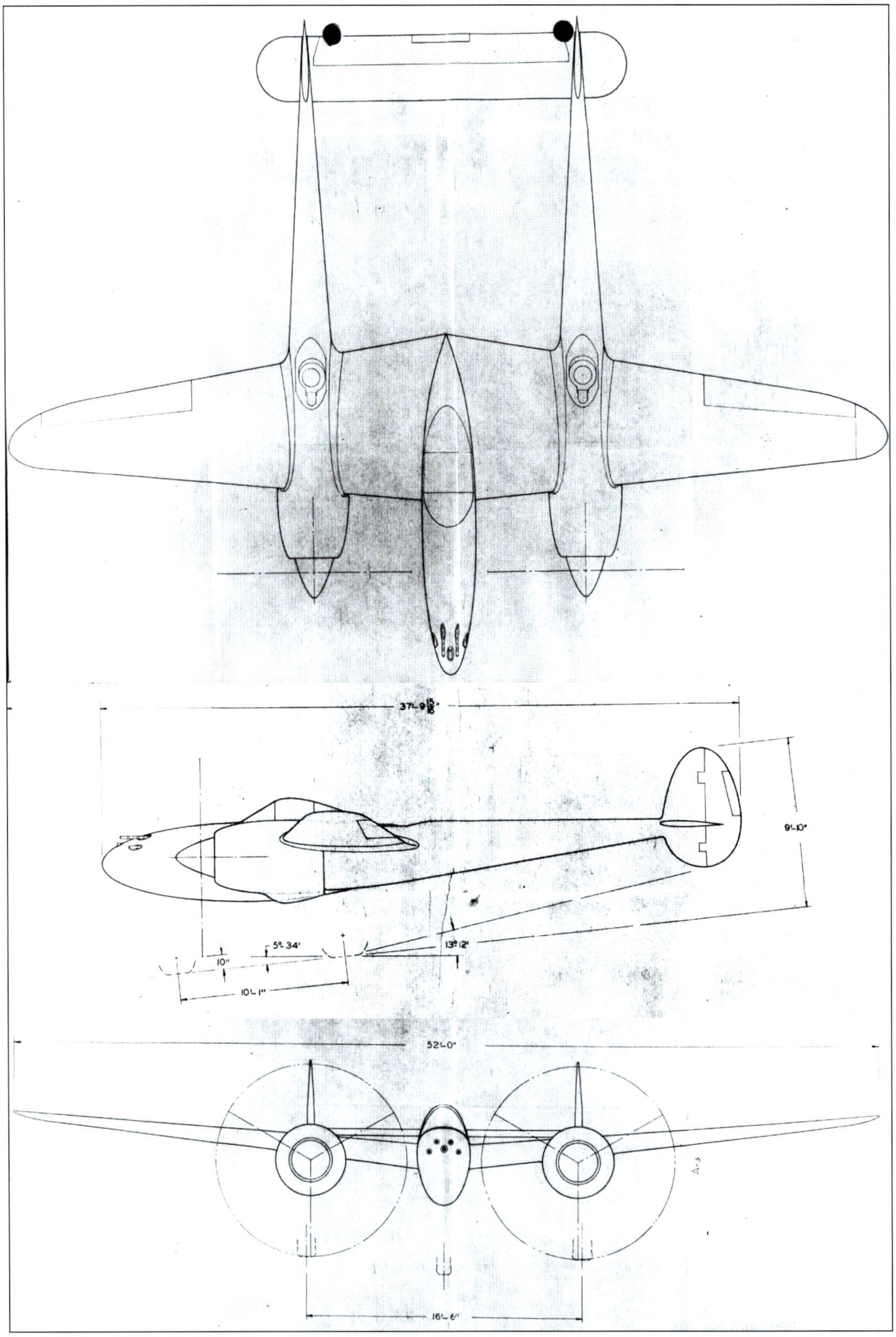

Drawing from the 39-775 design competition showing the Lockheed Model 222A fitted with Pratt & Whitney R1830 radial engines. Note the concentration of armament in the nose – four machine guns and one cannon (15.6.39). *US National Archives RG341 via Jared Zichek*

that both airplanes (the XP-49 and Grumman XP-50) warrant further development as advanced models of twin-engine interceptor pursuit aircraft, although the present status of their development does not warrant quantity procurement at this time." Nevertheless, consideration had been made towards ordering 66 production P-49s and indeed, at one point, authority was given to procure these machines. At this stage the XP-49 was some 4ft 6in (1.37m) longer and roughly 4,000lb (1,814kg) heavier than a standard P-38.

The AAF Board recommended the development of the Lockheed submission but with a new type of high power engine which, it was hoped, would result in a high estimated maximum speed, possibly

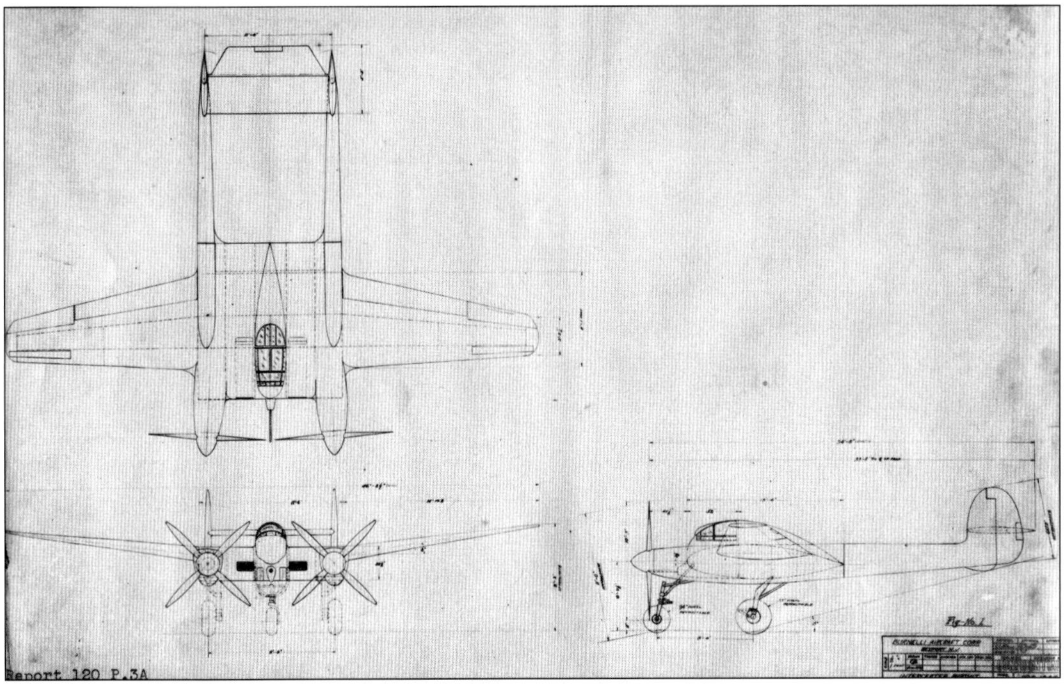

Official documents noted that the designs submitted by Bellanca and Burnelli were "not sufficiently reduced in practice to warrant consideration for either quantity of experimental procurement." This is the Burnelli proposal fitted with a tricycle undercarriage (17.6.39). *US National Archives RG341 via Jared Zichek*

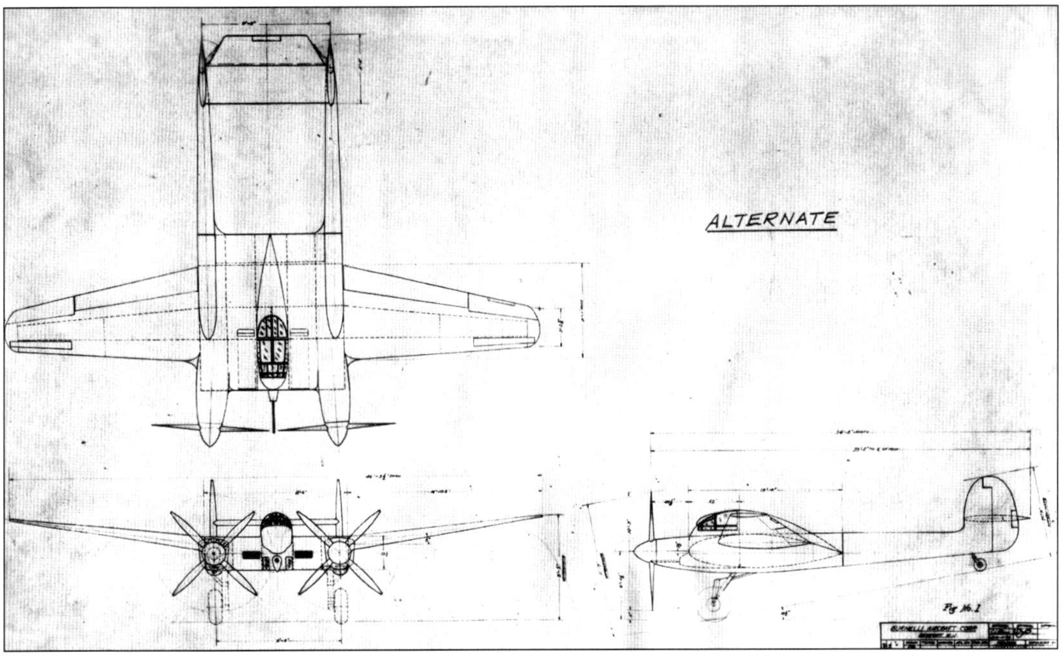

The same Burnelli Model XPB-1 design now fitted with a four-wheel undercarriage. Both Burnelli offerings had a span of 46ft 3.5in (14.11m) and length 35ft 2in (10.72m), the barrel of the 37mm protruded beneath the nose and they had four-blade propellers driving Allison V1710 engines. Note how the engine nacelles are angled slightly outwards to prevent the propellers from overlapping (16.6.39). *US National Archives RG341 via Jared Zichek*

in the region of 500mph (805km/h). In January 1940 the Chief of the Air Corps approved the ordering of two Pratt & Whitney X1800 liquid-cooled engines for the XP-49 but, once it had become clear that this manufacturer was no longer considering further developments in this form of aero engine, in March 1940 the Continental IV1430, fitted with turbo-superchargers, was confirmed instead as the powerplant for the new fighter.

The X1800 was an H-shaped unit designed to offer between 1,800hp and 2,000hp (1,342kW and 1,491kW) and at one stage this engine was earmarked to power, besides the XP-49, the Vultee XP-54, Curtiss XP-55, Northrop XP-56 and Lockheed XP-58, all of which have their own chapters in this book. However, on the test bench the engine's performance fell short of expectations, considerable further development was needed, and consequently in October 1940 Pratt & Whitney closed its development of the X1800, henceforth concentrating on radial piston engines; only one X1800 was completed. With the X1800 in place the XP-49's estimated top speed had been 473mph (761km/h) at 20,000ft (6,096m); the lower power rating of the Continental XIV1430 (1,600hp/1,193kW) meant that the XP-49's maximum would now be, most likely, rather less (one source gives 458mph/737km/h at 25,000ft/7,620m).

Lockheed did propose replacing the X1800s in production P-49s with two Wright R2160 Tornado

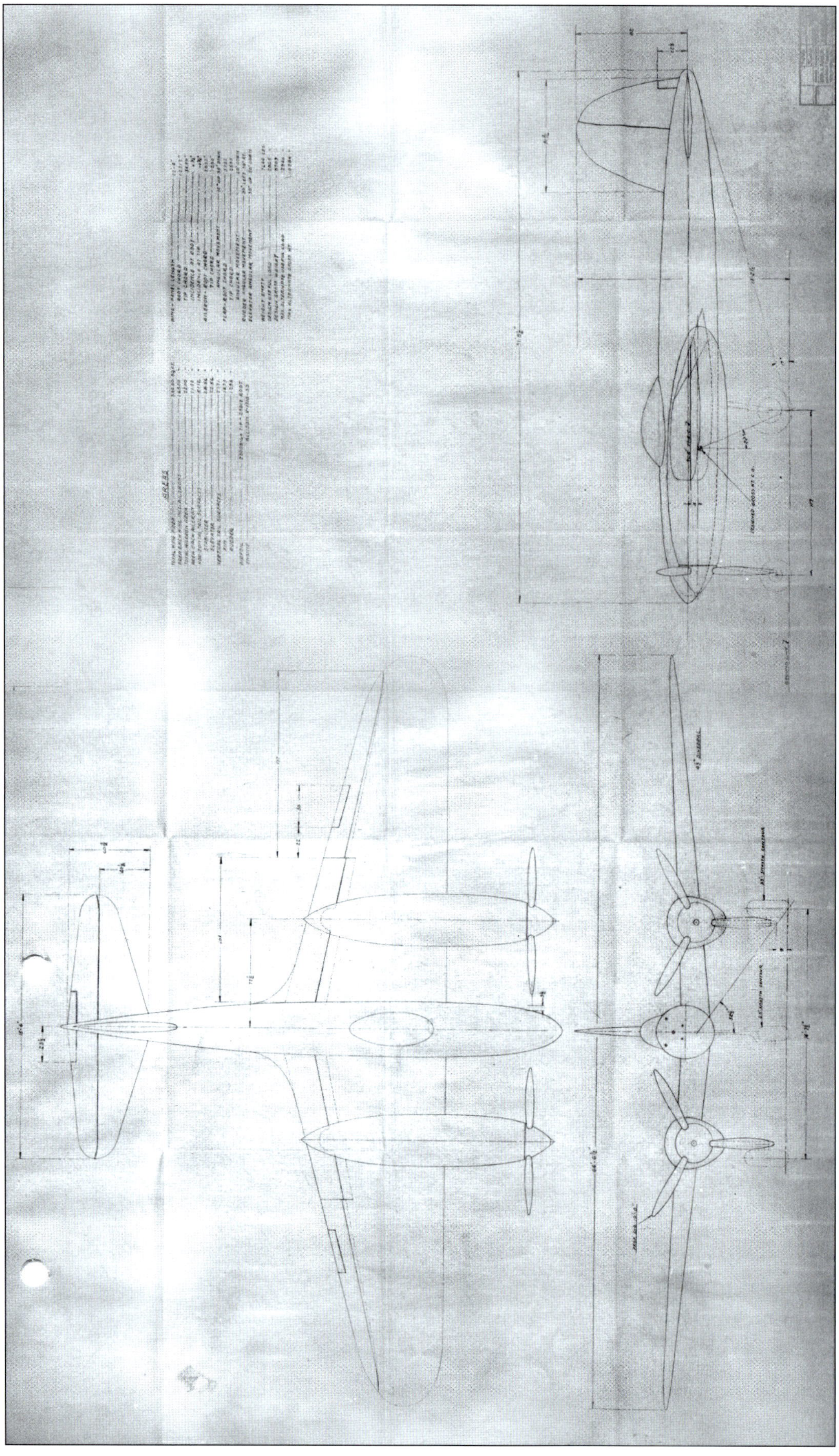

The Bellanca proposals to 39-775 used three-blade propellers for their V1710 power units (4.7.39). This is the Model 33-220. Span 44ft 6.5in (13.58m), length 31ft 8.25in (9.66m) and gross wing area 330sq.ft (30.69sq.m). Again all of the guns are in the nose. *US National Archives RG341 via Jared Zichek*

radial engines, a turbo-supercharged unit offering 2,350hp (1,752kW) which, it was estimated, would take the fighter to 500mph (805km/h) at 20,000ft (6,096m); the Tornado was also considered for the XP-58 (Chapter Eight) but this engine was another to be abandoned early in its development. The X1800 was later enlarged as the XH2600 and published sources indicate that the XP-49 fitted with either this engine or the R2160 would in fact have been overpowered.

To reduce the XP-49's structural weight wherever possible, the new fighter's airframe made extensive use of a new aluminium alloy called X74S (developed in 1939, X74S was one of the first high strength aluminium-zinc-magnesium-copper alloys to be produced for aerospace applications). The contract (W535-AC-13476) for just a single XP-49 prototype (serial number 40-3055) was dated 22 January 1940 and the official mock-up inspection, held at Lockheed's Burbank home at the same time as the firm's concurrent XP-58 mock-up inspection, took place from 25 August to 4 September 1941; in general it was considered satisfactory. A memo from 17 April 1940 noted that "in lieu of wind tunnel testing [on the XP-49] Lockheed will investigate the compressibility effects by running power-on dive tests in a P-38, which will be made available by the manufacturer." The detail design work for the XP-49 was undertaken under the direction of Lockheed project engineer M. Carl Haddon. Official comments made on 1 April 1941 noted that the XP-49 was a logical outgrowth of the P-38 and its anticipated design speed would make it superior to any new fighter type expected to appear in Europe within the next two years (and probably in the US as well). At this stage the only major drawback was the XP-49's estimated high landing speed, which needed to be reduced.

Work on the airframe moved forward rapidly, helped of course by having so much of the structure common to the P-38 Lightning, but progress with the Continental engines proved to be very slow and gradually the momentum behind the project began to fade. It was not until 22 April 1942 when Continental was finally able to deliver two XIV1430 engines to Lockheed, but then a change in the choice of supercharger was found necessary to match it with this engine (Continental had built a complete new factory at Muskegon in Michigan to produce the IV1430).

Then on 17 September 1942 a memo from Wright Field declared that several experimental fighters had proven to be substandard, and hence work on them should be halted. The XP-49 was among those listed (along with the XP-54 [Chapter Five], XP-67 [Chapter Eleven], and the Republic XP-69 and Curtiss XP-71 - neither of this last pair were ever completed). Colonel George B. Price, Acting Chief of Fighter Branch, Production Engineering Section, Wright Field, went so far as to state that the XP-49 would represent negative progress, it would pack a pressure cabin and have a fighting celling of 37,000ft (11,278m), "a ridiculous combination".

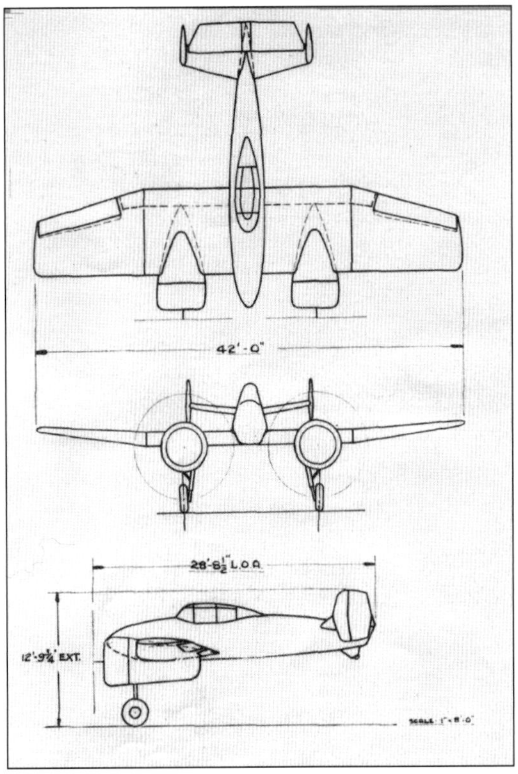

The Grumman G-41 as first proposed to CP 39-775 (c6.39). The story of this aircraft, built as the XP-50, will follow in the next chapter. *US National Archives RG341 via Jared Zichek*

Price added that "a severe shortage of engineering and supervisory personnel exists in the factories of most fighter contractors [and that] these contractors, in addition to trying to meet production schedules, are expending considerable engineering and supervisory time on experimental fighters. Untold man hours have been wasted on three fighters, two of which have been built and flown. These fighters (P-39E, P-60 and P-62) were obviously unsuited for production and service. It is believed that several other experimental fighters are substandard and that all work on them should stop."

This document's general subject matter takes the text away from the XP-49 for a moment, but it makes interesting reading. And Price closed by saying "Curtiss is building, on speculation, a [Packard-built] Merlin 61 engine into a P-40F. They should be ordered to quit wasting their time. North American's P-78 will undoubtedly absorb all Merlin 61 production." (Author's note: The P-39E version of the Bell Airacobra was a planned development which also received the designation P-76 and 4,000 examples were ordered, but then cancelled; it eventually formed the basis for the XP-63 Kingcobra. The P-40F did in fact achieve prolonged production, and the Merlin-powered version of the North American Mustang entered service as the P-51B, and not as the P-78. The Curtiss XP-60 and XP-62 follow in Chapters Nine and Ten.) The Technical Executive of Materiel Center at Wright Field concurred that the fighter development programme should be reviewed carefully and that types which would not materially aid the programme should be "ruthlessly" dropped.

In opposition to these opinions, the Experimental Engineering Section of AAF Material Center at

RIGHT A photograph taken at Lockheed's Burbank factory in November 1942 at around the time of the XP-49's maiden flight. It was the pressurised cockpit and different engine nacelles that identified this aircraft from a standard P-38 Lightning. *Lockheed/Gerald H. Balzer via Mark Nankivil, Greater St Louis Air & Space Museum*

A second view from November 1942 showing the aircraft as built. There are no known air-to-air photos of the XP-49. *Lockheed/ Gerald H. Balzer via Mark Nankivil, Greater St Louis Air & Space Museum*

Wright Field wrote on 24 September in reply that "a policy of discontinuing experimental projects which are nearing completion because such projects do not fit the immediate position is an extremely dangerous one." One reason given was that the effect on the moral of the various contractors and their engineering staffs would be disastrous. In addition the memo noted that "it is conceivable that a change in the military situation could completely change our estimation of the experimental project(s) in question."

Further, Colonel F.O. Carroll, Chief of the Engineering Section at Wright Field, was also averse to a curtailment of the experimental programme, although he was of the opinion that the XP-49 was now little more than a vehicle for the Continental engine, to gain flight experience on this power unit. Subsequently, on 10 November 1942 the Production Engineering Section at Wright Field recommended the cancellation of the Continental IV1430 contracts, since both Allison and Packard had by now not only produced engines with an output rating on a par with the Continental, but had also achieved volume production on these types. In addition, thanks to the improvements affected in the Allison V1710 engine, the Lockheed P-38H Lightning variant had come into the picture, the performance of which, particularly its rate of climb, was such that there was now little likelihood that the P-49 would go into production.

Suggestions made at around the time of the XP-49's first flight to scrap the Continental engine were deferred since it represented over three years of intense development. However, further developments of the IV1430 type, compared to the V1650 (Packard Merlin) and V1710, now appeared unfeasible because of the necessarily high supercharging required for the power output obtained.

Flight test

The XP-49 finally made its maiden flight, a sortie from Burbank which lasted 35 minutes and including a climb to 8,000ft (2,438m), on 11 November 1942; Lockheed test pilot Joe Towle was in the cockpit and the manufacturer reported that the flight was "entirely satisfactory". Flight 2 (on 13 November) lasted 47 minutes and reached 10,000ft (3,048m) and Flight 3 (14 November) 45 minutes and 5,000ft (1,524m). Then, after these initial trips, Lockheed moved to replace the engines with two torque meter units (XIV1430-13/15 engines fitted with devices to measure the torque or twisting force experienced by the engine). In addition P-38-type

A set of walk-around views was taken of the XP-49 with its original 'small' fins in place. *Lockheed/Gerald H. Balzer via Mark Nankivil, Greater St Louis Air & Space Museum*

As first built the XP-49 lacked national markings on its booms, but there were stripes on the fins, 'US Army' written under the outer wings, plus service roundels on the upper and lower wing surfaces. *Lockheed/Gerald H. Balzer via Mark Nankivil, Greater St Louis Air & Space Museum*

The XP-49 pictured after its fins had been enlarged, signified by the increase in the number of fin stripes. The nacelles for the Continental engines are well shown here. *Lockheed/Gerald H. Balzer via Mark Nankivil, Greater St Louis Air & Space Museum*

self-sealing fuel tanks were installed to help with problems experienced with fuel flow, and a flight engineer's seat was squeezed into the cockpit just behind the pilot's seat. The new engines were rated at 1,600hp (1,193kW) at 25,000ft (7,620m).

The second flight following the engine change took place on 30 December 1942, it lasted for 46 minutes and involved a climb to 19,000ft (5,791m) followed by level speed runs at 15,000ft (4,572m); the take-off weight here was 18,475lb (8,380kg). Continual problems were experienced with the hydraulics but these early flights did show that 40-3055 handled quite well and exhibited good manoeuvrability. Unfortunately, however, the IV1430 engines did not generate the hoped for power, with the result that the XP-49 showed a disappointing maximum speed of just 406mph (653km/h).

Next, on 1 January 1943 and after making another power run at 15,000ft (4,572m), 40-3055 was forced to make a crash landing at Muroc airfield. A cocktail of problems was behind this crash and included the failure of the hydraulic system, failure of the left landing gear to lock down, the faulty operation of the landing flaps and the inoperation of the electrical system. The XP-49 suffered major damage to its left-hand lower fin and rudder, to the left-hand undercarriage leg and closure doors and to both main tyres and tubes, and also minor damage to the left-hand boom and to the propeller blades.

In addition to the necessary repairs, while grounded the XP-49 had its vertical tail surfaces increased in height by 7¾in (19.69cm). The prototype flew again on 16 February 1943 (Flight 11), and by 15 April its weight had been increased by its various modifications from 18,788lb to 18,891lb (8,522kg to 8,569kg). Contractor's flight testing at the Burbank plant lasted until June and the preliminary performance data indicated a maximum speed just a few miles-per-hour higher than the production P-38, but certainly not sufficient to warrant a switch in production to P-49s, this also in the light of the questionable production future of the Continental IV1430 engine. As an aside, any move to fit the aircraft's guns had been held back until later, and in fact the aircraft's armament would never be fitted.

It was not until June 1943 that the XP-49 was considered ready for its official performance trials and an AAF pilot ferried the aircraft to Wright Field on the 26th of that month (a mere 27 months late from the initial schedule). However, from this point the aircraft was slated as 'under repair' by Wright Field's Flight Section until at least a week into July. In order to meet its guaranteed performance, 40-3055 still required further modifications by the manufacturer, but returning the aircraft to Burbank would impede Lockheed's war effort. As a result it was decided that the AFF should accept the XP-49 as it stood, and the Vultee XP-54 at the same time (Chapter Five), and to close out their contracts.

Prior to AAF testing further difficulty had been experienced with fuel leakage in the self-sealing tanks and in early August these were replaced, but the new installation still proved unsatisfactory. As a result all-new metal fuel tanks had to be specially fabricated since better self-sealing tanks were not available. This work was started in the Wright Engineering shops on 20 October 1943 but, due to the aircraft's by now low priority, they were not ready until March 1944, and then because of further difficulties their installation was not completed until May 1944.

Several flights were completed in early May 1944 but during one of these sorties the port-side engine failed, though 40-3055 was able to land without suffering any damage. The replacement engine had been installed by mid-August but during its first flight a severe leak was discovered in the fuel sump-tank. Due to the XP-49's continued low priority, and these complications surrounding the fuel system, this repair work had not been finished by the time that the Chief of the Engineering Division requested that all work should now cease on this aircraft.

Official performance flight testing was thus never started, and in fact it had been cancelled on 5 February 1944 in view of the higher priority work being conducted by the Flight Section at Wright Field. All of the XP-49's performance data has thus been complied from Lockheed's own trials and report. At a gross weight of 18,500lb (8,392kg) the

Front and rear views of the XP-49 in its modified form. *Lockheed/ Gerald H. Balzer via Mark Nankivil, Greater St Louis Air & Space Museum*

The XP-49 40-3055 pictured at Wright Field in October 1945 during a two-day Army Air Forces Fair and 'Victory Display' Open Day held at the secret base, which included many captured Axis combat aircraft and another AAF prototype, the Beechcraft XA-38 attack aircraft. The only example of the XP-49 was reportedly scrapped during the following year. *AAF/Gerald H. Balzer via Mark Nankivil, Greater St Louis Air & Space Museum*

maximum recorded speeds were 347mph (558km/h) at sea level, 384mph (618km/h) at 10,000ft (3,048m) and 406mph (653km/h) at 15,000ft (4,572m), and the 'guaranteed' maximum of 458mph (737km/h) was never determined.

However, in view of the Continental IV1430 being installed in the McDonnell XP-67 (Chapter Eleven), it was considered desirable to continue with the engine phase of the XP-49's flight trials, so any further sorties conducted after February were confined to the study of engine operation only. On 22 December 1944 the XP-49 was recommended for Class 26 status (grounded, possibly for ground instruction) and the aircraft was eventually scrapped at Wright Field in 1946. It is understood that the XP-49's final useful task was to be dropped several times from a hydraulic bridge crane in order to simulate heavy landings and then assess their effects.

XP-49 structure

Based on Lockheed's P-38 Lightning, the XP-49 was a twin-engine twin-boom single-seat interceptor fighter. The aircraft's fusleage was fabricated in aluminium alloy in the form of a stiffened monocoque structure, the centre body comprising a gondola attached to the centre wing section, while rearwards the two booms led back to the tailplane. The P-38's wing and fuselage had been retained but there were new engine nacelles for the change in powerplant, while the cabin was stressed for pressurised operation. Indeed as much as two-thirds of the XP-49 airframe parts were common to the P-38, but a further major change was the introduction of a strengthened undercarriage.

The cantilever wing was formed from a double web box centre portion between the booms with single web portions outboard. Fowler flaps were fitted. An internally braced horizontal tail was supported between the tail booms, while the twin vertical fins were full cantilever and attached rigidly to their booms. The wing structure was formed by aluminium alloy shear ribs and beams and was covered in smooth skinning.

Two experimental Continental XIV1430-9/11 twelve-cylinder inverted-vee liquid-cooled engines drove two three-blade 12ft 6in (3.81m) diameter Curtiss Electric propellers and to counteract torque these airscrews were handed (i.e rotating in opposite directions). The propellers were outward-rotating, so when viewed from behind the starboard propeller rotated clockwise, the port propeller anti- or counter-clockwise. The normal internal fuel load came to 300galUS (1,136lit), the maximum 600galUS (2,271lit), all in four tanks both forward and aft of the wing beam; these could be supplimented by two underwing drop tanks of 150galUS (568lit) capacity each.

XP-49 Data

Length:	52ft 0in (15.85m)
Wing span:	40ft 1in (12.22m)
Wing area:	327.5sq.ft (30.46sq.m)
Empty weight:	15,475lb (7,019kg)
Gross weight (no bombs):	18,885lb (8,566kg)
Powerplant:	2 x 1,600hp (1,193kW) Continental XIV1430 'Inverted-V' liquid-cooled piston engines
Maximum speed:	347mph (558km/h) at sea level, 406mph (653km/h) at 15,000ft (4,572m)
Sea level rate of climb:	3,300ft/min (1,006m/min)
Time to 20,000ft (6,096m):	8.7 minutes
Service ceiling:	37,500ft (11,430m)
Normal range at 18,885lb/kg weight:	679 miles (1,093km)
Maximum range:	1,800 miles (2,896km)
Armament:	4 x 0.50in (12.7mm) machine guns and 2 x 20mm cannon in nose (never fitted)

3 Grumman XP-50 Skyrocket

The second prototype to come out of the Circular Proposal 39-775 studies, and the second in that design competition's order of merit, was the Grumman XP-50 Skyrocket. In fact this aircraft was essentially a land-based version of the manufacturer's XF5F-1 naval fighter prototype first flown in April 1940 and covered in Chapter Twenty-Three.

39-775 prototype

A memo written to the Chief of the Air Corps on 8 August 1939, just after the assessment of the 39-775 proposals, stated that "the airplane offered by the Grumman Aircraft Engineering Corporation is 'substantially identical' to Navy Experimental Airplane Type XF5F. However, the modification and changes that are always necessary in the first article of a "substantially identical" airplane preclude freezing the design. The Navy design is now only in the process of construction. The design offered by Grumman provides for superior flying characteristics and efficiency in power to weight ratio. Procurement of a prototype of this basic design with improved engines is [therefore] justified. The manufacturer guarantees delivery of 48 airplanes in 22 months [but] this number is insufficient to meet the requirements of the Airplane Expansion Program." (The author of this memorandum is unknown because the relevant parts of the microfiche text is illegible; the document appeared in the Lockheed XP-49 Case History.)

The contract for a single XP-50 prototype was eventually awarded on 25 November 1939, the first such contract given by the Army Air Force to naval

The sole Grumman XP-50 to be built was given the military serial 40-3057, although none of the available photographs show this painted on, presumably because the aircraft was lost before being passed to AFF control. *Grumman via Mark Aldrich*

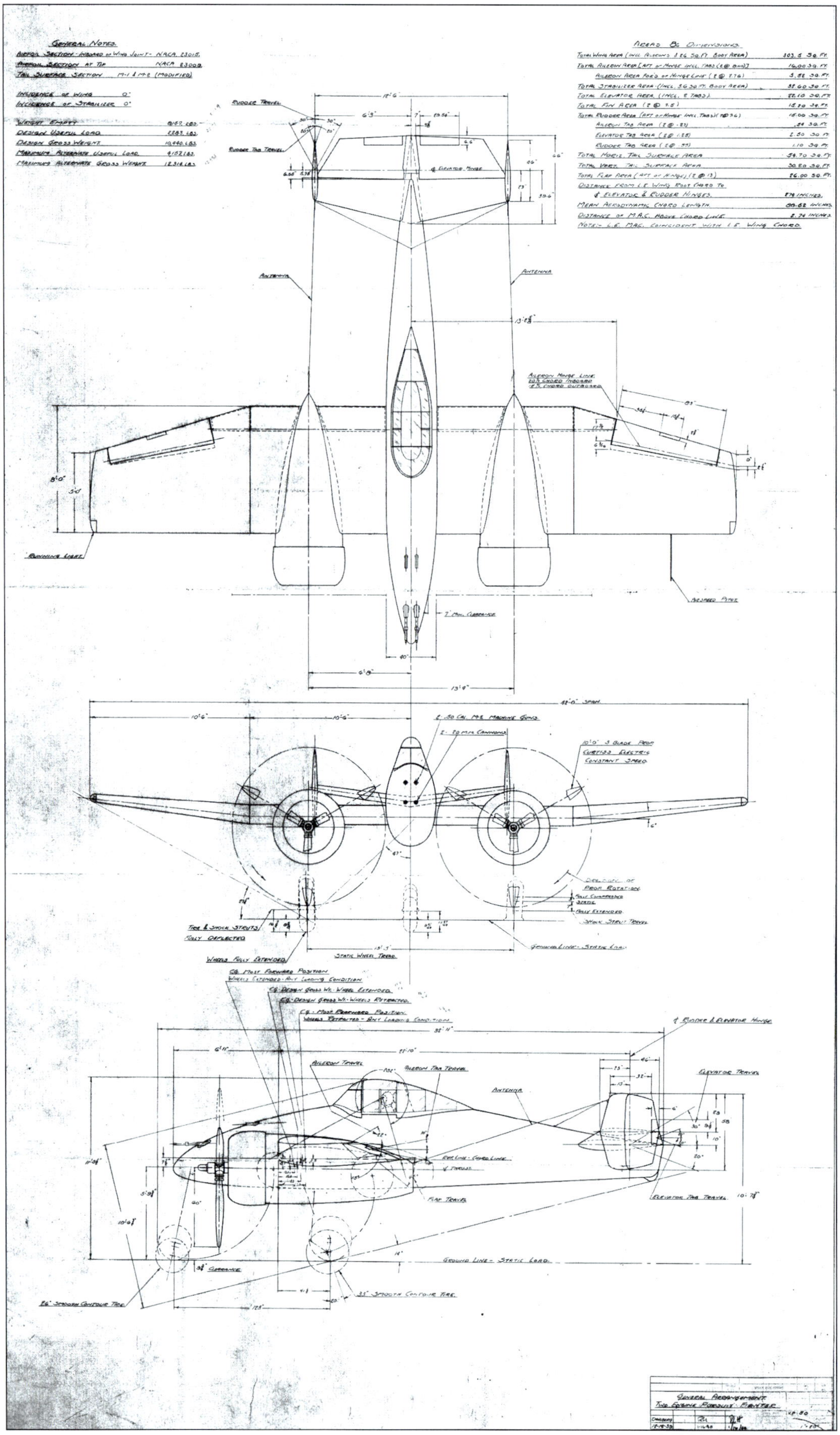

Original manufacturer's drawing of the XP-50 completed on 12 December 1939. *US National Archives via Tom Culbert*

aircraft specialist manufacturer Grumman; project engineer on the aircraft was Bill Schwendler. Major changes from the XF5F-1 included turbo supercharged Wright R1820 engines, a lengthened nose stretching past the propeller arcs and a tricycle undercarriage, this updated layout being submitted as Grumman's Model G-45. Provision was also in place to fit self-sealing fuel cells and to provide protective armour for the pilot. The mock-up was officially inspected on 22 April 1940, but then various official requests for changes began to put the XP-50 behind schedule.

A further memo, written on 1 April 1941 to the Chief of the Material Division by Lt Col J.G. Taylor AAF, Chief of the Foreign Intelligence Section, was more negative (this was composed after the flight trials had begun). He noted that the XP-50 "does not seem a likely airplane, but is desirable as an air-cooled prototype, which is needed because of the liquid-cooled 'bottleneck' [the Lockheed XP-49 and other types all underway at once – author]. As long as the liquid-cooled engine remains easier to protect with armor, its performance and installational advantages will cause this 'bottleneck' to remain. The altitude manoeuvrability of this design must suffer due to such a poor wing tip shape, as well as low aspect ratio. The span loading should be kept above 6.5 for altitude work, and spin tunnel testing completed before construction as it appears a dangerous spinner."

Flight test

Sadly, the flying career of the XP-50 lasted only for a short period. The prototype received military serial 40-3057 and first flew, from Grumman's Bethpage home, on 18 February 1941 piloted by manufacturer's test pilot Robert L. Hall. The initial sorties showed improvements in handling over its naval XF5F-1 counterpart, while the turbo supercharged engines provided a markedly improved performance at both medium and high altitudes. All very encouraging, but then on 14 March the ill-fated prototype suffered damage when the starboard main undercarriage leg collapsed on an icy runway.

Following repairs in was cleared to fly again but, having recorded just 20 hours of air time, the sole example of the XP-50 was lost on 14 May 1941 when the starboard R1820 turbo-supercharger exploded during a test flight. Both the engine and hydraulic system were disabled, test pilot Hall found that he could not lower the nosewheel to make a normal landing or retract the starboard wheel to try a belly landing. So he had no option but to abandon 40-3057 and bail out, which he did over Long Island Sound, the XP-50 coming down into Smithtown Bay. This loss of the prototype brought the XP-50 programme to a quite sudden end.

View of part of the full-size mock-up of the XP-50 at Bethpage. *Grumman via Gerald H. Balzer*

RIGHT AND BELOW Scenes of the XP-50 under construction. The hump-back shape of the fuselage is particularly noticeable. *Grumman via Gerald H. Balzer*

BELOW LEFT Starting the XP-50's starboard R1820 engine in 1940. No ear protection for those watching! *Grumman via Gerald H. Balzer*

BELOW RIGHT Cockpit inspection on what appears to be a chilly and part snow-covered day. *Grumman via Dave Ostrowski and Alan Griffith*

ABOVE Ground crew muster around the prototype as it is prepared for another trial. *Grumman via Gerald H. Balzer*

LEFT Three-quarter left front view of 40-3057 from above which gives an excellent view of the wing and empennage shapes. Once again the engines are undergoing a ground run. *Grumman via Dave Ostrowski and Alan Griffith*

XP-65

However, Grumman continued its development of twin-engine piston fighters and this work would ultimately result in the very successful F7F Tigercat naval fighter first flown in November 1943. And at one stage the AAF also came on board, using left over XP-50 funding to study a land-based version which was then designated XP-65 (under Project number MX-138). On 16 June 1941 authorisation was given to procure two prototypes, but on 7 January 1942 the XP-65 prototypes were cancelled. The following cancellation notice to Grumman, from Lt. Colonel F.O. Carroll, Chief of the Experimental Engineering Section and dated 16 January 1942, summed up the situation. He wrote:

> "1. A project covering the procurement of one or two twin-engine interceptor airplanes to succeed the XP-50 has been under consideration for some time. The procedure which the Division planned to follow consisted of coordinating the design of the Army version with the Navy, with the view of arriving at a design which would not depart basically from that of the Navy XF7F.
>
> 2. As a result of several conferences between representatives of the Materiel Division, the Bureau of Aeronautics, and your company, it has become apparent that the compromises necessary to obtain the Army version of this airplane are of such a nature as to make the anticipated advantages of the original plan somewhat questionable.
>
> 3. The Army requirements include a pressurised cabin, the installation of multiple 37mm cannon, turbo superchargers, and other changes.
>
> 4. The Bureau of Aeronautics is unwilling to accept any compromises which will result in increasing the weight of the basic XF7F design. This is understandable in view of the fact that the Navy version must be designed to meet the requirements for carrier landing and is already very heavy when considered from that standpoint.
>
> 5. It is realized that your organization would be working under a considerable handicap in endeavouring to design an airplane which represents a compromise between the requirements of the two services, rather than concentrating on a design intended to meet the specific requirements of either the Army or the Navy.
>
> 6. Accordingly, it is believed that the best interests of the Government and of your organization will be served if you are relieved from the necessity of building two XP-65 airplanes. You are, therefore, requested to discontinue your efforts along this line."

As a result the Army Air Force, and the Air Force that succeeded it in 1947, would never put a Grumman-designed fighter into production and service, and the XP-50 remained as the sole type to receive an AAF/USAF pursuit or fighter designation that was turned into hardware. At 20 June 1942 the XP-65 was expected to have a maximum speed of 345mph (555km/h) at sea level and 431mph (693km/h) at 27,000ft (8,230m), a sea level rate of climb of 4,400ft/min (1,341m/min), service ceiling 36,000ft (10,973m) and maximum range 1,000 miles (1,609km). The estimated gross weight came to 16,672lb (7,562kg).

The XP-50's very narrow fuselage, and the length of its nose undercarriage, are shown beautifully by this excellent nose-angle photo of the aircraft on the grass at Bethpage. *Grumman via Dave Ostrowski and Alan Griffith*

ABOVE Scene showing the XP-50 taxying out to begin a test flight. Just visible is the knuckled main landing gear aft of the struts, a move introduced to improve the aircraft's centre of gravity whilst on the ground. *Grumman via Rich Dann*

RIGHT With the engine covers in place, the size of the nacelles in comparison to the fuselage was noteworthy. *Grumman via Gerald H. Balzer*

BELOW The pilot had a relatively poor view out of the cockpit because of its position relative to the wing. A view taken at Grumman Bethpage in spring 1941. *Grumman via Gerald H. Balzer*

Although it completed just a few flights before being lost, the XP-50 did get its chance to be photographed air-to-air and a small number of shots have survived. The rudders were painted red and white with a vertical blue strip ahead of them. The rest of the airframe was painted silver and 'US ARMY' was applied to the wing undersides. *Grumman via Gerald H. Balzer*

On 14 March 1941 the prototype XP-50 40-3057 suffered damage when its starboard main undercarriage leg collapsed on the icy Bethpage runway. Grumman staff inspect the immobilised prototype, which resumed its flight trials in May. *Grumman via Gerald H. Balzer*

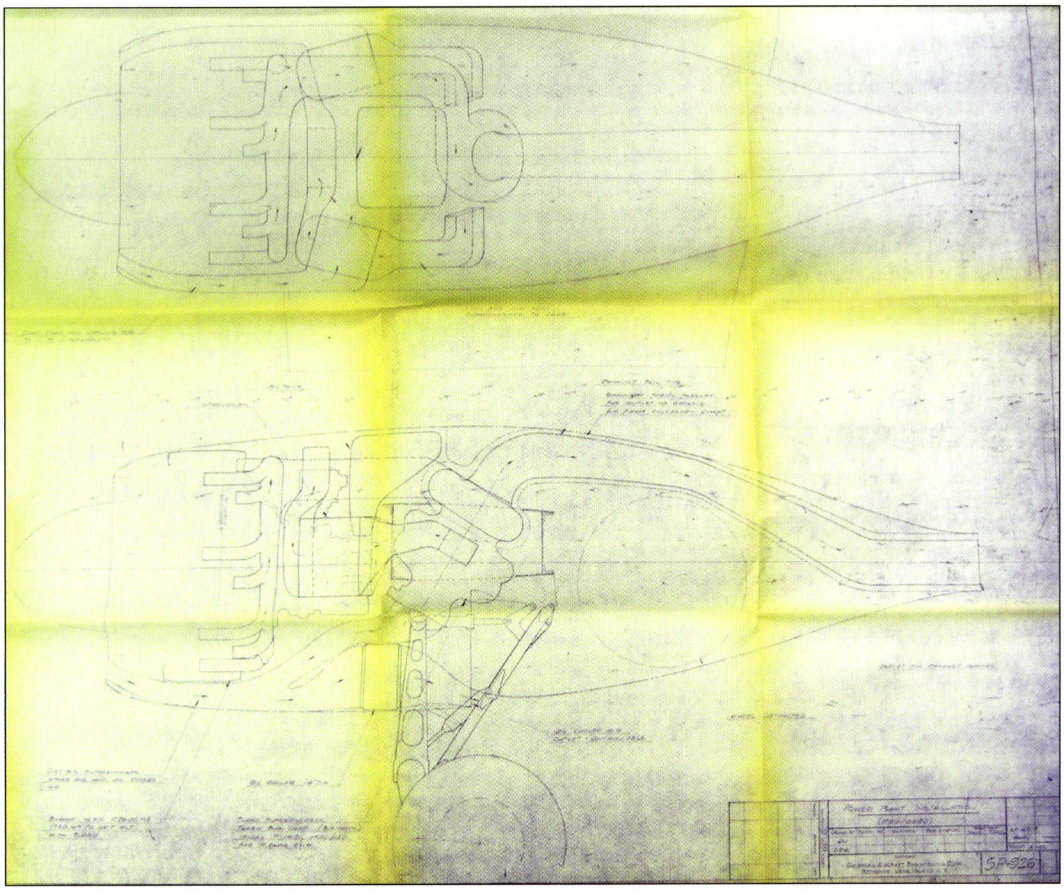

Internal detail for the proposed Grumman XP-65 powerplant installation. The drawing is dated 17 July 1941. *Grumman via Tommy Thomason*

XP-50 structure

In its design and structure the single-seat Grumman XP-50 had much in common with the manufacturer's XF5F-1 naval fighter prototype. It retained the latter's basic wing and empennage but the forward part of the fuselage was extended by over 2ft (0.61m), in part to make the accomodation of a different armament easier and to enable a tricycle landing gear to be fitted rather than the Navy aircraft's tailwheel form. As noted the Wright R1820-67/79 nine-cylinder radial engines were fitted with turbosuperchargers and these each drove a three-blade propeller.

XP-50 data

Length (on ground with nosewheel extended):	32ft 11in (10.03m)
Wing span:	42ft 0in (12.80m)
Wing area:	303.5sq.ft (28.23sq.m)
Empty weight:	8,183lb (3,712kg)
Gross weight (no bombs):	11,990lb (5,439kg)
Maximum take-off weight:	13,060lb (5,924kg)
Powerplant:	2 x 1,200hp (895kW) Wright R1820-67/69 air-cooled radial piston engines
Maximum speed (estimated and never achieved in flight):	424mph (682km/h) at 25,000ft (7,620m)
Sea level rate of climb:	c4,000ft/min (1,219m/min)
Time to 20,000ft (6,096m):	5 minutes
Service ceiling:	40,000ft (12,192m)
Normal range:	553 miles (890km)
Maximum range:	1,250 miles (2,011km)
Armament:	2 x 20mm cannon, 2 x 0.50in (12.70mm) machine guns, 200lb (91kg) bombs (bombs provision only)

4 North American XP-51 Lightweight Mustangs

The North American P-51 Mustang was one of the very best of the fighters operated by any nation during World War Two and, in theory, should never qualify for an entry in this book. However, three versions, the XP-51F, XP-51G and XP-51J, which looked very much like standard Mustangs, were essentially built to a new design with a lightened structure and thus had little in common with the earlier production variants. North American's designer for all versions of the Mustang was Edgar Schmued.

Three versions

The primary objective behind the procurement of this new series of experimental Mustangs was to assess a fighter aircraft designed with lower load factors than those specified previously by the AAF. A secondary plan was to consider along what lines the P-51 series might be taken forward in terms of improving the type's performance, its manoeuvrability and its accessibility for maintenance. The procurement of these prototypes was undertaken under the Research and Development Program for Fiscal Year 1943.

In January 1943 North American submitted a design to Air Material Command for a new fast and highly manoeuvrable fighter which also offered a high rate of climb. In plan view it resembled the production P-51B Mustang, but this was coincidental because here the similarity ended. North American's engineers had created the new fighter using British load factors rather than the equivalents specified by the Amy Air Forces. The structure throughout had been redesigned to make the airframe much lighter, in particular the main landing gear was new and had smaller wheels, and the wing area had been increased slightly with the leading edge now completely straight (the kink present in early Mustang versions had now gone). The fuselage fuel tank and the inboard wing guns from some P-51 versions had been taken out (leaving four guns in all), the engine mounting had been modified to save

A view of the first North American XP-51F prototype which shows what a neat and compact design this fighter was. *Gerald H. Balzer*

Walk around views of the first XP-51F serial 43-43332. The aircraft was fitted with a three-blade propeller. *Gerald H. Balzer*

With in particular its large canopy relative to the rest of the airframe (shown well in this side view) the XP-51F looked reasonably different from a standard Mustang. The need for such a large canopy was questioned by British test pilot Patrick Shea-Simonds. *Gerald H. Balzer*

weight and the engine and intercooler radiators were redesigned. The tail surfaces were also enlarged and there was a host of other detailed alterations and modifications. Finally, there was a new large teardrop canopy.

The resulting Model XP-51F was a low wing, single engine, all metal monoplane powered by a Packard Merlin V1650-3 engine driving a three-blade constant speed propeller. The prototypes of this, and the two follow-on versions, apparently never received any guns (at least none of the available photos show any, although one taken of the second XP-51F appears to have the gun ports covered by tape).

The XF-51G was structurally identical to the 'F' but introduced a British Merlin engine installed in lieu of the V1650-3 (the former supplied from England using the Reverse Lend Lease process). In addition the 'G' was to be flight tested with a British Rotol five-blade propeller (though in the end only on one flight). Any production aircraft would also have carried six machine guns rather than the 'F' and 'J's four. The XP-51J was again identical to the XP-51F in regard to airframe and armament, but the last of these lightweight Mustangs was powered by an Allison V1710-119 fuel metering engine. This featured an updraft carburettor and there were no air inlets around the nose in what was a very clean installation.

All of the XP-51s described here were covered by North American Model NA-105 and retained the name Mustang, though one wonders why they did not receive a new pursuit 'P-' number. Negotiations held during June 1943 between North American and the AAF resulted in a decision to order five

With the covers off, 43-43332 provides details for its Packard Merlin V-1650-3 engine. *Gerald H. Balzer*

prototypes (under Contract W535-AC-37857 and Project MX-356), three as XP-51Fs but with the last pair converted to the XP-51G variant with the British Merlin RM.14.SM engine; as such one XF-51F and one XP-51G would then be allocated to and sent to the UK.

A mock-up inspection of the XP-51F was conducted at the North American factory on 8 and 9 April 1943, and then on 4 September Col Mark E. Bradley Jnr, of the USAAF's Fighter Branch Engineering Section, wrote a brief report about the planned new type. In this he noted that "no definite quantity of production airplanes has yet been determined [but] a quantity of five thousand additional P-51-type airplanes has been procured [and] it is probable that they will be built as P-51Fs". Clearly, at this stage the new Mustang was very much in favour. Also, at this moment the intended armament was to be four 0.50in (12.7mm) machine guns, but with provision to fit four 20mm cannon; the estimated top speed was 460mph (740km/h) at 31,000ft (9,449m).

In October 1943 a message was sent from Air Technical Service Command (ATSC) to the AAF's Assistant Chief Air Staff (ACAS) requesting authority to procure a service test quantity of 25 P-51Fs. This proposal was rejected and a covering statement added that "No further production of the XP-51F will be considered until the ones now under construction have been thoroughly flight tested." However, in November the ATSC was authorised to procure the two further XP-51F-type aircraft specifically for the installation of the Allison V1710-119 engine, which were designated XF-51J. The reason for this move was that no new fighter type aircraft were being built which made use of the P-51's original V1710 engine.

The first XF-51F received the military serial 43-43332 and made a 40-minute maiden flight on 14 February 1944 in the hands of North American test pilot Robert Chilton, who reported the aircraft's flying characteristics as "satisfactory". The take-off gross weight for the flight was 6,296lb (2,856kg) and initial trials showed that the aircraft could exceed 490mph (788km/h) and climb to 20,000ft (6,096m) in little more than two minutes. Army Air Force pilots began their performance assessment of the XP-51F during March 1944 at North American's Inglewood plant, but these trials were limited because War Emergency ratings had not been released for the Packard power unit – only military power was available. Once the War Emergency ratings had been released the Army Air Force's pilots returned to the manufacturer to gather full official performance data.

Following North American's initial performance tests, on 16 September 1944 43-43332 was accepted by the AAF and official assessments of the XP-51's performance, engine behaviour and stability could now begin. The covering contract expired in May 1945 by which time the first XF-51F was no longer required by North American, so it was, therefore, delivered to NACA's Moffett Field base to be used in investigations into high speed phenomena.

Pictures showing the second XP-51F 43-43333, which also sported the three-blade propeller. The three-quarter front angle view suggests that this aircraft had gun ports in the wings, here covered over with fabric. *Gerald H. Balzer*

Serial 43-43333 was allotted to the second XP-51F which first flew on 22 May 1944. Following preliminary airworthiness flights at the Contractor's plant, in July the aircraft was ferried to Wright Field for an assessment to be made of the XP-51F's flying qualities. However, minor problems, such as the failure of the tail wheel fork, delayed the flying programme. The aircraft was accepted by the AAF in August 1944 and this programme roughly 70% complete when, in March 1945, 43-43332 was completely destroyed in a hanger fire at Wright Field.

It was the third XP-51F, serial 43-43334, which was allocated to the RAF under Lend Lease. It first flew on 20 May 1944 and, after a few check flights, the aircraft was then crated up in readiness for shipment to the UK, leaving on 30 June.

The first XP-51G carried serial 43-43336 and is seen at North American's airfield at Inglewood. *Gerald H. Balzer*

The decision to convert the fourth and fifth XP-51Fs into XF-51Gs with the Rolls Royce RM.14.SM was taken in January 1944. These engines arrived at the Contractor's plant in February and the first XP-51G, serial 43-43335, took to the air for the first time on 9 August 1944 in the hands of Ed Virgin, another pilot on the North American test team. No difficulties were encountered in a flight which lasted for 23 minutes, apart from a slight canopy vibration and some tail wheel shimmy – an Aeroproducts four-blade had been fitted for the first sortie and these issues were soon corrected. However, when the five-blade airscrew was fitted it was found that at cruising speed the XP-51G was totally directionally unstable and Chilton, flying the machine on its first flight in this form on 12 August, struggled to get it home. The four-blade prop was reinstated but, after North American had conducted only part of its preliminary performance tests, flying in this aircraft had to be terminated due to rough engine running.

The XP-51G was accepted by the AAF on 26 September 1944 and then returned to North American for the manufacturer to try and solve the problem of rough engine running, and afterwards to gather further performance data. But by January 1945 the engine roughness had become much worse, to the point that it was felt unsafe to conduct further flights. Since no more engines were available 43-43335 was now moved from North American to Wright Field and turned over to the Aircraft Laboratory for studies to be made of its airframe structure, with its reduced load factors.

The second XP-51G was 43-43336 and this aircraft accomplished its maiden flight on 14 November 1944. However, such was the current critical state with the Rolls Royce Merlin engines supplied for these prototypes that very few check flights were completed in this machine. It too had been allocated to go to Britain and it was crated and then shipped to England during February 1945.

The first XF-51J was serial 44-76027 and it completed its first flight on 23 April 1945 piloted by North American pilot George Welch. However, early flight trials revealed that the V1710-119 engine installed in this aircraft had not matured sufficiently for it to be used in any production machines. The V1710-119 incorporated fuel metering and it was this particular equipment which was not as yet developed fully.

As a result of the critical situation with the engine the second XP-51J, 44-76028, was never flown. It was accepted by the AAF and, in view of the fact that the V1710-119 clearly needed further development, both XP-51Js were now loaned to the Allison Division of General Motors at Indianapolis for further engine development and fuel metering research. The second XP-51J was supplied primarily to provide spare parts for the first example.

Walk around views of the first XP-51G. The aircraft is fitted with the five-blade propeller which, it is understood, was used for just one sortie, before being replaced by a four-blade fitting. Note the strip of dark colour paint on the lower part of the engine mounting and the black anti-glare panel in front of the cockpit. *Gerald H. Balzer*

The second XP-51G was 43-43336 which is seen here in a view also taken at Inglewood and dated 26 February 1945. It now has British markings in readiness for transportation across the Atlantic (as FR410) and the normal four-blade propeller. *Gerald H. Balzer*

British testing

RAF serial numbers FR409 to FR411 were allocated to three Mustangs, an XP-51F, XP-51G and an older P-51B respectively, that were acquired for evaluation by the British Aeroplane & Armament Experimental Establishment (A&AEE) at Boscombe Down. FR409 was the third and final XP-51F (ex-43-43334), it was passed to RAF hands as (unofficially) a Mustang V and then given its UK military serial. It was eventually Struck Off Charge on 18 February 1947, presumably for scrap. USAAF serial 43-43336 was the XP-51G which became Mustang IV FR410 and in British hands this aircraft was Struck Off Charge on 26 June 1947. The third aircraft in this series was P-51B 43-6565 which came under British control in November 1943 as FR411, but it was returned to the USAAF on 13 December 1943 having not seen any RAF use.

It is understood that FR409 was tested only briefly by Boscombe Down's pilots, in around October 1944 and at a loaded weight of 7,669lb (3,479kg) when carrying 150gallMP (682lit) of fuel. No performance data was collected but it was quoted as being a "marked improvement" over earlier Mustangs. The large canopy provided an outstanding view out and the handling was found to be "pleasant and easy". It appears that FR410 spent time with Air Service Training at Hamble but, as far as is known, it did not go to Boscombe Down.

However, in April 1945 British test pilots Jeffrey Quill and Patrick Shea-Simonds of Supermarine got the opportunity to assess the qualities of the XP-51F. FR809's controls for the 'Supermarine' flights were as follows:

Rudder: Plain, fabric covered, with anti-balance geared tab and small inset balance towards top of fin.

Elevators: Plain type, metal covered, with pronounced bulge in section and with similar type of small inset balance to the fitting on the rudder. Both elevators had geared tabs acting in the anti-balance sense.

Ailerons: Metal covered and hinged on the centreline with an Irving type of sealed balance. Also had a trimmer tab attached to the port aileron only which was operated from the cockpit.

The documents give no clue as to why these pilots were able to test fly this Mustang, but Quill was the first Supermarine pilot to try FR809 and he made a preliminary handling flight on 20 April 1945. He reported that the take-off was good with only a slight tendency to swing, and the undercarriage retraction was simple and rapid. However, the operation of the constant speed lever when it came to reducing rpm was very sluggish. Aileron control was positive and very effective right down to the stall, flaps up and flaps down, while above 350mph (563km/h) IAS it tended to become slightly heavy when compared to the concurrent Supermarine Spiteful. Elevator control was light and effective throughout the speed range and was considered "remarkably steady by comparison with Spitfire metal elevators". A brief stability check was made at 10,000ft (3,048m) and the aircraft showed a positive dynamic stability, while the level of static stability was estimated to lie approximately half way between the static stability of a Spitfire with a fabric elevator and a Spitfire with a metal elevator. This was borne out by the fact that when making a dive in the XP-51F from the trimmed condition in level flight, the stick force to hold the dive was appreciable but did not compare with that required on a fabric elevator Spitfire.

The rudder was not noticeably light and the directional characteristics were poor as far as stability was concerned. Firstly there were fairly considerable changes of rudder trim with speed and throttle opening. Then in dives the directional stability characteristics were what might be described as "lazy" and were somewhat similar to the directional characteristics of contraprop Spitfires, i.e. when disturbed the machine did not do a rapid directional phugoid but instead a "somewhat drunken side swipe".

All of the known photos of the less successful XP-51J depict the first example 44-76027 shown here. *Gerald H. Balzer*

All of the walk around views of the first XP-51J were taken on 24 April 1945. Note the white spinner and the very clean engine installation for the Allison engine with, compared to the 'F' and 'G' versions, no air inlets. *Gerald H. Balzer*

44-76027 carried the North American Aviation logo on the starboard side of its fin. It is an odd fact that no inflight photos were ever taken of the XP-51F, G, or J versions. *Gerald H. Balzer*

FR409 pictured on the ground after delivery to the UK, at A&AEE Boscombe Down. It has now been painted in RAF camouflage. *Phil Butler*

The stalling characteristics, both flaps and chassis down, were in Quill's words "perhaps the most remarkable point about this aircraft". FR809's stalling speeds were approximately as follows:

> All down – 83mph (134km/h) IAS. There was minor tail buffeting just preceding the stall.
> All up – 92mph (148km/h) IAS. No buffet.

The aileron control remained positive right down to the stall. There was no tendency towards aileron snatch or buffet and the lateral stability was "quite remarkable". The aeroplane displayed no tendency to drop a wing, but merely dropped its nose owing to a lack of elevator control if an attempt was made to hold the aircraft in a stalled condition.

Shea-Simonds flew FR809 on 21 and 23 April 1945 and endorsed Quill's comments. He added that the XP51F was "undoubtedly a very pleasant flying machine indeed from the handling point if view, although there is no doubt that its factors are too low to place it in the first class fighter category". He did highlight several small points which he considered to be undesirable.

> 1. The control column, "as is usually the case with most American fighter aircraft", seemed to Shea-Simonds to be too short and rigged too far forward.
>
> 2. The hood, although excellent from a vision point of view, seemed to be rather unnecessarily large. Something midway between this and the rear view Spitfire hood, say for the Spitfire Mk.XIV or 22, would appear to be the ideal.
>
> 3. The hydraulically-operated pilot's seat was in his words "an amusing toy but I hardly think a necessary feature. Surely a Spitfire type hand-operated adjustable seat would have saved a bit of weight, which seemed to be the object of the exercise throughout this aeroplane". However, Shea-Simonds regarded the power operation of the cockpit hood as a "first class innovation".

He also raised questions about the bad position of the mixture control lever, while the flap control and operation of the flaps did not seem very satisfactory.

Nevertheless, in spite of the above, Shea-Simonds considered this aeroplane to be a remarkably pleasant one and its handling characteristics, particularly at low speeds, were most satisfying. The directional stability at high speed was rather poor, however, and he felt that the lateral control and stability were a little deceptive; i.e. although at low and medium speeds the ailerons were very light, there seemed to be a delayed action response to lateral movements of the control column and the rate of roll was "by no means remarkable". At high speeds the lateral control became somewhat unresponsive and the lateral stability was, he felt, "rather less than one might expect".

The aircraft's behaviour at the stall had already been fully dealt with by Jeffrey Quill. However, as far as the stalling characteristics were concerned, it was very interesting to note (from the behaviour of wool tufts fitted to the port wing upper surface) the marked similarity between this aeroplane and a standard Spitfire fitted with Frise ailerons. Shea-Simonds concluded by saying "one excellent feature of this aircraft is the delightful smoothness of the

This series of Boscombe Down views of FR409 is dated October 1944, though it is thought that the aircraft first arrived at the airfield on 21 August. Note the large flap area. *Phil Butler*

Manufacturer's three-view drawing of the XP-51J. *US National Archives RG-342 via Tony Landis*

engine installation. This feature alone would be well worth achieving in many British fighters."

In the end neither 'F', 'G' or 'J' versions of the Mustang were taken to production by either the USAAF or the RAF and just the seven 'prototypes' were built. However, the knowledge and experience gained with the XP-51F and XP-51G was later incorporated into the P-51H production model, including the wing layout and aerodynamic improvements and landing gear, although the fuselage was made slightly longer. XP-51G 43-43335 has survived (in pieces) in private hands in La Cañada Flintridge in California.

XP-51F structure

The single-seat XP-51F's wings were formed from two panels and two tips and were manufactured primarily using stressed skin. Twin 0.50in (12.7mm) calibre machine guns were housed in the wings outside the propeller disc and a fuel tank was positioned in each panel just outboard of the centre rib. There was a 105galUS (397lit) tank in the starboard wing and a 75galUS (284lit) tank in the port wing, and with external fuel the total load came to 330galUS (1,249lit). The metal covered ailerons were internally balanced, while both the vertical and horizontal tail were stressed skin covered and had removable tips.

The fuselage consisted of two main sections – an engine section covered in sheet metal and then a main fuselage section, the latter formed from two beams comprising upper and lower longerons acting as spar flanges with the side skin then reinforced by frames that formed the webs. Rearwards, the after portion of the fuselage section had a shell-type sheet metal structure which housed the tailwheel assembly and the supporting structure for the empennage. The XP-51F had a Packard Merlin engine driving an 11ft 0in (3.35m) diameter Aeroproducts constant speed propeller.

Lightweight XP-51 data

Length:	XP-51F and XP-51G 32ft 3in (9.82m); XP-51J 32ft 11in (10.04m)
Wing span:	All 37ft 0.5in (11.29m)
Wing area:	All 235sq.ft (21.855sq.m)
Gross weight:	XP-51F 7,340lb (3,329kg); XP-51G 7,265lb (3,295kg); XP-51J 7,550lb (3,425kg)
Maximum take-off weight:	XP-51F 9,060lb (4,110kg); XP-51G 8,889lb (4,032kg); XP-51J 9,140lb (4,146kg)
Powerplant:	XP-51F 1 x 1,485hp (1,107kW) Packard Merlin V1650-3 liquid-cooled piston engine XP-51G 1 x 1,500hp (1,119kW) Rolls-Royce Merlin 145 (RM.14.SM) XP-51J 1 x 1,500hp (1,119kW) Allison V1710-119
Maximum speed:	XP-51F 491mph (790km/h) at 21,000ft (6,401m); XP-51G 470mph (756km/h) at 20,000ft (6,096m) – one source gives 498mph (801km/h) at c20,000ft (6,096m): XP-51J 471mph (758km/h) at 27,400ft (8,352m)
Maximum range (no bombs):	XP-51F 1,112 miles (1,789km)
Maximum rate of climb:	XP-51F 6,530ft/min (1,990m/min) at sea level
Service ceiling:	XP-51F 42,100ft (12,832m); XP-51G 45,700ft (13,929m); XP-51J 43,700ft (13,320m)
Absolute ceiling:	XP-51F 42,600ft (12,984m)
Armament (never carried):	XP-51F 4 x 0.50in (12.7mm) machine guns, 1 x 500lb (227kg) or 250lb (113kg) bomb; XP-51G 6 x 0.50in (12.7mm) machine guns; XP-51J 4 x 0.50in (12.7mm) machine guns

5 Vultee XP-54 'Swoose Goose'

The next subjects in this book, the XP-54 here, the Curtiss XP-55 and Northrop XP-56 in the following chapters, and then also the McDonnell XP-67 in Chapter Eleven, all resulted from a new design competition held during the winter of 1939/40. The common factor amongst these prototypes, and some of the rejected designs in the competition, was that their layouts were unconventional; indeed the four types under discussion in this volume could not have been more different. (For a much fuller account of this competition and the careers of the resulting aircraft, the reader is advised to read Gerald H. Balzer's excellent *American Secret Pusher Fighters of World War II*.)

Design competition

The competing designs were prepared against a document called R40-C and Specification XC-622 of November 1939, and one of the driving forces behind this move was that the previous 1939 competitions had failed to produce an outstanding aeroplane. Sufficient funding was to be made available to permit the ordering of twin prototypes of several different designs and their maximum speed was to be at least 425mph (684km/h) at altitudes between 15,000ft and 20,000ft (4,752m and 6,096m), but the desired maximum speed was the remarkably high figure for 1939/40 of 525mph (845km/h). The first of each of the pairs of prototypes or 'flying articles' was to be a flying shell and then, following flight testing, the second examples would be kitted out with full equipment.

Submissions from industry had been made by early April 1940. The top three designs were first a version of Vultee's V-70 project, second the Curtiss P-249C and third Northrop's N-2B; McDonnell's offering came some way behind, but the 'super-streamlining' of its Model 1 proposal generated enough interest that a prototype of a modified design was procured quite some time after the three 'winners' had been ordered.

Striking view of the first Vultee XP-54 prototype serial 41-1210. *Convair via Gerald H. Balzer*

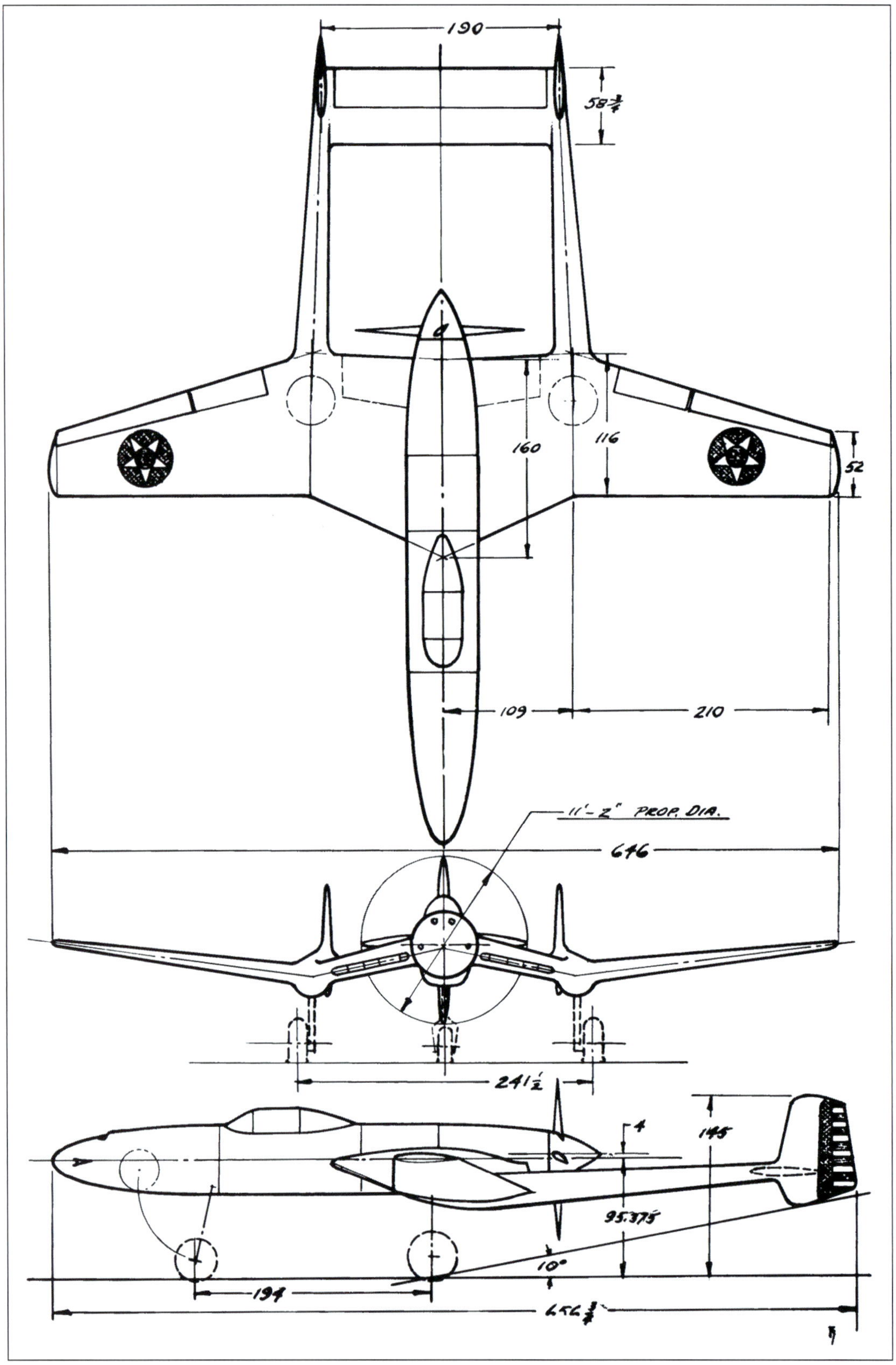

Early manufacturer's three-view drawing of the XP-54, with the original fin shape. In fact this came from a factory drawing retrieved from microfilm and then in essence redrawn by Gerry Balzer. *Convair via Gerald H. Balzer*

The initial contract with Vultee, W535-AC-15019 (Project number MX-12), was approved on 22 June 1940, and then on 16 September Materiel Division informed the manufacturer their intention to procure a second XP-54. The mock-up was officially inspected on 23 May 1941, but over time the original Vultee layout would be enlarged considerably through a series of design and requirement changes, and consequently it experienced substantial increases in weight. The path that the XP-54 followed from contract issue to end of career covered a mulitude of alterations,

Two views of 41-1210 undergoing final assembly at Downey, in a closed off security area, on 2 November 1942, over two months before first flight. *Convair via Gerald H. Balzer*

The first XP-54 is prepared for a test flight at Ontario, the view providing some detail for the fighter prototype's Lycoming XH2470-1 engine. *USAF via Gerald H. Balzer*

particularly to the engine and also through changes to the aircraft's role.

Firstly, the original plan had been to power the XP-54 with the experimental 1,850hp (1,380kW) Pratt & Whitney X1800 'H'-block engine, in fact the X1800-A4G fitted with a six-blade dual rotation propeller. However, on 4 October 1940 Wright Field advised the AAF's Material Division in Washington that Pratt & Whitney had decided to discontinue this engine; work on the X1800 had begun in 1938 but the manufacturer was now struggling with the project. As a replacement Brigadier General O.P. Echols at Wright Field recommended the 24-cylinder liquid-cooled Lycoming XH2470, and on 10 October Major F.O. Carroll, the chief of the Experimental Engineering Section at Wright Field, formally told Vultee to stop work on its X1800 installation and to concentrate now on fitting the XH2470. Lycoming's engine had been created by merging two opposed examples of its 12-cylinder 1,000hp (746kW) O1230 unit and it first ran on the bench in July 1940. The contra-rotating propeller was also now replaced by a single propeller, a step which automatically reduced the XP-54's estimated maximum speed and ceiling.

Then in May 1941 Echols took the decision to equip the XP-54 with turbo supercharging. Conferences held at Wright Field during September to discuss the fighter's future confirmed the procurement of two XP-54s with both to be powered by a supercharged XH2470-1; however, both machines were also to have space provision made to fit the experimental 42-cylinder Wright R2160 Tornado liquid-cooled inline radial engine, and if necessary with counter rotating propellers and two-speed gearing (the designation XP-68 was at one stage reserved for the Tornado version, but this project never went ahead and was cancelled on 22 November 1941 – see below). The chosen turbo supercharger for the XH2470-1 was the Wright Type TSBB, but this would be replaced on the second aircraft by the General Electric XCM turbo supercharger. One problem raised by turbo supercharging was that the hot turbo exhaust gases would run along the aft fuselage surface and thus overheat the aluminum skinning, so to deal with this a heat-resistant stainless steel cowling had to be installed behind the turbo outlets.

The reason behind the introduction of turbo supercharging was the decision by the AAF to turn the XP-54 from a high speed medium altitude aircraft, with an unsupercharged engine, into a high speed high-altitude interceptor with a rated altitude of 40,000ft (12,192m). A by-product of this move was that the cockpit now had to be pressurised and all of these changes brought heavy delays; in fact the aircraft was near redesigned entirely. For example, in its original form the XP-54 was to have been armed with six 0.50in (12.7mm) machine guns in the nose, but another change saw the introduction of 37mm cannon, along with armour and self-sealing fuel tanks, but it was to be the pressurised

41-1210 pictured outside Vultee's experimental hanger at Downey. *USAF via Gerald H. Balzer*

A further view taken at Downey that provides detail of the single-piece horizontal tail. *USAF via Gerald H. Balzer*

The purpose of the metal frame around the engine here is uncertain, but it was possibly to help align the engine/propeller fitting. The view is apparently dated late June 1943. *USAF via Gerald H. Balzer*

LEFT The XP-54 was a sleek and clean design, a point which contributed perhaps to disguising that this machine was a big beast. However, this close-up of thenose, taken at Muroc Army Air Base during an engine ground run in December 1942, does give an indication of how big it was. *Convair via Gerald H. Balzer*

BELOW Another view taken on the dry lake bed during December 1942. Ground crew are inspecting smoke coming from the main undercarriage brakes. This phenomenon appeared during the XP-54's high-speed taxi runs, during which the brakes tended to overheat. *Convair via Gerald H. Balzer*

BELOW A further Muroc view showing ground engineers working on the underside of the XP-54. *Convair via Gerald H. Balzer*

cockpit which added much of the extra weight. Finally, with the nature of this prototype fighter's pusher engine configuration, a novel method of escape for the pilot in an emergency was required, which is described later.

Many of these changes had been prompted by reports of the air fighting in the war over Europe. With a roughly 20% increase in size the XP-54 would now become one of the largest single-seat fighters ever flown. The two XP-54s (the new type was nicknamed 'Swoose Goose' at Vultee) received US military serials 41-1210 (first) and 42-108994 (second); however, all of the photos of the second prototype known to the author show it carrying the serial [4]1-1211 (all of these views appear to have been taken on the same flight, so was the correct serial ever painted up?). Vultee's XP-54 development team was led initially by chief engineer Richard W. Palmer, and then by A. P. 'Jack' Fontaine. At the start of the programme Vultee's chief engineer was E.G. Bunce, chief aerodynamicist William Curtis Rockefeller and chief designer M.F. Stoughton.

This was, incidentally, the last project undertaken as a pure Vultee aircraft before, in March 1943, the firm merged with Consolidated to become the Consolidated Vultee Aircraft Corporation, or Convair. In addition, the XP-54 flight test programme utilised one of the world's first telemetering systems; the Vultee Radio Recorder, designed by Harvey D. Gillis, had pickups that recorded variations in parameters such as pressure and temperature, which enabled it to supply real time data to the staff monitoring the flights on the ground.

Flight test

Having been taken by road from its Downey birthplace to Muroc, the first XP-54 had near completed its ground tests by Christmas 1942, and then its first flight, of 31 minutes duration, was accomplished on 15 January 1943. In the cockpit was Vultee chief test pilot, Frank Davis, who would perform all of the manufacturer's sorties with this aircraft. However, for this maiden flight 41-1210 had a Curtiss propeller fitted and the aircraft's take-off, acceleration and climb proved to be very poor – the Curtiss was simply the wrong choice to make full use of the available engine power. Consequently, prior to the second flight which took place on 27 January, a four-blade Hamilton Standard propeller had been fitted in its place and this improved the performance considerably. Overall, the XP-54's initial flights showed that it a was pleasant and easy aircraft to fly with good handling characteristics and, after just five flights at Muroc, on 20 February it was flown to the AAF base at Ontario in California. This was closer to Vultee's factory at Downey, which ensured that better engineering backup was close at hand.

It had been hoped that for landing the XP-54 would only have to use its outboard slotted flaps, with the split inboard flaps employed on engine and oil cooling alone, but flight nine on 7 March established that both sets of flaps were be required for landing; consequently, the two sets were now rigged together. The trials flying was not completely free of problems either; for example on one flight the air intake duct between the engine and supercharger blew out, forcing Frank Davis to make an emergency landing at El Toro. The testing conducted from Muroc and Ontario with 41-1210 would total 86 flights and just over 63 flight hours.

On 14 May 1943 the Engineering Division at Wright Field asked Consolidated-Vultee to provide results from the XP-54's preliminary tests. At this time the only information available to Wright Field was data accumulated during a test run made on 23 April, which indicated that (at normal power) the prototype would reach approximately 320mph (515km/h) at 10,000ft (3,048m). On 25 May Wright Field informed Washington that the test flights to date were indicating that the XP-54's maximum speed may be as much as 100mph (161km/h) below the guaranteed figures (in fact the loss in speed would prove to be considerable but not quite to this extent). On 28 May 1943 a maximum speed of 290mph (467km/h) was recorded at at sea level and 381mph (613km/h) at 28,500ft (8,689m); the gross weight here was 18,233lb (8,270kg).

Also during May 1943 the question of the XP-54's future was raised by AAF Headquarters in Washington. Air Material Command declared that it wanted to continue the project, although the lack of engine power and performance meant that production was now out of the question. But AMC wished to continue the flight trials to gain general aerodynamic data on pusher propeller type aircraft for future applications. However, during August 1943 the XP-54 was quoted by General Arnold, with several other experimental fighters, as being recommended for contract closure (as mentioned elsewhere in this book). Then on 18 August the AAF decided to accept delivery of the first XP-54 and close the contract.

The first XP-54 was flown from Ontario to Wright Field to come under AAF control on 28 October 1943. Throughout the trials so far the XH2470-1 had performed well, but it did suffer from oil foaming and scavenging at heights over 15,000ft (4,572m) and this problem was never fully resolved. Frank Davis told Wright Field about this weakness at altitude and the AAF's engineers made some immediate modifications. When Davis flew 41-1210 to check out these modifications, backfiring and a loss of power were experienced on the climb and he landed immediately. The Wright Field Power Plant Laboratory confirmed minor failures in the carburettor plus supercharger impeller damage, and it was clear that the cost of repairing the engine was not worth the effort. So 41-1210 was removed from flight status, it never took to the air again and instead was held as a spares source for the second prototype.

Reports on the XP-54's flying characteristics had, however, shown them to be pretty good. On the

ABOVE A seemingly very rare photo showing XP-54 Number 1 in flight. Here it still has the original fin arrangement. *Convair via Gerald H. Balzer*

RIGHT The first XP-54 lined up on the runway at Ontario Army Air Field. Now in place is the heat-resistant stainless steel cowling to the rear of the turbo outlets, which was intended to protect the aluminum skinning from overheating. *Convair via Gerald H. Balzer*

ground its control (in part due to the tricycle undercarriage) was very good and the take-off was achieved at speeds between 120mph and 130mph (193km/h and 209km/h), depending on the take-off weight. In the air stability and control was good about each of the three axes. The elevator was light and adequate, the rudder was light and virtually no trim change was necessary when power and speed were altered, and the loads on the ailerons did not increase at higher speeds. A controllable longitudinal instability was present when making power climbs at 180mph (290km/h), and with most of the fuel and ammunition expended the centre of gravity would move well aft, so the nose needed some ballasting. At a gross weight of 18,000lb (8,165kg), and with the inboard split flap set 10° down and the outboard slotted flaps 30° down, the stall occurred at 110mph (177km/h), and then with the flaps up at 120mph (193km/h).

During its flying career 41-1210 recorded true air speeds in a dive as high as 470 mph (756km/h), but the level speed performance was a disappointment. However, it was found that the quality of the external surface finish caused big variations in speed. Three conditions were assessed – factory finish (with camouflage), superfinish (with camouflage) and then superfinish with a waxed and polished surface. Taking the first and third conditions, the maximum speeds recorded at sea level in military power (at 18,360lb/8,328kg gross weight) were 287mph and 304mph respectively (462km/h and 489km/h), and then 380mph and 404mph (611km/h and 650km/h) at 28,000ft (8,534m), which was the critical altitude for the turbo running at 23,000rpm; the 'guaranteed' figure had been 479mph (771km/h) at 27,000ft (8,230m). At this weight the sea level rate of climb was really poor, at 1,620ft/min (494m/min).

After its arrival at Wright Field on 28 October 1943 the official cameraman took a series of walk-around views of 41-1210, which now has the enlarged dorsal fins and also the Vultee logo applied beneath the cockpit canopy. *USAF via Gerald H. Balzer*

Unusual photo showing 41-1210 parked on the ramp at El Toro Marine Air Base. This was after test pilot Frank Davis had been forced to make an emergency landing here following a blow out which had damaged the air intake ducting between the engine and supercharger. *Gerald H. Balzer*

Installing General Electric's new higher capacity XCM turbosupercharger delayed the second prototype, so that it did not make its first flight until 24 May 1944; this sortie, a trip from Downey to Ontario, lasted 20 minutes. The flying career of this machine is not well documented, but Frank Davis definitely flew it ten times between this 24 May flight and one on 2 April 1945, which in fact was the last occasion when an XP-54 would get airborne.

Six weeks after 42-108994's first flight Consolidated-Vultee advised that the engine and its turbo superchargers were clearly not totally compatible, this was causing serious damage to both parties and they needed to be returned to their manufacturers for rework. Convair also stated most strongly that it wanted to close out the XP-54 contract in order to give "greater attention to its new secret ship" (the XP-81 in Chapter Seventeen). However, by 16 October 1944 a new Lycoming engine had been fitted and at least seven more XP-54 flights were made with this unit in place.

On retirement the nose of the second XP-54 was removed at the San Bernardino Air Depot and then despatched to Eglin Field for some planned gun firing tests; the remainder of the airframe was dismantled for scrapping. The first XP-54 was then sent to Wright Field's Structural Test Laboratory who ultimately tested it to destruction.

XP-68

As noted, following the mock-up inspection of the XP-54 in its original form as a medium altitude fighter on 23 May 1941, Generals Echols and Kenny directed that the XP-54 should be equipped with turbo superchargers. That automatically meant further changes such as the application of a pressure cabin, all of such magnitude collectively that they required the redesign of the airframe referred to, including increasing the wing area and the weight. Installing the Tornado in one of the prototypes as the XP-68 was seriously considered, but the engine was dropped due to poor performance estimates, based mainly on the fact that the Tornado involved a 4 to 1 propeller reduction gear whereas Vultee's fighter design called for a reduction gear of approximately 2 to 1 with a dual rotation propeller. Conferences held during September 1941 determined that it would be practically impossible to use the Tornado because the gear ratio required a propeller of larger diameter than could be swung between the booms. As a result it was decided to proceed with the installation of the Lycoming H2470-1 engine in both XP-54s, and to have space provisions only for the possible future application of the Tornado R2160 with two speed gearing and opposite rotating propellers.

Frustratingly, there appears to be just one sequence of air-to-air photos, indeed any photos, of the second XP-54 prototype and incredibly they all look pretty similar. These views have been selected to try and show differing angles and detail. The author is not aware of any images showing the second machine on the ground. *Convair via Gerald H. Balzer*

As noted in the text, in all of the known pictures of the second prototype the aircraft carried an incorrect serial number on its fins. This has caused confusion over the years, because serial 41-1211 was in fact allocated to a BT-13A Valiant trainer, another product from Vultee. The XP-54's serial here should have been 42-108994. Note again the extension to the forward part of the fin above the rear boom. *Convair via Gerald H. Balzer*

The danger posed to the pilot by bailing out with a propeller directly behind, the XP-54's pressure cabin, and in addition the aircraft's height over the ground, meant that Vultee's designers had no option but to create this unusual pilot entry and exit arrangement and system. As shown here, the seat would drop down ready for the pilot to get aboard. The canopy was fixed because of pressurisation. *Convair via Gerald H. Balzer*

The XP-54's port side inboard split flap, which had twin panels with the smaller type outboard designed to control the air flowing past the radiators. The underside of the engine appears to have wool tufts attached to enable to airflow around the nacelle to be observed. *Convair via Gerald H. Balzer*

A series of drawings showing how the pilot would escape the XP-54 in an emergency. This extraordinary mechanism was designed to avoid him hitting the pusher propeller on departure. *USAF Museum*

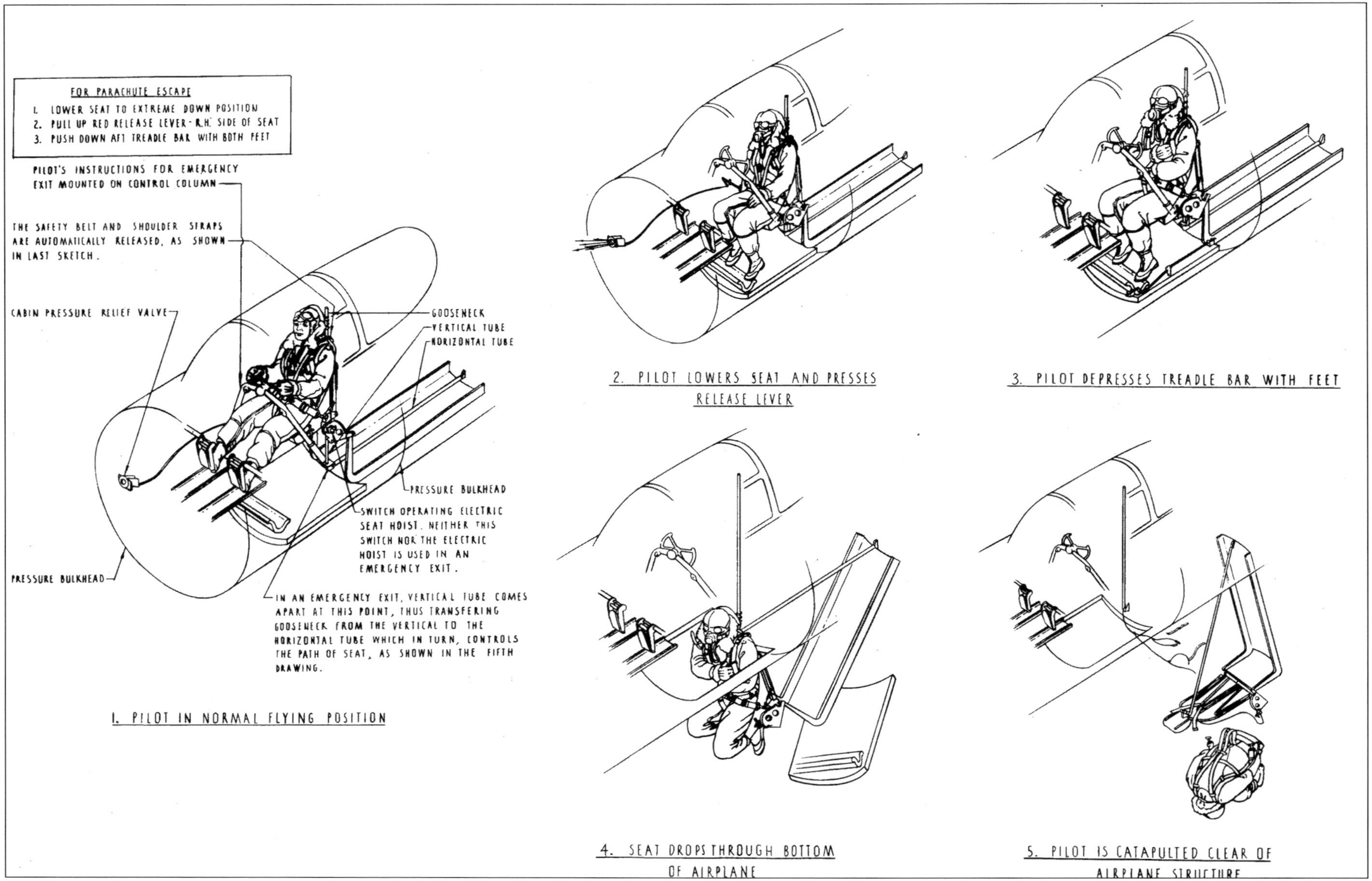

XP-54 structure

The XP-54 fighter had an all-metal structure manufactured entirely in aluminium alloy (reports that portions of the bullet-shaped forward fuselage were made in lightweight magnesium alloy are apparently in error). It had a twin-boom layout coupled with a low position gull-wing and a tricycle landing gear. The wing was of laminar flow section of a NACA-developed form described as a "ducted wing section". It featured two sets of flaps - split flaps between the booms and the fuselage and slotted flaps stretching outboard from the booms up to the ailerons. Air intakes for both oil and coolant were positioned within the inner wing, with the air passing through the leading-edge and flowing over the radiators before exiting via the trailing-edge flaps; thus there were no external radiators to disturb the aircraft's clean form.

Twin booms were faired into the wing, the tail was positioned inbetween the booms and each of the latter had its own fin and rudder; flight tests revealed that additional vertical fin area was necessary and so a 1.85sq.ft (0.172sq.m) dorsal section was attached subsequently to each fin. The wing-fuselage intersections were very clean, to the point that they were looked upon as an advance in state-of-the-art aerodynamics. A very clean circular cross section centre fuselage contained the pressurised cockpit, fuel tank, engine and in the nose the four guns. Both XP-54s had their guns installed but they were never fired in flight; in fact the elevation of the nose could be altered to permit these variable-range guns to fire more accurately – the nose could be depressed or elevated to accommodate the quite different ballistics of the machine guns and the cannon, without having to alter the fighter's flying attitude.

The Lycoming XH2470 drove a Hamilton Standard four-blade 12ft 2in (3.71m) diameter propeller and the two prototypes had different turbo superchargers. The first XP-54 had two Wright B turbos set in parallel while the second machine had a single General Electric type XCM turbo of greater capacity, in both cases all situated beneath the rear fuselage. Maximum overload fuel was 378galUS (1,431lit) with maximum internal fuel (on the second aircraft) 140galUS (530lit).

As noted earlier, if the pilot needed to bail out of the aircraft while airborne it was a problem and a worry for the design team to ensure he did not hit the rotating blades of the pusher engine. The chosen solution was a catapult arrangement that would push the pilot out through the bottom of the fuselage and clear of the propeller. For the pilot to first access the cockpit, his seat would be lowered through the bottom of the fuselage and then raised back up again to lift him into the normal flying position. If he then had to bail out, this process would be reversed but very rapidly, the 'swinging arm' automatically depositing him downwards and outwards and fast enough to clear the blades. Ejection seats were not yet on the scene and developing this facility, together with the pressurised cockpit, proved a most difficult process. This 'lift seat' principle to first get the pilot into the XP-54 was also necessary because the cockpit was around 6ft (1.83m) above the ground.

XP-54 data

Length:	54ft 9in (16.69m)
Wing span:	53ft 10in (16.40m)
Wing area:	455.5sq.ft (42.36sq.m)
Empty weight:	15,262lb (6,923kg)
Design gross weight (223 gal us/844 lit fuel):	18,360lb (8,328kg) – as delivered 18,735lb (8,498kg)
Maximum take-off (overload) weight:	19,735lb (8,952kg)
Powerplant:	1 x 2,300hp (1,715kW) Lycoming XH2470-1 'H'-shape liquid-cooled piston engine
Maximum speed:	304mph (489km/h) at sea level, 404mph (650km/h) at 28,000ft (8,534m)
Maximum rate of climb:	2,300ft/min (701m/min)
Service ceiling:	37,000ft (11,278m)
Normal range:	500 miles (805km)
Armament:	2 x 0.50in (12.70mm) machine guns and 2 x 37mm cannon in nose

6 Curtiss XP-55 Ascender

The second of the R40-C/Specification XC-622 prototypes to be ordered was the Curtiss XP-55 Ascender, a remarkable design since it had swept wings positioned towards the rear of the fuselage with the elevator attached to the nose. On seeing this 'reversed' foreplane configuration, which at the time was a major departure from previous fighter design practice, the St Louis Globe-Democrat newspaper for 11 March 1945 described the XP-55 as "the plane that seems to fly backwards". The XP-55 was preceded by a flying scale model research aircraft and then the prototypes themselves experienced serious delays, though the delays were more of a consequence of the greater priority given to Curtiss-Wright's current war production work.

Curtiss 24-B

Curtiss chose the tail first arrangement because it was believed this configuration would give less drag overall, which with extreme aerodynamic cleanliness should then provide good high speed performance. Meeting the specified performance requirements made it necessary to reduce the drag by a considerable margin since the engines then currently available offered relatively low levels of power, one of the reasons why the XP-54, XP-55 and XP-56 all employed unusual and unconventional configurations. Each of these aircraft used a pusher engine to eliminate propeller slipstream effects on airframe drag; further, both the XP-55 and XP-56 utilised what was termed the stable wing principle.

Curtiss Ascender serial number 42-78847 was the third and last XP-55 to be built and flown. *Curtiss via Gerald H. Balzer*

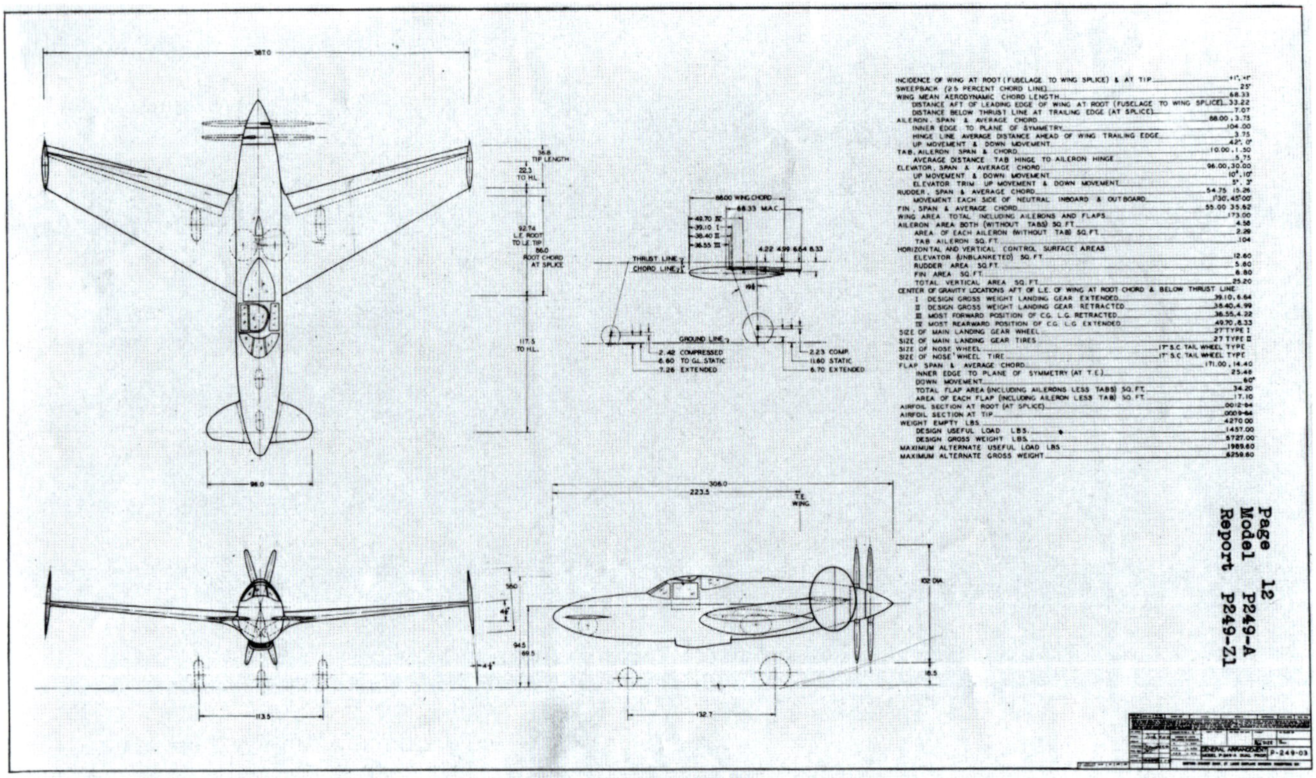

FIGURE 1
GENERAL ARRANGEMENT - P249-A

The Curtiss P-249A as proposed to R40-C and Specification XC-622 in April 1940. Powered by a Allison V1710-F3R engine driving a four-blade 8ft 6in (2.59m) diameter propeller, the P-249A had a span of 32ft 3in (9.83m), length 25ft 6in (7.77m), gross wing area 173sq.ft (16.09sq.m) and a design gross weight of 5,727lb (2,597kg). The planed armament was two 0.50in (12.7mm) and one 0.30in (7.6mm) machine guns plus a single 37mm cannon, and the guaranteed maximum speed was 480mph (772km/h) at 20,000ft (6,096m). To avoid the propeller in an emergency (which itself could be jettisoned) the pilot had an early form of ejection seat.

Two alternative versions were the P-249C (initially the most favoured by the AAF) with a Continental IV1430-3 engine and four-blade 8ft 3in (2.51m) diameter single rotating propeller, and the P-249T with a Wright Tornado 756-2-3 and a six-blade 10ft 0in (3.05m) dual rotation propeller. Apart from the powerplant portion of the fuselage, in each case the airframe was unchanged from the P-249A having the same wing and span. The P-249C had a length of 25ft 6in (7.77m), the estimated gross weight was 5,674lb (2,574kg) and its maximum speed 510mph (821km/h) at 20,000ft (6,096m). P-249T's length was 26ft 10in (8.79m), gross weight 9,157lb (4,154kg) - the Tornado having a marked effect on this figure - and maximum speed 525mph (845km/h) at 20,000ft (6,096m). *Gerald H. Balzer archive*

The design which became the XP-55 had been placed second in the competition and authority for the project to proceed (under Project number MX-13) was endorsed at the end of May 1940. However, apart from standard wind tunnel testing and a powered full-size model, the resulting contract (WC535-AC-15020 of 22 June) included only an option for purchasing a single experimental prototype. In due course it it was decided to drop the prototype and proceed just with the wind tunnel work and the scale model.

The tunnel testing, on a 1/4th scale powered model, was extensive. Conducted at the Massachusetts Institute of Technology between 5 November 1940 and 28 January 1941, it embraced 560 separate runs and, with such an unconventional layout, a very large proportion allocated to clearing the wing. In fact two different wings were assessed – Type I featured a conventional NACA aerofoil section and then Type II had a laminar flow section also designed by NACA . Although the Type I was considered the most suitable for the fighter, a decision was made to in fact use a laminar flow wing. These tests also enabled the wing sweep angle limits to be established, and they confirmed that this configuration did offer low drag.

In the end the AAF was not that happy with the tunnel data and so chose not to proceed further. However, the Curtiss-Wright Corporation design team felt the opposite, they considered that there was sufficient promise in these results and so they went ahead with building the low-powered full-scale flying model using the manufacturer's own finance. This was designated the Curtiss-Wright model CW-24-B and it had a very basic structure to

Manufacturer's artwork for the Curtiss P.249A. Note the contra-rotating propeller. *Curtiss via Gerald H. Balzer*

cut costs and to speed up its assembly. This determination was rewarded because, with the construction of the CW-24-B near complete, the AAF revived its sponsorship with the issue of Contract W535-AC-22239 of 26 November 1941 to cover this work. In addition the model was to be test flown from the AAF's Muroc Dry Lake base in California. Army serial number 42-39347 was assigned to the 24-B.

The CW-24-B's structure was a mix of metal and wood covered with fabric (a welded steel tube fuselage and an all wood wing), it was powered by a

Side view taken at St. Louis of the Curtiss CW-24-B full-scale research aircraft as built. *Curtiss via Gerald H. Balzer*

Rear angle photos of the 24-B which show firstly the aircraft in its original condition and then after the addition of vertical fins above and below the engine cowling, and with the wing fins moved much further out. *Curtiss via Gerald H. Balzer*

275hp (205kW) Menasco C6S-5 engine, its first flight took place on 2 December 1941 and the aircraft could reach a speed of 180mph (290km/h). The flying programme held at Muroc essentially covered two phases. There was an initial period during which certain modifications had to made to the airframe in order to establish the configuration that would give optimum flying qualities, then a second phase was devoted to collecting performance data.

The earliest flights had indicated that the CW-24-B possessed a certain degree of directional instability, but various experiments in altering the size and shapes of the wing-mounted fins and rudders, moving them further out to the wing tips, and introducing shallow vertical fins to the top and bottom of the engine cowling, improved the stability situation somewhat and gave good results. Eventually the vertical fins were placed 4ft (1.22m) further outboard from their original position, and at a later date wing tip extensions beyond the fins were introduced which improved the pitching moments of the 24-B's tips just prior to when the inboard part of the wings would stall.

Wing stall on any conventional aircraft of this time period would bring a change to the downwash and produce large diving moments from the horizontal tail surfaces. However, since the 24-B lacked a horizontal tail or any control surfaces aft of the wing, this breakdown in downwash would at most produce minimal effects on the aircraft's longitudinal trim. Thanks to the Menasco C6S-5 engine's unreliability, and the lack of sufficient power to get the 24-B up to a sufficiently safe altitude, deliberate spins were not attempted right through the aircraft's stalling trials. Nevertheless, the 24-B's manoeuvrability trials provided data that prompted an increase in the aircraft's nose elevator area by some 25%, which then improved the longitudinal control and the control during the take-off run.

The CW-24-B flying programme at Muroc lasted from November 1941 to May 1942, it totalled 169 flights and contributed vital information and data for the XP-55 design itself. The 24-B flight test report concluded and recommended that, "to facilitate take-off and flight characteristics the elevator area on the XP-55 should probably be increased 20% to 25% over the original elevator area of the flying model", and "the wing tip extensions improved the flying characteristics of the 24-B so much, especially at low speeds, that it is recommended that extensions of the type tested on the 24-B be incorporated in the XP-55." On completion of its flying career the CW-24-B was transferred to NACA for full-scale wind tunnel tests to be made in that establishment's laboratory at Langley Field in Virginia, which lasted from September to November 1942.

Separately, NACA had conducted a tunnel investigation of the 24-B's spinning characteristics using a 1/16th scale model and the results suggested that the aircraft's spin behaviour could be a worry. Any spin rotation could be halted but the model's vertical descent would continue unabated with the fuselage holding a horizontal attitude – in other words it appeared that a pilot would not be able to regain control from a spin just by using the aircraft's controls. Problems with spinning and stalling would prove to be the XP-55's Achilles Heel.

Here the 24-B demonstrates the wing tip fins assessed on this research aircraft. *Curtiss via Gerald H. Balzer*

Nevertheless, with the CW-24-B flying model programme finished (bar at this point the spinning trials) the AAF moved on to ordering three full XP-55 prototypes under Contract W535-AC-29013, approved on 10 July l942. Changes from the original R40/XC-622 proposals included the replacement of the Continental IV1430-3 engine of the P249C project to an Allison V1710-F16 (the P249A proposal to R40 was to have used an V1710-F3R) and the substitution of the original dual rotation propeller with a single rotation three-blade fitting. It was agreed that any production versions (as the P-55) would use newer engines, if they provided more power. There was also a revised guaranteed performance for the fighter which now included a maximum speed of 419mph (674km/h) at 19,300ft (5,883m). At this stage the armament comprised twin 20mm cannon mounts and twin 0.50in (12.7mm) calibre machine guns.

The XP-55 mock-up was assembled and duly inspected by AAF officials between August and December 1942 and the latter resulted in several detail changes, the most important being a reduction in fuel capacity and updating the armament to four 0.50in (12.7mm) machine guns (along with moving the guns' position to make accessibility easier). The unavailability of the V1710-F16 also brought a switch to a V1710-95, and the contract was later amended to cover the introduction of droppable fuel tanks. Curtiss chief engineer George Augustus Page Jr. and chief designer E.M. 'Bud' Flesh led the design team and serial numbers 42-78845 to 42-78847 inclusive were allotted to the three XP-55s.

Lovely view of the 24-B in flight late in its career. Note the fixed undercarriage. *Curtiss via Gerald H. Balzer*

XP-55 flight test

On 13 July 1943 the completed first XP-55 was delivered to AAF control at Curtiss-Wright's plant at Scott Field, St. Louis. It had been rolled out on 26 June, was taken by road to Scott Field on 7 July and began taxi runs on the 11th. Flight testing opened on 13 July with Curtiss' test pilot J. Harvey Gray in the cockpit. However, excessive ground runs were experienced during take off, so around 15% more area was added to the nose elevator which brought a considerable improvement to the run (and increased the foreplane span by 27in/68.7cm, from 8ft 11in/2.48m to 11ft 2in/3.40m).

On completion of these initial tests, now flying out of Lambert-St. Louis Airport the XP-55 programme moved on to an assessment of the flying qualities. By early October 42-78845 had had wing flow fences fitted immediately inboard of the ailerons and a major redesign of the engine's ventral air intake (only this XP-55 received flow fences, and also leading edge spoilers). However, on 15 November 1943 42-78845 was lost during a series of stalls. This sortie (Flight 27) had in fact been made with the objective of investigating the effects of wing spoilers on the XF-55's pitching characteristics in a stall. Two stalls completed with the aircraft's undercarriage and flaps retracted had proved entirely satisfactorily, but the third trial was to assess the situation with the gear and flaps now deployed. The resulting accident report detailed what happened next:

"The third stall was begun at an altitude of about 21,000ft (6,401m), landing gear extended, flaps full down, zero aileron trim, 20% elevator balance. At 86mph (138km/h) indicated 21,000ft (6,401m) altitude the plane pitched forward approximately 90°, hesitated momentarily, then continued [a further] 90° until it was on its back. There was no roll or yaw with the pitch, elevator control stick assumed position full aft against the stops. Power was immediately applied but the engine stopped running after approximately two seconds. Immediate application of controls did not effect recovery, therefore landing gear and flaps were retracted. No apparent recovery resulted.

The engine could not be started and the pilot [Gray] decided to bail out and [after some difficulty] fell free from the plane at approximately 5,000ft (1,524m). After falling clear, the pilot noticed that the airplane was descending at approximately the same rate as he was, even though he had not opened his parachute. The airplane was moving away from him horizontally, headed south but it gradually rotated 90° right during descent (heading

The first XP-55 42-78845 pictured at Scott Field on 11 July 1943 after final assembly, but as yet not flown. At this stage the serial number was painted on the nose sides. *Curtiss via Gerald H. Balzer*

east). The pilot observed that it was still upside down, 'parachuting' down steadily without oscillating. Its descent was so vertical and steady that there was no apparent change in its attitude when it struck the ground."

The pitch following this stall had progressed so quickly that the XP-55 had forwarded 180° onto its back and stabilised in a vertical, inverted descent, and it proved to be so stable under this condition - power off, inverted and at speeds below the stall - that recovery was impossible; incredibly, on impact with the ground there was no fire. The resulting imprint on the ground, with after first impact the aircraft having bounced forward by 21ft (6.4m) in the direction of the prevailing wind, showed that 42-78845 had descended upside down with practically no forward speed.

Previously, with the CW-24-B trials, when this research aircraft had fallen out of a stall its nose would point practically straight down until an indicated airspeed of 90mph (145km/h) had been reached, at which point the elevator became effective and recovery could be accomplished. The XP-55 accident report concluded the following (amongst a number of other points):

> "1. The longitudinal control characteristics at and below the stall in normal and inverted attitudes require further investigation by wind tunnel test and flight test. The use of spoilers is one satisfactory method of improving the control in the clean condition but gives indications of being inadequate for the landing condition.

The first prototype receives attention in one of the Curtiss hangers after the serial number had been moved to the dorsal fin. The picture shows the starboard flow fence positioned mid-wing, a feature which did not appear on the other XP-55s. *Curtiss via Gerald H. Balzer*

42-78845 in flight near St. Louis after the ventral air inlet had been redesigned to ensure the required boundary layer separation was present for the airflow to give sufficient cooling to the engine. *Curtiss via Gerald H. Balzer*

2. The XP-55 as loaded for Flight 27 is completely stable in inverted flight at speeds below the 'control out' stall, both in clean and landing conditions. This is the primary cause of the crash of the airplane.

3. Types of failure to the aluminium alloy and magnesium alloy sheet structural members indicate that the elongation characteristics of aluminium alloy sheet make this material the more satisfactory for aircraft structure."

So, as a result of this accident, further tunnel testing was needed prior to further stalling trials in flight. Several wing modifications were introduced with the intention of providing better stall characteristics. It had been learnt from the tunnel work that the XP-55's stall characteristics could be much improved by adding wing tip extensions of greater area, and by increasing the limits of nose elevator travel; also more area was given to the tip extensions to halt a decrease in rate of roll. However, at this stage these modifications would be incorporated into the third prototype only since this machine was still in fabrication.

The second prototype 42-78846 made its maiden flight on 9 January 1944 but in a configuration that was essentially the same as the first example, apart from a slightly larger nose elevator, an amended elevator tab system and a switch from balance tabs to spring tabs on the ailerons. Consequently, all of the flying conducted with 42-78846 was restricted to flight in conditions that were far outside the stall zone. Once the third machine had been completed, and had accomplished stall testing to a satisfactorily

The first XP-55 pictured again in flight. Pilots used to the conventional format of types such as the Curtiss P-40 and Republic P-47 must have been quite shocked to see this most radical design. *Curtiss via Gerald H. Balzer*

42-78845 following its most unusual accident, having dropped to the ground inverted without its pilot. It rather looks like a road roller had gone over the airframe, such is the compacting of the structure. And no fire! *Curtiss via Gerald H. Balzer*

level, the second airframe could go back to the factory for a rework and receive the necessary modifications to insure that its stall recovery behaviour would be satisfactory.

The third XP-55 42-78847 was completed in April 1944. Ground-based gun firing trials were started before any flight trials, but these resulted in further minor changes to the blast tubes and the addition of streamlined fairings to the forward end of these tubes. The aircraft's maiden flight took place on 25 April and it differed from the first and second airframes in having the increased elevator travel limits and the extended wing tip with what were called 'tailerons'. Once again, however, the take-off run proved unsatisfactory because the first sortie revealed that the increased elevator limits made the pilot hold such a high angle of elevator that it would stall; as a result the take-off run was far too long.

So another modification was a new automatic elevator stop that limited elevator down travel (nose-up) to just 17° during normal flight, but for inverted flight would be swung aside to permit the full 70° down travel. Also, before stall testing opened, a modification was introduced to 42-78847's fuel system to ensure that fuel would still reach the engine if the aircraft was inverted. This would permit several minutes of inverted operation and thus cover the situation of the XP-55 flipping on to its back again, with (hopefully) the pilot this time able to recover the aircraft.

The stall trials with 42-78847 proved satisfactory but did reveal two more shortcomings - a complete lack of any warning prior to the stall, and then the excessive loss of altitude needed to recover the machine to level flight. To deal with the first problem an artificial stall warning device was fitted in the form of a pressure pickup tube which would create a vibration that passed to the control column. Although helpful, this device still fell short of the normal stall warning associated with a conventional aircraft, i.e. experiencing buffet or vibration.

The AAF accepted 42-78847 on 5 November 1944 when Harvey Gray flew it to Eglin Field in Florida for gun firing trials, to see how an aircraft of this configuration might behave as a gun platform. Unfortunately, however, the gun mounts and blast tubes all failed during these ground-based tests and so in mid-December 42-78847 was flown to Wright Field.

The third XP-55 became the second to be lost in a crash and this occasion, on 27 May 1945, it proved tragic. The aircraft was piloted by Capt. William C. Glasgow who was leading a flight of five fighter types to display at an event at Wright Field. Having completed a slow roll, Glasgow began a second roll but the XP-55 wavered to left and right before making an inverted dive into the ground. He was killed and the XP-55 then broke through the airfield boundary fence and burst into flames, which killed a second person on the ground and severely injured several more.

Early photo of the second XP-55 42-78846 taken at its St Louis birthplace on 6 January 1944, just a few days before first flight. *Curtiss via Gerald H. Balzer*

42-78846 in November 1944 on the ground at Wright Field, now in its final condition which included redesigned undercarriage fairings. *Curtiss via Gerald H. Balzer*

In due course the second XP-55, 42-78846, was updated to conform to the configuration of the third. Army pilots performed its AAF performance tests at St. Louis between 16 September and 2 October 1944, the programme totalling 25 flights and 27 hours airtime. The second prototype was accepted by the AFF on 25 October and flown to Wright Field where, during November and December, a series of AAF pilot's observation flights was completed. But the pilots who sampled this XP-55 raised objections in the same areas that had previously caused trouble - an excessive take-off run and poor stall behaviour. The second XP-55 still survives and is on display at the Kalamazoo Air Zoo in Michigan.

The AAF aircrew who tackled the performance tests in 42-78846 in September and October 1944, in particular assessing the machine's high speed and climb performance at military power, were Maj. Everett W. Leach and Lt. Frank G. Morris, Jr. Gerald Balzer's book *American Secret Pusher Fighters of World War II* reviews their report in more detail; what follows here is a résumé.

On the ground the XP-55's handling was good and matched contemporary fighters with a tricycle undercarriage. The view out for taxiing was excellent except, thanks to the wing sweep, the wing tips could not be seen from the cockpit, so movements on a crowded airfield could be difficult. An unusually long take-off run, around 3,000ft to 3,500ft (914m and 1,067m) on a concrete surface with no wind, mainly the result of having no propeller slipstream over the control surfaces, had much in common with new jet fighters then coming under test. Incidentally, the pusher engine reversed the direction of propeller torque, to the right rather than to the left for tractor engine types.

Adjustable trim was available to both the rudders and nose elevator, but aileron trim was manually adjustable only and thus had to be done on the ground. In the air rudder control was sufficient to overcome adverse aileron yaw caused by an abrupt aileron deflection at speeds as low as 160mph (257km/h) IAS. Control effectiveness was

Excellent view of one of the XP-55s in flight. *Allison via Gerald H. Balzer*

LEFT AND BELOW CENTRE The third prototype 42-78847 was something approaching the definitive XP-55 and, in this form, it was hoped that it might have a future. But so much time and development effort had been expended in trying to improve its stall and spin characteristics, it was too late! *Curtiss via Gerald H. Balzer*

BELOW The nose of 42-78847 with the landing light positioned dead centre (on the first prototype this had been mounted on the undercarriage gear strut). Openings for the four machine guns are all above the centre line, lower left is the pitot tube, lower right the gun camera aperture. *Curtiss via Gerald H. Balzer*

good under all normal flight conditions. The elevator forces at low speeds were higher than average but for moderate to high speeds they were just a little over normal. Elevator response, however, was considered unconventional, and detrimental for a stable gun platform. A sudden elevator displacement with the stick held fixed would produce an oscillating pitching and a reversal of stick forces, which then gradually decreased in amplitude; a similar elevator problem was uncontrollable pitching in rough air. Aileron effectiveness was good but a little heavy. Slow rolls performed at cruising speed were smooth but the rate of roll only fair (and because of engine torque faster to the right).

The report noted that the stall behaviour was "both unusual and undesirable". Power-off stalls were performed both with the flaps and undercarriage down and in the clean condition. Approaching the stall there was no warning. Entry was abrupt, rolling to the right and simultaneously

pitching into a nose down attitude. The resulting manoeuvre changed the flight direction by some 135° and there was an excessive loss of altitude (3,000ft to 3,500ft [914m and 1,067m]). If the pilot made no attempt to correct using the controls, the XP-55 would enter a vertical dive until the airspeed was high enough to affect a safe recovery. But if he tried to prevent the post-stall roll or stop the rotation using rudder, the aircraft felt as though it had "re-entered the stall accompanied by negative acceleration (nose down) and a reversal of the direction of rotation". Here, releasing the controls would make the XP-55 return to its nose-down attitude with recovery as above, but the loss in altitude was 4,000ft (1,219m). In the clean stall the behaviour was nearly the same, with a recovery altitude for this condition of 3,000ft (914m); hence a stall during a landing approach could be disastrous.

Airspeeds of 390mph (628km/h) IAS had been recorded during Curtiss's own diving trials and the AAF pilots did not go any faster. Elevator sensitivity at speeds of over 300mph (483km/h) was high, but the 'feel' of the controls was satisfactory up to the 390mph (628km/h) figure. Problems with the engine had limited trials to a maximum altitude of 29,155ft (8,886m), but extrapolation of the test results enabled the engineers to estimate a service ceiling for the XP-55 of 35,800ft (10,912m) and an absolute ceiling of 36,800ft (11,217m).

Again the approach and landing were far removed from conventional fighter routine. With full flaps and power off the aircraft had an extremely steep glide angle. The normal approach speed was 140mph (225km/h), with power to reduce the glide angle, and the normal landing speed approximately 120mph (193km/h) IAS. Engine cooling was a massive problem. When ground running the power unit would consistently overheat, but then in level flight it was overcooled. Indeed, overcooling when running at lower power settings made rapid descents difficult, because when coming down a high power was necessary to maintain the coolant temperatures at or above 80°F.

In conclusion, Morris and Leach declared that the XP-55 did not meet contractor's guarantees and it did not compare favourably with contemporary production fighters. In addition, as it stood in its current level of development, the type's unconventional layout and flight characteristics meant it was not desirable as a combat aircraft.

It had been established that any advantages the XP-55 might offer over conventional fighter types did not justify its unusual configuration, and of course it had inherently severe stall characteristics and doubtful stability. Overall the development of the XP-55 had proved lengthy and difficult, mainly because the aerodynamic characteristics had required a considerable amount of wind tunnel and engineering work, in part because little experience had been available previously for an aircraft of this configuration. And in the meantime more conventional fighters such as the Republic P-47 and North American P-51 had now proved themselves as world-beating designs.

XP-55 structure

The XP-55 was a single-seat pusher-engine fighter prototype. Its fuselage had a semi-monocoque structure and was covered with aluminium light alloy sheet. Throughout the highly swept cantilever laminar flow wings (sweep angle 28.5° at quarter chord) employed all-metal stressed skin construction and they were attached to the middle and rear fuselage. Conventional metal ailerons and split flaps were fitted and the nose-mounted elevator was also made in metal, its leading edge having been designed to be continuous and to pass through the fuselage. An unusual feature for its time, this elevator was 'free-floating'; it was pivoted well forward and would only function when the pilot operated the control, so when stick free it tended to 'float' in the airstream. The rudders were all-metal and were mounted vertically on each wing with the fins protruding both above and below the aerofoil.

BELOW LEFT Close-up of the first XP-55s starboard wing root and inner wing, with a flow fence newly fitted. *Curtiss via Gerald H. Balzer*

BELOW RIGHT In this view the elevator on the first XP-55 has been increased temporarily to a span of 8ft 11in (2.72m), but the final version was of even greater span at 11ft 2in (3.40m). Note how the leading edge is continuous through the nose. *Curtiss via Gerald H. Balzer*

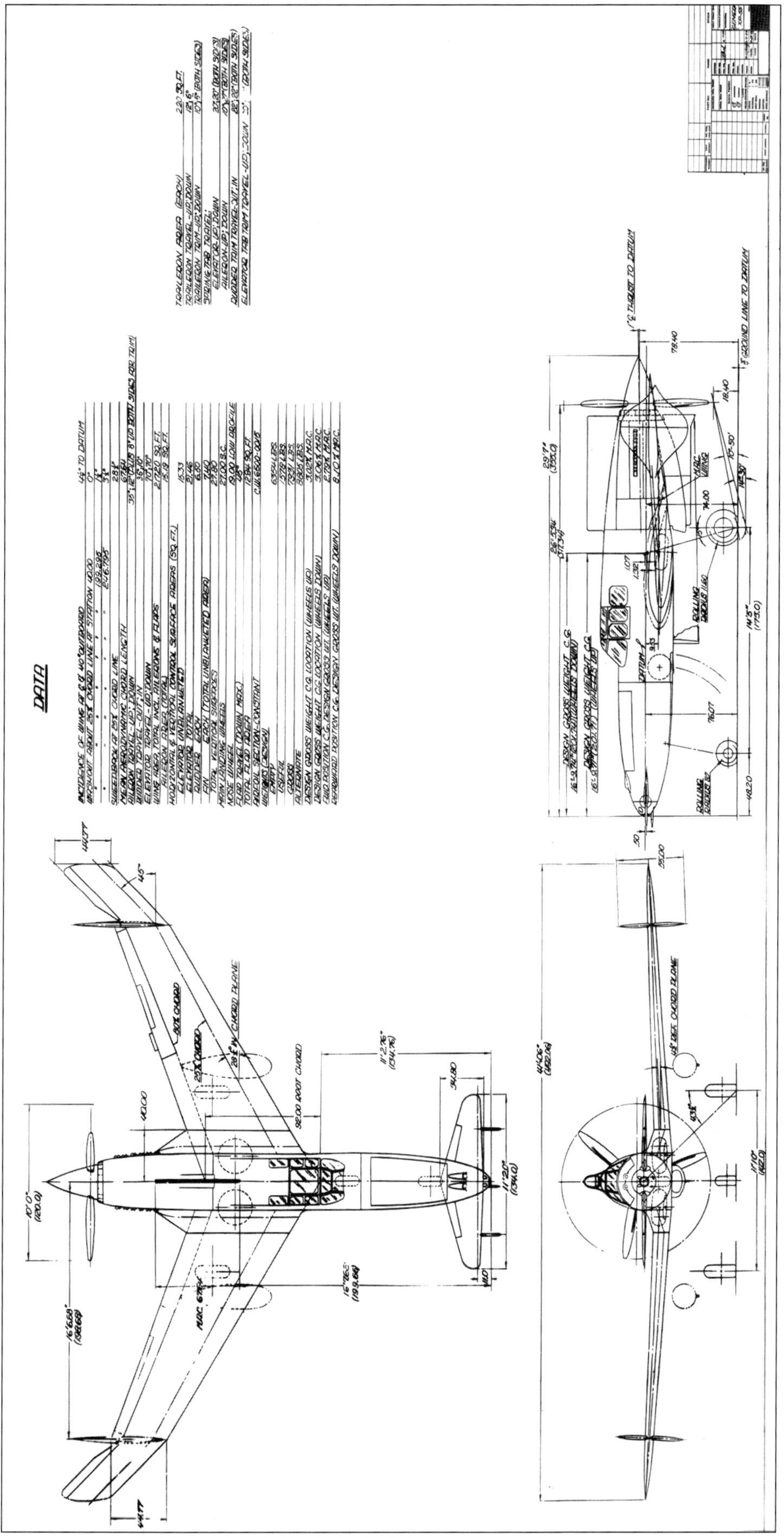

Manufacturer's drawing of the XP-55. *Curtiss via Gerald H. Balzer*

ABOVE LEFT The Allison V1710-95 installation on XP-55 No. 2 with the covers removed. This picture was taken at St Louis on 27 October 1943 during the aircraft's final assembly. *Curtiss via Gerald H. Balzer*

ABOVE RIGHT The tip extension and 'taileron' fitted to 42-78847's starboard wing. *Curtiss via Gerald H. Balzer*

LEFT 42-78847 demonstrates the final extended form of the XP-55's nose elevator. *Curtiss via Gerald H. Balzer*

BELOW LEFT Rear fuselage detail on 42-78847. *Curtiss via Gerald H. Balzer*

The engine, which was not fitted with a turbo supercharger, was mounted in the rear of the fuselage and drove a three-blade 10ft 0in (3.05m) diameter Curtiss Electric propeller; this could be jettisoned in an emergency. The radiators were positioned beneath the engine with a ventral scoop supplying the necessary cooling air, while the oil-cooling radiator was placed above the engine and fed by a dorsal air inlet. A tricycle undercarriage was fitted (the first time for a Curtiss fighter) and the guns were mounted in pairs in the upper half of the nose section. The internal fuel capacity was 110galUS (416lit), while the overload figure with two external tanks came to 210galUS (795lit).

The third XP-55 (and the second prototype retrospectively) had wing tip extensions which increased the wingspan a little and introduced a new moveable control surface to the trailing edge called a 'traileron'. The XP-55's configuration was unusual because this was not a true stable wing aircraft, nor a canard type - several sources in fact describe it as a stable flying wing with a controllable nose elevator.

This shot of the final XP-55 shows the aircraft carrying external fuel tanks of 50galUS (189lit) capacity. One source says that these tanks were carried on the underwing bomb racks, but others state that the XP-55 had no facility for carrying bombs. *Curtiss via Gerald H. Balzer*

XP-55 Data

Length:	29ft 7in (9.02m)
Wing span:	As built 40ft 6.9in (12.37m), 3rd prototype 41ft 0.6in (12.51m)
Wing area:	As built 208.9sq.ft (19.43sq.m), 3rd prototype 217.2sq.ft (20.20sq.m)
Empty weight:	6,354lb (2,882kg)
Design gross weight:	7,931lb (3,598kg)
Powerplant:	1 x 1,125hp (839kW) Allison V1710-95 12-cylinder liquid-cooled engine
Maximum speed (at 7,929lb/3,597kg weight – 3rd prototype):	377.5mph (607km/h) at 16,900ft (5,151m), 390mph (628km/h) at 19,300ft(5,883m)
Maximum rate of climb (at 7,929lb/3,597kg weight):	2,460ft/min (750m/min) at 13,700ft (4,176m)
Service ceiling:	35,800ft (10,912m)
Normal range:	635 miles (1,022km)
Maximum range:	1,440 miles (2,317km)
Armament:	4 x 0.50in (12.70mm) machine guns in nose

7 Northrop XP-56 Black Bullet

The next R40-C/XC-622 prototype was the Northrop XP-56, another unorthodox design – this time a flying wing with a pusher engine. The XP-54 in Chapter Five was unusual with its pusher powerplant, but the swept wing XP-55 in the previous chapter, the 'streamlined' XP-67 in Chapter Eleven, and now the XP-56, made the Vultee machine look almost conventional! However, the stocky aircraft described here did not make it into production, and its failure to do so meant that none of the XC-622 types would enter service.

Flying wing

A May 1942 memorandum from the Royal Aircraft Establishment at Farnborough reported that "the firm of Northrop are designing for the [US] Army a single-engine tailless fighter and a four-engine tailless bomber. The designer claims that he can save 30% of the drag and 20% of the weight of the structure on the normal arrangement. One prototype of each is being built and only the early stages have been reached. The fighter is estimated to do 467mph (751km/h) at 19,500ft (5,944m) at a total weight of 11,350lb (5,148kg). The four-engine bomber is estimated to carry 10,000lb (4,536kg) of bombs for 7,600 miles (12,228km) at 275mph (442km/h) and to have a maximum bomb capacity of 32,000lb (14,515kg). In both types the pusher engine arrangement has been adopted and a serious problem is that of jettisoning the airscrew to enable the crew to escape in an emergency."

The bomber would become the Northrop XB-35 which first flew in 1946. This had been preceded by Northrop's N-9M scale model which was built to test the flight characteristics of a multi-engine flying

The second Northrop XP-56 prototype pictured on Roach Lake in March 1943. The Northrop logo is just visible on the nose. *Northrop via Gerald H. Balzer*

Northrop's N-1M research aircraft taken during a test flight. *Northrop via Gerald H. Balzer*

wing aircraft (the B-35 programme would be cancelled before the bomber entered production). The fighter would become the XP-56.

The design of the XP-56 (company project number N-2) was based on another aerodynamic research aircraft, Northrop's N-1M flying wing first flown in July 1940. It even retained that aircraft's down-sloping wing tips, although the angle was not as acute. However, the N-1M was used primarily to conduct the manufacturer's initial investigations into the concept of the 'flying wing', and could not be considered exactly as a prototype of the XP-56. It could fly at speeds up to 200mph (322km/h) and heights of 4,000ft (1,219m) and by May 1941 Northrop had completed several flights with this flying mock-up, which had confirmed the stability of the aircraft about all three axes.

Authority for the XP-56 go-ahead was granted by General Arnold on 31 May 1940 and was covered by Contract TS535-AC-15021, which called for engineering data and wind tunnel models, though only an option to procure one experimental prototype. This contract was approved on 22 June, but then it was decided to take up the option for ordering the pursuit interceptor prototype, to be delivered within 12 months, plus a mock-up to be delivered in 120 days from the approval date. However, the XP-56 would fall victim, once again, to problems with engine availability.

In September 1940 the director of War Production issued a directive to terminate the development of the Pratt & Whitney X1800-AG3 engine, so that the company could devote its full time to production problems and other more important engine development work. The X1800 had been the chosen power unit for the XP-56 and so it became necessary for Northrop to seek an alternative. It was eventually agreed that the Pratt & Whitney R-2800-29 was best suited for the fighter (with a two-speed, two-stage supercharger added) and this was approved on 21 July 1941. However, this change resulted in a delay of five and a half months in producing the XP-56 prototype, a weight increase of some 2,000lb (907kg) and a decrease in maximum speed at the critical altitude of 14mph (23km/h). The X1800 had also been earmarked for the XP-54 and XP-58 prototypes (Chapters Five and Eight), but the R2800 as was in use in the Republic P-47 and Vought F4U-1 production fighters, for the AAF and Navy respectively.

Then in the spring of 1941 it became clear that, with only one airframe on contract, considerable

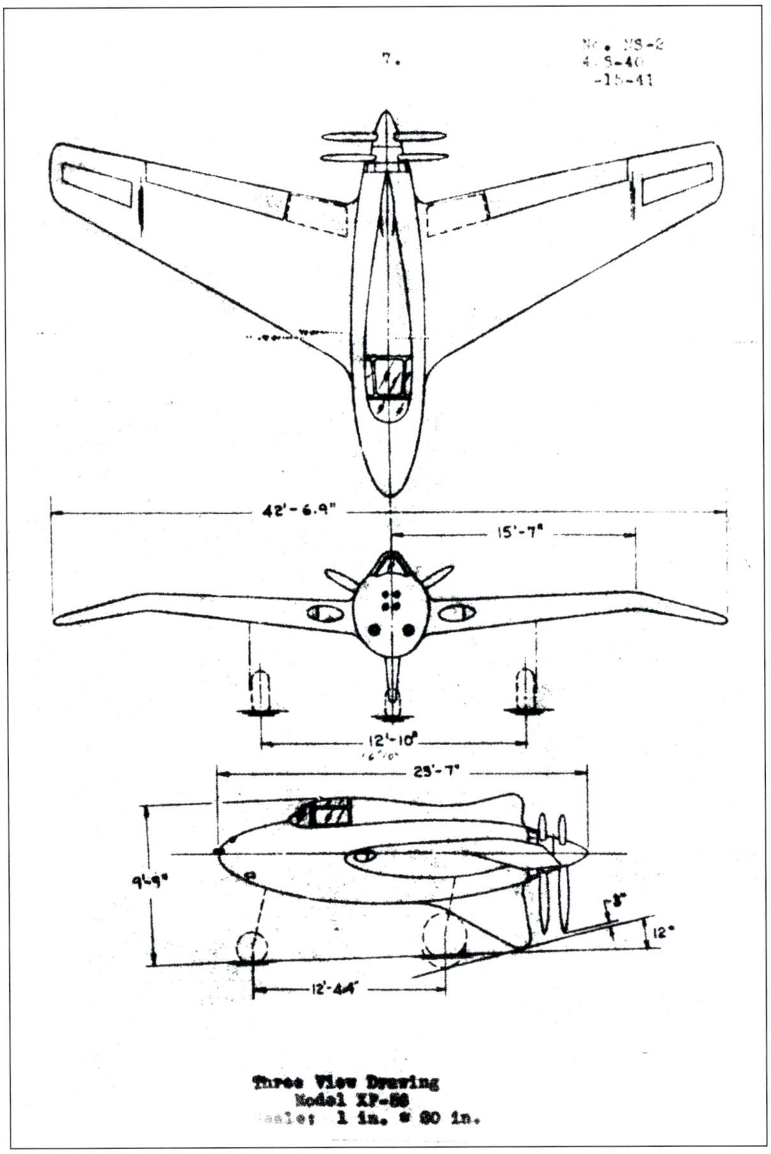

Manufacturer's three-view drawing showing the XP-56 in its original form. *Northrop via Gerald H. Balzer*

The original plan was to have the XP-56 powered by the Pratt & Whitney X1800 shown here, but this engine was abandoned in 1940. *Gerald H. Balzer*

delay would result if this machine were lost or damaged during flight testing. With Northrop's current workload, including the forthcoming P-61 night fighter and XB-35 bomber, there was some worry that ordering a second XP-56 might impede these programmes and overload Northrop's already extremely busy staff. Indeed, the AAF's Materiel Division even considered cancelling the XP-56 programme completely (by early May 1941 the XP-56 had been classed as secondary in priority to Northrop's XP-61 night fighter). Eventually, however, a second example was ordered under a separate Contract W535-AC-25060 approved on 13 February 1942, and the delivery of this XP-56 had to take place just 90 days after completion of the first aircraft.

The Mock-up inspection was held at Northrop's plant on 15 July 1941 and resulted in moving the landing gear forward to prevent the aircraft from flopping on to its nose wheel on landing when the main wheels touched the ground. In an effort to improve the armament installation a request was also made for a redesign of the XP-56's forward fuselage, by changing the originally proposed shape from circular to elliptical.

However, after the mock-up inspection, progress with the first prototype became extremely slow, in part through the interference of the XB-35 bomber project, also the late delivery of engine and gear box because of engine development difficulties at Pratt & Whitney, and then difficulties encountered by Northrop itself in developing a satisfactory method of welding the aircraft's magnesium structure. Finally, having overcome these difficulties, the contractor had the first airframe completed early in March 1943. The first XP-56 carried the AAF serial 41-786 and the fighter was covered by classified project number MX-14.

One new feature introduced by the XP-56 was the heavy use of welded magnesium alloy in its primary structure. The selection of magnesium for the XP-56, which is lighter than aluminium alloy and not a critical strategic material, was most desirable in terms of the weight it would save. But fabricating structures with this metal created problems – riveting parts together would induce a corrosive electrochemical reaction between two different metals, and welding was slow and brought problems with fire (magnesium is highly inflammable and, once burning, the flames are very difficult to extinguish). The solution, developed by Northrop's Vladimir Pavlecka and Russ Meridith, was a method of welding called the Heliarc (helium arc) Process.

The delivery of the XP-56's version of the R2800 engine also fell behind schedule. A propulsion rig had been built to try out the integration of the engine and its propeller within the fighter's airframe, which had proved troublesome for the engine manufacturer. Once the engine was installed inside the airframe, ground tests were conducted at Hawthorne between 15 and 26 March 1943 to ensure that propeller induced natural vibration frequencies would not create any problems with airframe vibration. However, considerable trouble was experienced with engine roughness and this took until early May to overcome.

Next, when preparing the XP-56 for shipment to Muroc Lake, it was learnt that a propeller blade had broken away from an R2800-29 under test at Pratt & Whitney. Since this was engine in use here, complete engine, gear box, and propeller vibration tests were conducted on the XP-56 to determine if this type of failure might occur in flight. Problems with the gear box installation only were discovered, which was now strengthened with more rigid mountings.

41-786 had been given a semi-gloss silver paint finish plus a yellow propeller spinner and Northrop chief test pilot John W. Myers began the aircraft's preliminary taxi runs on 12 April, which indicated that this prototype, particularly at high speed, would yaw sharply and quite dangerously. Taxi tests at Muroc Lake commenced early in September 1943 and high engine temperatures now proved a problem.

The first two 'flights', in reality 'hops', were achieved on 6 September. The first of these reached an altitude of around 4ft (1.2m), a speed of 110mph (177km/h) IAS and lasted about one mile (1.6km) in length and, with no attempt to alter the direction of flight, Myers reported satisfactory aileron control. The second flight, later that day and in slightly gusty conditions, recorded 25ft to 50ft (7.6m to 15m) height, 170mph (274km/h) IAS and around two miles (3.2km) distance. Here, however, the pilot reported a tendency for the right wing to drop, and the nose to yaw severely to the left with an accompanying diving moment. It seemed difficult to raise the wing with the ailerons and the stick needed two hands to regain control. Not good! The problem appeared to be the result of poor directional stability and it was calculated that more area was required for the upper vertical fin to correct it; when completed, nearly 12sq.ft (1.17sq.m) of area had been added.

The Northrop-assembled test stand for the replacement Pratt & Whitney R2800 engine for the XP-56. The contra-rotating propellers, and the internal shrouds used to adjust the flow of cooling air, are well shown. *Northrop via Gerald H. Balzer*

Now the scheduled taxi and flight tests could begin, in fact on 8 October 1943 at a gross weight of 11,010lb (4,994kg). Having twice successfully taxed across Muroc Lake at high speed Myers made a straight flight at between 10ft and 15ft (3.0m and 4.6m) height and with no apparent problems. The return was to be another high speed taxi run, but about half way back the left main wheel tyre burst at a speed of around 130mph (209km/h). The XP-56 performed a ground loop followed by rolls and gyrations, before coming to rest upside down - it was completely wrecked. Myers most fortunately survived having been thrown clear, but he suffered a broken

The first XP-56 41-786 photographed at Northrop during an engine run. *Northrop via Gerald H. Balzer*

ABOVE AND RIGHT
41-786 pictured on Rogers Dry Lake (Muroc) in early September 1943. The front-on view shows the air intakes well. The guns were never installed in this aircraft. *Northrop via Gerald H. Balzer*

John Myers checks the cockpit of the first XP-56 not long before the aircraft made its first, short, flight. *Northrop via Terry Panopalis*

Wreckage of the first XP-56 after the prototype had suffered a tyre failure during a fast taxi run. *Northrop via Gerald H. Balzer*

ankle and ruptured vertebrae. Mercifully, there was no fire, but the first XP-56 was written off.

As a result, the arrangement of the undercarriage was reviewed to prevent this happening again, though it was in fact decided instead to re-ballast the second prototype to move its CofG forward rather than make an expensive alteration to the landing gear. The rubber bumper in the lower part of the lower fin was also replaced on this aircraft with a small wheel to allow it to roll when touching the ground, rather than 'digging in'. New special nylon chord rubber tyres were installed as insurance against further blow outs, and the second prototype also introduced special wing tip-mounted 'aero boost ducts'; these were to provide power through ram air pressure to operate new enlarged split rudders. The crash investigation and these modifications held back the completion of the second prototype until early January 1944, when engine runs were started.

The first taxi tests were conducted at Northrop's plant and included one run of 110mph (177km/h). On completion it was intended to take the prototype to Muroc Lake to begin its flight trials. However, heavy rain now flooded the dry lakes in the area which brought yet more delay, and it was Roach Lake in Nevada which became the first of them to dry out sufficiently for enable flight trials to begin. The second XP-56 was thus taken by road to Roach Lake and was ready for flight on 22 March.

Flight test – Second prototype

The maiden flight of the second XP-56, serial 42-38353, took place on 23 March 1944, it lasted ten minutes and reached an altitude of 2,500ft (762m). The pilot was Harry Crosby who reported nose heaviness, to the extent of not being able to control the machine by the trim tab alone, and extreme rudder sensitivity. Otherwise, the aircraft appeared satisfactory and it flew again on 31 March with the CofG having in the meantime been moved rearwards to the point where the nose heaviness could be controlled by trim tab. A speed of 250mph (402km/h) IAS at 7,800ft (2,377m) was attained and Crosby took the XP-56 through various simple manoeuvres during which satisfactory behaviour was observed. However, he had to make various in-flight trim adjustments to counter a severe stalling moment which occurred after retracting the undercarriage, and then to deal with severe vibration when flying at more than 200mph (322km/h).

Next, Flights 3 and 4 on 6 April were used to assess the machine's flight characteristics and handling. At this stage it was yet to fly with the nose undercarriage doors fitted, but these were in place for Flights 5 and 6 on 18 April. By now manoeuvres

Rear angle view of the second XP-56 in the manufacturer's experimental hanger, jacked up to enable the undercarriage to be retracted. The drooped outer wings are well shown. *Northrop via Gerald H. Balzer*

On 22 March 1943, the day before first flight, the second XP-56 42-38353 posed for photographs on the lake bed at Roach Lake. *Northrop via Gerald H. Balzer and Terry Panopalis*

Two colour shots of 42-38353, also taken on 22 March 1943, which show the aircraft painted olive drab on top with gray undersides – standard Air Force colours. *Northrop via Gerald H. Balzer*

Poor quality view showing 42-38353 in flight during February 1944. Unfortunately not many photos were taken of the aircraft in the air – with so few flights one assumes that an official 'photo' sortie was never arranged. *Northrop via Gerald H. Balzer*

had been performed at speeds of up to 320mph (515km/h).

Following these six sorties, in May 1944 Northrop compiled for the AAF a summary report of flight testing to date. This noted:

"a). Pilot reaction to the airplane was unusually favourable considering the fact that it was a new and radical type, and that the first XP-56 had been involved in a major accident.

b). The chief difficulty experienced throughout the preliminary flight test was in longitudinal and directional instability. This condition made landings with flaps impossible since the diving moment induced on lowering the flaps could not be overcome using trim tabs. On several occasions the special nose wheel door designed to be used to overcome any nose heaviness was opened as the aircraft was on the approach to land and this helped to alleviate the nose heaviness, but did not overcome it to the extent that full flaps could be used.

c). On several occasions considerable wing heaviness had been experienced but in all cases could be trimmed out, and in Northrop's opinion could be completely eliminated by a re-rigging of the airplane."

Close up of the propeller cowling during a test run on the first XP-56. *Northrop via Gerald H. Balzer*

By May 1944 both Muroc and Harpers Lake had dried sufficiently for flying to resume, and both were better equipped than Roach Lake with the necessary back up facilities, so 5 May 1944 saw 42-38353 ferried to Harpers Lake. However, considerable wing heaviness was experienced throughout this journey, though Crosby did try several speed runs and checks for stability. On landing he also experienced lateral instability and control reversal at low speed. The cause proved to be the contra-rotating propeller – its control mechanism was allowing one of the propellers to move into full low pitch and it was thought that the wing heaviness stemmed from the torque reaction caused by improper propeller operation.

Thought now turned towards the NACA Ames Laboratories at Moffett Field in California to help Northrop with this programme. The vast experience of the NACA team with research in this field was felt to be possibly the best way to gather information and data from the XP-56 quickly, and to try and establish why this aircraft could not fly any faster. Its speed and power performances had proved disappointing and Northrop acknowledged that the guaranteed estimates were probably out of reach. In fact Material Command had used the data from Northrop to plot the XP-56s potential maximum performance, and as such had estimated a top speed of 340mph (547km/h) at 19,500ft (5,944m) - rather less than the 467mph (751km/h) at 25,000ft (7,620m), and 418mph (673km/h) at sea level, guaranteed in the original Northrop specification.

On 23 December 1944 Major Charles R. Hawks, chief of the Engineering Division Liaison Section, wrote a memo which stated that "the contractor [Northrop] is becoming quite concerned over the apparent lack of interest in this subject [the XP-56]." There had been a good deal of discussion as to the future of the aircraft, before it agreed that the necessary data could be more easily acquired in the Ames wind tunnel; however, the lack of priority now behind the XP-56 project meant that these test were consistently delayed. Finally, on 17 December 1945 the tunnel tests were cancelled altogether, in part because the hoped for data had been acquired elsewhere, and in part because the XP-56 was now considered obsolete and no longer of any tactical value.

In the meantime the second prototype had flown on three further occasions. Flights 8 and 9 from Harpers Lake were both made on 5 July 1944. Crosby took the first of these, but the second was a 35 minute familiarisation flight for Northrop pilot Alexandru 'Alex' Papană and on landing he buckled the XP-56's ventral fin. After repairs, on 11 August Crosby made the aircraft's final flight, No. 10, with a trip from Northrop Field (Hawthorne) to Muroc, but he reported extreme tail heaviness on the ground, an inability to obtain full power in flight, and an excessive fuel consumption.

When engineers checked the aircraft after this flight they found the linking rods for the pitch control mechanism between the propellers had failed once more. Here at last was the reason behind the heavy consumption of fuel and the shortage of power. Having occurred on four occasions, this linkage defect was now classed as a design deficiency and also a safety hazard for flight, and proved a major factor behind the change of emphasis to wind tunnel work rather than flying the XP-56 any more – the fighter just wasn't safe enough in the air to conduct flying wing research! After all of the design effort devoted to the XP-56, 42-38353's total air time came to just five hours and fifty-five minutes.

In late 1944 the XP-56 was in store at Muroc, but after February 1945 it was taken by road to Moffett Field. It came back to Northrop at Hawthorne, again by road, in April 1946, but thanks to the extended period of storage was by now in poor condition. It was transferred to National Air Museum, Smithsonian Institution, hands in 1947 and still awaits restoration.

In some quarters there had been a strong desire to use the XP-56 for general flying wing research. On 13 August 1945 Brigadier General Flying L. C. Craigie, Acting Chief of the Engineering Division, wrote "flying wing projects with the Northrop Aircraft Corporation date back to 1940. The oldest of these projects, the XP-56, is still uncompleted. Although we have expressed and evidenced considerable interest in the flying wing, it seems to me that we alternately blow hot and cold on it. The XP-56 encountered considerable difficulty, it was not an airplane that attracted pilots, and when one of the flying articles encountered serious trouble we sort of washed our hands of the whole mess. We never found out why the airplane did not conform closer to its computed performance. The second article has been at Sunnyvale in California for approximately one year, but its tests in full scale have been repeatedly delayed because of some higher priority project."

Craigie added, in more general terms, "The XP-79 [Chapter Sixteen] is scheduled for its initial flight test at an early date but the project has been lagging noticeably." Also "there are many indications that the Germans held high hopes for this configuration, particularly in association with aircraft and missiles intended for flight at high Mach numbers. We obviously need more basic data on this type of aircraft. NACA will be getting out of the 'fix it' business soon, we hope. It should put them in position to devote more attention to their primary job of getting basic data for us. I believe that we should re-energise the flying wing program, particularly the wind tunnel phase of it. It would appear smart too, at this time, to assign high priority to full scale tests of the XP-56 in the wind tunnel. Additional emphasis should be placed on the remaining flying wing projects."

Armament installation on the second prototype. *Northrop via Gerald H. Balzer*

Craigie's wish to see the XP-56 become more active again did not come to pass, but general research into flying wings would continue for many many years. In America this would culminate in the B-2 stealth bomber flown in 1989, and now the new B-21 Raider first flown in November 2023.

According to Tony Chong in his book *Flying Wings and Radical Things*, "designer Jack Northrop was never entirely happy with the configuration of the N-2 [XP-56] series. Ungainly looking, the aircraft was a compromised flying wing based on current N-1 thinking and the need for a bulbous body to house the guns, pilot, and engine. For a plane that size, however, there was no way around the large body, which was called a 'crew nacelle' by the company instead of a fuselage."

Other sources have suggested more strongly that, as built, the XP-56 should never have been flying. The crew nacelle made it too fat – the fuselage should have been extended both fore and aft. But much was learnt, both with flying wing flight and (with welding magnesium alloy) in the field of new manufacturing techniques. At one stage the XP-56 had been, in the Air Corps' eyes, "a truly experimental airplane if ever there was one", and in fact both the XP-55 and XP-56 were then described as "major engineering steps forward." But the XP-56 was fated not to be a success.

ABOVE LEFT Front view of one of the wingtip ducts that used ram-air to operate the split rudder boost system. *Northrop via Gerald H. Balzer*

ABOVE RIGHT Rear view of the boost ducting with the split drag rudder closed. *Northrop via Gerald H. Balzer*

RIGHT Engine run up prior to the XP-56's final flight on 11 August 1944. *Northrop via Gerald H. Balzer*

XP-56 structure

The XP-56 was a single-seat single-engine tailless pusher fighter (i.e. with no horizontal tail surface) powered by a buried or 'submerged' R2800-29 engine. It was an all metal aircraft with a wing made of magnesium alloy stressed skin construction assembled from built up sections. The wing was full cantilever and featured trailing edge 'elevons' and flaps and removable drooping outer panels. Lateral and pitch control was maintained by use of the elevons, with the elevon surfaces deflecting together for longitudinal control and differentially in opposite directions for lateral control.

Split type flaps were fitted and on the second prototype directional control was obtained by the use of bellows-opening split type 'trim' rudders or air brakes positioned near the wing tips. These were used as single surface ailerons for lateral control and then opened into upper and lower spoilers for making properly banked turns. Their actuation was novel - rammed air passed through a forward-facing intake on each wing tip, was routed through a duct and then diverted by valves to pressurise the bellows as required. In straight and level flight the duct was open at both ends, resulting in minimal drag.

The short stubby fuselage was of all metal, monocoque construction and divided into three major assemblies, with the armament installation concentrated in the nose section, the cockpit section next with the unpressurised cabin positioned well forward, and then the aft section behind the pilot which housed the engine. This had a two-stage two-speed supercharger and drove a Curtiss Propeller Division six-blade constant speed co-axial counter-rotating propeller 9ft 8in (2.95m) in diameter on the forward prop and 9ft 6in (2.90m) on the rear. The submerged engine drove its propellers through an extension shaft and independently mounted gear box and the choice of co-axial contra-propellers mades the resultant torque reaction on this gear box zero. The air intakes for cooling the engine were positioned on the wing leading-edge. A tricycle undercarriage was employed and the maximum fuel load was 320galUS (1,211lit).

The XP-56 had very large dorsal and ventral fins and the substantial-sized fin positioned on the rear of ventral centreline contributed to the lateral stability, but more importantly acted as a propeller strike guard. On the first prototype this had appeared just as a stub dorsal fin fitting, but was extended after the first two flights. The second XP-56 prototype brought with it quite a number of changes from the first – for example the dorsal vertical fin had been enlarged further and the centre of gravity relocated further forwards.

Harry Crosby about to take off for that last flight, to deliver the aircraft to Muroc from Hawthorne. *Northrop via Gerald H. Balzer*

XP-56 data

Length:	23ft 7in (7.19m)
Wing span:	1st prototype 42ft 6.9in (12.97m), 2nd prototype 43ft 1in (13.13m)
Wing area:	1st prototype 306.5sq.ft (28.50sq.m), 2nd prototype 311.0sq.ft (28.92sq.m)
Empty weight:	1st prototype 8,699lb (3,946kg), 2nd prototype 9,879lb (4,481kg)
Design gross weight:	12,000lb (5,443kg)
Actual gross weight:	1st prototype 11,350lb (5,148kg), 2nd prototype 12,588lb (5,710kg)
Powerplant:	1 x 2,000hp (1,491kW) Pratt & Whitney R-2800-29 18-cylinder air-cooled radial engine
Maximum speed (original guarantee at 12 February 1942 and 12,000lb [5,443kg] weight):	418mph (672km/h) at sea level, 467mph (751km/h) at 19,500ft (5,944m)
Maximum speed (estimate after flight test):	340mph (547km/h) at 19,500ft (5,944m)
Maximum speed achieved in flight:	320mph (515km/h)
Maximum rate of climb:	3,125ft/min (953m/min) at 15,000ft (4,572m)
Estimated service ceiling:	33,000ft (10,058m)
Maximum range:	660 miles (1,062km)
Armament:	4 x 0.50in (12.70mm) machine guns and 2 x 20mm cannon in nose. No bombs

8 Lockheed XP-58 Chain Lightning

The background to the creation of the Lockheed XP-58 Chain Lightning is most unusual and nothing like the path followed by the other subjects covered in this volume, and indeed by most new combat aircraft in general. At the beginning this fighter could be described as a total political beast, but subsequent changes of requirements and powerplants would ensure that the airframe became ever larger and heavier. In the end the XP-58 struggled to find a role and a purpose, and in fact failed to do so.

In its original form the XP-58 was looked upon as a high altitude medium range bomber escort fighter. On 17 April 1940, 20 months before entering the war itself, the American Government entered into a Foreign Lease Agreement whereby Lockheed would develop and deliver an improved version of its P-38 Lightning to the Air Corps (later AAF) without cost, in return for clearance for the manufacturer to sell the P-38 to the British to help the latter's war effort. At this time the Air Corps retained a right to block any sales by US manufacturers to overseas customers if it felt that such orders might seriously delay any deliveries of the same type(s) to the Air Corps itself.

For the new design, Lockheed project engineer James Gerschler drew a 20,000lb (9,072kg) 20mm cannon/0.50in machine gun aircraft, along with a second two-seat version which featured an additional remote-control 0.50in (12.7mm) machine gun at the end of each tail boom. On 6 May 1940 it was decided officially that the new type would be a two-seat twin-engine fighter, with the tentative designation XP-58. At this stage the fighter was similar in appearence to the P-38 and just a little bit bigger, but it would carry this more powerful armament while offering an estimated maximum speed in the region of 450mph (724km/h).

The Lockheed XP-58 prototype pictured in flight. *Lockheed via Gerald H. Balzer*

At a conference held at Material Division at Wright Field on 7 May 1940, between James Gerschler and L.V. Kerber of Lockheed and Capt. M.S. Roth. Chief Fighter Branch, Aircraft Projects at Wright Field, it was proposed by Kerber that the XP-58 should be used as the design model from which the XP-49 (Chapter Two) would evolve as a modification. It was suggested that in this manner two aircraft could be built differing only in their number of crew, armament, and engines. However, the course of the XP-58's development would in the end follow a far different route.

At first the Air Corps had planned to install Continental IV1430 engines in the XP-58, but these provided insufficient power and were subsequently replaced by Pratt & Whitney X1800-20 units, the purchase of which had originally been approved for the XP-49 by the Chief of the Air Corps in January 1940. But on 9 October 1940 the Air Corps was informed by Pratt & Whitney that further development of the X1800 engine had been dropped to permit the company to concentrate on its production of radial engines (we have have been here before in Chapters Two, Five and Seven, the XP-49, XP-54 and XP-56 prototypes were all similarly hampered by the closure of the X1800 programme).

One XP-58 prototype, serial 41-2670 under Contract W535-AC-13476 and Air Corps code number MX-2, was ordered in October 1940, by which time a second 20mm had been added to the nose weaponry and and the rearward-firing machine guns moved and combined into a remote-controlled dorsal turret. The gross weight now came to 24,000lb (10,886kg) with the guaranteed maximum speed reduced to 402mph (647km/h) at 25,000ft (7,620m).

On 8 November Lockheed, after considering various available powerplants to replace the X1800, selected the Pratt & Whitney GR2800 radial engine for the XP-58 fitted with a turbo supercharger. At the same time Lockheed stressed that if the Air Corps

ABOVE Views of the XP-58 Mock-Up showing the fighter with all of its armament in place, both nose and turret guns. *Lockheed via Mark Nankivil*

Pratt & Whitney X1800 engine pictured on 8 January 1940. *Gerald H. Balzer*

The XP-58 was eventually fitted with Allison V3420 engines, an example of which is shown here in a photo dated 27 January 1942. *Gerald H. Balzer*

It is thought that this picture shows the first and only XP-58 to be completed, serial 41-2670, on the day that it was first rolled out at the Lockheed factory. There are no gun ports in the nose. *Gerald H. Balzer*

requested the installation of the large Wright R2160 Tornado engine, then the XP-58 "must be practically redesigned" and the estimated gross weight would rise to 30,000lb (13,608kg). By this time Neil Harrison had taken over the role of XP-58 project leader and the GR2800s were expected to provide a maximum speed of 418mph (673km/h) at 25,000ft (7,620m) for a loaded weight of 26,000lb (11,794kg).

On 10 February 1941 Robert E. Gross, Lockheed Chairman, wrote to Brigadier Gen. Oliver F. Echols, Chief of the Air Corps Material Division at Wright Field, to express his "grave concern about the development of the XP-58, which was originally envisioned as an 18,500lb [8,392kg] airplane in which many parts from the YP-38 [Lightning] might, with minor modifications, be used. Lockheed was now committed to the construction of an airplane of 33,785lb [15,325kg] gross weight, or 6,785lb [3,078kg] more than double the gross weight of the YP-38." Lockheed's engineers had advised Gross that gross weight, wing area and amount of equipment had increased approximately as a function of the power of the engine. Since the first powerplant, the Continental IV1430, had 1,000bhp (746kW) at that time, comparatively the gross weight had increased 82%, while take-off power had gone up to 135%. Gross doubted the manoeuvrability of a 33,785lb [15,325kg] pursuit plane and was anxious to make certain that precious engineering hours were not being expended upon an experimental development. However, in reply Echols assured Gross that the War Department wanted to expedite the XP-58 programme.

In March 1941 the Corps stated that it wished to have the XP-58 powered by the Wright Tornado H2160 radial air-cooled engine, and then in May 1941 the Corps added cabin pressurisation for both pilot and rear-facing gunner, plus a further remotely-controlled ventral turret to supplement the dorsal fitting. These changes brought another big increase to the estimated gross weight plus a reduction in the estimated range. But more importantly the Tornado would push the XP-58's maximum speed up to 450mph (724km/h). At 7 July 1941, under a new Contract W535-AC-15867, the XP-58's data was given as two 2,350hp (1,752kW) Wright H2160-3 and -5 supercharged engines with Hamilton Standard Hydromatic propellers, an estimated maximum of 450mph (724km/h) at 25,000ft (7,620m), gross weight 34,242lb (15,532kg), span 70ft (21.34m), and forward-facing armament four 0.50in (12.7mm) and two 20mm guns.

As a result of the the official Mock-Up Inspection at the Lockheed plant on 25 August 1941 the XP-58 had been declared "satisfactory for purpose intended", although some changes to the design were required, such as the use of Curtiss Electric propellers instead of Hamilton Standard units. On 9 January 1942 the estimated maximum speed was reduced to 445mph (716km/h), and then on 16 March Lockheed proposed

Rear view of the XP-58 taken on 22 May 1954. *Lockheed via Gerald H. Balzer*

Walk-around views of the XP-58. A dummy shape has been fitted to represent the upper (dorsal) turret. *Lockheed via Mark Nankivil*

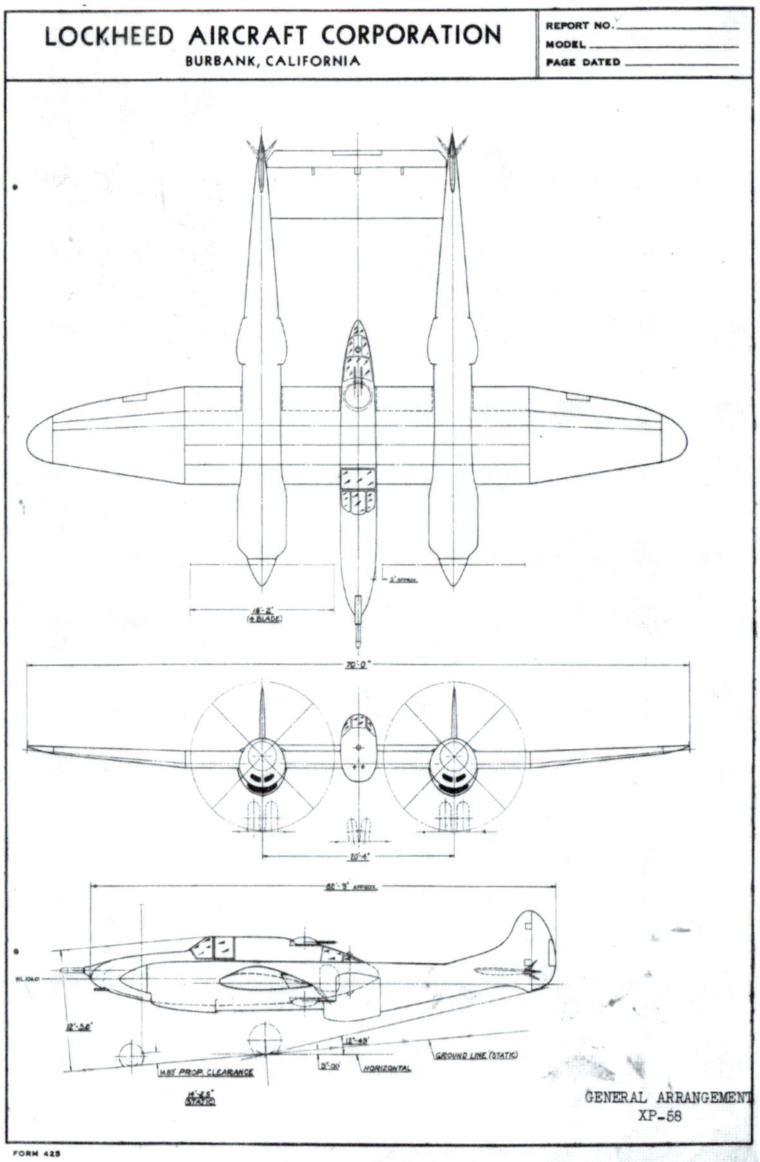

ABOVE Original manufacturer's drawing showing the 75mm-armed XP-58. Two machine guns are also mounted in the nose. *Lockheed via Mark Nankivil*

RIGHT Beautiful manufacturer's model showing the XP-58 fitted with the impressive 75mm cannon its nose. The turret guns are also in place. *Lockheed via Gerald H. Balzer*

the immediate construction of a second prototype to afford protection against loss of the first machine. Authorisation for a second XP-58 was given on 27 May 1942 under Contract W535-AC-39212. Before this, however, potential changes of role were in the offing.

On 1 April 1941 Lt. Col. J.G. Taylor, Chief of the Air Corps Foreign Intelligence Section wrote to the Chief of Material Division referring to "the 'convoy' type of twin-engine fighter, or escort pursuit, the lack of which is the weakest link in our program. It is true that the basic type specification has been a matter of controversy. Just how much range and armament are required of such an airplane have been in dispute for many years. So many that we have forgotten to provide a 'test tube' or prototype article. The GAF [German Air Force] cannot now bomb England in daylight because their single-engined convoy fighters have such short range, and their twin-engined planes lack defensive or even offensive fire power for the job. The GAF tried Me 109s for this, but could not stand their heavy losses and had to return to them as 'roving guards'. This was not good enough to permit them to do much day bombing. It cannot do this if it lacks defensive fire power."

Taylor added "The first article can be used as a prototype for the aerodynamic and engine problems. That means it will be a 35,000lb [15,876kg] job at least. It can be used to test large engines of the [Wright] Tornado and [UK Napier] Sabre class. The lack of this type [of fighter] is the greatest mistake apparent in our aerial defense plan."

On 3 September 1942 Lockheed suggested converting the XP-58 to a low-altitude destroyer fighter. The reasons behind this move were an expected five month delay in delivery of the Tornado engines (the delivery of the XP-58's Tornados had been pushed back from 15 November 1942 to 1 April 1943), anticipated troubles with compressibility at high speeds, and the inability of the XP-58 to compete with existing aircraft in its original category. The AAF requested data on 16 September, and then an AAF statement dated 19 September provided for the conversion of one XP-58 into a low altitude destroyer type, which was looked upon as "attractive".

But then, at a conference held on 19-20 October 1942 in the Office of the Director of Air Defense, it was concluded that the Beech XA-38 attack aircraft project would more than adequately fill the need for a low altitude destroyer type, and at a gross weight some 10,000lb (4,536kg) less than the XP-58. The meeting believed it was desirable to complete Lockheed's fighter as originally envisaged, except for the additional armament, for the following reasons – the XA-38 would be a better choice for a destroyer, there was a requirement for a high-altitude pressure cabin fighter to break up bomber formations, and the engineering work on the XP-58 as a high-altitude aircraft had reached final assembly. In addition, the bomber destroyer fighter was not expected to be regularly employed in terminal velocity dives, so any troubles brought about by compressibility should not be so serious. (The XA-38, armed with a 75mm nose cannon, never proceeded beyond two prototypes because it was not ready for production by the time the war in the Pacific came to an end.)

Front angle view of the only prototype. Note the especially long nose undercarriage leg. *Lockheed via Mark Nankivil*

As a result of recommendations from the Pursuit Board, the Experimental Engineering Section proceeded with the procurement of both XP-58s in their original form as high altitude aircraft with dorsal and ventral turrets, and with turbosuperchargers for the engines (which had been removed for the low level version). On 22 October 1942 Material Center at Wright Field wired Lockheed to tell the firm to cease its conversion to a low-altitude destroyer and to begin a new study of XP-58 armament. Now the first prototype would be armed with four 37mm in its nose (in lieu of the earlier two 20mm cannon and four 0.50in [12.7mm] machine guns) with the second having a single 75mm cannon with two 0.50in (12.7mm) guns. Gross weight now came to 38,275lb (17,362kg) and maximum speed 414mph (666km/h) at 25,000ft (7,620m).

However, by now any threat from enemy bombers, both in Europe and in the Pacific, was minimal, so production P-58s were unlikely ever to have to perform this bomber destroyer task. In January 1943 Lockheed recommended dropping the second prototype and instead having interchangeable noses for the first example, so that it could fly with either version of the forward-firing weaponry. At 2 February two alternative armament configurations were to be constructed by Lockheed.

But now, that same month, the problem-ridden Tornado programme collapsed, which meant Lockheed and the AAF had to look for another engine to power the unfortunate XP-58. The choice would be the turbosupercharged Allison V3420. This was authorised by the AAF on 12 February and this powerplant, together with the four 37mm cannon installation, would increase the weight to 37,800lb [17,146kg] and give a high speed of 425mph [684km/h] at 25,000ft [7,620m]. The expected first flight date was 30 August 1943. However, this date would be missed and further and very considerable delay to the project would follow when, in October 1943, most of the XP-58 personnel were diverted to the critical P-38 programme.

At 10 June 1943 the XP-58 specification had become a two-place twin-engine heavy cannon fighter of 40,294lb (18,277kg) gross weight with a guaranteed high speed of 430mph (692km/h) at 28,000ft (8,534m). The forward armament was an alternative installation of one 75mm cannon and two 0.50in (12.7mm) machine guns, or four 37mm high velocity cannon; the flexible armament remained two remotely controlled turrets, one upper and one lower, each containing two 0.50in (12.7mm) machine guns. At 17 April 1943 the first prototype was almost complete, except for the new engine installation, and the need for the second prototype was confirmed on 24 April.

Almost a year later an AAF memo dated 22 April 1944 reported that "from certain ground tests it had been determined that the first XP-58 had not met expectations [and] that in the interest of economy (since the second XP-58 on Contract AC-39212 was to be identical with the first), further effort on the second airplane was to be discontinued, this action thus making it possible to divert considerable manpower to the MX-409 project which had more promise of being direct benefit to the war." (MX-409 refers to the new prototype Lockheed jet fighter that would become the P-80 Shooting Star.) When the decision to discontinue further work on the second machine was made (by the termination of contract AC-39212 on 24 April) this aircraft was approximately 60% complete.

Two views of 41-2670 at rest at Los Angeles which provide excellent detail of the port side engine nacelle and rear boom.
Lockheed via Mark Nankivil

The one and only XP-58 prepares to take off on a test flight. *Lockheed via Gerald H. Balzer*

Flight test

The XP-58 was scheduled to make its initial flight on 5 June 1944, but during the preliminary taxi tests the emergency exit hatch pulled loose. So, after some four years in development, the prototype's maiden flight finally arrived the next day, 6 June; it lasted approximately 50 minutes and began at a take-off weight of 33,800lb (15,332kg). The flight began at the Lockheed Air Terminal at Los Angeles and included a climb to an altitude of 10,000ft (3,048m), before proceeding on to Muroc. En-route the Lockheed test pilot, Joseph C. 'Joe' Towle who had also flown the maiden flight of the XP-49, conducted preliminary directional, longitudinal and lateral stability checks, all of which passed satisfactorily. Flight testing continued from June to October when the Contractor's test programme was considered complete after twenty-five flights. The XP-58 lacked its forward-firing armament and cabin pressurisation and had dummy turrets, and the manufacturer's trials were hampered by turbo-supercharger torching which scorched both the twin booms and their tails. In addition, problems with longitudinal stability meant that the XP-58's original wooden elevator had to be replaced by a larger metal unit fitted with spring tabs.

On 11 October 1944 the XP-58 was classed as ready for delivery to the AAF and on this day Colonel

Here the XP-58's pilot runs up the aircraft's engines at Los Angeles (the engine covers are not in place). A small piece of nose art has now been applied, which appears in just a few photos but not in detail. *Lockheed via Gerald H. Balzer*

Cooper flew the aircraft on a familiarisation flight, but during his sortie the hydraulic fluid reservoir ruptured and drenched everything inside the cockpit, including the pilot who landed immediately. On 17 and 18 October flights were made to test the landing gear, but leaks with the hydraulic fluid meant that the landing gear down lock was slow to engage, so the entire emergency up system was removed which now made this fitting practically the same as that on the P-38. A flight made on 18 October found that the operation of the landing gear was now entirely satisfactory, so on the 19th the XP-58, crewed by Wright Field test pilot Major Frederic A. Borsodi and Mr. Ted Armitage, was ferried to Wright Field.

On receipt of the XP-58, Engineering Division's Flight Section (of Flight Test Engineering and Research Branch) was ordered to conduct brief performance tests on 41-2670 to acquire high speed data at critical altitude, and time to climb to critical altitude, with the engines operating at military power, and with increments of climb for each 5,000ft [1,524m]. Limited pilot evaluation flights were to follow on completion of these performance tests. In addition, by November 1944 arrangements had been made to have the second XP-58 placed in protected outside storage at Muroc, as a source of spares for the first prototype.

The official AAF flight tests were due to begin on 1 November 1944, but the XP-58 apparently remained grounded until early 1945. A memo written by C.R. Able of Flight Section in February 1945 (or possibly 31 March 1945) noted "airplane was out of commission due to turbo supercharger difficulties. Maintenance on plane has been very hard to contend with. Parts not available. Plane is constantly going out of commission after every flight. Project believed not worth the trouble and attempts have been made to cancel the project."

On 24 January 1945 First Lt. James L. Rust Jnr of Flight Section had outlined the future flight test programme, to be conducted by the Aircraft Projects Section of the Fighter Branch. The XP-58 first prototype was now at Wright Field in readiness for these trials and all of the tests were to be flown by Major Russell E. Schleeh, pilot, with Rust himself as engineer; Major C.R. Able was the AAF project engineer for the XP-58. For these flights the take-off gross weight was set at 39,000lb (17,690kg) and the aircraft would be unpainted for all tests. The V3420 engines would each drive a Curtiss Electric four-blade propeller.

Based at Wright Field, it was hoped that the flight testing would be completed in approximately six hours air time. Delays meant that the first flight did not take place until 17 February 1945, it lasted 30 minutes and the left-hand engine coolant experienced high temperatures. Flight 2 on 19 February lasted an hour and included a climb to 25,000ft (7,620m). Here it was noted that the limiting turbo rpm was reached approximately 10,000ft (3,048m) too low and so Schleeh returned to Wright Field. Another flight on 6 March was also terminated early because of engine malfunctioning.

Schleeh took 41-2670 on a 45 minute flight on 10 March 1945 where he climbed to 23,000ft (7,010m), and the critical heights of the turbos were reached at 19,000ft (5,791m) for the left engine and 21,300ft (6,492m) on the right side. On 22 March Schleeh had to terminate another flight and return to Wright Field after the cockpit had filled with smoke when flying at 27,000ft (8,230m). No information is available regarding any further flights.

The XP-58 proved to be a rather unlucky aircraft in that its progress was regularly and constantly interrupted by failures of engine programmes and changes to mission requirements. The only prototype to be completed was scrapped in 1946.

41-2670 in flight. It appears that all of the air-to-air photos of this aircraft were taken on just one sortie, on 2 September 1944, but then it never flew that often anyway. The XP-58 was one of Lockheed's least successful creations. *Lockheed via Gerald H. Balzer*

This air-to-air picture, though not of great quality, provides good underside detail, including the dummy ventral turret and the large air intakes beneath the booms. *Lockheed via Gerald H. Balzer*

Although only about half in picture, this shot presents some excellent cockpit, upper nose and engine nacelle detail. The XP-58 was never painted, always having an all-metal finish. *Lockheed via Gerald H. Balzer*

The seemingly laid-up XP-58, with covers removed and aircrew doors open, sits neglected during a winter day at Wright Field. *Lockheed via Gerald H. Balzer*

Another escort day fighter project was the XP-61E from Northrop, a streamlined version of that manufacturer's P-61 Black Widow night fighter. The latter's dorsal turret was removed and replaced by four machine guns in the nose, with a streamlined canopy covering two crew. Only two prototypes were completed (serials 42-39549 and 42–39557) modified from P-61B airframes, the first flying on 3 January 1945. Though a contemporary of the XP-58, and interesting to compare with it, the XP-61E was also in competition with the North American P-82. XP-61E had a span of 66ft 0in (20.12m), length 49ft 7in (15.11m), wing area 662sq.ft (61.57sq.m), and maximum take-off weight 40,181lb (18,226kg). Powerplant two 2,000hp (1,491kW) Pratt & Whitney R2800s giving a maximum speed of 376mph (605km/h) at 17,000ft (5,182m). Armament four 20mm cannon, four 0.50in (12.70mm) machine guns. *All Northrop via Gerald H. Balzer*

Excellent close-up photo of the XP-58 showing detail for the nose, nacelles and propellers, and for the heavy undercarriage. *US National Archives RG-342 via Tony Landis*

XP-58 structure

The XP-58 was a single-seat twin-engine heavy fighter prototype with an all-metal structure and pressurised cockpit. In configuration it was similar to Lockheed's earlier P-38 Lightning, having engine nacelles leading back to twin booms with the horizontal tailplane positioned in between. However, as the heaviest American fighter of World War II this machine was substantially larger, a fact reflected in the tricycle undercarriage having twin wheels on each gear. The tapered outer wing included the ailerons, whilst flaps were placed on the trailing edges of all of the straight sections of wing, inner and outer.

A large centre pod contained the cockpit and an enclosure at the rear to house the gunner who operated both remote-control turrets; however, none of the armament was ever fitted. The engines drove four-blade 14ft 8in (4.47m) diameter contra-rotating propellers and the XP-58's internal fuel capacity came to 800galUS (3,028lit), which with underwing drop tanks could be increased to 1,700galUS (6,435lit).

XP-58 data

Length:	49ft 5.5in (15.08m)
Wing span:	70ft 0in (21.34m)
Wing area:	600sq.ft (55.80sq.m)
Empty weight:	31,624lb (14,345kg)
Gross weight:	39,192lb (17,777kg)
Maximum take-off weight:	43,000lb (19,505kg)
Powerplant:	2 x 2,600hp (1,939kW) Allison V3420-11/13 24-cylinder turbo-supercharged double-'Vee' liquid-cooled piston engines
Maximum speed:	436mph (702km/h) at 25,000ft (7,620m)
Sea level rate of climb:	2,582ft/min (787m/min)
Service ceiling:	38,200ft (11,643m)
Absolute ceiling:	39,975ft (12,184m)
Normal range:	1,250 miles (2,011km)
Maximum range:	2,650 miles (4,264km)
Armament:	4 x 37mm cannon, or 1 x 75mm cannon plus 2 x 0.50in (12.70mm) machine guns in nose, 4 x 0.50in (12.7mm) in two twin turrets, 4,000lb (1,814kg) bombs under wings.

9 Curtiss XP-60 and XP-40Q

The main subject of this chapter, the Curtiss XP-60, although again never reaching production, did spawn a series of single-engine single-place prototype fighters in an attempt to produce a fighter interceptor with a high rate of climb and high speed. What follows is quite an involved story, and one could add that some of the later prototypes really should have carried all-new XP-designations. The chapter concludes with the XP-40Q.

XP-53

The story begins with an earlier unbuilt Curtiss project designated XP-53. This was to be a further development of the P-40 and XP-46 (Chapter One) and, as contracted for, would have a laminar flow wing and one 1,600hp (1,193kW) Continental XIV1430-3 engine, but retaining other elements of the earlier types. The projected maximum speed was 430mph (692km/h). A Curtiss Electric constant speed 11ft 2in (3.40m) diameter propeller was to be fitted and the internal fuel capacity was given as 204galUS (772lit). At Wright Field the XP-53 received Materiel Command Project Number MX-4. Initially a single prototype was planned but on 1 October 1940 the Air Corps asked if a Packard V1650-1 Merlin could go into a second airframe. Consequently, two prototypes were ordered later that month under contract W535-AC-15581 with serials 41-140 and 41-19508 (the fuselage and tail sections of the second would in fact be used for the XP-60). It is understood that there were plans to build 150 production P-53s under a no cost contract which resulted from a foreign release agreement

Superb photo showing the Curtiss XP-60C during a test flight. *Curtiss via Dave Ostrowski/Alan Griffith*

The first XP-60 prototype as first completed with the original fin shape carried over from the XP-53. *Mark Aldrich*

entered into by Curtiss-Wright at Buffalo and the Anglo-French purchasing commission. However, progress in developing the Continental engine was slow and in addition it was soon clear that the XP-53 would not provide the hoped for performance. In the end the XIV1430 failed to reach production, which also affected the XP-49 and XP-67 programmes (Chapters Two and Eleven).

XP-60 and P-60A

Designation XP-60 was assigned to the Merlin version (note – some official documents indicate that the XP-60 was originally designated XP-40F). Initially the project was to be a structural and aerodynamic study of a low drag laminar flow aerofoil on a standard P-40D Warhawk airframe (retaining the P-40D aft fuselage and tail) plus the Packard V1650 (though as first built the XP-60 would have a British-built Merlin XXVIII installed). Apart from the powerplant the XP-53 above was to be structurally identical to the first XP-60 from a point aft of the engine firewall, i.e. identical with the exception of the engine and cooling installation.

Agreement to procure the XP-60 was secured at a conference held on 14 November 1940 at the Air Corps Material Center between designer Donovan R. Berlin and Mr Nooman from Curtiss and Colonel Carroll, Major Bogert, Major Craigie and Captain Kelsey from the Air Corps. The aircraft would include a completely new flush-type inward-retracting landing gear and carry eight 0.50in (12.7mm) machine guns. At this stage it was deemed advisable to still provide for the Continental engine (in the XP-53) as an alternate installation to the Merlin XX. Contract W535-AC-18551 covering a single prototype was approved on 19 May 1941 and a full-size portion of the of the XP-60 wing suitable for testing in the tunnel at Langley Field was also to be supplied. Wright Field allotted Project Number MX-69 to the new design.

To accelerate the programme and make early assessments of the characteristics of the laminar flow wing, the original plan was to provide space provision only for the armament and to eliminate the self-sealing fuel tanks, armour plate protection and other minor items, but during the final assembly it was decided to complete the armament installation prior to delivery. Due to the similarity between the XP-60 and P-40, and this desire to fly the aircraft as soon as possible, there was no XP-60 mock-up.

In due course, however, interest grew in the type's production possibilities and as early as 1 February 1941 an AAF memo outlined a production schedule for 1,300 P-60s equipped with either the Packard/Rolls-Royce or Continental engine (this figure was later increased by a further 650). If the Packard was installed they would be P-60s, but if the Continental engine was put in then the designation would revert to P-53. On 14 May 1941 the AAF's General Echols directed that the XP-60 should be equipped with Rolls-Royce or Continental engines (as an aside, he also felt that too much attention was being given at this time to the XP-46 [Chapter One]). By 5 September 1941 the designation P-60A had been allotted to the production version, but with the single-stage two-speed Merlin XX in the XP-60 now replaced by the Allison V1710-F10R engine.

The choice of the low drag laminar flow wing would result in considerable delay to the programme,

Views of the first XP-60 after it had received a modified and enlarged fin. The air intake beneath the nose and the ports for the six wing-mounted machine guns are well shown. These photos are dated 19 November 1941. *Curtiss via Dave Ostrowski/Alan Griffith*

Well known but nevertheless excellent air-to-air shot of the XP-60. The aircraft carries no numerical markings of any kind. *Curtiss via Dave Ostrowski/ Alan Griffith*

but the XP-60's development did produce a solution to an ongoing problem of adequate aileron control coupled with a low drag aerofoil. In fact Curtiss succeeded in applying to the XP-60 the sealed gap type of aileron which resulted in unusually good aileron control with low stick forces throughout the flight envelope; this development would of course be made available to all fighter aircraft manufacturers (see the NACA Bulletin section below).

Taxiing tests started on 16 September 1941 and the XP-60, serial 41-19508, made its maiden flight on 18 September. Since very little experience was available with laminar flow wings, a considerable amount of flight testing (and wind tunnel testing) was necessary to obtain suitable aileron control characteristics. It was during these tests that two landing gear failures occurred which, in both cases, caused some damage. Following the correction of this and other minor difficulties, the official performance demonstration flights were conducted by Curtiss pilots at Buffalo in March 1942. The only difficulty encountered during these tests was a slight porpoising resulting from incorrect aerodynamic balancing of the elevator. This problem was dealt with at a later date, but additional dive tests had to be made to check the aircraft's safety.

In April 1942 AAF pilots began the type's official performance tests, at Buffalo. Here it was found that the XP-60 did not comply with the performance guarantee, due in part to the engine not delivering its guaranteed power output, but also because the wing surface was not finished to the degree of smoothness required for laminar flow. After the wing had been 'refinished', and a new engine installed, the prototype was tested again by the AAF in May when its performance now came within the allowable tolerance of the guarantee. Afterwards the XP-60 was delivered to Wright Field for final inspection and acceptance. It was accepted by the AAF on 11 July and then turned over to the Aircraft Laboratory for aileron control research and an investigation of the effects of the laminar flow wing. Then early in August 1942 it was returned to Curtiss for a Merlin 61 engine to be installed (as the XP-60D below).

On 18 November 1941, following a long period of discussion about the XP-53 and XP-60, a plan was submitted by Curtiss to convert the remaining XP-53 prototype into a static test article for the production P-60A. This was approved on 1 April 1942 and so the XP-53 with its Continental engine was never flown. However, just a day earlier, on 17 November, a memo written by Major Mark E. Bradley of the Pursuit Branch, Production Engineering Section, cast a cloud over the P-60A production plans. He wrote:

"The contract for 1,950 P-60A aircraft [W535-AC-22714] has now been signed and whatever is said now may be gate closing after departure of the horse, however, as project officer on the contract, it is my belief that it is my duty to present the picture as I now see it.

The P-60A airplane is starting out under an unsurmountable handicap. The airplane, as an airplane, is all right, but the power plant available for installation therein is completely inadequate. This lack of adequate power is a result of two things. First, the basic design of the airplane contemplated installation of the Continental engine. Second, the laminar flow wing necessitated more wing area, with the resulting increase in overall airplane size including the landing gear. It is my opinion, and the opinion of all Pursuit Project Officers in the Division, that at least 1,500hp [1,119kW] will be necessary in order to give the P-60A a reasonable chance of being a usable combat airplane. If we proceed on the supposition that that gross weight will be attained, the following comparison with other types is offered.

1. The power loading at military power is slightly over 7, identical to the P-40E. This means that at the military rating of the engine, the airplane can never have better manoeuvrability and climb than the P-40E has from sea level to 15,000ft [4,572m]. Tests show the P-40E to be inferior in combat to other current types.

2. The P-60A will maintain its performance to 25,000ft or 50,000ft [7,620m or 15,240m] but will will be inferior in flying characteristics to airplanes with adequate power. After discussion of desirable fighting qualities with RAF pilots, I am more than ever convinced that the P-60A, even though it meets every guarantee, will be considered unfit for combat even against airplanes now being produced in quantity.

3. The present gross weight of 9,451lb [4,287kg] is without some thirty items of special equipment and changes which have not yet been included in the airplane, but most of which we have been forced to install in present models due to operational requirements. I do not believe the airplane will weigh less than 9,700lb [4,400kg] when completed. I feel that the performance guarantee will be reduced due to the addition of some of the above items.

4. I believe that the P-40F, an airplane weighing more than 1,000lb (454kg) less than the P-60A and carrying the same armament, will be a far superior airplane in all combat qualities.

5. The P-60A performance guarantees are as follows:
Speed at Military Power 1,325hp [988kW] at 5,000ft [1,524m] = 324mph [521km/h],
Speed at Military Power 1,325hp [988kW] at 20,000ft [6,096m] = 375mph [603km/h],
Climb to 15,000ft [4,572m] in military power, 1,325hp [988kW] = 6.95 minutes.

6. According to the specification the estimated ceiling of 34,700ft [10,577m] is not guaranteed.

The above performance is poor. The P-40F will have at least the same performance at 5,000ft and 15,000ft [1,524m and 4,572m], and will climb to 15,000ft [4,572m] in 6.0 minutes. The ceiling is too low to make the airplane pay its way at high altitude and the guaranteed performance at lower altitude is inferior to our present types. There is nothing to indicate that the Lockheed P-38 and Republic P-47 will not completely outclass the P-60A at all altitudes.

7. It is recommended that:
   a. The Curtiss Company be required to redesign the P-60A to a military power loading of not over 6; until such a design is available the production of P-40Fs should be continued, possibly with the Merlin 61 engine.
   b. An engine of at least 1,500hp [1,119kW] military power be developed and that no P-60As be built until such an engine is available.
   c. If neither of the above plans are possible, the P-60A contract be cancelled and … let Curtiss build P-47Bs or P-38s."

The outcome of this strongly worded document was a conference held on 26 November, involving General Kenney, Colonels Page and Crawford of Wright Field with Messrs Jansen, Crosswell, Flader and Wright of the Airplane Division. Burdette S. Wright wrote an account of the meeting in which he noted:

"It seems that the P-47 is considered to be the outstanding pursuit plane now flying and that there is a strong question in the minds of the visiting officers as to the continuation of the P-60A production, rather than considering now a discontinuation and arrangement with Republic whereby the P-47 type could be built in the Buffalo plants. Plans were suggested for the P-47 to be built in other companies, but Wright was worried that the question of Curtiss dropping out of the P-60A would result in the elimination of a turbo Allison tractor pursuit aircraft, and the continuation of Curtiss' experiments and developments of liquid cooled pursuit. Wright felt that this was a vary serious matter and strongly recommended that they not discontinue the P-60A production, but that the Army arrange for Republic to increase P-47 production through increasing subcontracting, and that Curtiss continue the P-60A as it would than have an air cooled and a liquid cooled pursuit type of high altitude performance."

The author has reproduced extended excerpts from these memoranda since they provide an indication of the planning that went on behind the scenes into creating the nation's new combat aircraft, and an idea of the problems that had to be considered and the decisions made to build the best aircraft.

Nevertheless, the engineering inspection for the P-60A was conducted at Buffalo between 1 and 5 December 1941, with the armament inspection following a week later. A number of necessary changes were required, but these were not to be made to the prototype. The P-60A would incorporate alterations to the wing panels, tail surfaces and landing gear, plus a fuselage modified to accommodate the Allison engine and its supercharger.

At 13 December Curtiss had flown 41-19508 at Buffalo for about 23 hours. On 15 December Major Chidlaw reported to General Echols that the XP-60 had obtained 384mph (618km/h) at 22,000ft (6,706m), instead of (the guaranteed) 387mph (623km/h), so it was just a little short. Unfortunately, although this figure was almost equal to the guarantee, the XP-60 was slower and carried less armament than the P-47 Thunderbolt, which was undergoing development at the same time as a parallel project. By 27 May 1942 the data now accumulated indicated a rammed critical altitude of 21,000ft (6,401m) and a high speed in just military power of 330mph (531km/h) maximum at 5,150ft (1,570m). The aircraft was then repainted and rubbed smooth immediately before flight testing, all of the wing seams were covered with Scotch tape, and all eight machine guns in the wings covered over. At 20,000ft (6,096m) with guns covered the speed was 380mph (611km/h), but then with dummy blast tubes fitted this dropped to 371.5mph (598km/h). The XP-60 took 10.2 minutes to reach 20,000ft (6,096m).

(Author's Note: The critical altitude for a piston aero-engine is the maximum height at which the turbocharger will maintain a pressure to the engine equivalent to sea level standard pressure. Once the aircraft exceeds this critical height the engine provides less power, though of course it still delivers more than a non-turbocharged (normally aspirated) unit would at the same air density. The benefit of a ram air intake was that the engine's rated altitude would be increased by several thousands of feet - in the case of the Merlin-powered P-51 Mustangs by over 5000ft [1,524m] - compared to an engine on a test bench where a turbo would do all of the work [provided the intake was well designed, which did not always happen]. In addition, as the aircraft's forward speed was increased the air would be 'rammed' into the intake with greater force.)

During the war the British Aeronautical Committee/Council and the Royal Aircraft Establishment (RAE) at Farnborough reported on various Confidential Bulletins circulated by NACA, and these included information for the XP-60 series (and for the XP-62 in the next chapter and the XP-81 in Chapter Seventeen).

In May 1942 these bodies looked at NACA's review of preliminary drag results obtained in flight on the XP-60's low-drag wing. The drag measurements were made in spite of the fact that some easily corrected imperfections were evident, particularly in the incomplete filling of a skin joint and rivets at the leading edge. Some filling was then applied as far back as the forward edge of the ammunition door, and the surface condition was generally improved

These photos of the XP-60A were taken on 14 October 1942 prior to first flight and indeed first engine runs. The new fuselage shape is most marked. Once again the aircraft is yet to receive any identity markings and indeed it still lacks items such as the undercarriage doors. Problems with the turbo-supercharger made necessary the addition of standard exhaust stacks protruding out of the engine cowling. *Curtiss via Dave Ostrowski/Alan Griffith*

by repainting and sanding, before the drag measurements were repeated. The results showed that, even with the wing having a comparatively poor surface near the leading edge, it showed a drag coefficient markedly less than could have been obtained with a conventional wing section. At the time it was hoped to make comparable measurements on the conventional wing of a P-40 Warhawk. Here the XP-60 had the Packard-Merlin engine equivalent to the Merlin XX and was fitted with eight machine guns, armour plate, bullet-proof glass and tank protection, plus of course the laminar flow aerofoil and completely flush landing gear.

Further work followed in July which saw brief flight assessments of the aileron characteristics of the XP-60 fitted with internally balanced, sealed ailerons, which had been developed by NACA for use particularly on low-drag-type wings. The results showed that light and effective aileron control was obtained without evidence of overbalance or undesirable shaking of the control system over any part of the deflection range within the level-flight speed range. This work had been undertaken at the request of the AAF, with NACA co-operating with Curtiss in developing satisfactory lateral-control characteristics for the XP-60 with its low-drag wing.

After comparing the results against similar data for the Hawker Hurricane and Supermarine Spitfire, RAE Farnborough added that the XP-60's ailerons showed up well against those of the other types. In addition to providing exceptionally light and effective lateral control at high speeds, the ailerons apparently give adequate effectiveness at low speeds and with flaps down. However, the maximum speed at which test were made was just 268mph (431km/h), so estimates for higher speeds were going to be uncertain. Nevertheless, RAE felt that these results showed considerable promise and the development of such ailerons should be watched closely.

The XP-60C prototype pictured at Buffalo, apparently prior to first flight and certainly before the painting of USAAF roundels. Note the contra-rotating propeller (though official American documents seem to prefer the term dual-rotation, rather than counter-rotating). *Curtiss via Dave Ostrowski/Alan Griffith*

These later views of XP-60C 42-79424 are apparently dated 24 February 1944 and show the bulged turbocharger intake positioned beneath the middle fuselage. *Curtiss via Dave Ostrowski/Alan Griffith*

279424

Another excellent view of the XP-60C in flight. From this angle the aircraft looks quite neat and compact. By this stage very little P-40 content remained in the design. *Curtiss via Dave Ostrowski/ Alan Griffith*

XP-60A, XP-60B, XP-60C

So, towards the end of 1941 discussions were underway as to whether the P-47 was better than the production P-60A, with suggestions that the latter should be dropped. However, by 15 December a P-60A fitted with an improved Allison engine of increased altitude rating was offering an estimated 394mph (634km/h) at 25,000ft (7,620m); it also weighed slightly more that the XP-60 at 9,450lb (4,287kg) as against 9,297lb (4,217kg).

Then, on 2 January 1942, General Kenney notified Curtiss that the entire production run of P-60As, 1,950 aircraft, was to be cancelled, but three new experimental prototype airframes – XP-60A, XP-60B and XP-60C - would be procured under a new contract W535-AC-28113 (issued on 24 July 1942). However, it was not until 29 August, and following a decision that Curtiss was to manufacture the P-47 Thunderbolt instead, that the production contract was finally closed. This cancellation proved to be a pivotal moment for Curtiss because never again would it put an all-new fighter type into production. For the remainder of the war it would build P-47s under licence and further variants of its P-40 Warhawk.

On 28 January 1942 it was confirmed that the three new prototypes would have three different powerplants. The new XP-60s would be structurally identical with the XP-60A having a 1,425hp (1,063kW) Allison V1710-F13R engine, the XP-60B the same, and the XP-60C the 16-cylinder 2,300hp (1,715kW) Chrysler XIV2220 liquid-cooled engine (later XI2220). The latter would retain its 'X' for experimental label during its entire existence and was eventually dropped for being too heavy; it was flight tested only by the Republic XP-47H (Chapter Twelve). The differences in the XP-60A and B came with their turbos, the former having a General Electric B.14 turbo-supercharger, the latter a Wright Aircraft Corporation Type 'B' (SU-504-2) turbo-supercharger (in fact the latter was not completed in this form and would eventually emerge as the XP-60E). MX-313 was allocated to the XP-60C (and to the XP-60E below).

Since (at this time) two out of three of these aircraft were still being considered as prototypes for production P-60s, a very heavy flight test programme was planned for them. Curtiss noted that these aircraft will be large and relatively complicated, especially because of the two-stage supercharger with ducting and intercoolers and the counter-rotation propeller to be used by the XP-60C.

To accommodate the Allison 1710-3 engine the contours of the XP-60A's nose and fuselage were altered extensively, while the gun armament was reduced to six 0.50in (12.7mm). Ground taxi runs began in late October 1942 but the fighter suffered serious troubles with cooling in the exhaust shrouds, which on one occasion resulted in a minor fire. This all happened before first flight and, since this particular aircraft had no future, the turbo and long exhaust ducting were thus removed, so that the aircraft was left with short exhaust stacks.

The XP-60A serial 42-79423 finally made its maiden flight on 11 November 1942 but was short on performance. The AAF accepted the aircraft on 13 October 1943 and, when all possible aerodynamic data had been garnered from its flight test programme (for application to the XP-60C, below), the XP-60A was then to be disassembled and sent to Wright Field to provide spare parts for the XP-60C and XP-60E. A plan to convert the XP-60A into a second XP-60E was dropped on 19 March 1943. This aircraft was classed as Class 26 (Instructional Airframe) at Wright Field on 15 April 1944.

When the above cooling difficulties were encountered on the XP-60A, it was decided to remove both the turbo and Allison engine in the XP-60B and install a Pratt & Whitney R2800-10 with single-rotation four-blade propeller instead, as the XP-60E (below). Thus, the XP-60B was never completed in its original form. Materiel Center at Wright Field changed the designation from XP-60B to XP-60E on 31 October 1942, the aircraft listed now as being identical to the XP-60C (in the form that that aircraft had become - below) apart from its reduction gearing and the latter's dual rotation propeller.

On 5 September 1942 a proposal from Wright Field to fit the R2800 in the XP-60C instead of the Chrysler unit was taken up with General Echols, who in fact initially disagreed with the idea, particularly in view of the modified aircraft's expected performance being substantially the same as for the Bell XP-63 Kingcobra. But on 5 October 1942 Echols decided that the R2800-10 should go into the XP-60C and that this must "proceed with all speed". Part of the problem was that the Chrysler's weight meant that several hundred pounds of lead needed to be loaded into the tail to balance the airframe. The armament was also reduced to four 0.50in (12.7mm) weapons.

In fact, such was the potential improvement in performance with the R2800 that, for a brief period, there was a second production order. With the R2800, and at a gross weight of 10,000lb (4,536kg), the XP-60C was expected to have a high speed of 430mph (692km/h) at 22,000ft (6,706m) in war emergency power and a climb rate of 4,600ft/min (1,402m/min) at sea level. As such it would be a possible immediate answer to the Director of Pursuit's urgent plea for a fast climbing interceptor.

Contract W535-AC-35373 of 13 March 1943 covered 500 R2800-powered P-60s of which the first 26 were to be produced as YP-60As and delivered as service test articles with single rotation propellers, in lieu of the main run fitted with dual-rotation props. The former would carry serials 43-32763 to 43-32788 and the remaining 474 airframes (43-32789 to 43-33262) were to be designated P-60A-1. However, all of these aircraft bar 43-32763 were cancelled in June 1943, with this single example being completed as a YP-60E (below). The assembly of 43-32764 was started but never completed.

The cancellation was in part prompted by in an Inter-Office memorandum of 22 March 1943 within AAF Material Center (and also by flight trials in late April described later). In this document Brig. Gen. K.B. Wolfe, the Chief of the Production Division, compared current USAAF fighter projects and programmes, including the P-60 which in his eyes looked inferior. For his report he used estimated data for the forthcoming Republic XP-47J and XP-72 (Chapter Twelve), both still some way off first flight, and noted:

"The P-47J should be put into production due to its superior high altitude characteristics. It rate of climb at 35,000ft [10,668m] is 1,100ft/min [335m/min] better than the nebulous P-72, and 900ft/min [274m/min] better than the Lockheed P-38H [Lightning]. Speed at 35,000ft [10,668m] is 93mph [150km/h] better than the P-38H. The P-47J should be our number one high altitude fighter."

He added that above 25,000ft (7,620m) the P-47J is better than the P-72. Below 25,000ft (7,620m) the P-72 is excellent (except it will be 'un-manoeuvrable') and at 10,000ft (3,048m) it is:

45mph (72km/h) and 800ft/min (244m/min) better than the P-47J,
45mph (72km/h) and 800ft/min (244m/min) better than the P-60,
35mph (56km/h) and zero better than the P-63,
40mph (64km/h) and 1,250ft/min (381m/min) better than the P-51,
70mph (113km/h) and 1,000ft/min (305m/min) better than the P-38.

Wolfe added that he wanted to disapprove a Curtiss request to initiate a new P-40 (the version in question is not given, but may have been the XP-40Q below). He stated that "this should be a good aircraft next month, but would be too sub-marginal to put into production in January 1944." Also, "Curtiss is designing the P-60 for the dual-rotation nose on the R2800-C, but due to the non-availability of the nose they will deliver 500 to 700 with single-rotation. Curtiss and Republic each require this nose. The P-60C will gain a maximum of 250ft/min [76m/min] by using dual rotation. The P-47J will gain at all altitudes, and at 35,000ft [10,668m] the gain is 840ft/min [256m/min]. It is essential that the P-47J be given priority for the production installation of the dual rotation nose."

The original XP-60 now converted into the XP-60D with a deeper nose to take a Packard V1650-3 engine. The fin area has been increased and Curtiss altered the radiator intake several times, but when photographed it still had a three-blade propeller. *Curtiss via Dave Ostrowski/Alan Griffith*

Wolfe recommended that, if it became necessary to reduce the quantity of fighters being produced, that the "first airplane to be eliminated should be the P-60. It is going into production in September and under no circumstances will the dual rotation version be available prior to February 1944. At this time there will be 3,000 P-63s out of the factory with superior performance, armament and range. In fact there seems no logical reason for producing the P-60." He suggested switching production at Republic's Farmingdale factory from the P-47D to the P-47J, and that at Evansville from the P-47B to the P-72. Had this been done then the story of USAAF fighter procurement during the later stages of the war might have been very different, but clearly the P-60 was out of favour.

On 9 May 1943 a Board set up after Wolfe's memo, under the chairmanship of Maj. Gen. Barney M. Giles, Chief of Air Staff for Operations, Commitments and Requirements, released a report which made a thorough appraisal of the entire USAAF fighter programme, with a view "to reducing the number of.....fighter types from being produced unless they [were] outstanding." With this in mind, the Board recommended that the planned and actual production of the P-60 should be eliminated immediately. As a result, on 13 May 1943 Washington directed that P-60 production was to be discontinued after just 20 aircraft had been built for experimental and service test use; this further change of plan which was confirmed on 7 June.

The XP-60C made an initial 10 minute flight on 27 January 1943. The pilot reported that its general characteristics were good, with no torque reaction (from the contra-rotation propeller). Shake-down flights in the XP-60C followed on 8 and 9 February 1943, the aircraft handled well and its stability and flight characteristics were considered good, with all major items reported to be satisfactory, apart from relatively high elevator and rudder forces.

XP-60D

The next designation, XP-60D (to AAF Project MX-280), was applied to the original XP-60 after a two stage, supercharged Packard V1650-3 (Merlin 61/63) engine had been installed during August 1942, along with a four-blade propeller. Turning the XP-60 serial 41-19508 into the XP-60D also required the vertical tail and fin to be enlarged and these alterations were completed later in 1942.

On 6 May 1943, during a demonstration performance dive test at Rome Air Depot in New York, the tail came off the XP-60D. The pilot had just entered his final dive to reach the 464mph (747km/h) indicated speed specified for the pull out. The pull out was started at approximately 10,000ft (3,048m) and the pilot was recorded saying "I am going into a dive – there goes the tail – I am getting out." Fortunately, he landed safely by parachute. Prior to this Curtiss had experienced some difficulties with the tail and had been trying various configurations on account of buffeting. All indications were that the accident resulted from compressibility. The XP-60D was destroyed.

A review of current XP-60 variants was made by the AAF on 27 March 1943 showing how they stood at the time:

XP-60 – None on Contract – Merlin XX engine and no supercharger. This model had been "obliterated by rework into the XP-60D".

XP-60A – One on Contract – Allison engine but in other respects is similar to the XP-60

The XP-60E, seen here early in its career in 1943, was powered by an R2800-10 engine driving a four-blade propeller. *Curtiss via Dave Ostrowski/Alan Griffith*

except for centre section leading edge projections which house cooling ducts and some changes in the tail surfaces. It has a General Electric turbo.

XP-60B – None on Contract – Allison engine and a Wright turbo. It resembled the XP-60A so much that no spin tests were necessary. This aircraft was modified into the XP-60E.

XP-60C – One on Contract – Pratt & Whitney R2800-B with two-stage supercharger. Dual rotation propellers are used.

XP-60D – One on Contract – Much like the XP-60 but powered with a Merlin 61 engine with two-stage supercharger.

XP-60E – One on Contract – Much like the XP-60C but has a single-rotation propeller. The engine is further forward, it has a larger nose and smaller spinner combination, which compensate as far as the fin area is concerned.

XP-60F – One on Contract - Pratt & Whitney R2800-C engine with two-stage supercharger and dual rotation propellers, but the fuselage lines aft of the cockpit, instead of being straight, are concave. (Author's note: The XP-60F was cancelled well before completion.)

YP-60 – Twenty on Contract – Like the XP-60C but will have the fuselage and tail surfaces of the XP-60E.

Walk-around views of the XP-60 42-79425 with markings now applied. One of the prints is dated 17 April 1944 and clearly all of these shots were taken on the same day. The aircraft carried just two machine guns in each wing. *Curtiss via Dave Ostrowski/Alan Griffith*

One assumes that this selection of air-to-air pictures of the XP-60 were all taken during the same sortie, on 10 October 1944. They provide particularly good detail for the laminar flow wing shape and for the underside, both front and rear. This aircraft was exactly the same as the XP-60C with the exception of the single rotation propeller. *Curtiss via Dave Ostrowski/Alan Griffith*

XP-60E

As part of its conversion to XP-60E condition, ex-XP-60B serial 42-79425 had its engine moved forward by 10in (25.4cm) in comparison to the XP-60C. This was because the 'E's four-blade propeller was rather lighter than the 'C's six-blade contraprop and the repositioning was necessary to maintain the CofG. One reason for this latest conversion ('B' to 'E') was that (while plans for production were still live) the contra-rotating propeller and its associated gearing were unlikely to be ready for the first airframes off the production line, so fitting one airframe with a single rotation substitute would at least provide early in-flight data.

Because of delays, including problems with the engine during ground running, 42-79425 did not make its maiden flight as an XP-60E until 26 May 1943. Then on 14 August it had to force land at Niagara Falls Airport after engine failure. The underside of its fuselage and the propeller were damaged but the aircraft was repaired using the undercarriage and wing now available from the retired XP-60A.

Since no AAF performance information was available as yet on 42-79425 as an XP-60E, on 22 November Colonel R.P. Swofford, the Chief of Fighter Branch, wrote that "it is considered advisable to convert the XP-60C to an XP-60E so that performance data could be obtained to evaluate the advantages of the dual rotation propeller over the single rotation form. It is considered desirable to have two identical aircraft, one equipped with a single rotation propeller and the other dual rotation, to be used in further propeller development by the Propeller Laboratory and general evaluation by AAF personnel." Thus, the AAF planned to make a direct comparison of single and dual rotation propellers.

For this reason Curtiss was authorised to repair 42-79425 and convert it from an XP-60E into an XP-60C. Both the R2800-53 engine and its contra-rotating propeller were taken out of 42-79424 and put into 42-79425 to make the latter an XP-60C, while 42-79424 itself had an R2800-10 and single-rotation propeller installed to become an XP-60E. This very confusing situation meant that the two prototypes had now switched configurations and type categories. As an XP-60C 42-79425 was flown for 19 hours before it was considered ready for assessment by AAF pilots.

An event which finally killed off any long-term future for the P-60 series was some trials flights made between different fighter types at Patterson Field late in April 1943. The AAF wanted the XP-60E to be involved here, but at this stage it was still to fly and so the XP-60C went instead. Unfortunately, the 'C's engine would not deliver full power, and its wing surface was in poor condition which ruined the smooth laminar-flow characteristics and cut the aircraft's speed. In these trials both the Republic P-47D Thunderbolt and North American P-51B Mustang exhibited superior performance so, in terms of production, the XP-60 line of Curtiss fighter development was dropped from further consideration.

However, in January 1944 the XP-60E was delivered to the AAF Proving Base at Eglin Field in Florida to undergo official testing. In the air this prototype's performance proved little better than current types – maintaining flight in a steady condition necessitated constant close attention from the pilot to the aircraft's trim, its level flight stability was poor, and having just four guns meant that the armament was weaker compared to other current types. In general, at Eglin the XP-60's speed performance fell short of the competition, although its sea level rate of climb was considered to be very good. The AAF accepted the aircraft on 13 May 1944 and it was later written off following a severe landing accident.

BELOW AND OPPOSITE There appears to be a good supply of photos of the XP-60s, but many are walk-around shots like these taken on 24 February 1945. This is the final version, the YP-60E 43-32763 which, with its bulky fuselage and bubble canopy, is so different to the first XP-60 and has now almost morphed into a P-47 Thunderbolt! The turbo-supercharger intake is set in the chin position at the very bottom of the engine cowling and the six-gun armament has been restored, but this aircraft flew very little. *Curtiss via Dave Ostrowski/Alan Griffith*

332763

332763

332763

An image depicting the YP-60E after it had passed into civilian ownership, in the hand of Jimmy DeSanto who named the aircraft *Connie II* after his wife. It arried civil registration NX21979. Note the staining from the engine exhaust on the side of the fuselage. The Thompson Trophy was one of America's National Air Races and in 1947 was won by a Goodyear F2G Corsair (described briefly in Appendix Two). *Curtiss via Dave Ostrowski/ Alan Griffith*

YP-60E

Despite the problems experienced with the XP-60 series, there was to be one further version. On 22 June 1943 the YP-60E designation was assigned to two aircraft after the order for 20 YP-60s had been cut (serials 43-32763 and 43-32764, still covered by Contract W535-AC-35373). The YP-60E had an R2800-18 engine and was similar to the XP-60E, except for in particular the introduction of a bubble canopy, but with other modifications including a revised fuselage and vertical tailplane, plus six wing-mounted machine guns rather than four. This aircraft first flew on 15 July 1944 but the AAF showed minimal interest in it. After just one more flight in Curtiss hands 43-32763 was transferred to AAF responsibility at Wright Field on 16 September 1944, but it was never flown and just set aside. Previously, on 9 May, it had been announced that work on the second airframe 43-32764 was to be discontinued with some of the machine's components to go for spares.

The YP-60E was Struck Off Charge on 22 December 1944 and put up for disposal on the 27th. It was bought by engineer Art Knapp who modified the engine to take water injection, to provide 2,440hp (1,820kW) of power for short periods. With civil register NX21979, and only three hours airtime all told, in late 1946 the aircraft was sold on to James DeSanto who, before entering it for the 1947 Thompson Trophy Race, stripped out all of the military equipment. In addition, he took 5ft 1in (1.55m) off each wing tip to reduce the span to just 31ft 2in (9.50m), and in the process took away about one third of the aileron area. Test flights revealed a top speed of 422mph (679km/h) but, during preparations to qualify for the race in early September 1947, parts the aircraft's tail unit broke away and DeSanto was forced to take to his parachute, fortunately reaching the ground in safety. The XP-60 prototype series had finally closed after a long period of gestation which produced little reward. None of the P-60 series survives today.

XP-60 structure

All of the XP-60 series prototypes were all-metal single-seat low-wing monoplanes with a tail-wheel undercarriage. Each of them retained a straight tapered NACA low drag laminar flow wing, the same horizontal tailplane and roughly the same fin shape (but with variations in size for the latter). However, the different engine installations brought changes to the fuselage. In general the original XP-60 (and as the XP-60D) had a relatively slim fuselage while the follow on members of the family featured fatter, more chunky forms. Both wing and tail surfaces were of full cantilever construction and the wing always carried the full armament installation.

Reviewing the individual powerplants and fuel loads, the XP-606 had a Merlin XXVIII driving a Curtiss Electric constant speed three-bladed propeller of 11ft (3.35m) diameter. It had an internal fuel capacity of 228galUS (863lit). The XP-60A introduced an Allison V1710-75 driving a 11ft 8in (3.58m) diameter Curtiss Electric constant speed four-blade propeller and had 200galUS (757lit) of internal fuel. XP-60B also had a Curtiss Electric constant speed four-blade 11ft 8in (3.58m) diameter propeller. The XP-60C's Pratt & Whitney two-speed two-stage supercharged R2800-53 had a Curtiss Electric constant speed (two x three) six-blade dual rotation propeller 12ft 2in (3.71m) in diameter and 225galUS (852lit) of fuel housed internally, while the XP-60D's powerplant was a Packard Merlin V1570-3 with a two stage supercharger and four-blade 11ft (3.35m) diameter Curtiss Electric propeller. Here the internal fuel capacity was 228galUS (863lit).

For the XP-60E it was an R2800-10 and General Electric turbosupercharger driving a four-blade 12ft 11in (3.94m) diameter single rotation Curtiss Electric constant speed propeller plus an internal fuel capacity of 225galUS (852lit). The YP-60E had an R2800-18 two-speed two-stage supercharged unit driving a four-blade, single rotation Curtiss Electric prop 12ft 2in (3.71m) in diameter. This aircraft carried fuel in

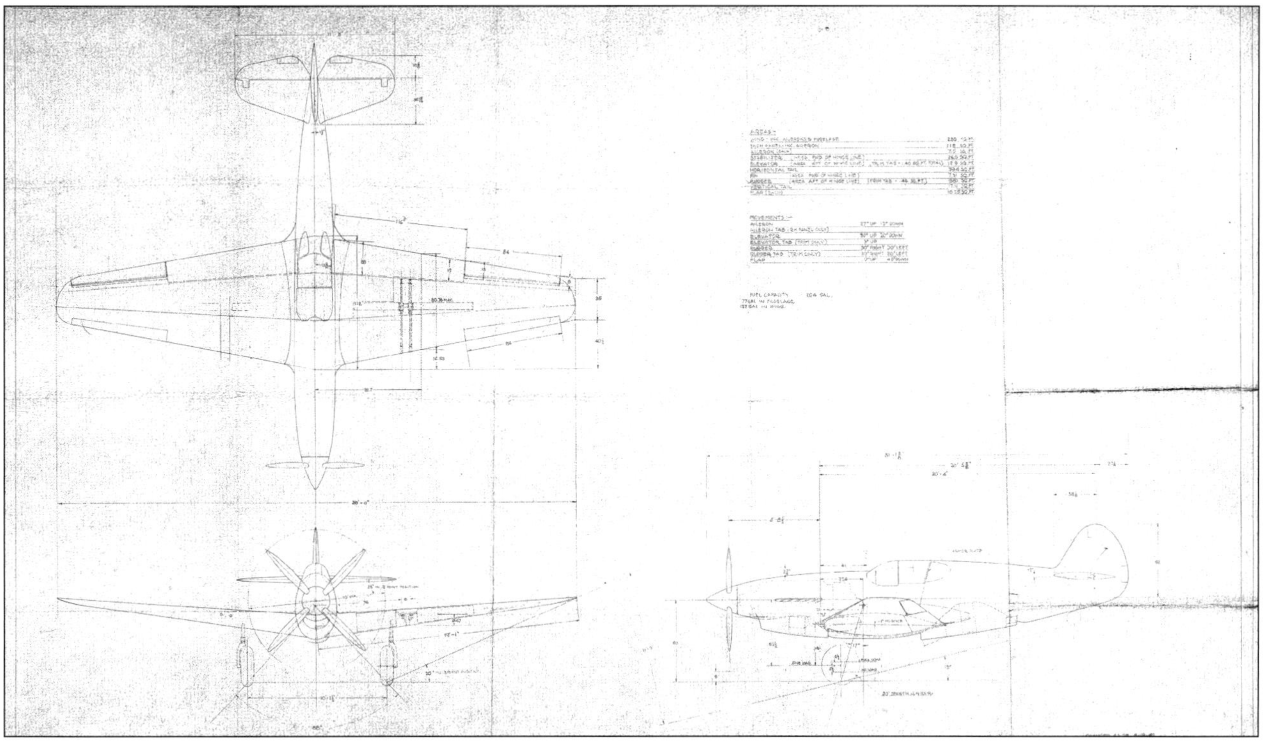

ABOVE Three view drawing of the Curtiss XP-53 dated August 1940. Span 38ft 0in (11.58m), length 31ft 1.375in (9.48m), wing area 230sq.ft (21.39sq.m). *US National Archives, College Park, RG-342*

RIGHT AND OVERLEAF Original manufacturer's drawings of the P-60 series of experimental prototypes. *All Maxwell AFB Archives*

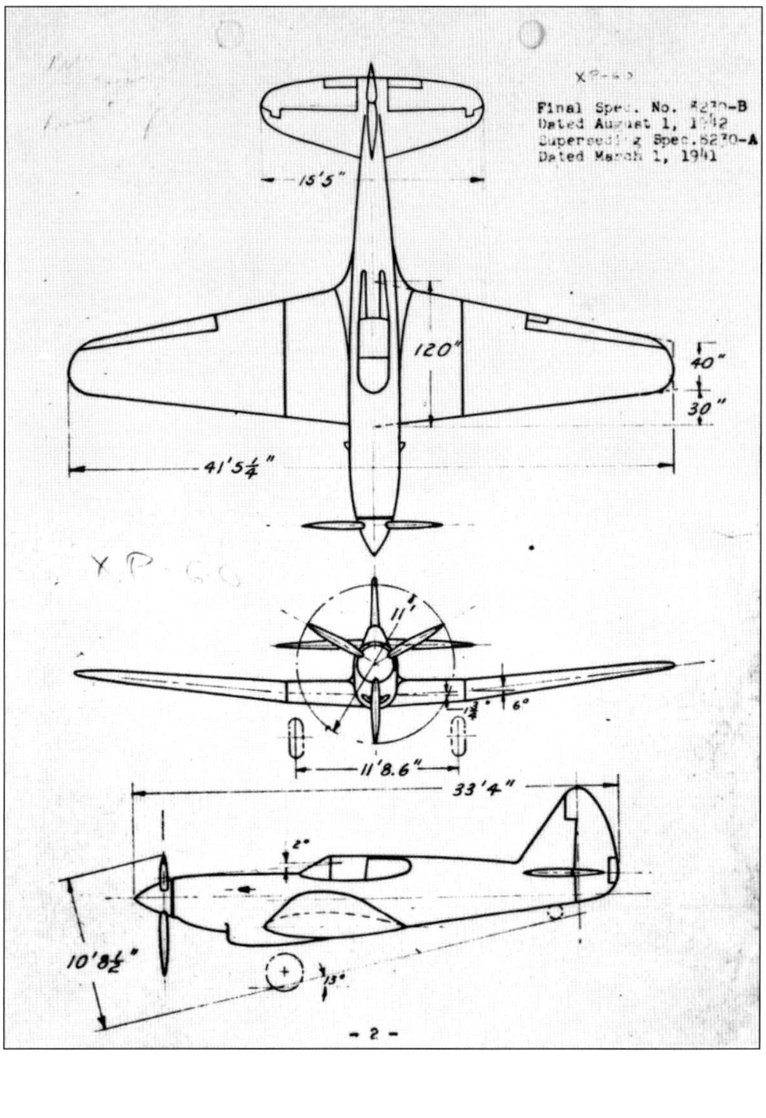

The original XP-60 layout, drawing dated March 1941.

both wing and fuselage tanks for a total of 368galUS (1,393lit) internally, and another 400galUS (1,514lit) could be carried in external tanks. YP-60E also introduced a cut-down rear fuselage and bubble canopy for an improved view for the pilot, but it still had the laminar flow wing.

For the record, the serial numbers were:

41-140 – XP-53.
41-19508 – XP-53, later XP-60, later XP-60D.
42-79423 – XP-60A.
42-79424 – XP-60C.
42-79425 – XP-60B, later XP-60E.
43-32762/32787 – YP-60A, 43-32763 to YP-60E, remainder cancelled.
43-32789/33262 – P-60A-1-CU all cancelled.

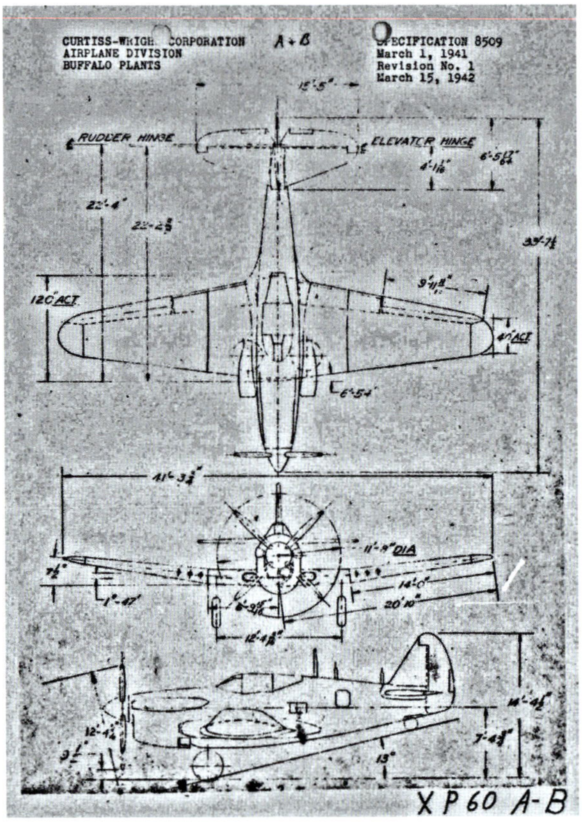

Configuration for the XP-60A and XP-60B, dated March 1942. This poor quality drawing is the only three-view available to the author.

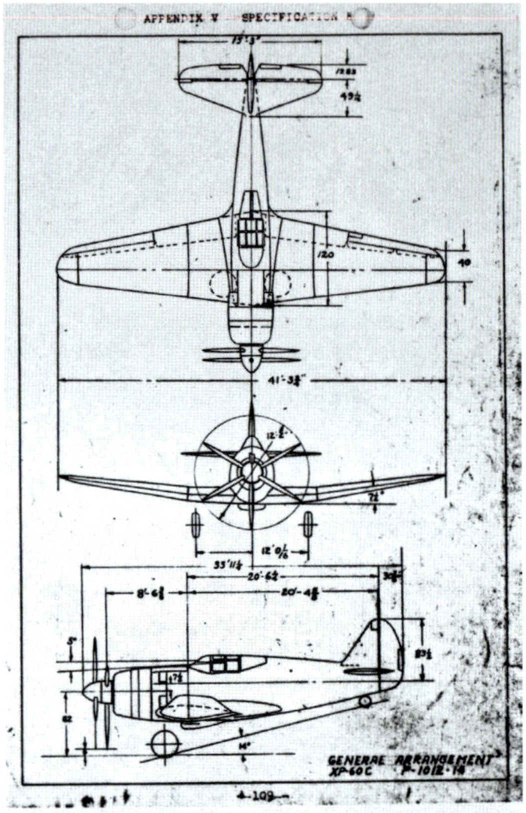

The XP-60C with dual rotation propeller. The drawing is undated but is marked as number P-1012-14.

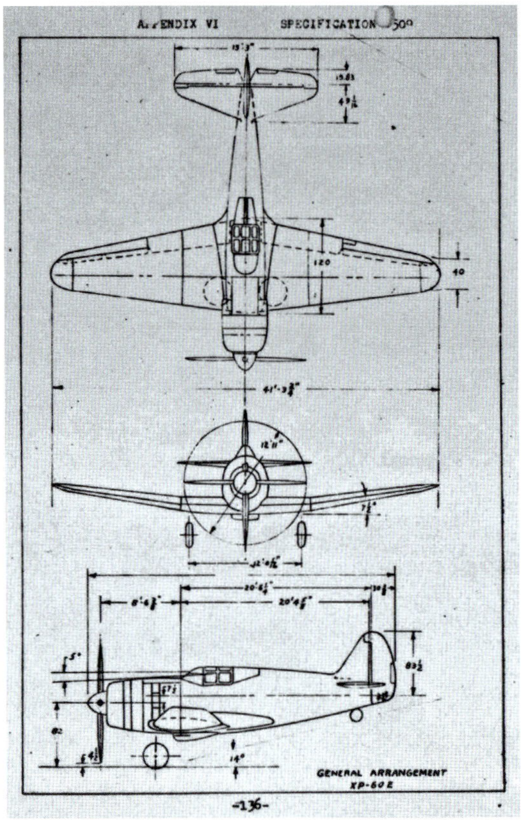

General arrangement of the XP-60E.

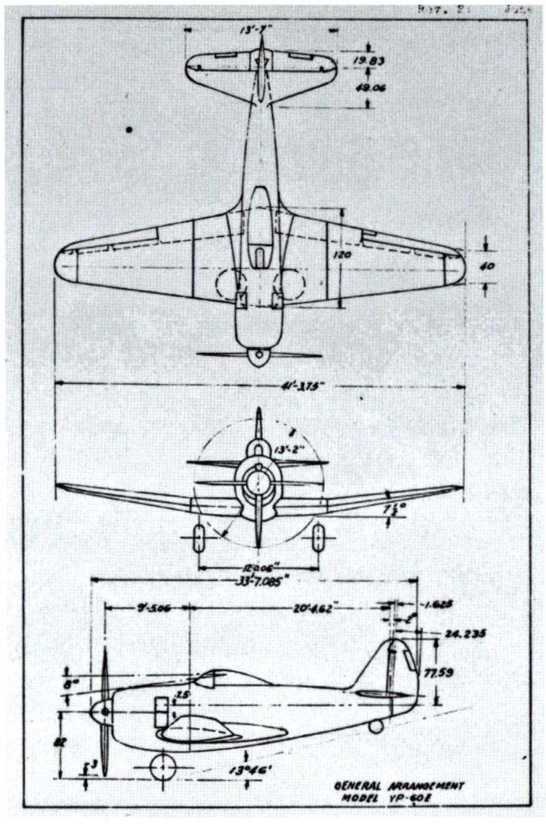

General arrangement of the YP-60E.

XP-60 data

Length:	33ft 4in (10.16m)
Wing span:	41ft 5.25in (12.63m)
Wing area:	275.4sq.ft (25.61sq.m)
Empty weight:	7,008lb (3,179kg)
Gross weight:	9,351lb (4,242kg)
Powerplant:	1 x 1,300hp (969kW) Packard/Rolls-Royce Merlin V1650-1 two speed, single stage, supercharged liquid-cooled engine
Maximum speed:	380mph (611km/h) at 20,000ft (6,096m)
Rate of climb:	7.3 minutes to 15,000ft (4,572m)
Service ceiling:	29,000ft (8,839m)
Normal range:	800 miles (1,287km) at 365mph (587km/h) at 16,500ft (5,029m)
Maximum range:	1,100 miles (1,770km) at 314mph (505km/h) at 15,000ft (4,572m)
Armament:	8 x 0.50in (12.70mm) machine guns

XP-60A data

Length:	33ft 11in (10.34m)
Wing span:	41ft 4in (12.60m)
Wing area:	275sq.ft (25.575sq.m)
Empty weight:	7,806lb (3,541kg)
Gross weight:	9,616lb (4,362kg)
Maximum take-off weight (overload gross weight):	10,160lb (4,609kg)
Powerplant:	1 x 1,425hp (1,063kW) Allison V1710-75 turbo supercharged 12-cylinder liquid-cooled engine
Maximum speed (estimated – never achieved):	324mph (521km/h) at sea level, 420mph (676km/h) at 25,000ft (7,620m)
Rate of climb:	2,560ft/min (780m/min) at sea level
Service ceiling:	32,500ft (9,906m)
Normal range:	375 miles (603km) at 375mph (603km/h)
Armament:	6 x 0.50in (12.70mm) machine guns in wings

XP-60B data at 26 October 1942

(Never flew in this form – performance estimated)

Length:	33ft 7.5in (10.25m)
Wing span:	41ft 3.75in (12.59m)
Wing area:	275.15sq.ft (25.59sq.m)
Empty weight:	7,806lb (3,541kg)
Design gross weight:	9,615lb (4,361kg)
Powerplant:	1 x 1,425hp (1,063kW) Allison V1710-F13R
Maximum speed (at design gross weight):	340mph (547km/h) at 5,000ft (1,524m), 420mph (676km/h) at 20,000ft (6,096m)
Rate of climb (at design gross weight):	6.5 minutes to 15,000ft (4,572m)
Service ceiling:	32,500ft (9,906m)
Armament:	6 x 0.50in (12.7mm) machine guns in wings

XP-60C data

Length:	33ft 11.25in (10.34m)
Wing span:	41ft 3.75in (12.59m)
Wing area:	275sq.ft (25.575sq.m)
Empty weight:	8,601lb (3,901kg)
Gross weight:	10,525lb (4,774kg)
Maximum take-off weight:	11,835lb (5,368kg)
Powerplant:	1 x 2,000hp (1,491kW) Pratt & Whitney R2800-53 18-cylinder supercharged air-cooled radial engine
Maximum speed (war emergency power):	340mph (547km/h) at sea level, 354mph (570km/h) at 3,600ft (1,097m), 414mph (666km/h) at 20,350ft (6,203m)
Best speed on military power:	397mph (639km/h) at 18,800ft (5,730m)
Rate of climb (war emergency power):	3,890ft/min (1,186m/min) at sea level, maximum 4,140ft/min (1,262m/min) at 12,800ft (3,901m)
Service ceiling:	35,000ft (10,668m)
Normal range:	315 miles (507km)
Armament:	4 x 0.50in (12.70mm) machine guns

XP-60D data

Length:	33ft 7in (10.24m)
Wing span:	41ft 5in (12.62m)
Wing area:	275sq.ft (25.575sq.m)
Gross weight:	9,980lb (4,527kg)
Powerplant:	1 x 1,380hp (1,029kW) Packard Merlin V1570-3 two stage supercharged liquid-cooled engine
Maximum speed:	390mph (628km/h) at height
Armament:	Uncertain

XP-60E data

Length:	33ft 11in (10.34m)
Wing span:	41ft 4in (12.60m)
Wing area:	275sq.ft (25.575sq.m)
Empty weight:	8,574lb (3,889kg)
Gross weight:	10,320lb (4,681kg)
Maximum take-off weight:	10,667lb (4,839kg)
Powerplant:	1 x 2,000hp (1,491kW) Pratt & Whitney R-2800-10 air-cooled radial engine
Maximum speed:	410mph (660km/h) at 20,200ft (6,157m)
Rate of climb:	4,200ft/min (1,280m/min) at sea level
Service ceiling:	38,000ft (11,582m)
Normal range:	315 miles (507km)
Armament:	4 x 0.50in (12.70mm) machine guns

YP-60E data

Length:	33ft 11in (10.34m)
Wing span:	41ft 4in (12.60m)
Wing area:	275.15sq.ft (25.59sq.m)
Empty weight:	8,285lb (3,758kg)
Gross weight (four guns):	10,270lb (4,658kg)
Maximum take-off weight:	11,520lb (5,225kg)
Powerplant:	1 x 2,100hp (1,566kW) Pratt & Whitney R-2800-18 air-cooled radial engine
Maximum speed:	405mph (652km/h) at 24,500ft (7,468m)
Maximum speed (estimated at 20 january 1944):	367mph (591km/h) at sea level, 446mph (718km/h) at 25,000ft (7,620m)
Rate of climb:	4.8 minutes to 14,000ft (4,267m)
Rate of climb (estimated at 20 january 1944):	4,600ft/min (1,402m/min) at sea level
Service ceiling:	34,000ft (10,363m), Estimate at 20 January 1944: 40,800ft (12,436m)
Armament:	6 x 0.50in (12.70mm) machine guns

The first XP-40Q was serial 42-9987, seen here in a photo which shows the extended nose very well. This shot has the aircraft in original XP-40Q-2 form with the P-40-style canopy. *Jeremy Collins*

ABOVE LEFT AND RIGHT Later 42-9987 was further modified with a bubble canopy and other changes. *Curtiss*

RIGHT Ground views of 42-9987 as fully converted to XP-40Q standard. Note the four-blade propeller. *Jeremy Collins*

XP-40Q

With declining fortunes during the war Curtiss made several attempts to hold its place in the fighter development market and their resulting programmes fill several chapters within this book. Another was the experimental XP-40Q which, like the XP-60, was a development of the long standing P-40 Warhawk series; hence its inclusion in this chapter. Here, the effort directed towards producing a much more modern fighter than the current P-40, equal to or surpassing the performance of newer types, produced such drastic alterations that the XP-40Q had relatively little in common with the standard fighter and indeed looked quite different.

Work began in 1943 and three XP-40Q prototypes were built, all rebuilt from former P-40 airframes originally manufactured during 1943 and 1944 – P-40K serials 42-9987 and 42-45722 and P-40N 43-24571. Each of them received a two-stage supercharged water-injected Allison V1710 engine, revised cooling systems, a four-blade propeller and carried an armament of just four 0.50in (12.7mm) machine guns (proposals for P-40Q production aircraft showed either four 20mm cannon or six 0.50in guns).

The first prototype 42-9987, which as a P-40K had incurred some damage in a landing accident on 27 January 1943, was designated XP-40Q-2 (and not XP-40Q-1 as reported in some published sources). It retained the standard P-40 wing and canopy but the nose was extended to take the 1,500hp (1,119kW) V1710-101, the air intake was above the cowling and the radiator and oil cooler in the centre wing between the undercarriage. XP-40Q-2's length was 33ft 4.15in (10.16m) and span 37ft 4in (11.38m), but the latter was reduced to 35ft 2.5in (10.73m) after the wings were clipped when 42-9987 had become an XP-40Q-2; the wing area in clipped form was apparently 232sq.ft (21.58sq.m).

It is understood that the XP-40Q-2's maiden flight took place from Buffalo on 13 June 1943, but very quickly the aircraft was modified further and by November it was sporting a cut back rear fuselage and a bubble cockpit canopy. Now the radiators were located in the wing leading edges just outboard of the undercarriage (leaving room for just the four guns) and it had a shallow air intake in the chin position; the engine was unaltered. In the air the XP-40Q-2 flew beautifully and AAF test pilot Capt Gustav Lundquist, who evaluated 42-9987, declared the aircraft as "the best P-40-type he had flown", and recommended that flight testing should be taken further. As a result, in December 1943 AAF Air Materiel Command recommended that two more XP-40Qs should be procured.

In January 1944 42-9987 was taken to Eglin Field for trials, but in March it was back at Curtiss's Buffalo facility for further testing, by which time an 1,800hp (1,342kW) V1710-121 engine had been installed and the wingtips clipped. Between 8 and 24 March 1944 Lt Robert M. Edholm of the AFF piloted 42-9987 on 20 sorties, for around 25 hours airtime, before the aircraft suffered damage on the 24th after nosing over following a test flight. With repairs completed, in mid-1944 it went to Wright Field but was damaged again on 31 July, this time extensively, after experiencing a ground loop on landing.

The second prototype 42-45722 was designated XP-40Q-2A. Very similar to 42-9987 in final form with a 1,800hp (1,342kW) V1710-121 plus clipped wings, the second example did have automatic radiator and cooler shutters. It first flew before the end of March 1944 but in the air was bedevilled with engine problems, which resulted in several forced landings. A good deal of time was spent on repairs before the machine was passed to Allison for engine trials. It was declared surplus in March 1946 and sold privately to Joe Ziegler with civil registration NX300B. Unfortunately, on 1 September 1947 when flying in the Thompson Trophy Race, the V1710 caught fire, Ziegler had to bale out and the aircraft was destroyed when it crashed (the second Curtiss fighter prototype to fall victim during this event).

The third prototype, 43-24571 designated XP-40Q-3 and the only XP-40Q recognised as such by the AAF, was very similar to 42-45722 with the same engine; however, it had a slightly smaller and revised canopy, with amended nose contours, which improved the pilot's view still further. Span was 35ft 3in (10.74m) and length 35ft 4in (10.77m) and the aircraft was passed to AAF hands in April 1944. However, during an early flight it suffered engine failure, the pilot had to make a forced landing and 43-24571 was damaged; it was not repaired and was written off. The P-40Q was one of the best ever Curtiss fighters but, unfortunately, it was matched and equalled by rival products.

XP40Q flight test

Lundquist's report (above) was dated 2 November 1943 and he flew 42-9987 at a gross weight of 8,203lb (3,721kg) with 160galUS (606lit) of fuel on board, and with unclipped wings. Taxiing and ground handling qualities were satisfactory and on take-off the aircraft left the ground after a short run and then climbed steeply with considerably less torque affect than with earlier P-40 variants. The XP-40Q was statically and dynamically stable longitudinally and directionally, and neutrally stable laterally. Lundquist wrote that the handling characteristics were "excellent and the airplane is very manoeuvrable. Control forces, although slightly heavy, are well coordinated and highly effective from the stall up to the present limiting IAS of 400mph [644km/h]. An exceptionally short radius of turn and fast rate of roll are characteristic of this airplane. Trim qualities are good and, unlike earlier P-40 models, there is very little change in directional trim during transition from dive to climb. The airplane stalls rather abruptly with very little warning and exhibits a strong tendency to roll over to the left; however, this condition is not too

Excellent air-to-air photo of 42-45722 which shows the bubble canopy well. The third XP-40Q, serial 43-24571, had a smaller and more streamlined canopy. *Curtiss*

Serial 42-45722 was the second XP-40Q conversion and, unlike the first example with drab AAF camouflage, this aircraft had a natural metal finish. *Curtiss*

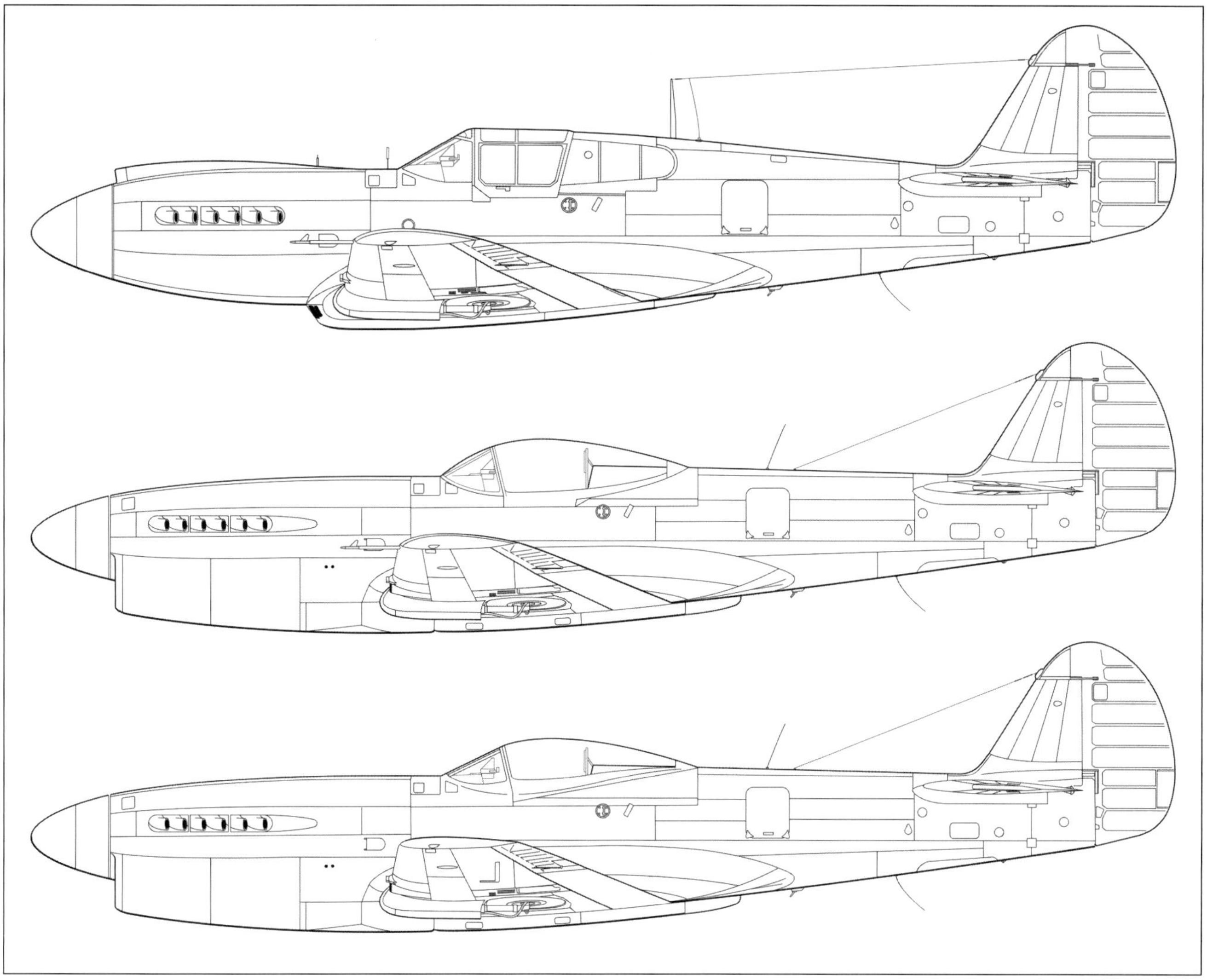

Side view lines drawings prepared by Rich Dann showing the three different XP-40Q configurations – top the original XP-40Q-2, middle the XP-40Q-2A, and bottom the XP-40Q-3 with its slightly altered and smaller canopy. *Rich Dann*

objectionable since good control is maintained at the stall. A bubble type canopy is installed .... giving excellent all around visibility." On the approach for landing Lundquist commented that "the airplane has a normal glide angle and a three point landing can be made easily."

Lt Norman A. Krause of the AAF compiled a report of his flight testing with 42-9987 for the AAF's Flight Test Engineering Branch. His review was dated 5 April 1944.

The aircraft was tested at Buffalo in a 20-flight programme between 8 and 24 March 1944. He repeated Lundquist's observations of how the performance and handling characteristics were a decided improvement over previous models in the P-40 series. With the engine in war emergency power, with water injection, a high speed of 420mph (676km/h) at 15,000ft (4,572m) was obtained along with a maximum rate of climb of 4,410ft/min (1,344m/min) at 5,000ft (1,524m); in military power a maximum of 407mph (655km/h) at 24,000ft (7,315m) was obtained. Here the take-off gross weight was 9,000lb (4,082kg) which included full fuel plus ballasting for four 0.50in (12.7mm) machine guns and their ammunition.

In the air steep right-hand turns (against the engine torque) were executed easily, and the control forces about all three axes were light and well balanced. At high speed up to 425mph (684km/h) IAS all of the controls were moderate in force and very effective. Manoeuvrability over previous P-40s was greatly increased due to the [now] squared/clipped wing tips, the rate of roll was very good and rolls, loops and Immelmann turns could be performed with ease (an Immelmann turn or roll-off-the-top is a manoeuvre where an aircraft half rolls at the top of a loop so that it can return to level flight but now in the opposite direction, and at greater altitude). The XP-40Q-2 had good diving characteristics and no buffeting of the airframe or its controls was detected at speeds up to 425mph (684km/h) IAS. At higher altitudes the general operation of the aircraft and the effectiveness of its controls were satisfactory.

The overall maximum speed in level flight for the XP-40Q-3, again with water injection for the engine, was 422mph (679km/h) at 20,500ft (6,248m), the climb to 20,000ft (6,096m) took 4.8 minutes, service ceiling was 39,000ft (11,887m) and range 700 miles (1,126km).

10 Curtiss XP-62

The XP-62 was another attempt from Curtiss to develop a new fighter, although this was an altogether bigger and heavier machine than the P-60 series in the previous chapter. Much effort was expended on this project over a long period, but again it would lead to a dead end. This massive machine was designed to enable the new Wright Aeronautical Corporation R3350 engine to go into a pursuit/fighter type aircraft. At this time the R3350 was the most powerful aero engine in development in the United States (to the point where it was ready for quantity production) and would be the heaviest engine as yet mounted in a fighter; it would also power the Boeing B-29 and Consolidated B-32 bombers and the Lockheed C-69 transport.

Following consultations between General H. H. Arnold and Curtiss, Arnold cleared the way the manufacturer to being work on an experimental high altitude pursuit prototype powered by a turbo-supercharged R3550 and fitted with a pressure cabin and either twelve 0.50in (12.7mm) machine guns or eight 20mm cannon. At this stage the guaranteed maximum speed was 468mph (753km/h) at 27,000ft (8,230m), and the designation XP-62 and Project number MX-88 were assigned in mid-January 1941. On 29 April Curtiss submitted proposals to Wright Field for the construction of two airframes, designated XP-62 and XP-62A, with delivery of the first within 15 months from date of contract and with the second to follow three

Side view of the Curtiss XP-61 taken on 19 June 1943. *Curtiss via Dave Ostrowski and Alan Griffith*

months later. The supply contract, W535-AC-19440, was approved on 27 June with first delivery to take place in October 1942 and the second in January 1943. The fighter was designed by Donovan A. Berlin before he departed from Curtiss-Wright in December 1941.

For this schedule to be met, the original discussions had assumed that both engines and propellers would be ready in time for the prototypes. However, on 1 July 1941 Curtiss notified the Materiel Division that the R3550 equipped with its exhaust driven supercharger and co-axial propellers would not be ready for installation in time for the required XP-62 delivery, so slippage had begun. Next, a revised specification was issued on 2 August with the principal differences an increase in weight by 1,537lb (697kg) and a drop in top speed from 460mph (740km/h) down to 448mph (721km/h) (Curtiss had reduced this speed figure when the eight 20mm cannon armament replaced the 12 machine guns); nevertheless, the new figures were still considered as "most satisfactory" by the Experimental Engineering Section.

On 18 September a conference held at the Langley Memorial Aeronautical Laboratory looked closely the powerplant and propeller installation and decided that the first XP-62 should have a single four-blade 14ft 2in (4.32m) diameter propeller. Eventually a dual-rotation propeller was to be developed with a 13ft 2in (4.01m) diameter prop for the rear blades, and both of these installations were to be tested on a 19ft (5.79m) tunnel model (in the event, the only XP-62 completed would have contra-rotating propellers). Authority to purchase 100 P-62A aircraft was prepared during November 1941 and the official mock-up inspection took place at Buffalo on 15 and 16 December; the latter resulted in a request for numerous design changes, but the review concluded that the mock-up was "fairly complete and, in general, very satisfactory for the purpose".

From the start of 1942, however, the programme came under close scrutiny. On 1 January, in a review of the project, the AAF's Major Swofford observed that "the military power loading of the XP-62 was considerably lighter than desirable for that type of aircraft and that the wing loading was slightly greater than it should be for good manoeuvrability and for overall performance at high altitude." He presented for comparison the basic characteristics of some concurrent types, namely, the German Messerschmitt Bf 109F, the British Supermarine Spitfire Mk.V and Hawker Hurricane Mk.IIC, and the American Lockheed P-38B and Republic XP-47B. The XP-62 was heavier than any of these (the latest weight estimate was 15,568lb/7,062kg), it had a larger wing area, its wing loading was greater than for the foreign models but less than the American, its power was greater than all of the types except the P-38F, but its power loading was the highest of all. Swofford recommended that the XP-62's weight should be reduced to 14,000lb (6,350kg) by taking out four of the cannon plus the propeller anti-icing equipment, and by a close and thorough restudy of its structure.

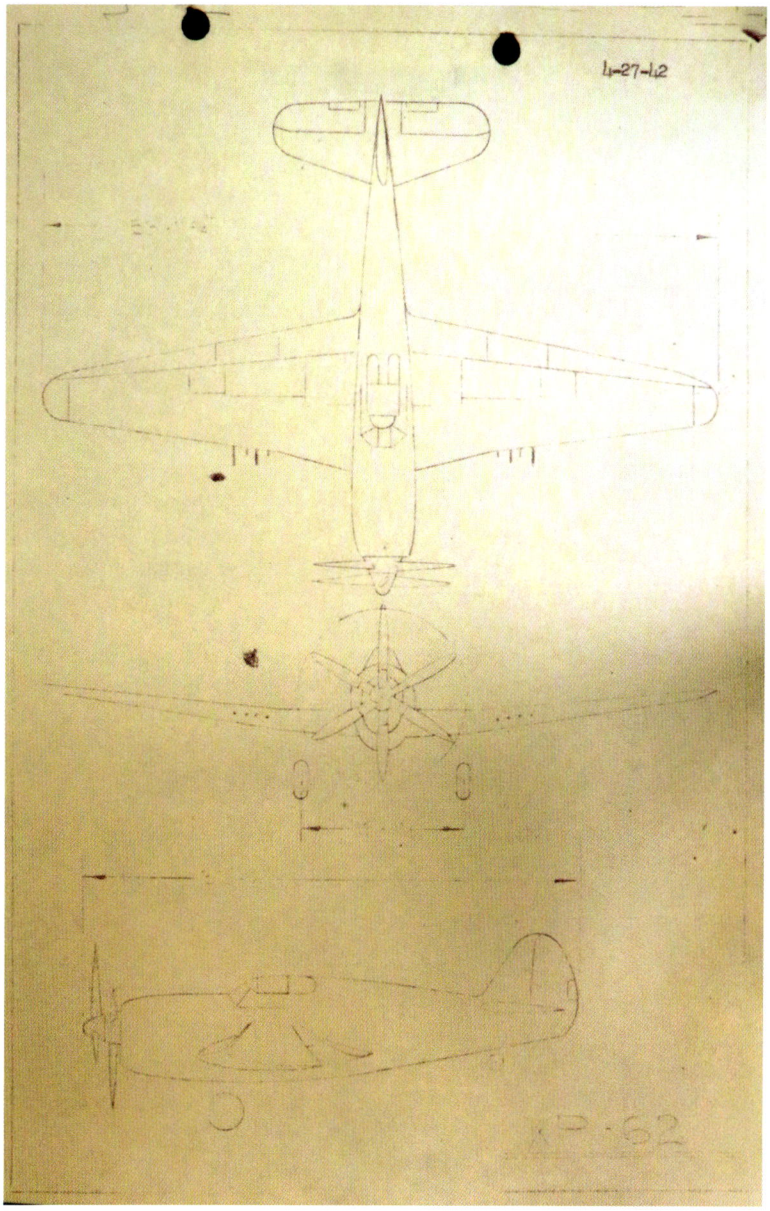

Original AAF drawing for the XP-62 as the design appeared at 27 April 1942. *Curtiss*

Wright Field and the Materiel Division approved these weight reduction recommendations later that month. At a conference held on 30 January, looking at both the XP-60 (Chapter Nine) and the XP-62, it was confirmed that Curtiss should look for ways to lighten the airframe and indeed to eliminate four of the 20mm guns. The manufacturer was told that the four excess cannon could be carried as an alternate load, but the wing structure would not be changed. At a later date the fighter's manoeuvring flaps were also removed since these added weight without offering any benefit.

Next, on 20 June 1942, after the letter contract with Curtiss covering 100 P-62s had been arranged, Brigadier General K.B. Wolfe, the Chief of the Production Division at Wright Field, recommended that only one experimental XP-62 should be built (this is the same officer who's observations in March

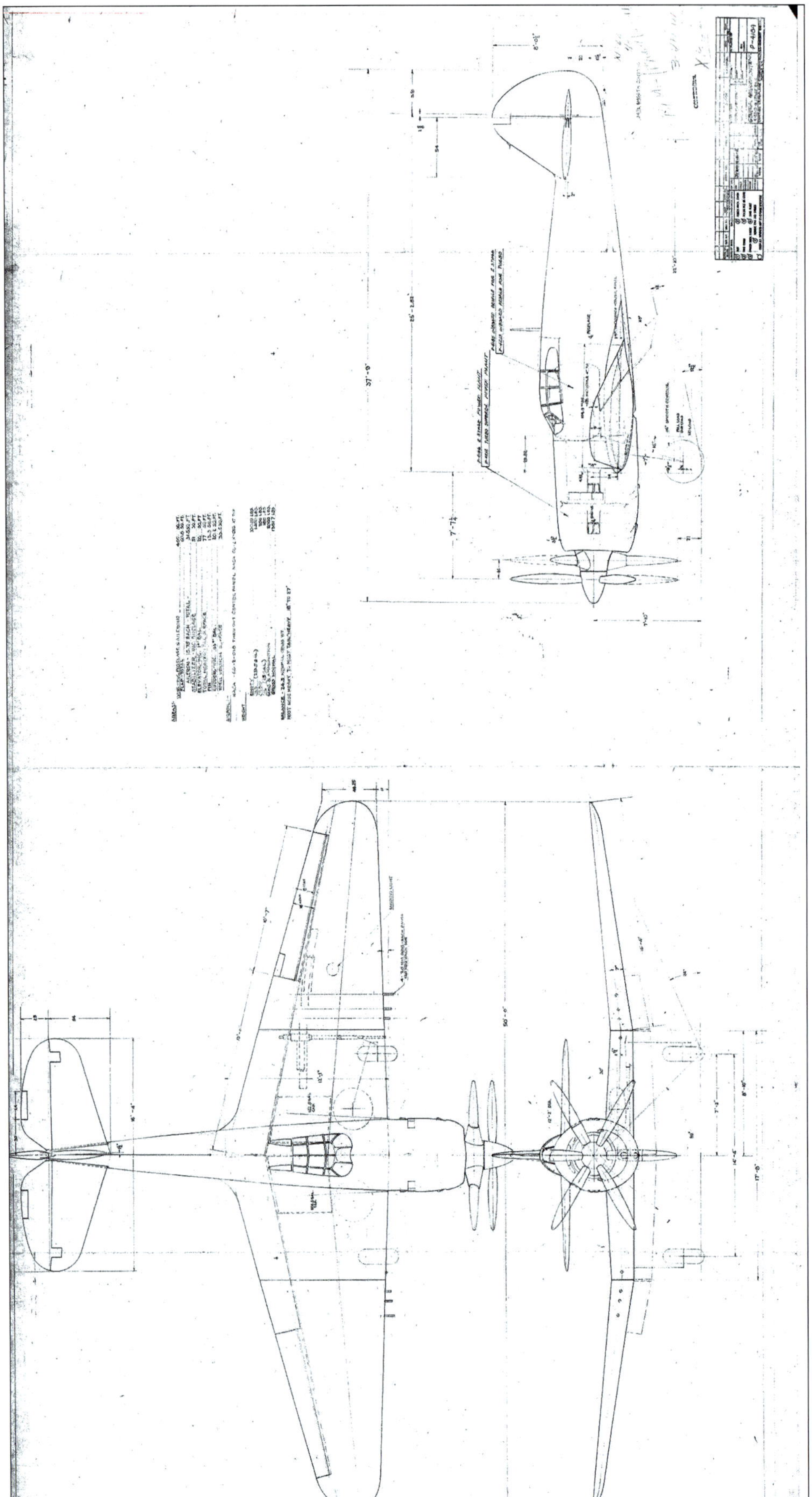

Manufacturer's drawing of the XP-62 as it looked on 16 April 1941. *Curtiss*

The full-size mock-up of the XP-62 photographed on 17 December 1941. *Curtiss via Gerald H. Balzer*

Three-quarter angle starboard front view of the XP-62 prototype. The covered over gun ports in the wings are visible. *Curtiss via Gerald H. Balzer*

1943 had done much to kill the P-60 production programme in the previous chapter). The production contract was dated 25 May and the first machine (designated P-62A-1-CU) was to be delivered in May 1943, after which the rate would rise to 30 a month by October of that year. In a memo to the Commanding General, Materiel Command at Washington, Wolfe called attention to the (at this stage estimated) performance characteristics of the XP-62 in relation to other pursuit aircraft and he drew unfavourable conclusions.

Wolfe compared the XP-62 with the Bell P-39E and the P-60A. The production contracts for the two latter types were cancelled due to their poor performance, particularly in terms of rate of climb, and he clarified just how weak the P-62's performance was. It had a rate of climb at 20,000ft (6,096m) of 1,570ft/min (479m/min), only 125ft/min (38m/min) better than the all time low set by the P-39E, and this compared very unfavourably with the 2,450ft/min (747m/min) figure for both the P-63 and P-47. Thus, in view of the reported climbing capabilities of the latest German and Japanese fighters, the pilot of a production P-62 would be hopelessly outclassed. Wolfe recommended that P-62 production be limited to a single experimental model for the following reasons (1) the very poor rate of climb, (2) no advantages in speed over the P-47 and P-63, (3) the fighting ceiling was too low to require a pressure cabin and (4) a production contract would interfere with Curtiss' P-47 production. On 27 July the AAF's Contract Section notified Curtiss that the letter contract for P-62 production was cancelled.

Work on the prototypes did continue, however, and on 1 August 1942 the Engineering Division at Wright Field reported that the first XP-62 was between 75% and 80% complete. The development of the pressure cabin supercharger equipment was, however, being watched with particular interest because this was one of the first such installations to go into a pursuit/fighter type aircraft. In fact there were numerous delays with the delivery of several important pieces of equipment and the manufacturer of the pressure cabin, the York Ice Machinery Company of York in Pennsylvania, was very late in supplying this vital item.

The XP-62 seems to be another wartime prototype which was never photographed in flight, though in this case the aircraft appears to have stayed on the ground for most of its life. Fortunately, there is a reasonable selection showing it 'at rest'. This side view is dated 10 August 1943. *Curtiss via Dave Ostrowski and Alan Griffith*

On 30 April 1943 the engineering on the first XP-62 was reported as virtually complete, except for a few minor details. Then on 20 May Curtiss proposed a major modification to the second XP-62 airframe by converting it into a low altitude fighter-bomber or support aircraft. The proposal document in fact came in two parts, the first detailing the removal of the supercharger and allied high altitude equipment followed by the installation of a Pratt & Whitney XR4360 engine. A second separate proposal introduced an all new and improved fuselage constructed to fit the original wings, landing gear and tail surfaces of the XP-62. Both of the proposals looked attractive and both compared well with other close support aircraft then under development for the AAF.

They were reviewed by the Engineering Division's Lt Col Victor R. Haugen. He noted that the second design was considerably lighter while the new fuselage offered several advantages over the converted XP-62 arrangement. All of the bombs on both designs were to be carried externally, a feature that would provide very good high speed performance when no bombs were carried, and the speed with bombs on board was also very attractive – 352mph (566km/h) at sea level. The selection of stores that could be carried was, however, somewhat limited in that only three bomb stations were provided, and hence an efficient load of smaller calibre bombs was not possible.

The gross weight was 16,523lb (7,495kg), maximum speed 410mph (660km/h) at 15,500ft

The XP-62 had a relatively small tail (with a dorsal extension to the fin) but this was not problematic since the contra-rotating propeller would eliminate any effects of torque. This view is another secured on 19 June 1943. *Curtiss via Dave Ostrowski and Alan Griffith*

Further three-quarter front views of the sole XP-62 prototype, which illustrate the fighter's massive nose and propeller. *Curtiss via Dave Ostrowski and Alan Griffith*

(4,724m), the aircraft would take five minutes to reach 15,000ft (4,572m), and the armament was two 37mm cannon and four 0.50in (12.7mm) machine guns, plus one 1,000lb (454kg) or 2,000lb (907kg), or three 250lb (113kg) or 500lb (227kg) bombs. Length was 41ft 8in (12.70m), the gross weight of the other proposal 18,330lb (8,314kg), and the maximum speed at sea level in military power when not carrying a bomb was 376mph (605km/h). However, in view of the number of attack types already under development for the AAF, it was recommended that no action should be taken to convert the second XP-62 into a low level aircraft.

On 29 May 1943 Major Norman W. Weidenheimer reported that engineering was virtually complete on both the first and second XP-62s, though the first article was receiving some slight modifications. However, on 10 July the AAF's Capt Logan reported that considerable minor difficulties had been experienced in the operation of the first example whilst

A selection of photos showing the XP-62 parked on a taxiway, which shows the type's all-round heavy and bulky appearance. *Curtiss via Gerald H. Balzer*

preparing it for flight. To begin with the engine had cut out before take-off, a problem finally attributed to carburettor failure, and then during several engine runs a small fire had developed in the turbo.

On 18 August General Echols had given Wright Field a list of experimental aircraft projects classified according to the disposition for each type. In the case of the XP-62 he specified that one prototype was to be accepted while the other should now be cancelled. A month later Wright Field's Procurement Division notified Curtiss that the portion of the contract covering the second prototype with spare parts was cancelled, and formal notification of this termination followed on 21 September.

The XP-62's contra-rotating propeller. *Curtiss via Gerald H. Balzer*

Flight test

The first flight of the only XP-62 to be completed, serial 41-35873, was finally accomplished on 21 July 1943 and lasted for 15 minutes; this was twenty-five months after the contract had been approved rather than the scheduled fifteen months. In addition the pressure cabin was still not ready, it was not in place for the maiden sortie and indeed would not be for all of the limited flight testing completed up until February 1944. At that point installing the pressure cabin for general trials did begin, but it is understood that this was never completed and the prototype never flew again.

Flight trials with the surviving aircraft had progressed slowly because of its by now low priority, but there were various attempts to find a role for 41-35873. For example in October 1943 the aircraft was earmarked to go to Wright Aeronautical to conduct development work on the R3350, and then in August 1944 it was to be made available for testing the pressure cabin, but little seems to have been done. On 25 August 1944 Colonel Roth reported that it had been delivered to Wright Field where it had been inspected and found satisfactory for acceptance. The XP-62 was formally accepted by the AAF on 5 September and passed into storage at Wright Field. It was classified Class 26 (instructional airframe) on 2 March 1945, and then went for reclamation/scrap at Wright Field on 26 September 1945.

According to the project engineer the XP-62 was never airborne for long enough to secure full flight characteristics and maximum limits for its performance data. At the time of writing no information had been uncovered by the author relating to how the XP-62 actually behaved in the air, or what minimal in-flight characteristics were established during its brief flying career.

In May 1944 the UK Aeronautical Research Committee issued a report discussing the information in a NACA wind tunnel report dated October 1943. To determine the effect of a dual-rotating propeller on the aircraft's static longitudinal stability, tests had been made in the Langley Memorial Aeronautical Laboratory 7ft by 10ft

Photo dated 18 April 1942 detailing the forward section of the XP-62's air induction system. *Curtiss via Gerald H. Balzer*

(2.13m by 3.05m) tunnel on a 1/9th-scale model of the XP-62 with its flaps retracted. It had been found that the dual-rotating propeller decreased the longitudinal stability of the model to a greater extent than did a single-rotating propeller of the same diameter and solidity. The rate of change of downwash angle with model angle of attack, as well as the direct effect of the propeller normal force, was also greater with the dual-rotating than with the single-rotating propeller. But there was very little difference between the dynamic pressures at the tail with the dual- and single-rotating arrangements.

XP-62 structure

The Curtiss XP-62 was a low-wing single-seat cantilever monoplane with a retractable landing gear and tailwheel. It had an all metal airframe, a laminar flow type aerofoil, pressurised cockpit and a Curtiss Electric constant speed dual-rotation six-blade propeller 13ft 2in (4.01m) in diameter. The normal and maximum fuel capacities were 245galUS (927lit) and 384galUS (1,454lit) respectively. The engine's turbo-supercharger was positioned beneath the middle fuselage, which then required the engine exhaust to be directed forwards some 10ft (3.05m) to the engine. The pressure cabin was designed to maintain an 'altitude' of 10,000ft (3,048m) up to 35,000ft (10,668m).

XP-62 Data

(All performance figures are Curtiss estimates at design gross weight and published in Army documents)

Length:	39ft 6in (12.04m)
Wing span:	53ft 7.75in (16.35m)
Wing area:	420sq.ft (39.06sq.m)
Empty weight:	11,773lb (5,340kg)
Design gross weight:	14,660lb (6,650kg)
Maximum take-off weight:	16,651lb (7,553kg)
Powerplant:	1 x 2,300hp (1,715kW) Wright R-3350-17 turbo-supercharged 'Duplex Cyclone' twin-row eighteen-cylinder air cooled radial engine
Maximum speed:	358mph (576km/h) at 5,000ft (1,524m), 448mph (721km/h) at 27,000ft (8,230m)
Maximum rate of climb:	2,300ft/min (701m/min)
Service ceiling:	35,700ft (10,881m)
Normal range:	900 miles (1,448km)
Maximum range:	1,500 miles (2,414km)
Armament:	4 or 8 x 20mm cannon in wings

11 McDonnell XP-67

With its faired wings and fuselage the subject of this chapter, the McDonnell XP-67 single-seat high-altitude fighter prototype, looked very unconventional for its time. The first prototype aircraft to be built by the then new McDonnell company, this unusual design was at one stage looked upon with favour by the US Army Air Force, but the manufacturer's trials programme did not proceed without incident. And then, just as it was about to begin its official USAAF test flights, the first XP-67 was wrecked by fire. That brought the end to a most interesting project, though any production plans would most likely have been halted by the arrival of the first jet fighters.

The XF-67 long range interceptor fighter was designed and built by the McDonnell Aircraft Corporation at St. Louis in Missouri. As a project it started life during the first half of 1940 when McDonnell submitted its Model I (Model 1) design against the competition for a new Army Air Force fighter under R-40C and Air Corps Specification XC-622. Model 1 featured a submerged Allison V-3420 engine driving twin propellers, but the competition was won by the proposals from Vultee, Curtiss and Northrop which resulted in the XP-54, XP-55 and XP-56 prototypes being test flown (Chapters Five, Six and Seven respectively). However, despite coming well down in the final assessment list, the unconventional Model 1 did generate some interest, to the point that in June 1940 the Air Corps decided to purchase engineering data and a wind tunnel model.

Impressive air-to-air photo of the only XP-67 to fly, AAF serial number 42-11677. *Gerald H. Balzer*

RIGHT Colour artwork by McDonnell's Mr L. Mihalovsky of the unbuilt but direct predecessor of the XP-67, McDonnell's Model I. *Mark Nankivil, Greater St Louis Air & Space Museum*

BELOW These images show McDonnell's full-size part mock-up of its XP-67 design as first accepted by the Army Air Force. Many detail changes had to be made to this design following the official review of this structure. *Gerald H. Balzer*

The purchase order was dated 6 June 1940, but in the meantime McDonnell continued to revise and develop its fighter design. A Model II (Model 2) was submitted on 30 June but this too was turned down by Materiel Division in late July. Then, much later, after the firm's designers under Garrett C. Covington had made a series of changes to the layout, this was followed on 24 April 1941 by the Model II-A (2-A) proposal. The new 2-A was generally of more conventional twin-engine form and, after a further revision in early May, it was now acceptable to the AAF.

On 22 May 1941 official Project code MX127 was assigned to the Model 2-A, and on 29 July pursuit designation XP-67 was allocated to the fighter. At this stage the aircraft had a "guaranteed high speed of 462mph (743km/h) at 25,000ft (7,620m), time to climb to this altitude guaranteed at 12 minutes, and the service ceiling approximately 41,500ft (12,650m)". Contract W535-AC-21218 was finalised in October 1941 and then approved by the Under Secretary for War; the programme was covered by Project number MX-127. It described two XP-67 prototypes, full-size mock-up, spinning model, wind tunnel testing (which in fact would take over two years to clear and at times hold up progress) and engine nacelle testing. These prototype long range fighter aircraft "of novel design" were now based around two Continental IV1430 engines. The allocated AAF serial numbers were 42-11677 and 42-11678 but the names 'Bat' and 'Moonbat', which have often been applied to the XP-67 in publications, were both unofficial (although quite appropriate).

LEFT The full scale ground-based engine nacelle which was tested by McDonnell during May 1942. *Gerald H. Balzer*

There were to be periods when the future of the project, and whether it should be continued, came into doubt. The first occasion saw the Aircraft Project Section at Wright Field attempting to establish the merits of the XP-67 by comparing it to the XP-49, a similar machine under development by Lockheed (Chapter Two). In fact the XP-67 appeared to compare very favourably, since it incorporated the same powerplant but carried more armament and fuel, it appeared to have a slightly higher maximum speed, and offered more than double the range. In addition the XP-49 had the higher gross weight by some 400lb (181kg).

In mid-August 1941 further official 'justification' for the project was made on the grounds that there was a need for an experimental aircraft type, at a time when the major established aircraft companies were so overloaded with production orders that they were not well placed to take on further experimental work. Indeed, in addition to providing "an aircraft having desirable characteristics", the XP-67 project presented "an opportunity to develop another [new] source of supply" for fighter-type aircraft (i.e. McDonnell). Attention was also called to the fact that the original proposed armament, four 20mm cannon and six 0.50 calibre machine guns, had on official recommendation now been altered to six 37mm cannon, and as such offered the earliest opportunity to investigate the value and potential of a battery of this type of weapon.

On 20 October 1941 the Pursuit Board approved the McDonnell project, in part because it believed that there was a definite need for this aircraft when no other type with a comparable performance was currently under development. At this point the estimated high speed was now rather lower at 405mph (652km/h) at 25,000ft (7,620m) and 357mph (574km/h) at 10,000ft (3,048m). The Mock-Up Inspection took place on 15, 16 and 17 April 1942 and resulted in substantial detail changes, while throughout May McDonnell ran engine ground runs on the full scale test nacelle which enabled numerous minor problems to be corrected.

Views showing the first XP-67 in course of assembly. The later front-on view, taken just before painting, is dated 19 November 1943 and shows the wing root gun ports covered over. *Gerald H. Balzer*

One of the Continental XIV1430 engines which would be installed in the first XP-67. *Gerald H. Balzer*

Support was forthcoming from Wright Field. On 24 September 1942 Colonel F.O. Carroll, Chief of the Engineering Section, wrote in a memo "the airplane represents a new approach to the fighter problem. It is obviously not a fighter versus fighter airplane. It embodies a very potent armament installation. When one considers the defensive armament on modern bombers, it should be obvious that an anti-bombardment type of fighter which is capable of delivering extremely heavy fire will be a 'must' in the not too distant future. It will be unwise to drop this and other similar projects merely because the design with its present characteristics does not fit current production and/or war plans." (This same report is referred to in Chapter Two in respect to Carroll's comments about the Lockheed XP-49.)

In November 1942 the XP-67 was described by the Experimental Engineering Section as a "true experimental model representing the ultimate in aerodynamic refinement of a conventional arrangement with the fuselage and nacelles merging smoothly into the wing itself". Usually the interface between an aeroplane's fuselage, wings and engine nacelles created some turbulence (what was termed interference drag) with the result that many designs had their wings curved in to try and reduce this problem. The streamlining of the XP-67's centre wings, between in particular the fuselage and nacelles, was some of the most extreme yet seen (but in the end would not provide the hoped for benefit).

On 1 January 1943 Engineering Division at Wright Field decided against modifying the XP-67 into an attack aircraft, as had been suggested by Mr. McDonnell during December 1942, because it did not meet new military requirements for a light bomber. It more nearly met the requirements for a support type machine, but the XP-67 programme as it stood was not going to be altered. Later studies would find that the XP-67 was also unsuited to the long range photographic aircraft role.

Then on 1 April 1943 the Air Defense Branch in Washington requested that action be taken to discontinue development work on the XP-67 and on the concurrent Republic XP-69 and Curtiss XP-71 projects. In reply, Material Division in Washington presented detailed reasons for their continuation, describing for example new developments in the fields of aerodynamics, engines, propellers, instruments and other equipment, and how the work load should be distribution throughout the country. They stressed that "new designs were laid down to meet military characteristics and to develop technical ideas and, from a research and development point of view, it was wise to start more than one design. Although desired military characteristics might suddenly change in the midst of a programme, rendering one of the airplanes under development obsolete from a tactical standpoint, certain of these airplanes might still be of vital interest from a technical standpoint. The XP-67 belonged in that category, because it had a new and promising type of wing planform believed worthy of experimentation." (Author's note: in many respects these comments can apply to many of the prototypes described in this book. Neither the XP-69 or XP-71 ever flew.)

At a conference held on 23 October 1943 McDonnell was told verbally to halt assembly work on the second prototype because wind tunnel testing had revealed some potential problems, and that the official requirements had also been changed. Now it was planned to make any necessary modifications to the second machine based on the in-flight results of the first aircraft. An official inspection of the first near complete XP-67 followed at the McDonnell plant between 1 and 3 December to determine any changes that might be needed prior to first flight, prior to delivery to the AAF, and in the event of production orders.

Taxi tests began immediately afterwards and continued until 8 December, on which date fires started in both nacelles during engine run-up. The cause was the failure of the exhaust manifold slip rings to operate correctly, thereby causing the manifold to collapse and set the self-sealing oil tanks alight. The first flight was thus delayed while McDonnell replaced the self-sealing tanks with metal tanks. On completion the first XP-67 was trucked to Scott Field at Belleville in Illinois to be reassembled and prepared for its maiden flight.

Flight testing

The first flight of the first XP-67 finally took place on 6 January 1944 with McDonnell test pilot Everett Edward Elliot in the cockpit, but the sortie had to be terminated abruptly when the engine's turbo superchargers began to overheat and start some minor fires. The flight lasted approximately six minutes and consisted of a quick circuit of the field, but the airframe suffered no major damage. The principal outcome was the installation of a stainless steel bulkhead to seal off the turbo compartment

This pair of photos was taken on 29 November 1943, possibly after the prototype had been rolled out. An official inspection was made a few days later in early December, and taxi trials commenced straight after that. The 'humped' fairings around the nacelles and curved air intakes are most pronounced, and the tailplane is in the original position. *Mark Nankivil*

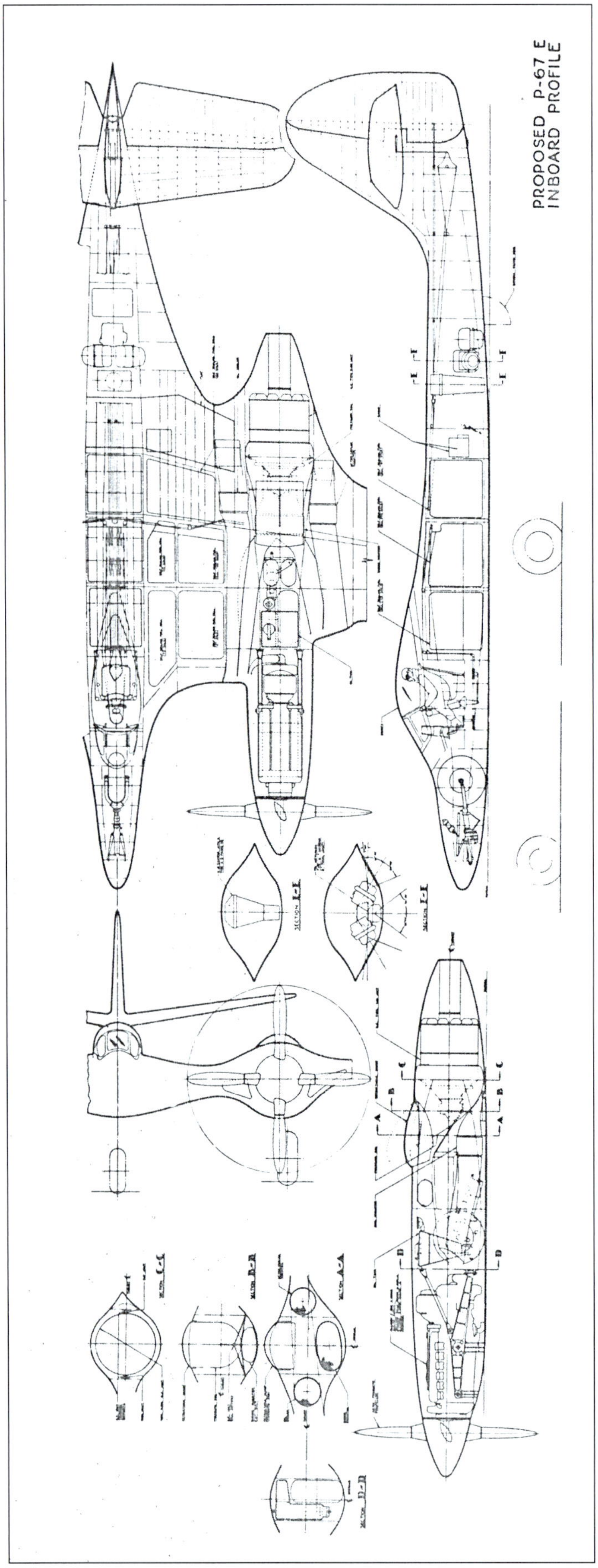

Internal detail drawing of the proposed XP-67E project to be powered by a combination of Rolls-Royce/Packard V-1650 Merlin engines and General Electric I-20 jet units. *Mark Nankivil, Greater St Louis Air & Space Museum*

from the main nacelle, better circulation of cooling air within the compartment, and a reduction to the length of the cowl around the turbo hood.

Flights 2 and 3 followed on 26 January and 28 January 1944 and proved satisfactory without major incident, but Flight 4 on 1 February again lasted just a few minutes. With the XP-67 still above the runway, the port engine main centre bearing burned out after the engines had been unintentionally over speeded. If that was not enough, around 200 yards beyond the end of the runway the aircraft lost its cockpit canopy and so Elliot landed straight away. Replacement engines were not immediately available and so 42-11677 was trucked back to Lambert Field at St. Louis where, after wind tunnel testing had indicated such changes to be highly desirable, the ducts were modified and the horizontal tail was also moved up by 12in (30.5cm).

The XP-67 flew next, twice in a day and this time from Lambert Field, on 23 March 1944, and it was found that the elevated tail gave an improvement in stability; the cooling had also improved. Next came a period of contractor's testing which lasted until 5 May, with all sorties flown by Everett Edward Elliot, before the first flights by AAF pilots began on 11 May 1944. During this period the main problems needing attention were engine roughness, balancing the ailerons and difficulties with closing the main undercarriage door.

In the meantime, during the period preceding the maiden flight, the AAF had held discussions with McDonnell over possible revisions to the second airframe and to the production P-67. The most attractive option offered by the manufacturer seemed to be a switch to Allison two-stage or Rolls Royce 14.SM piston engines in the forward portion of the nacelle, with Westinghouse jet units replacing the turbos in the rear. In addition, Continental engines were not expected to be available for any production machines, so to fit these in the second prototype seemed a waste.

Through 1944 McDonnell made numerous proposals along these lines. One resulting mixed powerplant proposal was called the XP-67E and featured twin 1,925hp (1,435kW) Packard V-1650-11 engines (war emergency rating) driving four-blade propellers, plus a pair of 2,300lb (10.2kN) thrust General Electric I-20 jets in the rear of the nacelles (the V-1650 was the licence-built version of the Rolls-Royce Merlin). The airframe dimensions were unchanged and the maximum internal fuel load came to 1,290USgal (4,883lit) with another 300USgal (1,136lit) carried externally. This proposal was studied thoroughly by the AAF, but it was found that it would need new nacelles, new outer wing panels, a modified tail, a strengthened undercarriage, a raised cockpit, and as a result of these a full refairing. All through, however, Material Command wished to complete the tests on 42-11677 before making any decisions about further developments and, since official performance data was never obtained before the first prototype was destroyed

Side view of the XP-67 prototype taken on 29 November 1943. *Gerald H. Balzer*

(below), these various developments suggested by McDonnell would never progress beyond the drawing board.

However, on 10 April 1944 Materiel Command did release the second airframe to allow its construction to resume. By now the second XP-67 was intended to have dual-rotation propellers which were expected to add 7-10mph (11-16km/h) to the maximum speed.

A preliminary flight test report put together by the AAF's pilots on 19 May 1944, and included in the official Case History for the type, was quite extensive. Three pilots, Col. M. F. Cooper, Lt. Col. C. J. Ritland and Major F. A. Borsodi, completed five flights in the XP-67 from Lambert Field from 11 to 13 May 1944, totalling around four and a half hours of air time. For the assessment the aircraft's six 37mm cannon ports had been covered and carefully smoothed over while the airframe itself was camouflaged with all surfaces polished and made very smooth. All flights were made at a take-off gross weight of 21,700lb (9,843kg), which equated to the design useful load with 300USgal (1,136lit) of fuel on board plus ballast for the guns and their ammunition.

As an opener there was criticism of the cockpit and instrument layout, which needed rearranging. The aircraft was considered fairly comfortable but the control column was too high and the rudder pedals were not close enough together, an arrangement that would make extended periods of flight fatiguing for the pilot. The engines were very quiet with a low level of noise, a point helped by the fact that the cockpit had been designed as a pressure cabin.

In general the ground handling characteristics were considered satisfactory, though taxiing out at slow speeds was not simple because the fighter itself produced quick responses to both a burst of engine power and to the brakes and the nose wheel would castor quite easily. However, the brakes were good and these problems seemed to be overcome if the machine was taxied at a faster speed.

These same problems also made the start of the take-off roll difficult, but once the speed had reached the point where the rudder became effective the control was good. However, the take-off run was described as "unusually long and gives the pilot the sensation that the aircraft is under powered". As a result full military power (1,600hp/1,193kW) was employed by the pilots for all take-offs rather than the normal 1,550hp (1,156kW) take-off rating. The XP-67 left the ground at approximately 130mph (209mph) and the initial climb was poor. In addition,

ABOVE LEFT The date of this view is given as 3 December 1943 and may show the first occasion when the XP-67s engines were started in readiness for taxi trials. *Gerald H. Balzer*

ABOVE RIGHT Here McDonnell test pilot Everett Edward Elliot takes his turn to pose in front of the XP-67. *Gerald H. Balzer*

the forward vision was considerably restricted immediately after take-off while the acceleration to the minimum safe single engine speed was slow.

The report continued stating "the rate of climb is low at all altitudes for fighter type aircraft; indicating at sea level only 2,100ft/min (640m/min) at military power and approximately l,500ft/min (457m/min) at normal rated power. On two short climbs it took 14 minutes 34 seconds to climb to 20,000ft (6,096m) at normal power and 4 minutes 45 seconds to climb to 10,000ft (3,048m) at military power [both climbs were made at 185mph (298km/h) IAS]. At 22,000ft (6,706m) the aircraft begins to feel mushy and the response to controls is slow. Cooling during all climbs was good.

All controls are effective from high speeds to the stall except the elevators may be blanketed out at high angles of attack near the stalling speeds. The rudder becomes somewhat ineffective at slow speed with the gear and flaps extended but aileron control is good throughout the stall. At less than 200mph (322km/h) all control forces are light; however, at higher speeds (350mph/563km/h IAS) the aileron loads become increasingly heavy. Elevator forces are too light at all speeds [while] the rudder forces are heavy for single engine operation

The gentleman standing in front of the XP-67 here is thought to be McDonnell chief designer Garrett C. Covington. *Gerald H. Balzer*

but are otherwise satisfactory. Rate of roll seems good at high speeds.

In dives at high speed with the aircraft trimmed for cruising level flight the aircraft tends to nose over into the dive and requires tail heavy trim to maintain a steady dive; then, as the airspeed is reduced, the aircraft requires nose down trim. Stick forces per 'g' in tight turns and pull outs are very light and tend to decrease in tight turns at speeds below 180mph (290km/h) IAS so that the aircraft tends to tighten up into the turn; once again nose down trim is required to make a steady turn.

In spite of the above mentioned stick force changes the aircraft appeared to be longitudinally stable when the nose was displaced from a trimmed level flight attitude. The resulting oscillations took an excessively long time to dampen out. Laterally the aircraft is neutrally stable bordering on divergence. The aircraft's directional stability is poor. The damping is slow and the aircraft has a peculiar 'swim' or 'Dutch roll' during the oscillations [which] occur at a rate of approximately 24 per minute [with] little tendency to dampen out. This condition was easily induced when flying in rough air. When trimmed for level flight, the ship tends to gradually fall off on either wing. It is felt that the aircraft would not be a good gun platform with its present handling characteristics.

In the clean configuration the aircraft stalls at 118mph (190km/h) indicated, and with the gear down and flaps one half down it stalls at approximately the same speed. The stall warning is excessive, as a slight buffeting starts at around 140mph (225km/h) indicated and increases down to the stall. The stall itself is not violent; however, it is apparent that the wing is not completely stalled and that the tail is stalling out. The ailerons are effective at the stall and no tendency to spin was noted [but the] rudder becomes ineffective near stalling speeds."

No aerobatics were performed during the assessment but the XP-67's in-flight manoeuvrability and radius of turn were compared against a single-engine North American P-51B Mustang, with the P-51B possessing better manoeuvrability and a much smaller turn radius. It also had greater acceleration in level flight and in a dive. The rate of roll at high speed was good in spite of heavy ailerons.

A major problem for the XP-67 was the pilot's view out of the cockpit for manoeuvring. His forward view was good despite considerable distortion around the edge of the front wind shield panel, but he was seated so low against the wing that his side vision was hampered by the engine nacelles, the rear view was poor because of the wing, and the downward vision was restricted by the fuselage fairings. Indeed, it was not possible to see the wing tips from the cockpit, so formation flying would be "difficult if not hazardous". In general the XP-67's cockpit vision was described as "very poor".

With one engine, using military power in the clean condition, satisfactory control could be held down to 140mph (225km/h) indicated, while the minimum safe speed to continue flight if an engine failed on take-off was 165mph (265km/h) IAS. Very little change in trim was experienced when operating the landing gear and flaps, the XP-67 would become slightly nose heavy as the flaps and gear were extended, but retrim was not necessary due to the very light elevator forces. Even with power on the approach was steep and it proved difficult to slip the aircraft during an approach, but the aircraft would land easily despite possessing a

McDonnell's XP-67 prototype was from most angles quite an unusual-looking machine. This rear angle shot shows again the extreme fairings around the wings, body and engine nacelles. *Mark Nankivil, Greater St Louis Air & Space Museum*

In many ways the XP-67 was pretty orthodox but it was the heavy fairing to wings and body that made it appear so different, as shown once more by this well-known picture taken during a test flight. *Gerald H. Balzer*

Here the substantial size of the XP-67 engine nacelle is shown well. It stretched for over half of the length of the whole aeroplane and also housed one leg of the main undercarriage. *Gerald H. Balzer*

high landing speed at contact of about 120mph (193km/h). The tail would drag quite easily on landing.

The AAF pilots did not collect any flight test performance data, but speed checks were made at military power against a calibrated P-51B at both 10,000ft and 22,000ft (3,048m and 6,706m) altitude. The maximum level speed at 22,000ft came to 272mph (438km/h) IAS, which corrected to approximately 393mph (632km/h) true, while the 10,000ft run at the same power corrected to approximately 357mph (574km/h) true airspeed.

The report concluded that the performance of the XP-67 "was not good in comparison to present fighters, particularly in rate of climb, take-off and landing characteristics and service and combat ceiling". In respect to stability and manoeuvrability the flying characteristics left a good deal to be desired and pilot visibility was poor for all conditions of flight. In fact with its present long take-off run and high landing speed the aircraft was not considered safe for the average military pilot.

Finally, with such a poor rate of climb the only tactical role for which the XP-67 appeared suitable

The very large flap fitted to the XP-67 can just be seen in this picture, which shows the aircraft landing after an early test flight. *Gerald H. Balzer*

Photos taken during a test flight after special markings had been applied to the sides of the nose and end fuselage. It appears that the tailplane now has the increased dihedral, and it has certainly been moved to its slightly higher position, by some 12in (30.5cm). *Gerald H. Balzer*

was to operate as a long range escort fighter, but such missions would need more fuel taking the gross weight to over 25,000lb (11,340kg), thus worsening the already poor take-off and climb. However, with an improved pilot's view McDonnell's aircraft could be employed on ground support duties.

Following official performance tests, on 30 May 1944 McDonnell was authorised by Material Command to install dual rotation (contra-rotating) propellers in the first prototype to enable performance data to be collected at an earlier date for when the engines were running at war emergency power. Since the contra-rotating propellers, and the Continental engines to go with them, would be available for the second XP-67 prototype in June, the manufacturer had asked that they should be installed on the first prototype instead as replacements for the original Curtiss Electric airscrews, and this had been agreed.

On 30 June 1944 an official named Miller declared that the XP-67 had been flying for about six months and, having now been modified, "it appeared to have satisfactory flying qualities except for a low rate of roll and a long period control-free lateral oscillation. The aileron effectiveness was about 50% lower than had been predicted, and large control forces limited the available aileron deflection to small values at high speeds." Plans were being made to correct the latter while the lateral oscillation did not feature in the AAF's requirements; although the lateral motion was not seen as being objectionable to pilots in general, the AAF pilots had felt that it was undesirable.

Further changes were considered as the flight test programme proceeded through the summer of 1944. Various solutions were assessed in an effort to increase the lateral stability, including wires on the rudder trailing edge, a dorsal fin and lastly an increase in dihedral from 5° to 7°. One of the proposed changes again involved the propellers. Tests undertaken by Continental had determined that, with 150 grade fuel, a war emergency rating of 2,100hp (1,566kW) could be realised without using water injection, while studies made by both McDonnell and Material Command had suggested that a single rotation Aeroproducts propeller blade, known as design H-20-156 and 11ft (3.35m) in diameter, would prove suitable for this rating. Accordingly, the dual rotation plans were now replaced by this new fitting and approved by Engineering Division on 20 July. However, because of the destruction of the aircraft, this change was never carried out.

During this period the XP-67 was test flown by several more Army Air Force pilots including Colonel M. S. Roth, while McDonnell's 'contractor' flight trials also included a programme of drag reduction (which embraced smoother fairings and the elimination of extraneous items). Roth appears to have had strong opinions about the XP-67 and declared that it "was becoming too expensive and the last thing which was to be done on it would be the installation of dual rotating propellers". He added that the "XP-67 made the runway look short, and something was wrong with the propeller".

However, on 18 July 1944 the Requirements Division at Washington advised that the poor take-off quality of the XP-67 was realised, but otherwise "the general flight handling characteristics of the aircraft are delightful. It handles exceptionally well, has beautiful stall characteristics, and the roll characteristics are good, although the control forces are high. Mounting twelve 0.50 calibre machine guns or eight 20mm guns, the space available for gun installation made possible the future installation of the .60 calibre gun, probably to a greater extent than in other fighter aircraft under development. These features were of greatest interest from a long range fighter and strafer viewpoint." So it appears that, at this stage, opinions as to the quality of McDonnell's fighter were somewhat mixed.

By 24 August McDonnell had completed an extensive rework and repairs to its XP-67 prototype. Ground tests were made that day, and then on 28 August a five-minute flight was recorded, though this had to be terminated suddenly by a drop in engine oil pressure, the result of defective oil seals. Brief flights followed on 31 August and 2 September but further defects came to light which necessitated more repairs and refitting.

Finally, almost everything was in ready for the XP-67 to start its official AAF trials when, on 6 September 1944, the aircraft was damaged beyond repair by fire. Having taken off from Lambert Field, Elliott was conducting checks at 10,000ft (3,048m) when there was a loss of power in the starboard engine. The first indication of fire appeared when the aircraft had descended to 3,000ft (914m), but by the time he landed smoke and flames were coming out of the nacelle. Elliot attempted to stop 42-11677 at such an angle to the wind that the flames would be contained, but the starboard brake would not hold and the aircraft turned crosswind, coming to rest on the ground in such a position that the fire was able to spread, with wind assistance, across to the fuselage and to the port wing. The fuselage, right engine nacelle and wheel well were all eventually burnt out and the left wing and its nacelle damaged considerably. Fortunately, Elliot was not injured.

Examination of the starboard engine revealed that the fire was the result of the rocker arm on the No 1 cylinder failing, which by staying closed from then on allowed hot exhaust gases to enter the intake manifold; this caused a backfire which made the induction system fail and allowed the fire to start. In view of the very long time required to effect repairs to the aircraft, or to finish the second prototype (which at this time was just 15% complete), it was decided to terminate the XP-67 contract. Another factor was the potential superior performance of the upcoming first generation of jet-propelled fighters, which made any P-67 production plans unlikely to go ahead anyway.

Photos showing the sorry state of the McDonnell XP-67 following its landing fire on 6 September 1944. The aircraft was never repaired and soon went for scrap. *Gerald H. Balzer*

In all 42-11677 had accumulated a total of 43 hours flying time, every sortie having been conducted from Lambert Field bar the first four flights which had been made from Scott Field. Neither the armament installation or the pressure cabin were ever fitted or tested since these had been given secondary priority over obtaining flight test data and information.

Contract termination was mutually agreed between McDonnell and the AAF on 13 September 1944, the contractor having requested the abandonment. Formal cancellation of Contract W535 ac-21218 was made effective on 24 October, although two weeks before this McDonnell had been cleared to begin dismantling the aircraft. No further work was undertaken on the second prototype, which was thus never completed. Nevertheless, despite failing to win a production order for P-67s, McDonnell had done enough to become established as a manufacturer of fighter aircraft and during the 1950s it would produce a string of ever more impressive jet fighters for both the US Air Force and Navy.

Structure

The XP-67's general arrangement and planform were quite unusual and the result of having a laminar flow aerofoil section throughout, not just for the wing itself but also for the engine nacelles and for the fuselage as well. Overall the aircraft's external configuration gave the appearance of extremely large fillets between the wing, nacelles and fuselage. This was the outcome of making the basic design an attempt to maintain true aerofoil sections throughout the entire airframe. Indeed, the XP-67 was known by AAF pilots at least as the 'Flying Fillet' due to any longitudinal cross section through the airframe being an aerofoil section.

All-metal stressed skin construction was employed on the full cantilever wing, principally in aluminium light alloy. Each wing was assembled in two sections, both having two spars, with the inner section (attached to the fuselage side) housing the gun compartment, an engine nacelle and a split flap, while the outer section contained the aileron. All flying surfaces had a metal torque box at their leading edges and an aft section built up using metal ribs and skinning. The control surfaces were also built entirely in aluminium alloy with the aileron controlled by a single horn. The rudder had a control quadrant at its lower bracket, while the elevators were interconnected by a torque tube on which a control quadrant was located.

XP-67's semi-monocoque aluminium alloy fuselage had Alclad covering and contained the nose wheel, a pressurised cockpit (the pressurising equipment was never installed) and a portion of the split flap. The tail surfaces were mounted on the aft fuselage in a conventional manner and the normal fuel load was 280USgal (1,060lit) with the maximum capacity 735USgal (2,782lit), all distributed in four main tanks located both in the wings and in the fuselage.

A fully retractable nosewheel-type tricycle landing gear was fitted which had a wheelbase of 15ft 8in (4.78m). The main gear retracted rearwards into the engine nacelles and the nose gear rearwards into the forward fuselage and both the undercarriage and its doors operated hydraulically. The nose wheel could swivel but was non-steerable. As flown the two Continental piston engines each drove a Curtiss Electric 10ft 8in (3.25m) diameter, single rotation, four-blade electric propeller.

XP-67 Data (as at 25 July 1942)

Length:	44ft 9.25in (13.66m)
Wing span:	55ft 0in (16.76m)
Wing area:	414sq.ft (38.50sq.m)
Empty weight:	17,745lb (8,049kg)
Design gross weight (with 280usgal/1,060lit fuel):	22,114lb (10,031kg)
Maximum take-off weight (with 735usgal/2,782lit fuel):	25,400lb (11,521kg)
Powerplant:	2 x 1,600hp (1,193kW) Continental XIV1430-17/19 (RH/LH respectively) liquid-cooled piston engines (war emergency rating 2,100hp/1,566kW)
Maximum speed:	405mph (652km/h) at 25,000ft (7,620m) and 22,000lb (9,979kg) weight
Sea level rate of climb:	2,100ft/min (640m/min)
Service ceiling:	37,400ft (11,400m)
Absolute ceiling:	38,000ft (11,582m)
Maximum range:	2,385 miles (3,837km) with 735USgal (2,782lit) fuel.
Armament:	six 37mm M-4 cannon mounted three in each inner wing (not fitted)

12 Republic XP-47H, XP-47J and XP-72

Republic Aviation's single-seat P-47 Thunderbolt was another of the great fighters of World War II and was built in prolific numbers and in numerous versions. However, the basic design experienced a steady increase in weight as the fighter matured and there were attempts by the design team to produce lighter versions. Two of these are described here, the XP-47J and another which received a new number in the US Army Air Force's designation system, XP-72. But this chapter opens with a Thunderbolt engine test bed, the XP-47H.

Republic's designer Alexander Kartveli was responsible for the manufacturer's aircraft programmes right through the war and for many jet aircraft designs as well. On the P-47 programme, his first really successful design, he was assisted by Murray Burkow.

XP-47H

The objective behind the development of this aeroplane was to have a fighter type available to serve as a test bed for the new Chrysler XI2220 (initially XIV2220) inverted 16-cylinder liquid-cooled engine, which was the outcome of a major design effort to produce a 2,000hp (1,491kW) unit specifically

Early photo of the Republic XP-47J 'Superbolt' taken before any nose art had been applied. The cooling fan vanes around the spinner can be seen inside the cowling. *Republic Aviation*

for fighter type aircraft applications. Chrysler was of course an established car manufacturer and this was its first foray into aero engine design, work on the engine having started in June 1941. Initially Air Materiel Command had felt that the XI2220 should be incorporated into a specially designed airframe but, to obtain the quickest results, it was subsequently decided to adapt the P-47 as a test bed, since this fighter was best suited to take the new power unit.

In fact the first studies looking into the feasibility of a trial installation in a P-47 had been requested during the early part of 1942, when consideration was also being given to install this engine in a Curtiss P-60 (Chapter Nine). The XI2220 first ran on the bench in December 1942 but, because of slow progress, the P-47 installation was held in abeyance

ABOVE The Chrysler engine in XP-47H 42-23297 is given a ground run. Note the strip of blocker wood in front of the main undercarriage wheels. *Republic via Dave Ostrowski*

RIGHT Further views taken during almost certainly the same engine run (note the tail wheel position) which provide nose and then port side detail. *Republic via Gerald H. Balzer*

until August 1943. Then, after a conference, a request was made for Chrysler itself to be allowed to install the XI2220 in a P-47, but this was not confirmed until spring 1944. The new Thunderbolt was designated XP-47H but it would serve simply as a test bed – any plans for potential production machines with Chrysler's engine were dropped in 1944 before first flight. The XP-47H was ordered under contract W535-AC-18195 and covered by Project number MX-260.

In September 1944 orders were given to convert two additional P-47s, but on 23 October 1944 this directive was modified to cover "the modification and test of two XP-47H airplanes and the procurement or one complete set of spare parts, except engine, for a third airplane." The XP-47H was in fact a standard P-47D-15 modified to take a XI2220-11 in combination with a General Electric CH-5 turbo supercharger (Chrysler having failed to develop a planned axial-flow supercharger of its own) and the conversion involved extensive changes to the airframe, which included the following:

a. The complete redesign of the aircraft forward of the firewall, including a new primary cowl, engine controls, fuel and oil system, new exhaust manifold and shrouds, and the engine mounting. The engine was over 10ft (3.05m) long and the new nose would give the XP-47H something of a shark-like appearance.

b. A redesign of the belly cowl from the firewall to a position aft of the rear fuel tank, although here none of the changes would affect the fuselage structural members.

c. The redesign aft also included provision for mounting the supercharger, the engine cooling radiators and the liquid-cooled intercooler.

d. Finally there was the installation of the engine itself along with its associated equipment.

A 13ft 0in (3.96m) diameter four-blade Curtiss-Wright propeller was fitted and the aircraft carried 305galUS (1,155lit) of internal fuel. Initially, the intention had been to have Chrysler undertake these conversions at its Detroit plant, but eventually the work was moved out to Republic's Evansville factory in Indiana, with Republic now acting as a sub-contractor. The two airframes received the serials 42-23297 and 42-23298 under project number MX260, a mock-up was inspected on 11 November 1944 and general vibration tests were conducted at Evansville on 6-13 July 1945, which met the contractor's requirements. Finally, the first example flew for the first time on 27 July 1945, immediately after an official inspection of the aircraft had been made on 25 and 26 July. In total

One final view of the ground run with 42-23297. The large air intake, and its position relative to the nose, accentuated the likeness of the aircraft's forward fuselage to a shark. *Republic via Gerald H. Balzer*

the contractor conducted approximately 18 hours of tests on 42-23297 to gather flight data.

Unfortunately, air trials revealed no significant improvements over the standard P-47's performance and the top speed proved to be well short of the 490mph (788km/h) figure estimated prior to flight. In addition, engine overheating meant that its cooler-regulator doors needed to be near continuously fully open, which added to the aircraft's drag quite considerably. Then in November 1945, on Flight 27, 42-23297 experienced propeller shaft failure when flying at 18,000ft (5,486m), a problem caused most likely by power surging of the engine, and the pilot had to make a dead-stick landing.

In consequence it was decided to install the second XI2220 in 42-23298 in readiness for its delivery to Wright Field, but by now there was little interest in this project, with a requirement for either the XP-47H or its Chrysler engine no longer active. So instead the second example was ferried, in September 1945, to Freeman Field in Indiana for disposition/disposal.

XP-47J

By July 1942 it was apparent that the weight of the P-47 was becoming excessive. The objective of the XP-47J project was to continue the Thunderbolt's development but to take out some of this weight while also introducing a more powerful engine and a dual-rotation (contra-rotating) propeller. The designation XP-47J was assigned to this new 'lightweight' version in early November 1942. In fact in its conception the XP-47J was a similar step to that taken by North American in producing lightweight versions of its P-51 Mustang (Chapter Four), but it was also Republic's first effort in developing an ultra-high-performance fighter capable of exceeding the 500mph (805km/h) mark.

The 'J's maximum performance would be improved by the installation of a Pratt & Whitney R2800 engine with water injection and fan cooling,

TOP Views of the XP-47H in flight are very rare – this one is well known. *Republic via Gerald H. Balzer*

ABOVE From the rear the XP-47H still displayed its P-47 Thunderbolt ancestry. *Republic via Gerald H. Balzer*

RIGHT The reason for the XP-47H's long nose was the need to accommodate the enormous Chrysler XI2220 engine, which is seen here in position but with covers off. *Republic via Gerald H. Balzer*

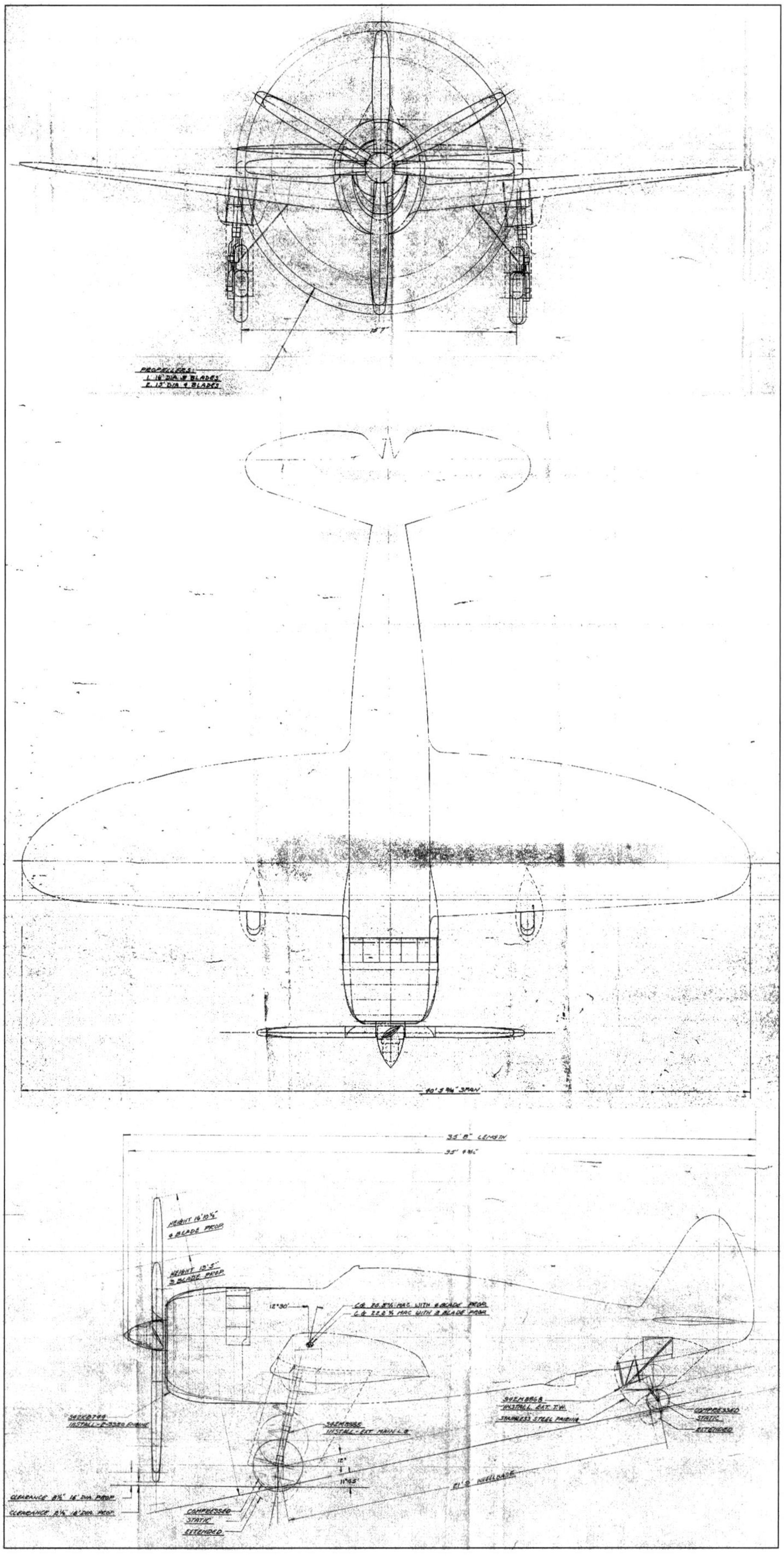

It is not well known that Republic drew a version of its P-47B Thunderbolt fitted with a Wright R3350-23 engine. This was against official requirement MX192, which appears to have been a general 'all-embracing' document for "Studies to improve performance and tactical utility of service aircraft". The drawing is dated 28 April 1942. *US National Archives via Alan Griffith*

Views of the second XP-47H, serial 42-23298, are also pretty rare. This picture shows off the aircraft's large flaps and rudder. *Republic via Dave Ostrowski*

XP-47H data

Span:	40ft 9.4in (12.43m)
Length:	38ft 4in (11.68m)
Gross wing area:	300sq.ft (27.90sq.m)
Gross weight:	14,010lb (6,355kg)
Maximum take-off weight:	15,135lb (6,865kg)
Powerplant:	1 x 2,500hp (1,864kW) Chrysler XI2220 liquid-cooled piston engine
Maximum speed:	414mph (666km/h) at 30,000ft (9,144m)
Maximum rate-of-climb:	2,740ft/min (835m/min) at sea level
Service ceiling:	36,000ft (10,973m)
Absolute ceiling:	37,700ft (11,491m)
Maximum range:	1,000 miles (1,609km)
Armament:	6 x 0.50in (12.7mm) machine guns in wings (not fitted)

the new propeller, an improved General Electric turbo-supercharger, eliminating two 0.50in (12.7mm) machine guns (to leave six), and removing the rear fuel tank (the XP-47J's main fuel tank held 287galUS/1,086lit). In addition, to keep the aircraft clean for high speed flight, no provision was made for external stores under the wings or fuselage, while the basic structure itself was refined.

Though similar in appearance to a P-47B Thunderbolt, the XP-47J was in fact an entirely new type. Two prototypes were planned (against contract W535-AC-39160) which were to be ready in July and September 1943 respectively, and a mock-up was inspected between 19 and 23 April 1943. By 7 April it had been agreed that the XP-47J should have an Aeroproducts dual-rotation propeller, and on 31 May the decision was taken to install a bubble-type canopy on the second prototype, rather than the heavily framed and partially faired form used on the first airframe. Next, on 31 July Republic furnished proposed delivery dates for the XP-47J and the XP-72 (below) and, for new models such as these, it was stated that engineering, tooling and obtaining the necessary materials would take ten months. In addition, although the XP-47J appeared to offer a remarkable performance, particularly at

Near side-on view of the XP-47J prototype 43-46952. Differences from a standard P-47 were the additional plexiglass panel behind the pilot and the lack of intercooler exhaust doors on the sides of the rear fuselage. *Republic via Gerald H. Balzer*

The size of the air intake for the Pratt & Whitney R2800-57 is well shown by this front-on view. Note the six wing guns. *Republic via Gerald H. Balzer*

When this view of the 'Superbolt' was taken, on a snow-covered runway, both sides of the nose had been adorned with artwork showing the Superman cartoon character holding a lightning bolt. *Republic via Gerald H. Balzer*

Republic's XP-47J preparing to land at Farmingdale sometime around August 1943. On 4 August 1944 this aircraft recorded a speed of 505mph (813km/h), which approached the limits of what could be achieved with a piston engine and propeller aircraft. A remarkable accomplishment that was all the more noteworthy because it used a mass-produced engine and propeller. *Cradle of Aviation Museum*

heights over 30,000ft (9,144m), the overall performance would fall far short of the XP-72. Republic added that it would not be possible to go into production on both of these models in less than nine months.

The XP-47J was ordered on 18 June 1943. However, Republic did not have sufficient engineering personnel to handle both this programme and the XP-72 together. Consequently, it was decided that the production possibilities for the XP-47J were remote and that the project should be continued on a limited basis only, with a view to obtaining all the necessary performance data from just one prototype. In view of these points, Republic recommended that the P-47J programme be dropped completely except for the completion of flight testing of the first experimental XP-47J, and that all efforts should now be directed towards the successful development of the XP-72, to be followed as rapidly as possible by the production of the P-72.

The AAF concurred and the second prototype and the static test airframe were officially cancelled on 8 October; as of 30 September the assembly of the second example was 50% complete and that of the static test specimen quoted as 99.9%. The surviving first XP-47J prototype carried the serial 43-46952, it was completed early in November 1943 and its maiden flight took place at Republic's factory airfield at Farmingdale on Long Island on 26 November. The machine was fitted with a single rotation propeller, the length of the flight was 35 minutes and the pilot stated that the aircraft had functioned satisfactorily.

However, after about ten hours of flying had been accumulated, metal chips were found in the oil system, which meant an engine change. Other features such as the water injection were now added to permit operation at a war emergency engine rating of 2,800hp (2,088kW - a water injection system sprays anti-detonation fluid, a mixture of water and alcohol, into the induction system to reduce the charge temperature and prevent detonation inside the cylinders). The new engine was installed in February 1944 and the flight test programme was underway again by the end of the month. However, Pratt & Whitney warned that the R2800-57 now in use did not have the safety features for a full flying programme. Instead, it should be used just for the preliminary flight tests at war emergency power, and then replaced quickly with an R2800-14 (a water-injected R2800-14W engine was fitted during April).

In March 1944 the picture concerning the dual rotation propeller changed considerably. It had been planned to fly the XP-47J with both single and dual rotation types, but Republic had conducted comparative tests using a standard P-47D Thunderbolt equipped with a dual rotation propeller. These tests did not show any marked improvement in the performance of the dual rotation over the single rotation type. It was however, considered that the advantage of the dual propeller would be realised at higher levels of horsepower than were available with the P-47D, and that the XP-47J would provide that increase in performance.

Then, that same month, Pratt & Whitney reported that, due to engineering problems, the dual rotation R2800-61 engine for the XP-47J would be delayed for such a long time that it was suggested that this installation should be dropped from the XP-47J altogether. The sole prototype thus continued flying with its single-rotation unit and

Republic's own flight trials established a maximum speed of 493mph (793km/h) at 35,550ft (10,836m), this data being recording during a flight made on 11 July 1944. But the manufacturer believed that higher speeds could be attained by fitting a better propeller and by increasing the critical altitude of the engine by installing a different turbo-supercharger. Authority to do this was granted on 9 August and a new experimental 13ft (3.96m) diameter Curtiss propeller was fitted which had an additional 2in (50.8mm) on its trailing edge to increase the width.

A Republic flight test report stated that on 4 August 1944 43-46952, in the hands of test pilot Mike Richie, attained a maximum speed of 505mph (813km/h) over a calibrated course and at an altitude of 34,450ft (10,500mm). Then on 8 December Air Corps pilot Capt George D. Colchagoff took delivery of the XP-47J at Farmingdale and ferried it directly to Wright Field, where the aircraft's official AAF flight trials commenced during January 1945.

The first part of this programme saw the aircraft undertake maximum power trials at various heights. This section of the flying was almost complete when there was a serious failure of the exhaust manifold system in flight at 36,000ft (10,973m). Investigations revealed that the original (unstrengthened) exhaust system had proved inadequate to accommodate the increase in engine power (2,800hp/2,088kW). In addition there was the larger capacity supercharger and the supercharger exhaust had been constricted to take advantage of the jet thrust available in the exhaust gases, all of which had produced higher temperatures and pressures than the exhaust system could cope with.

Although maximum power was never achieved during the AAF flight tests (because of the limitations of the special exhaust system), a true airspeed of 484mph (779km/h) was obtained at 25,350ft (7,727m). When corrected to standard atmospheric conditions the data obtained indicated a top speed of 482mph (776km/h) at 30,000ft (9,144m), while the Official Performance Summary eventually quoted a speed of 507mph (816km/h); Republic's own test report from January 1945 gave 502mph (808km/h).

It is thought that the Republic XP-47J was the first piston fighter to exceed 500mph (805km/h). Indeed it was one of the fastest piston-powered fighters ever built and the 505mph (813km/h) figure recorded above was certainly the highest speed in level flight recorded by any propeller-driven aeroplane during the Second World War. Thanks to its speed performance the XP-47J was dubbed the 'Superbolt'.

Structure

The XP-47J's wing used full-cantilever all metal stress-skin construction. Flush riveting was employed on all external surfaces and the structure itself was built mainly in aluminium alloy, but with some magnesium alloy and some steel fittings. The control surfaces were constructed of built-up spars and sheet metal ribs and the wing had NACA-type slotted flaps.

The fuselage was of all-metal semi-monocoque construction, composed of transverse bulkheads and continuous longitudinal stringers and covered by Alclad aluminium alloy. Corrosion resistant steel was used to cover the structure in regions of excessive high temperatures and the cockpit was enclosed by a 'Vee'-type windshield.

Pratt & Whitney's R2800 engine was housed in a close-fitting cowling, it had a fan to assist with cooling, and an intake under the nose provided air to the turbo-supercharger. Also the exhaust ejection system was so designed that some forward jet thrust could be extracted from this flow. A large propeller spinner was also fitted and the XP-47J had a wide-track undercarriage.

XP-47J data

Span:	40ft 9.4in (12.43m)
Length:	33ft 3.2in (10.14m)
Gross wing area:	300sq.ft (27.90sq.m)
Gross weight:	12,400lb (5,625kg)
Maximum take-off weight:	16,780lb (7,611kg)
Powerplant:	1 x 2,800hp (2,088kW) Pratt & Whitney R2800-57 air-cooled radial piston engine
Maximum speed:	507mph (816km/h) at 34,300ft (10,455m)
Maximum rate-of-climb:	4,900ft/min (1,494m/min)
Service ceiling:	45,000ft (13,716m)
Maximum range:	1,070 miles (1,722km)
Armament:	6 x 0.50in (12.7mm) machine guns in wings, no bombs carried

The first XP-72 'Super Thunderbolt' or 'Ultrabolt' leaves its hanger for a test flight, possibly in July 1944. The 14ft 2in (4.32m) diameter Curtiss propeller was one of the largest used during World War II. The engine had a cooling fan positioned behind the spinner. *Republic via Mark Aldrich*

Republic XP-72

By now engine manufacturer Pratt & Whitney had produced what would prove to be the last important reciprocating engine to be used by US military air arms before they moved on to turboprops and jets, the massive 28-cylinder turbo-supercharged R4360 Wasp Major. Republic's follow-on XP-72 long-range high-altitude high-speed fighter was designed to make use of this engine, the first example of which ran on the bench on 28 April 1941.

In 1943 some examples were made available as experimental units for prototype aeroplanes. One recipient was to be the Republic AP-19 project, essentially a bubble-canopy P-47D fitted with an R4360 and two-stage supercharging, which was subsequently given the AAF designation XP-72 (under project number MX189). It also had a close-fitted engine cowling and the R4360 had a remote-mounted, engine-driven auxiliary stage supercharger behind the cockpit. This was run by a long shaft that passed back to the supercharger from the engine through the cockpit and between the pilot's legs. The wing and empennage were similar to the standard P-47D, but the airframe had been enlarged and the lower fuselage modified for a large underside air intake. Dive recovery flaps went under the wings.

Like the XP-47J, the engine drove a fan at the front of the cowling to help keep it cool and air exiting this cowling was mixed with the exhaust gases being expelled through side ejectors to produce a small amount of additional jet thrust. The XP-72's internal fuel capacity was 370galUS (1,401lit) and more could be carried externally in two 150galUS (568lit) drop tanks, one under each wing. Each underwing hardpoint could also take a 1,000lb (454kg) bomb.

Two prototypes were ordered on 18 June 1943 under contract W535-AC-37879 (and Project MX-189) and the type became known as the 'Super Thunderbolt' or 'Ultrabolt'. Once more the objective was to fit a dual-rotation (contra-rotating) propeller, but here again development problems with the Aeroproducts fitting meant that the first prototype, serial 43-36598, made its maiden flight with a conventional four-blade propeller. However, the second, 43-6599, did get the six-blade propeller.

Completed on 29 January 1944, 43-6598 made its first flight on 2 February from Farmingdale with an R4360-13 installed, a single-rotation engine which normally could not have contra-rotating propellers fitted. The second XP-72 first flew on 26 June 1944 with a six-blade 13ft 6in (4.11m) diameter Aeroproducts dual-rotation unit. Over time there has been much discussion as to what mark of engine went into 43-6599, possibly the planned R4360-19, though a specially adapted -13 may have been used (the Pilot's Handbook refers to the -13). Test pilot Carl Bellinger flew the prototypes.

The four-blade Curtiss Electric propeller on 43-6598 was even bigger at 14ft 2in (4.32m) diameter, making it possibly the largest ever fitted to a fighter. Indeed, the propellers fitted to the two XP-72s were so big that, to avoid them hitting the ground, the pilots had to take off and to land in a three-point attitude. The four-blade version left only 5in (12.7cm) of ground clearance with the aircraft horizontal, the six-blade just 9in (22.9cm)!

The XP-72's potential performance resulted in a contract placed in late 1944 for 100 P-72s. Production machines would receive the 3,650hp (2,722kW)

The position of the air intake on the XP-72, well back beneath the cockpit, is shown by this early view of the first aircraft 43-36598. On production aircraft the six machine guns were expected to be replaced by four cannon. *Republic via Mark Aldrich*

Nose angle shot of 43-36598 with that enormous four-blade propeller. *USAF via Mark Aldrich*

Prototype XP-72 43-36598 seen from the side. The port oil cooler air outlet is just visible on the lower fuselage, beneath the wing's trailing edge; another was in the same spot on the opposite side of the aircraft. The underside notch which is visible just ahead of the tailwheel was the air outlet from the intercooler. Note the bubble canopy. *USAF via Mark Aldrich*

The XP-72 in its original single-propeller form stands on the apron waiting for another test flight. In the author's opinion this was the best-looking of all of the P-47 developments and versions. *Mark Aldrich*

R4360-19 with a dual-rotation propeller, which it was estimated would give a top speed of 504mph (811km/h) at 25,000ft (7,620m). There was also to be an upgraded wing with more fuel which increased the span by approximatley 2ft (0.61m), and four 37mm wing cannon would replace the machine guns. However, by the time the XP-72 flew, other versions of Republic's P-47 Thunderbolt and the North American P-51 Mustang escort fighters were flying high altitude operations over Germany. There was no need for another high-altitude piston fighter and consequently the P-72 production order was cancelled on 4 January 1945. Officially the XP-72's top speed was given as 490mph (788km/h) at 25,000ft (7,620m) and both prototypes achieved this figure.

In an interview XP-72 test pilot Ken Jernstedt said nothing about any difference between the fighter's performance with the two different propellers, but he did observe that the fighter "was exceptionally fast". Other sources indicate that it was quite responsive to the controls and "a joy to fly". However, there were some problems with the six-blade propeller which experienced jumps in rpm to 'over-speed' levels. The dual-rotation propellers also produced a slight destabilising effect on the XP-72, though for the pilot this was manageable. The Pilot's Handbook of Flight Operating Instructions noted that the XP-72 was stable under all loading conditions but the trim tabs were very sensitive. The aircraft was very heavy and after landing required considerable distance to stop rolling. The stalling speed with flaps and undercarriage up was 110mph (177km/h) IAS, with flaps and gear down 93mph (150km/h) IAS.

One day, as Jernstedt was taking off from Caldwell in New Jersey in 43-6599, an oil seal failed on the supercharger which started a serious leak. Hot oil was sprayed onto the pilot's legs, into the cockpit and on the outside of the cockpit canopy, and he had to make an emergency landing. Some accounts state that the aircraft had been damaged beyond repair, but Jernstedt denied this. It could have been repaired, but it was not because the programme was closed soon afterwards. In August 1946 one prototype (without its engine) went to an Air Scouts group based on Long Island. The other XP-72 was scrapped.

The XP-47J was overshadowed and eventually pushed out of the picture by the XP-72, the ultimate development of the original P-47 Thunderbolt which received the most powerful aeroengine of the war. Each type was full of unrealised promise and potential and in the end both were victims of the pace of developments in fighter design, with the turbojet once again becoming the dominant source of power for the future. Neither of these very high performance piston fighters ever had a chance of entering squadron service. A pity since both of them were very fast indeed!

Close-up of the XP-72's six-blade dual-rotation (contra-rotating) propeller installation. The XP-72 was roughly the same size and weight as the P-47D but was more aerodynamic and possessed about 50% more power. *Republic Aviation*

It was the second XP-72, 43-36599, which flew with the dual-rotation propeller and this rear angle photo shows the aircraft after the contraprop had been fitted. The blades were hollow but the propeller unit still weighed in the region of 765lb (347kg). *Republic via Mark Aldrich*

Neither XP-72 prototype had their serial number painted correctly on their tails – here it should have been '336599' to conform to AAF guidelines. There are no known photos showing the XP-72 in flight. *Republic via Mike Machat*

XP-72 Data

Span:	40ft 11.7in (12.49m)
Length:	36ft 7.8in (11.17m)
Wing area:	300sq.ft (27.90sq.m)
Empty weight:	10,965lb (4,974kg)
Gross weight (no bombs):	14,760lb (6,695kg)
Maximum take-off weight (maximum fuel plus bombs):	17,492lb (7,934kg)
Powerplant:	1 x 3,000hp (2,237kW) four-row, 28-cylinder Pratt & Whitney R4360-13 air-cooled radial piston engine
Maximum speed:	405mph (652km/h) at sea level, 490mph (788km/h) at 25,000ft (7,620m)
Sea level rate of climb:	5,250ft/min (1,600m/min)
Service ceiling:	42,000ft (12,802m)
Maximum range with drop tanks:	1,330 miles (2,140km)
Armament:	6 x 0.50in (12.7mm) machine guns in wings (production aircraft four 37mm cannon in wings), two 1,000lb (454kg) bombs.

13 Hughes XF-11

During the 1940s American tycoon Howard Hughes made a serious and concentrated effort to turn his company at Burbank in California into an established aircraft manufacturer. Perhaps the firm's most famous product was the enormous H-4 Hercules flying boat, the 'Spruce Goose', which flew briefly in November 1947. This machine was preceded by a high performance reconnaissance prototype called the XF-11 which did complete a flying programme, but also nearly claimed the life of Hughes himself! The full XF-11 story embraces a series of twin-engine twin-boom designs, designated D-2, D-3, D-5, XP-73, XA-37 and XF-11, and it passed through numerous phases including long range pursuit (fighter), medium bomber, bomber escort and long range photo reconnaissance.

From December 1939 the Hughes company had begun to push hard for a contract (W535-AC-1079) to build an aircraft of its own design for the US Army Air Force. On 19 March 1940 authority was granted to build its D-2 bomber project which primarily would

The second Hughes XF-11 pictured in flight off the coast of California during a sortie from Eglin. *Gerald H. Balzer*

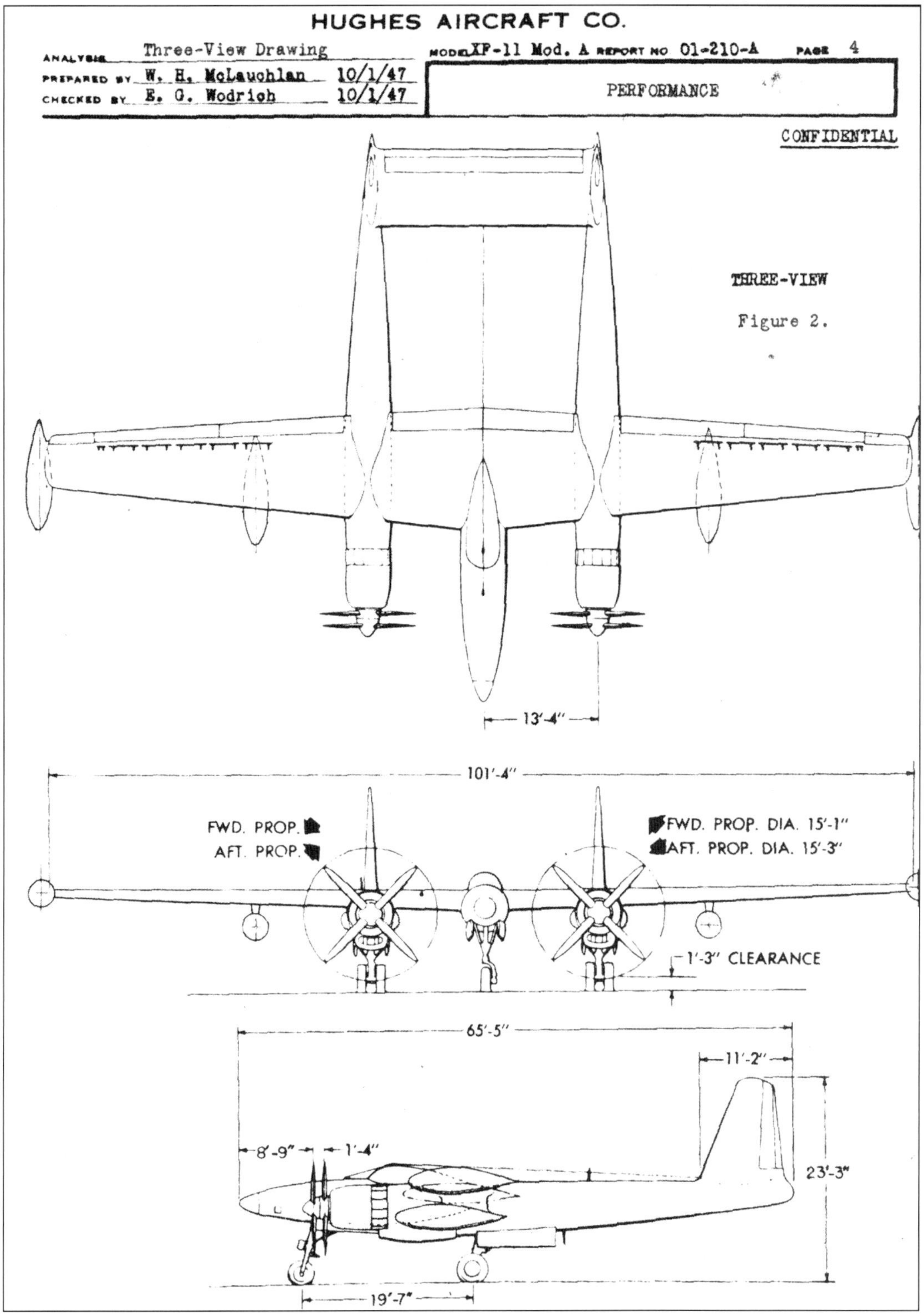

Manufacturer's drawing from 1947 showing the XF-11 in its original form with counter-rotating propellers (and also external fuel tanks). The front propellers had a diameter of 15ft 1in (4.60m), the rear props 15ft 3in (4.65m). *US National Archives via Ryan Crierie*

have a wooden structure formed using the Duramold Process. In mid-1942 AAF Material Division at Wright Field decided to purchase the D-2 prototype and a USAAF memorandum from June 1942 noted that the Hughes machine "has been submitted as a convoy protector, convoy destroyer, pursuit airplane, fighter, and light bombardment type, but the latest specification....calls it a fighter. If the present airplane is completed as a military weapon, it will have armament substantially as on the XP-58 [Chapter Eight]....it is considered advisable to call it the XP-73 for the sake of administering the contract."

In fact XP-73 proved to be just a temporary designation because, inside three days, the D-2 had been redesignated XA-37. The prototype was test flown from 20 June 1943 but in the air it performed poorly due to problems with high control forces. A full redesign of the main wings was considered necessary, but then the aircraft was destroyed by fire on 11 November 1944 having flown very little.

Views of the first XF-11 fitted with its contra-rotating propellers. These were taken at Culver City on 3 July 1946. *Gerald H. Balzer*

A new project

In June 1943 General 'Hap' Arnold, Commanding General of the Army Air Forces, commented on the lack of night fighters and reconnaissance aircraft within the AAF, and he suggested that the Hughes machine might suit these roles. The design would have to be revised and as such became known as the D-5 (the Lockheed XP-58 fighter prototype was also considered for the reconnaissance role at this time, and Wright Field's engineers did feel that this would be a better option). However, assessments suggested that a force of 16 of Hughes aircraft could do much to possibly even shorten the war and on 11 November 1943 the D-5 was officially designated F-11; it was covered by Project number MX-575. (Note: the 'F' designation referred here to photography, not fighter, which was covered by the 'P' pursuit designation. Only in 1948 did 'F' come to represent fighter in US military aircraft listings, at which point [in July] the prototype XF-11 became the XR-11 with 'R' for reconnaissance.)

From March 1942 there was considerable debate regarding Hughes' ability to manufacture aircraft using the Duramold process. The company had acquired some rights to use this composite material formed of birch ply impregnated with phenolic resin and which offered certain advantages over aluminium. However, the AAF considered it unsatisfactory for use in combat aircraft that were expected to be airworthy under all climatic conditions, and so ordered that the F-11 should have an all-metal (aluminium) airframe.

Turning the D-5 into the F-11 proved a considerable task for the team led by chief engineer Stanley Bell. Plans were laid down for two XF-11 prototypes, a static test airframe and 98 production machines and on 5 April 1944 contract approval was given for the latter to be built at Hughes' Culver City plant; it was hoped that production would reach 10 aircraft per month by September 1945. At 30 September 1944 the requirements stated a maximum speed of 315mph (507km/h) at sea level and 450mph (724km/h) at 33,000ft (10,058m), sea level rate-of-climb 2,025ft/min (617m/min), a range without bombs of 5,000 miles (8,045km) and a service ceiling of 42,000ft (12,802m).

The programme, however, experienced difficulties and constant delays. For example by October 1943 the wings were to be sub-contracted to Fleetwings since it was considered that Hughes could not produce the complete aircraft to the proposed schedule, but this plan collapsed in February 1944 after Fleetwings complained about the difficulty of acquiring the necessary information to do the job. Delay was also experienced in the delivery of engines and propellers, and Hughes was itself affected by the shortage of manpower within the aircraft industry. Finally, at times, the negotiations between manufacturer and customer proved fractious, Hughes for example asking for a refund on the D-2 which it described as a prototype of the F-11, something to which the USAAF retorted as "ridiculous".

By the end of July 1944 the design was 85% complete and at this stage the project was considered vital. On 7 June Gen Franklin O. Carroll, chief of the experimental engineering section at Wright Field, had written that "no other aircraft being developed at this time...could meet all of the F-11 Specification"; it was superior to any other photo reconnaissance aircraft in existence. At a conference in August representatives from the AAF's Operations, Commitments, and Requirements Office were very enthusiastic and believed that, in combat, they would rather fly it than the Republic F-12 because it was smaller, had higher strength factors and a better view to the rear (a new rival, the four-engine XF-12 Rainbow, would also progress no further than prototype flight).

At 3 November 1944 the first XF-11 was scheduled to be completed in March 1945 and it would have eight-blade propellers which were the best available at the time (high altitude propellers would need another 18 months before they were ready). Next, the loss of some bases in China by 28 February 1945 made the programme more secure since many target areas were now out of range of any photo-reconnaissance aircraft apart from the F-13 (a modified Boeing B-29 bomber), but these aircraft were needed as bombers. So producing the F-11 was now "of the utmost importance". Indeed, on 29 March the F-11 was given Group 1 Preference Rating, which signified that these machines were needed urgently.

However, by 6 April 1945 it was becoming doubtful if they could be produced in time to be of material value in the war effort, in part because of the lack of skilled labour working on the project at Hughes (there was at this time a manpower shortage throughout the US aircraft industry). By May the project was running late and it had become expensive.

As a result, on 26 May all 98 production aircraft (tail numbers 44-70157 to 44-70254) were cancelled, although the two prototypes (44-70155 and 44-70156) would continue. The first, however, would not be ready now until the spring of 1946. The F-11 mock-up was completed in September 1945 and by late January 1946 the first machine was 93% complete. It was accepted on 5 April, at which point the second aircraft was some 65% complete.

Taxi trials commenced on 15 April 1946 with Howard Hughes himself in the cockpit. This was on the grass runway at his company's home airfield at Culver City, rather than the usual venue for AAF aircraft first flights of Muroc Base in the Mojave Desert, Hughes having apparently persuaded the Air Force to let him fly the plane from its birthplace. On 20 April the XF-11 was flown 20ft (6m) in the air to check the effectiveness of the surface controls, before landing and stopping (it did not clear the airfield). It was then grounded until the contra-rotating propellers could be delivered.

Hughes accumulated a considerable amount of taxiing time and on occasion was accompanied by

Howard Hughes runs up the engines of XF-11 No.1 on the ramp. *Gerald Balzer Collection, Greater St. Louis Air and Space Museum*

Frank J. Prinz, a service engineer from Hamilton Standard who supplied the propellers. On one occasion this proved fortunate when Hughes, watching the instruments closely, failed to notice how close they were to the end of the runway. Prinz put all four contra-rotating propellers into reverse pitch while Hughes applied full brake, just enough to stop the plane in time. Another run, on 26 June, revealed that the rudder forces were too high, which brought further delay while this had to be remedied. Ominously, thanks to a small internal leak, after each taxi run several ounces of oil were needed to replenish the tank for the starboard propeller (some sources indicate that Hughes was not aware of this).

Disastrous crash

Phase I flight testing was to be conducted by the contractor. Hughes took 44-70155 on its maiden flight on 7 July 1946 after having completed two further hours of taxi runs that day. As per AAF instructions the sortie was to be limited to one hour's duration and a total of 600galUS (2,271lit) of fuel was to be carried. However, when the aircraft took off at 5.20pm it had 1,200galUS (4,542lit) aboard at a weight of 44,000lb (19,958kg). Hughes clearly intended to stay airborne for rather longer and he had also chosen to fly alone, but two of his engineers followed in a Douglas A-20 chase plane.

Another AAF stipulation had been to keep the undercarriage extended, but Hughes duly retracted the landing gear. However, an unsafe red light on one gear showed in the cockpit and he had to recycle the landing gear handle several times and perform low g manoeuvres to ensure that it became fully retracted. Hughes flew above Culver City at around 5,000ft (1,524m) altitude for about forty minutes before at one point flying across the base airfield at low level with the gear deployed once again.

Then at 6:35pm, after 75 minutes airborne and still at 5,000ft (1,524m) altitude and about two miles (3.2km) from base, the oil leak in the starboard propeller's self-contained supply suddenly put the rear propeller into reverse pitch. To counteract the resulting drag the forward propeller went into high pitch, which meant the thrust from the starboard engine was lost. The pilot applied full left rudder and aileron deflection to hold the aircraft level, but began to lose altitude. However, there was no radio communication and the A-20 crew thought that Hughes was preparing to land.

Unfortunately, he was unable to reach the airfield. The aircraft came down in a plush area of Los Angeles, it hit a house and then a large extent of brush, the latter helping to slow the XF-11 down. Hughes crawled out and was pulled to safety by a bystander, but 44-70155 was burnt out. It was quite simply a miracle that Howard Hughes survived this catastrophe, but he did sustain severe injuries and burns.

Hughes also suffered in the resulting enquiry held on 16 August 1946. By then he had reported how the blades on the rear half of the right propeller had

Front view of 44-70155. *Hughes*

ABOVE The first XF-11 takes off on its first and, sadly and near tragically, its only test flight, on Sunday 7 July 1946. *Gerald Balzer Collection, Greater St. Louis Air and Space Museum*

LEFT The second XF-11, serial 44-70156, was essentially the same in most respects as the first prototype, apart from the change of propellers. *Gerald H. Balzer*

inadvertently reversed pitch, and how he had unsuccessfully attempted to remedy the situation by reducing power on the left engine and retaining power on the right. Preliminary investigations indicated that once again there had been a leakage in the oil seal around the propeller shaft, and that the loss of hydraulic fluid had permitted the blades to reverse pitch and render the propeller controls ineffective. In fact similar leakage had been seen with these propellers on other aircraft types, particularly on the Northrop XB-35 bomber. Furthermore, this propeller had not passed a type test, nor had it been tested at Wright Field (the propellers were eventually rejected and did not complete their type test).

Cameras in the plane had recorded flight information for an hour and 35 minutes. The Enquiry report stated:

1. Because of his record, Hughes' request to personally make the first flight had been granted; however, the initial test flight was supposed to have been limited to one hour.

2.The engine used in the XF-11 had passed its military test and there was no indication from the examined wreckage that the engine had failed.

3.Previous difficulties had occurred with the Hamilton Standard dual rotation reversible propellers on the test stand and on other aircraft. The damaged XF-11 propellers were still undergoing investigation at Wright Field.

4. Hughes had started on a 45-minute flight, but stayed in the air almost twice that time and concentrated mainly on landing gear issues instead of following the approved flight programme. During the last few minutes a drag developed on the plane's starboard side and Hughes did not have time to find the cause before the plane crashed.

5.It appeared that the loss of hydraulic fluid had caused the failure of the pitch change mechanism of the right rear propeller. Hughes had maintained full power on the right engine and reduced that of the left engine, instead of trying to fly with the right propeller windmilling without power.

6.Wright Field's Engineering Division felt that he should have been able to continue flying on one engine. Indeed, it was Wright Field's understanding that the crash was attributed to pilot error.

On 28 August, after a careful review of the Investigation Board's report, and of the recommendations from the Propeller Laboratory and Wright Field's Engineering Division, the following action was taken. Hughes was asked to name a pilot, "other than Howard Hughes", to test the second XF-11 prototype 44-70156, which would now have single-rotating four-blade propellers. Hughes was also directed to conduct the first 10 hours of flight testing at Muroc, after the aircraft had been transported there by road for assembly.

The Hughes photo-reconnaissance aircraft was a massive beast. These pictures, thought to have been taken at Muroc, show the flying surfaces very well. Wings spoilers were positioned just forward of the outer flaps. Note that the rear of the fixed canopy is missing, and the insignia on the side of the boom has no horizontal red stripe, a feature introduced around this time. *Hughes*

The XF-11's wing flaps stretched from outside the tail booms to almost the wing tips where they met the relatively small ailerons. The trailing edge between the tail booms also carried a flap. Note the ports for the cameras under and on the sides of the fuselage nose. *Gerald H. Balzer*

Nose view showing detail for the new propeller arrangement on the second machine. These had a diameter of 14ft 8in (4.47m) and spinners were fitted later on. The camera operator would use the Plexiglas bubble nose whilst lying in a prone position. *Hughes*

Walk around views of 44-70156. The bulges on the nacelles under the wings were the exhaust outlets for the inner turbo-superchargers. The airframe surface finish was natural clad aluminium. *Gerald H. Balzer*

This picture of 44-70156 was taken on 31 December 1948, possibly after its move to Eglin Field. It now wears the revised Air Force insignia with an additional red stripe. *Photo credit???*

Second best

Incredibly, and after much lobbying, Hughes was permitted to take the second aircraft on its first flight as well, from Muroc on 5 April 1947. This time there were no problems and indeed Hughes went on to complete numerous sorties in the aircraft as part of manufacturer's testing. On 14 April 1948 44-70156 was accepted by the Wright Field test section, who operated and assessed the aeroplane until December, after which it was flown to Eglin Field in Florida to undergo operational suitability testing by the Air Proving Ground Command; this lasted until July 1949. Finally, on 26 July 1949 the XR-11 (as it had now become) was transferred to Sheppard Air Force Base in Texas where it was used for ground maintenance instruction by the 3750th Technical Training Wing. It was finally released from the USAF inventory in November 1949 and subsequently scrapped.

Test pilot Lindell C. Hendrix provided a little insight on what the second XF-11/XR-11 was like in the air. The first impression was that this "was a huge machine", but for the photo-reconnaissance role it seemed like just another modified fighter. On take-off he measured the initial rate of climb at over 5,000ft/min (1,524m/min) and then recorded a maximum altitude of 48,000ft (14,630m). Hendrix reported that 44-70156 was "a remarkably stable aeroplane and at high speeds the lateral control was excellent, but it left a great deal to be desired at low speeds. The XR-11 had an aileron-spoiler combination for lateral control but [he considered] the ailerons were much too small for low-speed flight". The aircraft's massive wings also enabled it get down to only 80mph (129km/h) before it stalled. Hendrix added that in the air the XR-11 felt more akin to "an interceptor rather than a photo-reconnaissance machine".

As one of the last high-power piston aircraft built for the Air Force the XF-11 had a acceptable performance for a reconnaissance type and an interceptor, but the arrival of jet-powered aircraft meant that it was obsolete by the time it flew. The project proved a commercial failure for Hughes, but the company would soon achieve success as a supplier of air-to-air missiles and avionics.

Structure

The Hughes XF-11 was an elegant, stylish and very clean design with a structure built in semi-monocoque flush-riveted aluminium alloy. Each engine nacelle extended aft of the wing to form a boom to either side of the short centrally located needle-nose cockpit and fuselage. The straight and slightly tapered wing had spoiler-type ailerons for roll control. The first prototype, with eight-blade Hamilton Standard Super-Hydromatic dual rotation constant speed fully feathering propellers, had Pratt & Whitney R4360-31 units fitted; the second, with conventional four-blade Curtiss-Electric single-rotating propellers, received R4360-37s.

Production aeroplanes would have carried up to 12 cameras in total in the nose of the central nacelle and in the booms to the rear of the wings. The F-11 was a two-seater (pilot and observer) but an additional 'photographer' could also be taken on board. The cockpit was pressurised and a tricycle undercarriage was fitted, at the time still a relatively new feature. Self-sealing bullet-proof fuel tanks were used and the XF-11 never carried weaponry.

This in-flight study of 44-70156 flying off Southern California was taken on 20 July 1948. Although the second prototype, this aircraft was in fact the third to be completed, after 44-70155 and then the static test airframe which was situated at Wright Field. *Gerald Balzer Collection, Greater St. Louis Air and Space Museum*

Test pilot Lindell C. Hendrix. *Hughes*

The second XF-11 pictured during an early test flight. No colour photos appear to exist of this aircraft, despite the US aircraft industry having made use of this medium through much of the war. *Hughes*

44-70156 seen just after take off with the nose gear retracting and doors about to close. The pylons positioned under each outer wing could take 310galUS (1,173lit) drop tanks. *Gerald Balzer Collection, Greater St. Louis Air and Space Museum*

Despite its size the XF-11 was a most attractive and impressive-looking machine. The spinners have now been fitted to the propellers. *Gerald Balzer Collection, Greater St. Louis Air and Space Museum*

Splendid view looking down on 44-70156 during a test flight. *Gerald Balzer Collection, Greater St. Louis Air and Space Museum*

XF-11 Data

Span (not including tip tanks):	101ft 4in (30.89m)
Length:	65ft 5in (19.94m)
Wing area:	983sq.ft (91.42sq.m) - some sources state 989sq.ft (91.98sq.m)
Empty weight:	37,100lb (16,829kg)
Loaded weight:	47,500lb (21,546kg)
Maximum take-off weight:	58,315lb (26,452kg)
Powerplant:	2 x Pratt & Whitney R4360 28-cylinder 3,000hp (2,237kW) turbo-supercharged air-cooled radial piston engines
Maximum speed:	420mph (676km/h) at 30,000ft (9,144m)
Absolute ceiling:	48,000ft (14,630m)
Range:	c5,000 miles (8,045kg)

14 Fisher XP-75 Eagle

The fighter programme discussed here, the Fisher XP-75, differs from the others in this book specifically in two ways. Firstly it was the creation of a company that was not part of the traditional aircraft industry (though designer Donovan Berlin had a long track record with Curtiss), and second it did reach production, though only just before cancellation.

Initially, the object of the XP-75's development was to provide, with minimal delay, a new type of fighter for the AAF with an exceptional rate of climb. To help accelerate the project the airframe was to involve the use of certain major assemblies, such as wing panels, empennage, and landing gear, from existing production types. This would (in theory) save time in designing new parts and would also require rather less in the way of new tooling. Added to this the fighter would use the most powerful liquid cooled piston engine available, but the work was to be undertaken by car manufacturer Fisher Body in Detroit, part of General Motors, and not by the established aircraft companies.

As part of the war effort the Aircraft Development Division (or Section) within the Fisher Body Division of the General Motors Corporation already had contracts covering other manufacturer's aircraft (and tanks) – namely the final assembly of Boeing B-29 bombers plus wing sections and other major

Superb air-to-air image of production Fisher P-75 44-44550. This top view shows the aircraft's square wingtips and horizontal tail. Only a minimal extension was made to the wings during the programme, but the area of the horizontal tail was increased considerably. The machine guns are installed on this aircraft. *Greater St Louis Air & Space Museum*

assemblies for the North American B-25 light bomber and attack aircraft. Nevertheless, moving into the realm of aircraft design and development was a step into the unknown for Fisher but, to back up its plans, the firm acquired the services of Donovan R. Berlin. He joined the team (apparently on request of the Federal Government) after leaving Curtiss in December 1941 and became the Director of Fisher's Aircraft Development Section.

What would become the XP-75 was Berlin's first job. Fisher's initial submission for an interceptor type fighter, with contra-rotating propellers and an engine positioned aft of the cockpit, was submitted in September 1942. This was against an AAF Request for Proposals for a new fighter having a rate of climb of 5,600ft/min (1,707m/min) and a maximum speed of 440mph (708km/h) at 20,000ft (6,096m). As first proposed the fighter would utilise North American P-51 outer wing panels in an inverted gull wing

ABOVE The first XP-75 seen at a late stage of assembly. *Gerald H. Balzer*

LEFT Photos taken on the ground and in the air of the first Fisher XP-75 Eagle prototype 43-46950. Engine exhausts are positioned all around the central fuselage. For the author, the original heavily framed canopy looked somewhat old-fashioned for the latter war years. Yet subsequent aircraft which had the tear drop canopy looked far more modern! Nevertheless, the Eagle family had a very sleek fuselage. *Alan Griffith and Greater St Louis Air & Space Museum*

43-46950 seen from head on. The aircraft lacks armament and undercarriage strut fairings. *Gerald H. Balzer*

For comparison one of the later aircraft with guns and main gear covers fitted. *Gerald H. Balzer*

A final ground view of the first XP-75, here showing the unusual fairing at the rear of the cockpit canopy and the original fin shape. *Gerald H. Balzer*

arrangement, the tail assembly from a Douglas A-24 attack aircraft and the undercarriage from a Vought F4U Corsair navy fighter. However, this was soon modified to the extent of substituting a straight wing with Curtiss P-40 outer wing panels. The powerplant was an Allison V3420 liquid cooled engine driving an Aeroproducts dual rotation propeller through twin shafts running under the cockpit. Letter contract W535-AC-33962 dated 11 September 1942 was issued to Fisher for two prototypes (serials 43-46950 and 43-46951).

Allison was also owned by General Motors and the V3420 was effectively two of this manufacturer's V1710 units (used in types such as the Bell P-39) mated to a common crankcase side-by-side in a W-type arrangement. This new engine appeared to offer an excellent power-to-weight ratio and it was also selected for the Lockheed XP-58 fighter (Chapter Eight) and the Boeing XB-39 bomber, but in the end neither type went into service and only about 150 examples of the V3420 would be produced.

With the need for a high rate of climb, and with the project in the hands of a 'new' design team, on 7 November 1942 the AAF's General Echols specifically instructed Brigadier Gen. F. O. Carroll, Chief of the Experimental Engineering Section at Wright Field, to monitor the weight of the XP-75 closely. This was the designation now allotted to the fighter, it was also named Eagle and project/code number MX-317 covered the programme. At 21 October the XP-75's estimated performance included a maximum speed of 440mph (708km/h) at 20,000ft (6,096m), a rate of climb at sea level of 5,600ft/min (1,707m/min) and a service ceiling of 38,000ft (11,582m). Its weight would be in the region of 12,000lb (5,443kg) and the armament four to six 0.5in (12.7mm) calibre machine guns, though there might be the possibility of mounting 37mm cannon later on.

By March 1943 Fisher had made sufficient progress for a mock-up inspection to be held at the manufacturer's facility in Detroit, in fact on 1 to 3 March. In all three complete full-scale, wood-frame XP-75 mock-ups were to be constructed, two during the development of the original design and one more after the long range fighter version had been authorised (below). A fourth, an all-metal mock-up, was also planned to serve as a model for production aircraft. One of the comments to come out of the inspection was that Fisher should initiate a new development around the installation of P-51 wings with four 20mm cannon, but this was not taken up.

In June a conference was held with NACA to determine what corrective action could be taken to improve the predicted poor rolling characteristics of the XP-75 (as defined in the wind tunnel). It was decided to supply NACA with a Curtiss P-40 to investigate ways of increasing aileron effectiveness. Tests conducted in the NACA spin tunnel during September 1943 also revealed a condition which ultimately resulted in the installation of a ventral fin on production P-75s to improve the spin characteristics.

The following month the changing tactical situation in the war resulted in a change in the development programme - a new long range fighter type was now required. Increasing pressure was being brought to bear on Material Command to produce a well-armed fighter with sufficient range to escort the AAF's B-17 and B-24 heavy bombers on missions deep into Germany. In response Fisher submitted data showing how a modified XP-75 could accomplish this task. The result was that six additional long range escort fighter prototypes were requested (before the definitive contract was issued in October 1943) to cover the necessary extra flight testing that this version would entail. These were designated XP-75As and received the serial numbers 44-32161 to 44-32166, they had extra fuel in wing tanks and V3420-23 engines.

On 7 July 1943 Maj Gen Stratemeyer, Chief of the Air Staff, quoting information received from the UK, reported that inside of six months the latest Messerschmitt Bf 109 and Focke-Wulf Fw 190 fighters would out perform the current P-47, and that General Arnold was very concerned as to what fighter the AAF was planning to use to meet this challenge. Stratemeyer stated "We are all thinking about the P-75 and are in hopes that it will be the airplane that we should put into production. If that is true then we should be planning to stop the production of the P-47 and put in the P-75."

Very quickly plans were laid down for substantial P-75 production with Contract W535-AC-41011 for 2,500 machines; the Letter of Intent for these aircraft was approved on 16 July 1943 but the formal contract was dated 19 April 1944. Such a programme would make necessary changes to the arrangements to build B-29 bombers at Fisher's Cleveland plant – these would have to be moved to other factories. Indeed as early as 6 July AAF High Command had informed the manufacturer that it was now relieved of its commitments to build B-29s (200 examples at a peak rate of 20 per month) to provide adequate production floor space for the P-75.

All of the XP-75s and P-75s would be built at Cleveland, with the exception of the first two interceptor prototypes which were constructed in Detroit. The armament now comprised six 0.50in (12.7mm) machine guns in the wings and another four in the nose. With changes required for production aircraft, contract AC-41011 now included a static test article, but the Letter of Intent specifically stated that if the first production P-75 did not meet requirements, then the entire production order might be cancelled.

Over time, particularly now with a new version of the aircraft, Fisher's engineers had to incorporate numerous minor changes to the airframe. As the detail design and then the manufacture of the XP-75s began, more problems began to surface and the hoped for easy and smooth coming together of this somewhat 'composite' aircraft into a complete machine started to fade. This situation would get worse once flight testing had begun.

ABOVE LEFT The first XP-75 takes to the skies for its maiden flight on 17 November 1943. *Gerald H. Balzer*

ABOVE RIGHT A line-up of Eagles – left to right airframes 6, 9, 2 and 3. *Chris Gibson*

BELOW Rear view photo of an XP-75A taken on 30 March 1945. *Alan Griffith*

Nevertheless, at this stage Fisher was still very confident of success, as shown by its Operating Report for the six month period to 1 November 1943, and which also provides some background detail to the programme up to this point. It described the 'P-75 Long Range Fighter' as "the only American airplane ever to be designed and built outside the aircraft industry, and the automobile industry's first." The report continued saying "the Army Air Forces' High Command told us that the need on the fighting fronts for this type of airplane [long range fighter] was grave and immediate, and that our XP-75 was the only development in prospect that offered any hope of being modified to meet the new need. Adapted to the design of the XP-75 were the following assemblies from other airplanes – from the Curtiss P-40: Outer Wings, Retracting Strut, Instrument Panel, Control Stick and Pedal Assemblies – from the Douglas A-24: Empennage Assembly and Tall Wheel installation - and from the Vought-Sikorsky F4U-1: the Oleo Strut Assembly."

Work on the XP-75 prototypes had started immediately after the issue of the original letter contract in October 1942. However, in March 1943 progress had to be sidetracked in favour of Fisher's work on the XB-19A and XB-39 projects (this was adapting the Allison V3420, respectively, to the gigantic Douglas XB-19 experimental bomber prototype for trials and then to the Boeing B-29 heavy bomber) - these too had become urgent programmes. Consequently, late in June, when the demand for a long range fighter suddenly "sky-rocketed" the XP-75 to the number one position on the list of critical military requirements, the engineering on the fighter was only 60% advanced (and would require revision to meet the new specifications), and only 10% of the fabrication on the prototype had been completed.

Fisher's report concluded that, "with its 3,000hp [2,237kW] engine and reduction gear assembly by Allison, its six-bladed dual rotation propeller by Aeroproducts, its electrical system by Packard Electric, and its design and airframe by Fisher, the P-75 long range fighter will be truly a General Motors Airplane."

V3420-23 units mounted in conveyors. These were used for the installation of accessories and controls and for fitting the exhaust manifold and stack assemblies. *Gerald H. Balzer*

Photos providing detail of the fighter's main undercarriage and its long forward fuselage. *Gerald H. Balzer*

Walk around views of the second XP-75A 44-32162 dated 10 May 1944. This aircraft has its guns installed. *Gerald H. Balzer*

44-32164 has a fin with a rounded tip and a modified but still heavily-framed canopy; the cockpit position was well forward in the fuselage. *Gerald H. Balzer*

Flight test

Sub-assembly work on the first prototype 43-46950 began on 25 August 1943 and the first flight took place on 17 November, 11 days after it had been removed from the final assembly fixture. On this first sortie the XP-75 was aloft for about 25 minutes and it was taken to an altitude of approximately 6,000ft (1,829m). Fisher's test pilot Russell Thaw reported after the flight that the longitudinal stability appeared satisfactory but that stability in yaw was questionable, possibly indicating a need for larger tail surface area; otherwise the aircraft was very satisfactory except for minor difficulties with equipment. At this stage the first and second prototypes had the fuselage fuel tank only, but the third and subsequent (long range) prototypes would have additional fuel in the centre section.

On 25 November General Echols advised Material Division in Washington that the P-75 was one of AAF's highest priority projects. After four flights the first XP-75 had accumulated approximately 2.5 hours airtime and on that fourth flight, made on 24 November, 43-46950 was accompanied by a calibrated fighter aircraft from Wright Field for the purpose of calibrating the XP-75. However, during low speed runs the latter's engine backfired and stopped, on reaching cruising speed during this flight the engine had also appeared to be running rough, and so the flight was terminated. The prototype was grounded for one week, during which time (to prevent further backfiring) the air intake was changed from the cold side of the radiator duct to the warm side.

At a conference held on 29 November 1943 between Fisher Body and Material Command Washington personnel, it was decided to locate an experimental set of dive recovery flaps on the centre section of the XP-75's wing. Although the fuel tanks housed in the centre section would interfere with the operating mechanism if these flaps were installed, it was decided to go ahead with this trial fitting.

On 20 January 1944 43-46950 was flown by Col Ernest K. Warburton and Lt Col Estes from Wright Field's Flight Section while on a visit to Fisher Body. After two hours flying time the pilots reported that:

1. Stability and control forces on the XP-75 were unsuitable for a fighter. When making tight turns the aircraft felt as if it were going to stall or go into a spin, and none of the controls particularly inspired confidence in the pilots.

2. The second prototype was to have some of the friction removed from its control systems, a larger fin was to be installed, and the engine was to be made to operate without carburettor heat.

3. The fighter did not give the impression of being particularly fast; however a loss in power due to carburettor heat had accounted for the loss in speed. The vision out of the cockpit was excellent, as a whole the XP-75 was quite conventional and very easy to fly, and pilots should have no trouble transitioning to it.

As the trials continued and additional prototypes were flown, a number of major troubles became apparent. Chiefly these were instability (caused by a poor estimation of the centre of gravity position), loss of engine power, sloshing of fuel in the fuselage tank, poor cooling, and a low rate of roll (i.e. high aileron forces at high speeds). The flight test and engineering programme throughout 1944 would be chiefly concerned with eliminating these and many other minor flaws. This effort resulted in several major and numerous minor modifications to the aircraft, including revamped tail surfaces, an extension of the nose to adjust the centre of gravity (especially after the tail had been enlarged), the extension of the ailerons to the wing tips, the introduction of a booster control installation to improve aileron operation, the addition of the dive recovery flaps, and the improvement to the engine cooling; a bubble canopy was also introduced. Some of these changes seriously impaired the original plan to utilise production of ready-built components and there were extensive delays caused by the reworking of production tooling.

Fisher was now learning just how much skill and effort was necessary to create new aircraft, as opposed to just manufacturing other firm's products. The AAF's official history of the XP-75 indicated that the reasons for some of the problems probably lay in the use of an experimental engine (the V3420 engine's first flight was actually in the XP-75), an engineering and production organisation largely inexperienced and physically separated geographically (Fisher's engineering was performed in Detroit with construction in Cleveland) and then the tremendous pressure for immediate production which did not allow sufficient time for a carefully planned development programme.

By 28 January 1944 the first prototype had completed 42 flights totalling 32 hours 50 minutes airtime. The second XP-75, 43-46951, made a ten-minute first flight on 27 January, but the engine did not work satisfactorily. The third, 44-32161, made during its second flight a high speed run at 20,000ft (6,096m) and the follow-up examination revealed that, again, the carburettor heat control had failed. The resulting excess heat had caused some loss in engine power, but the pilot did report that the installation of a larger fin on the third machine had corrected some of the weakness in directional stability.

Vibration and flutter tests were held in February 1944, while critical performance tests were attempted in June 1944 using the sixth prototype, but due to improper engine operation the results were questionable. No further official performance tests were tried until a production aircraft was made available in September 1944.

On 24 February 1944 Don Berlin reported that the third XP-75 had made a speed run that day and recorded a true air speed of 410mph (660km/h) at 20,000ft (6,096m). This was achieved with an unretracted tail wheel and a narrow blade propeller and Berlin indicated that with a wide blade propeller installed (which was being shipped from Aeroproducts), together with a retracted tail wheel plus a bubble canopy, that the guaranteed high speed of 430mph (692km/h) would be attained. On 8 April a speed of 415mph (668km/h) at 24,600ft (7,498m) was obtained, and by 26 July the third XP-75 had reached 420mph (676km/h) at 22,000ft (6,706m), but the rate of climb attained by this aircraft was approximately 3,000ft/min (914m/min) compared to the originally projected 5,600ft/min (1,707m/min).

On 6 April 1944 General Chidlaw reported the results of flight tests by Materiel Command officers on the second XF-75, which by now incorporated numerous changes resulting from flight experience. Many of the points which previously had caused difficulty were now sorted (the landing and take off characteristics were excellent, vision good, lateral stability satisfactory, and the aircraft accelerated rapidly), but several deficiencies were still present. These were: (a) unsatisfactory longitudinal stability, (b) completely unsatisfactory ailerons, (c) engine cooling remained inadequate, (d) the propeller had been throwing considerable oil, (e) the speed of the aircraft was mediocre compared to other late model fighters, and (f) the rudder forces were somewhat high.

It was around this time that the decision was made between the contractor and Material Command to extend the ailerons to the wing tips and to redesign the tip to approximately a rectangular plan form. By now five prototypes were flying, though 44-32163, the fifth XP-75, was lost on 8 April in a fatal accident at Cleveland, in which it was believed that the Fisher civilian pilot (Hamilton Wagner) had engaged in low-level aerobatics beyond the established restricted limits. An investigation of the wreckage disclosed that the entire tail section was lost in flight due to structural failure, the right aileron had also detached, and these failures resulted in an uncontrolled descent and crash. This particular aircraft had been restricted to certain speeds and manoeuvres due to longitudinal instability but this had been corrected by the installation of a completely new tail which had moved the centre of gravity forward. A subsequent investigation showed that the tail had been structurally sound, but the XP-75's current longitudinal instability had possibly imposed unduly high air loads on the tailplane; the basic cause of the accident was thought to be longitudinal instability.

The eighth and final XP-75 prototype, 44-32166, was to receive all of the new features - dive flaps, bubble canopy, new production type tail installation including retractable tail wheel, compensating gun sight and automatic pilot; when completed it was to go to Eglin Field for tactical trials. By 10 August this aircraft had made five flights and some further unsatisfactory characteristics had been discovered, but a dorsal fin had been added as suggested by Material Command Wright Field. Meanwhile a report on progress dated 16 May 1944 called attention to the fact that the reasons for producing the P-75 had now been lost in redesign, that Fisher's design engineering was behind schedule, and that flight tests so far still indicated an unsatisfactory performance.

On 5 June 1944 personnel from the Resources Control Section at Wright Field visited Fisher Body to determine the contributing factors behind the delayed production of the P-75. Currently 3,000 people were engaged at Fisher on the project, with sub-assemblies also being built in several Fisher plants. The following conclusions were reached – again, the contributing factor causing delay to comply with the work schedule was engineering. The structure of the wing had been changed so much that essentially it was an entirely new wing. Another factor was the redesign of the empennage, though if the first newly designed tail assembly proved satisfactory on the eighth XP-75, production would accelerate rapidly. And, as noted above, it had also been necessary to move the centre of gravity forward by 11in (27.9cm), which change had been made in the forward fuselage immediately forward of the engine.

Six XP-75s had flown by 16 June (with one lost), though none had been accepted by the AAF. The pressure on the project increased during the summer of 1944, Engineering Division stating on 17 July that performance data on the XP-75s was not coming through quickly enough; again the principal reason appeared to be that the engines were not providing the required horsepower. Consequently, on 27 July Materiel Command ordered that one of the XF-75s should go to the Allison Division at Indianapolis for investigations into this shortcoming. By now the programme was being reviewed regularly and at a meeting on 31 July General Echols conceded that it was highly possible that the then new P-47N long range version of the Thunderbolt could perform the function for which the P-75 had been developed.

On 5 August 1944 the third XP-75 – the first XP-75A 44-32161 - was destroyed in a crash at Cleveland while the pilot was making speed runs at 23,000ft (7,010m). It appeared that an explosion jarred the plane and started a fire in the engine compartment, the pilot lost elevator control and he was attempting to make an emergency landing when the fire got out of control. Immediately after he bailed out (safely), the plane appeared to disintegrate in the air due to another explosion.

Information supplied on 30 August by the AAF's Operations, Commitments, and Requirements (OC&R) Department in Washington stated that a high speed of 427mph (687km/h) at 25,000ft (7,620m) had been recorded in the XP-75. It was also stated that the type did not offer the possibilities offered by the P-47N which had a high speed of 463mph (745km/h) at 30,000ft (9,144m) and a combat radius of action of 1,300 miles (2,092km). Therefore, OC&R now recommended that the P-75 should be eliminated.

With bubble canopy and polished metal surfaces 44-32165 looks an altogether cleaner aircraft. Apart from national markings all of the examples built seem to have sported a predominantly natural metal finish. *Gerald H. Balzer*

The last of the prototypes was 44-32166. The first shot shows it with a rounded fin tip, the second with the fin squared off, just an example of the alterations and modifications made to the P-75 family in an effort to improve the aircraft's performance and flying qualities. Note the fairings for the nose guns directly behind the contra-rotating propeller. *Gerald H. Balzer*

The first production P-75A was 44-44549 which is seen here outside the control tower (it is thought) at Cleveland. *Gerald H. Balzer*

Speed runs were showing that the fighter had fallen short of its high speed guarantee by some 30mph (48km/h). In an attempt to correct this, to provide substantial increases in engine power, production aircraft 44-44551 did have an experimental intercooler installed for the first stage of the engine supercharger. This may have recovered part of the shortfall in performance and, had not programme termination intervened, the change would have been incorporated in the production run.

The first production P-75 44-44549 flew at Cleveland on 15 September 1944 and, at a gross weight of 17,800lb (8,074kg), it recorded the following official performance data – high speed 404mph (650km/h) at 32,000ft (9,754m), sea level rate of climb 2,400ft/min (732m/min), range 2,030 miles (3,266km). Tests with this aircraft showed that the engine temperature was at times 29°F above the allowable maximum (the V3420's tendency to overheat was always a disappointment).

This aircraft had completed seven flights by 27 September, at which point it was flown to Eglin Field in Florida. In fact in September and October 1944 the first two production aircraft were both sent to Eglin Field for tactical suitability trials, but these were not completed because of the termination of the production contract early in October. And 44-44549 was destroyed in a crash on 10 October when flying

44-44549 again, here shown on 22 September 1944 with square wingtips and rounded fin, but after having had small finlets attached to the ends of the horizontal tail in another attempt to improve the aircraft's stability. *Greater St Louis Air & Space Museum*

Another excellent air-to-air shot of 44-44550 which here provides good underside detail, including the substantial two-section air intake scoop located just to the rear of the wings and the unusual undercarriage doors or covers (the main gears were never fully enclosed). *Greater St Louis Air & Space Museum*

This photo of 44-44551 highlights the much revised fin design compared to the form employed on 44-32164 and other prototypes. *Gerald H. Balzer*

One of the Eagles receives attention outside the Aeroproducts hanger (on the left). A North American B-25 Mitchell (serial 42-87550) stands behind. *Gerald H. Balzer*

An unidentified production P-75 (possibly 44-44550) showing the Eagle in its final form with the final square fin and horizontal tail. It has the two-section belly scoop and F4U Corsair main landing gear, and the upper fuselage on this aircraft has been painted over in a dark colour to prevent reflected sunlight affecting the pilot's vision. *Terry Panopalis*

from Eglin Field. Mechanical failure of the propeller made the pilot, Major Harry Bolster, attempt a dead-stick landing in rough country; tragically, he was killed.

The following is taken from an original Fisher 'Advance Descriptive Data' brochure dated 20 May 1944 and gives an idea of how a pilot would have to approach flying the aircraft. In manoeuvres, snap rolls at speeds greater than 180mph (290km/h), and outside loops, were prohibited, but all other manoeuvres were unrestricted. The maximum permissible speed in a dive was 500mph (805km/h) IAS at heights from to 10,000ft (3,048m), and then 425mph (684km/h) IAS at 20,000ft (6,096m). The

An unidentified Eagle is prepared for gun-firing trials. The instruction on the top of the front of the building states "Caution: Aircraft and Guns must be securely fixed in immovable position before firing". *Gerald H. Balzer*

One of the P-75s taxis out for a test flight. *Gerald H. Balzer*

The last Eagle to fly was 44-44553 and the aircraft is seen here possibly after having been 'put out to grass'. Again, the final fin shape is well shown. *Gerald H. Balzer*

predicted maximum diving speed was 540mph (869km/h) IAS, but this speed would not be attained until a dangerously low altitude had been reached. In a dive it was recommended that longitudinal trim be maintained at approximately zero stick force.

The stalling characteristics were described as "excellent" and a deliberate stall in straight level flight would result in a warning buffet 5-6mph (8-10km/h) above the stall. At the stall the nose would drop with the wings level and adequate aileron control was maintained while the nose was dropping. The altitude loss during the stall and the recovery was very small. In a tight turn the warning buffet was again felt 5-6mph (8-10km/h) before the stall, and when the stall occurred the aircraft did not tend to whip. In the landing approach condition, with flaps and gear extended, the warning was not as pronounced as in the clean condition, but it still advised the pilot of the impending stall 2-3mph (3-5km/h) before the nose would drop. There was no tendency to fall off on a wing.

Intentional spinning was not recommended since there is no combat utility in this manoeuvre, and spins were prohibited when external fuel tanks were carried; inverted spins were also prohibited. However, there were no restrictions on aerobatics except those imposed on inverted flight by the reduction in oil pressure resulting from failure to scavenge the engine. Finally, when taxying the wide tread main undercarriage made the fighter easy to control through gentle use of the brakes. Because of the high power installed in the aircraft, the application of take-off power with brakes locked would raise the tail off the ground.

On 3 October 1944 the Aircraft Requirements Board, Operations, Commitments and Requirements, met and recommended a limit to the production of P-75s to no more than 30 examples. The primary reason behind this move was that the fighter's performance still did not compare favourably with that offered by the P-47N and the North American P-51H, and that flight tests by the Proving Ground Command had confirmed that the true performance fell short of the original estimated figures. It was also stated that by the time the P-75 could attain full production it would have become surplus to AAF requirements anyway. After the cancellation of all except 30 P-75s had been cleared, a conference held at Fisher's Cleveland base on 18 October resulted in a further decision to cancel the experimental contract altogether, and to deliver just the remaining aircraft as they were.

The initial production machines were to be retained for experimental purposes. In fact the closure of the production contract left five production P-75s flyable or very nearly complete - numbers 2, 3, 4, 5 and 6. These were to be turned over to the Engineering Division for experimental work and to help with the development of the V3420 engine. A new contract was negotiated with Fisher calling for the completion of production airframes 2, 3, 4 and 5 and then to store number 6 (44-44554) in Cleveland as a source of spare parts; apart from the completion of the wing panels, no further work was to be done on this aircraft. The five completed production machines were serials 44-44549 to 44-44553.

Number 2 (44-44550) was assigned to the NACA Ames Aeronautical Laboratory and ferried to Moffett Field. Here drag and propeller tests were conducted in the full scale wind tunnel, followed by flight correlation tests to provide information against the tunnel data; additional sorties would assess the P-75's flying qualities, its stability and control and performance. With this research programme completed, 44-44550 went to McClellan AFB on 24 May 1946 for reclamation and scrapping.

In the early part of 1943 General Motors had decided to transfer all activity connected with its P-75 fighter to its Allison division. The intercooler installation in number 3 (44-44551) was completed and the aircraft was then delivered to Allison for engine flight testing on 28 June 1945. The trials had not started by V-J day but, since the airframe had been instrumented and was ready for flight, Allison requested that 44-44551 be assigned to them under a blanket bailment contract for 10 hours of flight testing. When this work was concluded the fighter was passed to the War Assets Administration on 3 August 1946.

The fourth and fifth production P-75s were flown to Patterson Field and placed in storage in case they might be needed for future V3420 development work. By March 1945 the second, fourth, sixth, seventh, and eighth experimental XP-75s had been delivered to the AAF and upon arrival at Wright Field were placed in Class 26 (i.e. articles of all classes of property which were set aside for ground instructional purposes); they were later scrapped. By 12 March 1947 the remaining P-75s, with the exception of 44-44551 purchased by Allison, had been declared excess and were disposed of through the War Assets Administration. However, the last production P-75A (44-44553) has survived and is on display at the Wright-Patterson Air Force Base Museum in Dayton.

However simple and straightforward the idea of producing a new first class fighter design might have seemed, in a process utilising as many available sub-assemblies as possible from other types to ensure that the new type is ready in a much shorter time than normal, the P-75 showed that in practice this is extremely difficult to achieve. But with the stress of war it was worth a try. Outwardly, the P-75 story and programme look rather a mess but it must be stressed that, for an organisation new to aircraft design, Fisher had achieved much. Sadly all of this effort came to nothing and in total just 13 XP-75s and production P-75s were flown.

XP-75 Structure

Fisher's XP-75 and P-75 were single-seat low-wing interceptor and long-range escort fighters of all metal construction. Their wing was the full cantilever stressed skin type and consisted of a straight centre section with two outer panels that were five-spar Curtiss P-40 wing panels with modified tips. The ailerons had a longer span than the original P-40 ailerons and split trailing edge flaps were fitted; the control surfaces were fabric-covered. The empennage, with modifications and a fixed tailwheel, came from the Douglas A-24 attack aircraft and comprised conventional internally braced and rigidly fixed horizontal and vertical stabilisers with all metal rudder and elevators. A fully retractable landing gear was used with components taken from the Vought F4U Corsair naval fighter.

There was some variation in the shape and size of the tail and fin, with later airframes having a much larger tail and squared off fin. For example, to begin with the last two XP-75A prototypes and the first pair of production P-75As had a tall round fin, but in due course 44-44550 was modified and received the enlarged and square-tipped form for both the horizontal and vertical surfaces.

The all metal semi-monocoque fuselage, made in 24ST aluminium alloy, was divided into three sections, forward, mid, and rear, with the wing centre section assembled as an integral part of the fuselage. Built around four longerons, the forward section contained the gun compartment, pilot's cockpit and main fuel tank, with the canopy consisting of front and side panels from a Curtiss P-40. The mid-section housed the engine compartment (which extended into the rear section), a stainless steel fire wall was located forward of the engine, and then the rear section supported the tail gear, tail cone and tail surfaces. The large oil and coolant air intake scoop and radiators were positioned beneath the mid/rear fuselage.

Power came from an Allison V3420 with variable-speed two-stage supercharger mounted in the fuselage to the rear of the cockpit and driving either a 13ft [3.96m] diameter narrow-blade propeller (on early examples) or an Aeroproducts 12ft 7in (3.84m) diameter six-blade constant speed contra-rotating propeller (on later airframes) with wider blades. Two long extension shafts, rotating in opposite directions, connected the engine to the propeller through a reduction gear box; this arrangement, used for balancing, was similar to that employed by the Bell P-39 fighter. As noted in Appendix Two, contra-rotation of the blades eliminated torque at the propeller – here, similarly, contra-rotation of the shafts eliminated all torsional reaction between the powerplant and the aircraft.

The normal fuel load came to 535galUS (2,025lit), with 321galUS (1,215lit) in a fuselage tank and 214galUS (810lit) in the wings; two 75galUS (284lit) or 110galUS (416lit) drop tanks could be carried to give a maximum load of 755galUS (2,858lit). Apart from the changes to the empennage and wings the various prototypes were unalike in other certain details, especially so in relation to the cockpit canopy.

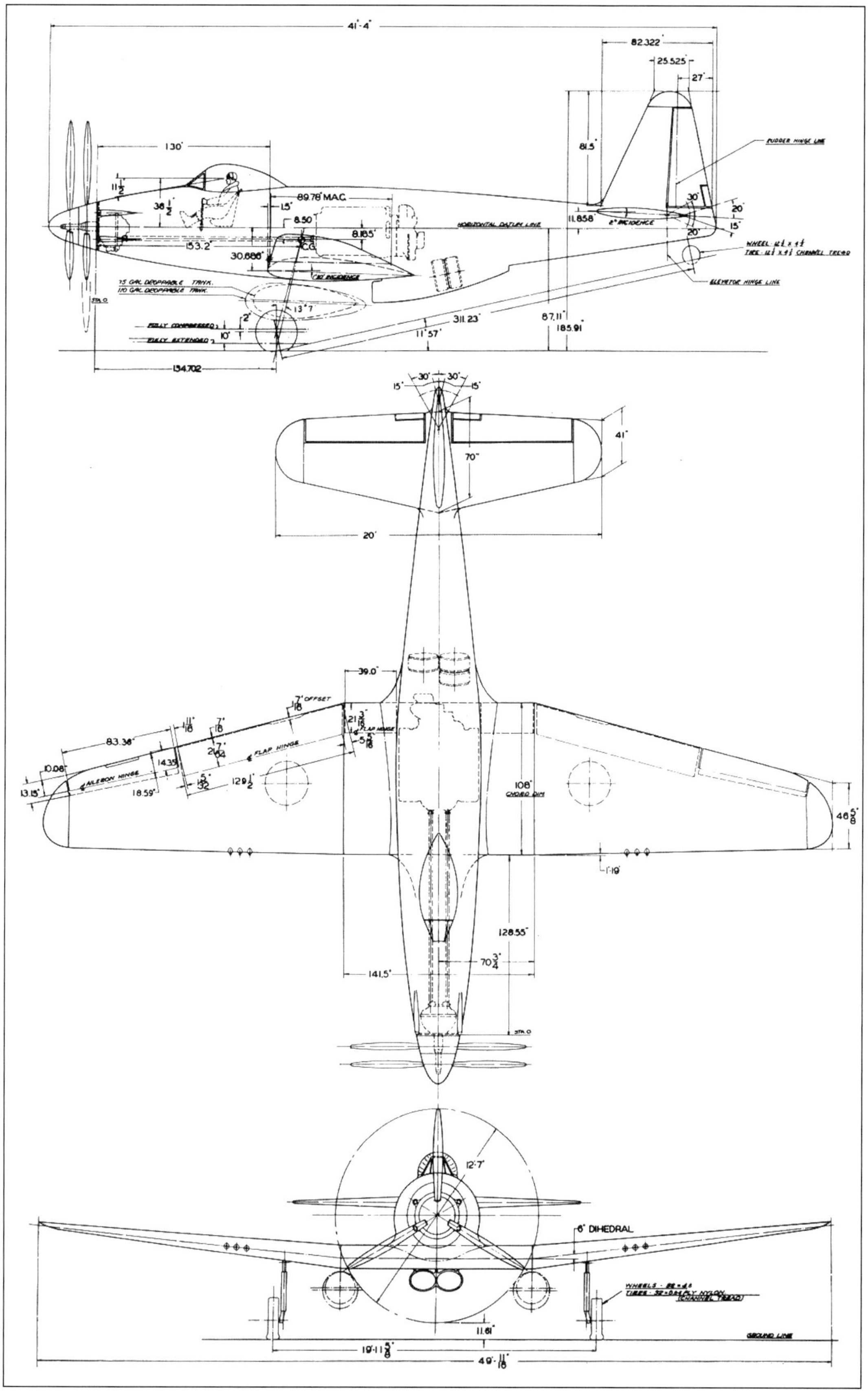

ABOVE A big player in the future of the P-75 Eagle while the fighter was an ongoing programme, and indeed with all of the wartime AAF fighters included in this volume, was General Oliver P. Echols who was the Army Air Force's Chief Materiel Officer throughout World War II. *USAF*

LEFT Original manufacturer's drawing of the Fisher P-75 as at 20 May 1944. *Fisher via Chris Gibson*

Views of 44-44550 in flight taken on 25 September 1944. Note the almost fully open rear shutter of the underfuselage air intake.
US National Archives via Alan Griffith

XP-75 data

Note: the data given below comes from original documents and should be accurate. However, sources differ considerably and, with variations between individual airframes (and with no official tests having been conducted on the type), the performance figures are estimates. With the extended wing the span became 49ft 4in (15.03m) and wing area 347sq.ft (32.27sq.m).

XP-75 Data at 23 March 1944 as Long Range Offensive Fighter

Length:	41ft 6in (12.65m)
Wing span:	49ft 0.75in (14.95m)
Wing area:	342sq.ft (31.81sq.m)
Design gross weight (no bombs):	13,543lb (6,143kg)
Maximum take-off weight (with external tanks):	18,665lb (8,466kg)
Powerplant:	1 x 2,600hp (1,939kW) Allison V3420-23 24-cylinder liquid-cooled double 'V' inline engine (War Emergency Power rating = 3,000hp/2,237kw)
Powerplant (first two prototypes):	1 x 2,600hp (1,939kW) Allison V3420-19
Maximum speed:	389mph (626km/h) at sea level, 439mph (706km/h) at 20,000ft (6,096m)
Maximum rate of climb:	3,600ft/min (1,097m/min) at sea level (War Emergency Power)
Service ceiling:	37,000ft (11,278m)
Armament (all versions):	10 x 0.50in (12.7mm) machine guns – six in outer wing panels outboard of the propeller arc, four in nose, 2 x 500lb (227kg) bombs on racks under centre wing panel.

P-75 Production Aircraft data at 20 May 1944

Length:	41ft 4in (12.60m)
Wing span:	49ft 0.75in (14.95m)
Wing area:	342sq.ft (31.81sq.m)
Empty weight:	11,308lb (5,129kg)
Design gross weight (maximum internal fuel and ammunition):	17,217lb (7,810kg)
Maximum take-off weight (with external tanks):	18,665lb (8,466kg)
Powerplant:	1 x 2,600hp (1,939kW) Allison V3420-23 24-cylinder liquid-cooled double 'V' inline engine (War Emergency Power rating = 3,000hp/2,237kw)
Maximum speed:	?
Maximum rate of climb:	4,850ft/min (1,478m/min) at sea level
Maximum range (with external tanks):	3,850 miles (6,195km)

15 Bell XP-77

The Bell XP-77 was designed as a lightweight, highly manoeuvrable wooden interceptor, it was built to test the practicability of 'small fighter theory' and also to study the feasibilities of mass production of a wooden fighter at a fraction of the time and cost of the average all metal fighter type.

This concept of a very light fighter had been considered previously with two other projects. The first, the Douglas XP-48 powered by a Ranger XV770 engine, was rejected early in 1940. The second was the Tucker XP-57 (with a Miller L510 engine) which died as a programme when Tucker went bankrupt in February 1941. Neither project had progressed beyond the drawing board when halted.

The early part of the war brought a huge increase in the production of fighter aircraft within the overall war programme. This threatened the supply of certain critical metals and materials used in aircraft manufacture, so research was directed towards new types of fighter which would make use of so-called 'non-strategic materials', and for designs that would permit the simplest and quickest manufacture by factories and workers not previously employed in aircraft production. The existing American fighters had generally concentrated on heavy armament, high speed and rugged airframes, at the expense of a fast rate of climb and maximum manoeuvrability. Demonstrations in combat of these latter capabilities by the Supermarine Spitfire and Messerschmitt 109, and later by the Mitsubishi A6M Zero, emphasised the importance for certain tactical operations of having such an interceptor.

Well known but nevertheless excellent photo showing the Bell XP-77 in flight. This is the second prototype 43-34916. *Bell via Gerald H. Balzer*

The XP-77 was small enough for the complete airframe to be tested inside a wind tunnel. *Bell via Gerald H. Balzer*

On 30 October 1941 AAF personnel met at Wright Field representatives from the Bell Aircraft Corporation of Buffalo in New York, including chief designer Robert J. Woods, to discuss the design of a lightweight interceptor. The resulting Bell proposal was called the Tri-4, and later D-6. Equipped with a supercharged Ranger XV770-9 engine, this would have a high speed of 410mph (660km/h) at 27,000ft (8,230m), a design gross weight of around 3,700lb (1,678kg) and would carry a 20mm cannon firing through the propeller hub plus two 0.50in (12.7mm) calibre machine guns in the nose synchronised to fire through the propeller. It would have a laminar flow wing and, with the critical situation regarding the supply of metals, Bell planned to use wood for the wings and metal just for the fuselage and tail surfaces. This would be the ultimate in small lightweight interceptor aircraft and Bell submitted a proposal to build six examples, with the first to be delivered within six months of contract approval.

On 16 May 1942 General Arnold authorised the procurement of 25 Tri-4 aircraft with provision to carry one 325lb (147kg) depth charge or one 300lb (136kg) bomb. However, the Tri-4 hinged on a modification of the Navy's Ranger V770-6 engine, in which form it would not be available in quantity for at least a year. The maximum number available from the Navy at present was six units, so General Echols recommended procurement of six aircraft using the available Ranger engines in lieu of twenty-five. The new type was designated XP-77, it was covered by project MX-272 and the order would come under Contract W535-AC-30864 of May 1942. Bell's project engineer for the XP-77 was Sam Treman.

Bell's original D-6 specification had called for a wood wing, metal fuselage and metal tail surfaces, but a second version was offered which called for construction entirely in wood. A study of both forms revealed that there were several advantages to the original design and Bell agreed to make either, but

LEFT Air-intake detail. *Bell via Gerald H. Balzer*

BELOW A picture taken during the assembly of one of the prototypes. *Bell via Gerald H. Blaze*

The Ranger V770 engine installation during assembly of one of the prototypes. The engine was attached to the airframe without any shock mounts and as a result, at certain power settings, the V770 produced unacceptable levels of vibration. *Bell via Gerald H. Balzer*

indicated that a delay of one month could be expected if the original mixed wood/metal design was selected. Wright Field proposed ordering the latter all-wood type, this was agreed and the contract now included the six XP-77s, one skeleton airframe for static testing, plus wind tunnel models.

The mock-up Committee conducted its inspection of the XP-77 on 21 and 22 September 1942. It pronounced the mock-up "fairly complete, and, in general, very satisfactory for the purpose intended." However, a total of 54 changes to the design were recommended.

The XP-77 project schedule suffered its first setback in January 1943 when Bell advised Materiel Command that the first flight aircraft would be completed on 1 May, which represented a four-month set back from the contract schedule. The reason behind the delay was that the new fighter incorporated materials (wood and plastic plus magnesium alloy), and hence processes, that were entirely foreign to Bell's experience, so the firm had had to subcontract work to specialists in these areas of construction. This move had not proved as successful as first hoped, as explained by Colonel H. F. Cooper, former XP-77 project officer.

He declared that "the progress of this project has been disappointing both in time as well as cost. One of the original selling points for this type of airplane was the opinion of Bell that a wooden airplane of light weight construction could be produced with a minimum of man hours and cost as compared to present day conventional fighter types. This had proven a mistaken idea. The majority of this airplane was subcontracted by Bell to manufacturers who were supposed to be familiar with wooden fabrication methods, yet, due to the nature of high strength requirements of fighter airplane construction, training of fabrication personnel and the trial of new methods, construction was considerably delayed. The wing contract with Gosen Veneer ran to such a high cost, as well as delayed deliveries on the wing, that Bell, on 1 October 1943, cancelled the subcontract with Gosen and turned the wing subcontract for the flight wings and one static test plane over to the Vidal Research Corporation."

The first wing was not delivered until 3 February 1944 (but the Chief Army Inspector reported that the quality and workmanship was greatly improved over the wings obtained from Goshen). However, by May 1943 Material Division was expressing serious concern, not only about the XP-77, but also with over-time running to high levels on the Curtiss XP-60 and XP-62 (Chapters Nine and Ten) and on the Douglas XB-19A, Boeing XB-29 and Douglas XA-26 bombers. All of these programmes were falling behind.

Then, on 26 May 1943, Engineering Division recommended that the XP-77 contract be terminated immediately. The main reason given was that the contractor had undertaken more experimental development than it could satisfactorily handle and, unless relief was afforded work on higher priority Bell projects, the concurrent P-63 and P-59 fighters would suffer. In addition, by the second half of 1943 any worries regarding problems with the supply of aluminium and other aircraft alloys had faded. In fact Bell was working on versions of its P-39 and P-63 piston-powered fighters and the new P-59 jet fighter, there seemed little future for the XP-77 and the manufacturer pushed for delays in the light weight fighter programme to help keep these other types on schedule.

On 2 August 1943 General Echols advised that action had been initiated to terminate the XP-77 project, except for the completion of tests on the static test airframe and to complete two flight articles. This action was considered advisable in order to obtain valuable flight data for this type of 'plywood aircraft'. The next day Bell was instructed to proceed with the construction of the two flying articles in lieu of the six previously required, purely for academic interest. The serial numbers carried by the two completed XP-77s were 43-34915 and 43-34916, while 43-34917 to 43-34920 had been allocated to the now cancelled airframes. The static test airframe was delivered to Wright Field on 20 July 1944.

On 11 August Wright Field notified Bell that, in an effort to reduce additional costs and engineering work, it was considered advisable to fit the two prototypes with the standard unsupercharged Ranger V770-7 engine (the AAF version of the Navy's V770-6). This unit offered the same level of power up to 12,000ft (3,658m) altitude but the move killed off any chance of installing the supercharged XV770-9. A memo from Air Material Command, written by Colonel H.Z. Bogert of Engineering Division on 11 August 1943, stated "our action on the P-77 has been very discouraging to the Ranger Engine people, since it is apparent that there will be no large production of the V770-9."

Walk-around views of the first XP-77 43-34915 taken at Bell's factory soon after completion. The name of the manufacturer's test pilot, Jack Woolams, is stencilled just beneath the cockpit canopy. Note the gun ports to the sides of the propeller spinner. *Bell via Gerald H. Balzer*

ABOVE The small size of Bell's fighter prototype made 43-34915 easy to move around on its own tricycle undercarriage. *Bell via Gerald H. Balzer*

RIGHT This view appears to show the first prototype undergoing an engine ground run at the Bell plant. *Bell via Gerald H. Balzer*

Flight test

The XP-77's maiden flight took place at Niagara Falls on 1 April 1944 with the aircraft crewed by Jack V. Woolams, Bell's senior experimental test pilot. The flight lasted for only 25 minutes due to to weather conditions, wherein the ceiling dropped from 2,500ft to 1,200ft (762m to 366m) and accompanied by snow. This was purely a shake-down flight with no attempt being made to obtain exact performance data. Woolams reported that the aircraft handled very satisfactorily with light controls and no apparent vices; engine operation was normal and the cooling system proved very effective. The pilot further stated that very little effect upon longitudinal stability was caused by the operation during flight of the landing gear or flaps. By now the second prototype was way behind schedule, its present status being approximately 78% complete, and its wing panel had still to be delivered to Bell.

Army Air Force tests were conducted in late July and early August 1944 by the AAF Proving Ground Command at Eglin Field in Florida, the second XP-77 having been ferried to Eglin from Bell's Niagara Falls plant on 22 July by the aircraft's Project Officer, Captain George D. Colchagoff. The arrival of the first prototype at Eglin was, however, delayed by two weeks after it had been grounded due to damage incurred from a failure of its nose wheel.

The official flight tests to determine the XP-77's operational suitability were conducted using 43-34916. The resulting report noted that "the general handling characteristics of the XP-77 are satisfactory, although restrictions on the airplane prevented any dives, spins, or violent manoeuvres to be performed. One objectionable feature of the control system was the fixed trim tabs on the ailerons and rudder. Only the elevator tabs may be controlled from the cockpit, and this results in only one condition of flight in which the airplane will fly stick and rudder free for each ground setting of the aileron and rudder tabs. However, stick forces are light and control can be easily maintained by holding the stick and rudder through all speed ranges encountered during these tests. Visibility is good for all conditions of flight and ground handling. Noise and vibration in the cockpit is considerable. The cockpit becomes very cold and uncomfortable in cold weather and at high altitude when cockpit heat is not available."

The high/maximum speeds attained during these tests was 316mph (508km/h) at 5,000ft (1,524m), instead of the 346mph (557km/h) contained in the model specification, and then 304mph (489km/h) at sea level, 295mph (475km/h) at 20,000ft (6,096m) and 258mph (415km/h) at 30,000ft (9,144m); the rate of climb at sea level was 2,900ft/min (884m/min) as compared with the 3,050ft/min (930m/min) contained in the a model specification. And the gross weight was 3,857lb (1,750kg) as against the design gross weight of 3,700lb (1,678kg). War Emergency Power was available only to 2,000ft (610m), above which the manifold pressure dropped off rapidly.

43-34915 seen after suffering a mishap through failure of the nose wheel undercarriage, not long before it was to have been ferried to Eglin Field for AAF trials. The pictures give a rare opportunity to see upper and underside surface details. *Gerald H. Balzer*

As a result of these trials, on 18 August 1944 Colonel Kenneth P. Bergquist, Assistant Chief of Air Staff at Operations, Commitments and Requirements (OC&R), recommended that no further consideration be given to production of the XP-77. Although the prototype's fuel consumption was very low, its performance and armament was so inferior to other AAF types, and to enemy fighters, that the type's use in combat "should not be contemplated". General Arnold approved this decision, though for a short period Bell's aircraft was considered for use as a trainer.

On 17 October 1944 Colonel C. B. Overacker, the Director of the Proof Division, reported on the XP-77's capabilities as a possible advanced trainer, and in doing so gave a graphic illustration for what the XP-77 was like in the air. He wrote:

"**1. Poor Take-off and Landing Characteristics.** Due to the mushy feel at low speeds, it is necessary to land the airplane at speeds about 20mph [32km/h] higher than current fighter types. There is not sufficient elevator control to hold the nose wheel off the ground, and the nose falls through as soon as the main wheels touch. With all three wheels on the runway the

Further walk-around views of the first XP-77, taken this time after delivery to AAF control and dated 7 August 1944. They are probably taken at Eglin Field. Little change has been made to the airframe, but the test pilot's name has now been removed and various official notes stencilled on the side of the fuselage, including "suitable for aromatic fuel". Also, the gun ports have been faired over. *AAF via Terry Panopalis*

drag of the airplane is low, and an excessively long distance is required to bring the airplane to a stop. The take-off run is excessively long, as the airplane does not become airborne until about 130mph (209km/h) is attained.

2. Unsuitable Handling Characteristics. Although the airplane is statically stable about all axes, it combines very light stick forces with extremely rapid response. The effectiveness of the controls is so great as to give the impression of instability. These characteristics are not dangerous to an experienced fighter pilot, but the extreme sensitivity of the airplane would provide many opportunities for an inexperienced pilot to get into trouble. The elevator trim tab is not sufficient to trim the airplane for high speeds. No aileron or rudder trim are provided, lateral and directional trim are unnecessary in this airplane, because of the very light aileron and rudder forces, but this detracts from the value of the airplane as a trainer.

3. Unsuitability for Gunnery. The airplane is entirely unsuited for gunnery work, having very little visibility over the nose (about 2°). The airplane's extreme sensitivity makes it a poor gunnery platform; the very light rudder forces result in a tendency to yaw the airplane inadvertently.

4. Low Ceiling. The airplane is equipped with a sea level engine, which gives good performance up to about 15,000ft (4,572m). But a fighter trainer of this type should provide good altitude performance so that it can be used for oxygen indoctrination.

5. Insufficient Ruggedness and Durability. During the tests conducted at this station, the airplane was continually out of commission for repairs to minor items such as cowling formers, oil cooler mountings, exhaust stacks and shrouds, and landing gear door fittings. Many of these failures appeared to be the result of vibration. Although no failures of landing gear structural members were encountered, it is doubtful if the airplane would stand up under continuous rough landings. Wooden construction is considered unsuitable for a trainer; repairs are difficult, and it is doubtful if the airplane could withstand a belly landing. The whole airplane is too delicate to stand the rough handling that a training airplane is required to withstand."

In July 1944 Bell's own pilots had themselves flight tested the second prototype. During spin tests it was found that all spins were violently oscillatory, but that recovery was rapid and positive. Also, the V770 had been hung rigidly on the airframe without the use of shock-mounts, so excessive vibration was experienced at certain speed settings.

On 2 October 1944 the second XP-77 43-34916, which was being prepared for a return flight to Wright Field for further official AAF performance testing, crashed near Eglin Field. The pilot's statement was that he was attempting to perform an Immelman manoeuvre and the aircraft had inadvertently fallen into an inverted spin. He added that he had been able to effect recovery of the aircraft from this type of spin, but here the XP-77 immediately went into a normal but flat spin from which he was unable to extricate the aircraft. The pilot therefore bailed out and was uninjured, but 43-34916 was a total loss.

The first prototype was delivered to and accepted by the AAF; the second was delivered but was lost in this crash before it could be accepted at Wright Field. The XP-77 contract was terminated by the end of 1944, although the first prototype was used for further flight trials and spent time both at Wright Field and at Elgin. It also attended several postwar air shows before becoming an air base gate guard; weather took its toll and eventually 43-34915 was destroyed.

The basic concept that a fighter incorporating the requisite strength requirements could be constructed efficiently and expeditiously by the use of wood was not borne out by the XP-77 programme. This became apparent as more and more delays were encountered during the fabrication of the airframes. Consequently, when the flight performance also failed to reach expectations it was decided that the XP-77 should not go into production.

The short-lived second prototype 43-34916 parked alongside Boeing B-29 Superfortress serial 42-63408. The huge bomber stresses once again the XP-77's diminutive size. AAF *via Gerald H. Balzer*

XP-77 structure

The XP-77 was a single seat, lightweight interceptor fighter. Its laminar flow cantilever wing panels, detachable from the fuselage, consisted of a single spar covered in stressed skin and fabricated primarily using resin bonded laminated wood. The fixed position vertical and horizontal stabilisers were full cantilever and again the control surfaces had external and internal structures in laminated wood; the flap had 60° maximum deflection. XP-77's fuselage employed the same style of resin bonded wood structure, here using a stressed skin/stringer combination with transverse frames and built as a single unit.

To match the inverted V-12 power unit the fuselage cross-section was of triangular shape and the engine itself was a Ranger V770 incorporating a two-blade Aeroproducts 9ft 0in (2.74m) diameter propeller. The engine was covered by an extended cowling which pushed the cockpit well to the rear of the aircraft. A tricycle undercarriage was fitted and the armament was two 0.50in (12.70mm) machine guns mounted in the fuselage nose and synchronized to fire through the propeller arc. Normal internal fuel capacity was 53galUS (201lit) and an auxiliary 37galUS (140lit) external drop tank could be carried under the fuselage, to give a maximum 90galUS (341lit); maximum bomb load was 325lb (147kg).

TOP And another photo which illustrates graphically how small the XP-77 was, with the pilot here seemingly squashed into the cockpit. AAF *via Gerald H. Balzer*

ABOVE This shot of 43-34915 appears to have been taken after its retirement and while the airframe was in use as a gate guard. It has acquired some additional markings. *Gerald H. Balzer*

RIGHT Air-to-air pictures of the XP-77 seems to be very rare. This one again shows the second prototype. AAF *via Gerald H. Balzer*

43-34915 on show at the airbase at Wright Patterson in 1946. *W.T. Larkins via Gerald H. Balzer*

XP-77 data as at 26 June 1945

Length:	22ft 10.5in (6.97m)
Wing span:	27ft 6in (8.38m)
Wing area:	100sq.ft (9.30sq.m)
Empty weight:	2,855lb (1,295kg)
Gross weight:	3,671lb (1,665kg)
Gross weight with 325lb/147kg store:	4,028lb (1,827kg)
Powerplant:	1 x 520hp (388kW) Ranger XV770-17 12-cylinder air-cooled inline inverted Vee piston engine (War Emergency Power 670hp/500kW)
Maximum speed:	330mph (531km/h) at 4,000ft (1,219m), 328mph (528km/h) at 12,600ft (3,840m)
Maximum rate of climb:	3,630ft/min (1,106m/min)
Service ceiling:	30,100ft (9,174m)
Absolute ceiling:	31,000ft (9,449m)
Normal range:	305 miles (491km)
Maximum range:	550 miles (885km)
Armament:	2 x 0.50in (12.70mm) machine guns in fuselage, 1 x 100lb (45kg) or 300lb (136kg) bomb or 1 x 325lb (147kg) depth charge

16 Northrop XP-79

The Northop XP-79 was a remarkable machine for its time – a short range jet-propelled flying wing interceptor fighter that in concept was far ahead of most types then under development. The story of its creation is quite involved but the Flight Test section of this chapter is relatively short, because the sole prototype was lost in a tragic crash just minutes into its maiden flight.

Scale models

The XP-79 was preceded by scale model research aircraft, in fact a series of gliders that were known by their AAF project numbers MX-324 and MX-334. Because of the unusual nature of the flying wing for fighter applications, it was felt that data on such a type's flying qualities would be desirable so that what would become the XP-79 prototype would not be a completely unknown quantity. To this end Air Technical Service Command decided to build a flying mock-up. Northrop agreed to undertake the construction and flight testing of this aircraft, but their engineering staff was not of sufficient size to assume the added burden brought about by the necessary design work. Consequently, it was agreed that Air Technical Service Command would engineer the project and then forward the necessary drawings on to Northrop.

In all three experimental glider models were built, all in plywood but with a welded steel tubing centre section, and test pilot John Myers conducted the first unpowered flight on 2 October 1943. The

The sole XP-79B seen on the ramp at Northrop's Hawthorne facility in June 1945. In the left is the low loader which was about to take the aircraft to Muroc for its flight trials. *Northrop via Harvey Mudd/Alan Griffith*

LEFT Avion artwork showing the rocket-powered XP-79 as it appeared at 29 April 1943, without any fins. *Alan Griffith*

BELOW By 7 December 1943 Avion's three-view drawing was showing an XP-79 with twin fins. *Alan Griffith*

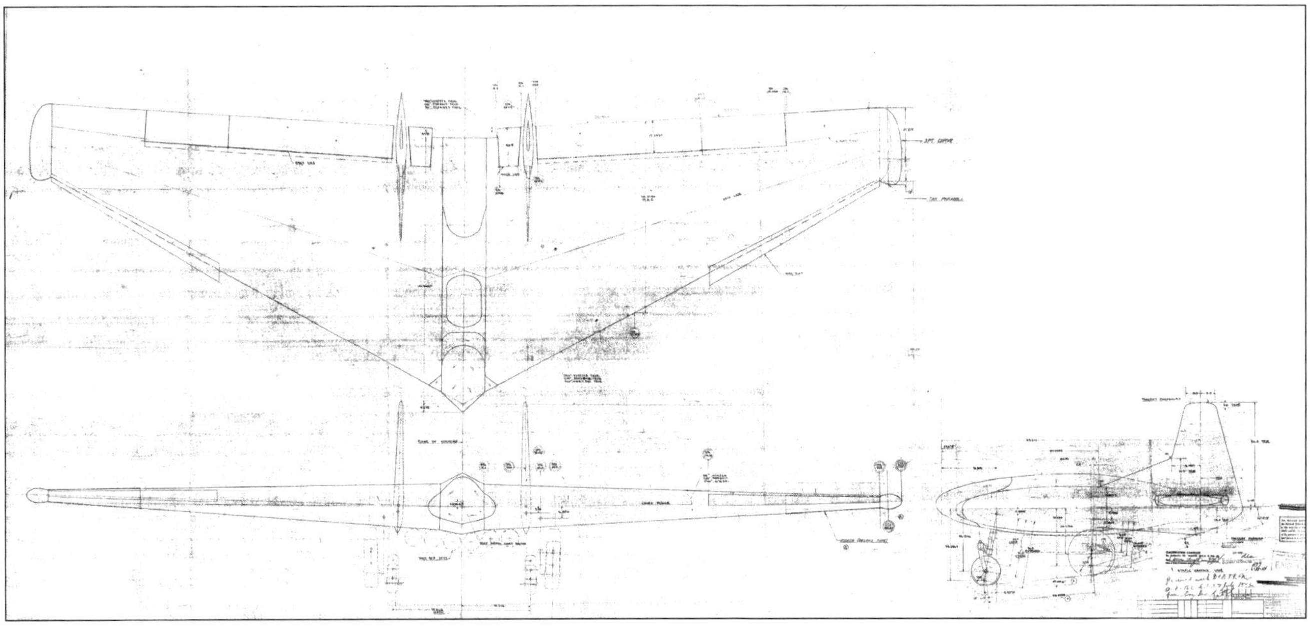

second glider was lost in an accident, but one had a small 200lb (0.9kN) thrust Aerojet rocket motor installed and on 5 July 1944 test pilot Harry Crosby completed the maiden powered sortie of this 'Rocket Wing'. For control the MX-324/MX-334 family had elevons which for roll operated asymmetrically and then in pitch symmetrically, leading edge slats placed close to the wings tips, and finally, inboard on the trailing edge, combined rudders/speed-brakes known as 'brudders'. These would split both above and beneath the wing and were a form of elevon augmentation that combined the rudder and air-brake functions into the control system (some sources call these 'split-flap rudders' or 'drag rudders'.

In September 1942 Northrop presented Air Materiel Command with a design proposal for a rocket propelled flying wing fighter (at the time the

One of the MX-324 gliders seen on the Muroc lakebed. *Alan Griffith*

One of the three MX-324 craft was fitted with a low power Aerojet rocket motor. Northrop's 'Rocket Wing' was completed under the strictest secrecy and the world did not learn of its existence until 12 February 1947. Its first flight was made on 5 July 1944 at Harper's Dry Lake in California and Northrop stated that the prone cockpit enabled the pilot to lie flat to withstand higher accelerations, and it also made possible a thinner aerofoil. *Alan Griffith*

designers called it the P-999). The company considered this to be a worthwhile project, but at this time its factory workload meant that it did not have sufficient engineering manpower and shop facilities to take it forward itself (Northrop was a small company and a shortage of work space and manpower was a problem throughout the war). A letter written by John Northrop on 20 March 1945 clarified the proposal, saying "the basic arrangement of what is now known as the XP-79 airplane appeared to have important military characteristics including high speeds in the order of 560mph (901km/h), rates of climb in the order of 7,000ft/min (2,134m/min), ceilings in the order of 100,000ft (30,480m), very high allowable manoeuvre factors both positive and negative due to the use of a prone pilot's position, ability to ram enemy aircraft without damage to itself, and numerous others [author's note: this is the only known reference to the XP-79 being used as a ram aircraft].

After lengthy conferences it was decided that the fighter was to be procured from Northrop, but with the understanding that the manufacturer would then subcontract 100% of the engineering and fabrication work. As such Northrop would be responsible for the general supervision of the project only, and would not undertake any of the design or construction. Air Materiel Command, however, wanted Northrop to make available its experience in the design of flying wing aircraft, along with its knowledge of fabricating magnesium structures.

As first proposed the XP-79 rocket powered prone pilot fighter interceptor was to have an airframe been built entirely in welded magnesium alloy, It was to be powered by a 2,000lb (9kN) thrust Aerojet rocket and the fuels/propellants for this motor were red fuming nitric acid and monoethylaniline (aniline). The former will readily react with magnesium and consequently, for this reason and for the potential effects of both propellants mixing away from the combustion chamber, the fuel tanks needed to be protected from any potential battle damage. Thus, the XP-79's magnesium alloy monocoque wing structure was to have skin thicknesses varying from 3/4in (19mm) at the leading edge down to 3/16in (4.75mm) at the trailing edge. Special protective coatings would also have to be developed for the fuel tanks themselves since the XP-79 was to have integral tanks and it was vital to have their walls screened by a coating not affected by the acid.

Welded magnesium was not classed as a strategic war material and Northrop also used it in its XP-56 fighter prototype (Chapter Seven), but new fabrication techniques had to be developed such as the Heliarc (helium arc) welding process. The prone pilot would have a pressure cabin and, initially, a retractable skid type undercarriage was to be fitted - four skids in all with two on each side of the centre section. The take off would involve a wheeled dolly, a catapult or greased tracks, though later two expendable 1,000lb (4.5kN) thrust jet-assisted take-off rockets became the choice. However, by early July 1943 the skid undercarriage had been abandoned and replaced by a retractable quadricycle arrangement. The airframe itself was to be stressed to withstand +/-12g.

The firm selected by Northrop to build the fighter prototypes was Avion Incorporated near Maywood in California, which had recently been established and was run by several former employees of the Vultee company (the XP-79 would be their first and indeed only project). Procurement action for three prototypes, a static test airframe, wind tunnel models and engineering data was started on 12 January 1943 and resulted in Contract W535-AC-36997. Northrop allocated its N-14 designation to the project and the AAF's Materiel Division assigned Project Number MX-365; the allotted serials were 43-52437 to 43-52439.

Unfortunately Avion did not prove up to the task, as will be seen shortly. Referring to John Northrop's 1945 letter once more: "Avion was given complete information and full responsibility on the project for the first year. For the next six months Northrop assumed more active direction of aerodynamic matters and became specific rather than general in its recommendations concerning the project. After 18 months Northrop assumed complete direct supervision of the Avion engineering department through the assignment of a project engineer with full authority on the project. After about 22 months the whole operation was moved to the plant of Northrop Aircraft under complete Northrop jurisdiction."

The manufacturer of the rocket motor was the Aerojet Engineering Corporation based at Azusa in California. American firms had looked at both solid and liquid propellant engines for aircraft propulsion and Aerojet favoured solid propellants, but its XCALR-2000A motor was quite unique since it had a turbopump which was driven by arranging the exhaust nozzle to spin; this was made possible by having the thrust slightly offset. A total of 8,400lb (3,810kg) of propellants would be carried in the wings with the aniline and oxidiser tanks separated by the gun bays.

In March 1943 a decision was made to modify the third XP-79 to incorporate two Westinghouse 19B axial flow jet engines instead of the rocket motor. This would provide more range and endurance than was available to the basic XP-79 (almost 2.5 hours compared to the rocket version's 35 minutes), since the rocket's fuel consumption was expected to be very high. In addition, the higher combined thrust of the two jet units, compared to that from the single rocket motor, indicated that a considerable gain in high speed could be expected. As such the new version was designated XP-79B (initially a low thrust Westinghouse engine was to have been fitted with the aircraft in this form designated XP-79A, but availability of the more powerful 19B stopped this plan). However, the Westinghouse 19B (which was officially designated J30) was a Navy procurement and so during April 1943 arrangements had to be made to obtain four engines direct from the Navy.

In May 1943 Northrop submitted proposals to build thirteen YP-79 aircraft and a further thirteen YP-79Bs. However, the AAF did not move to procure these machines, because the experimental prototypes themselves had not yet progressed to a point where it could be established whether the P-79 was a practical fighter design or not.

Mock-up of the XP-79 showing how the 2,000lb (9kN) thrust rocket motor would have slotted into the centre of the airframe. *Northrop via Alan Griffith*

Because of the secrecy surrounding the project at this time, on 3 June 1943 a 'Limited Engineering Inspection' was made of the XP-79 mock-up, rather than the more usual 'Mock-up Inspection'. The evaluation team concluded that the XP-79 would offer superior performance in climb, high speed and ceiling and was thus worthy of continued development, but certain weaknesses with the rocket motor and the prone pilot position would have to be solved before the type could be considered

One of the Westinghouse 19B (J30) engines used to power the XP-79B. *Northrop via Alan Griffith*

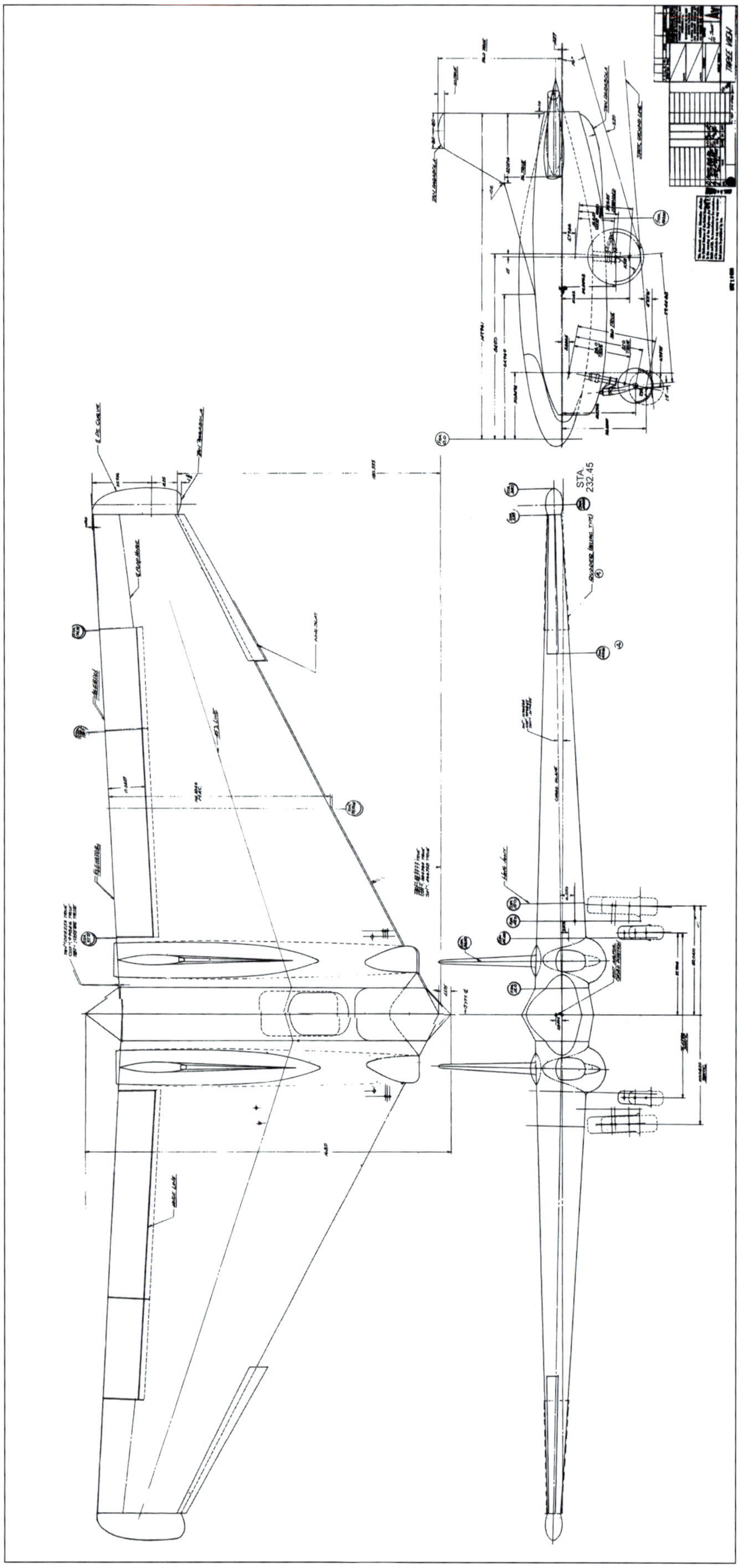

Three view drawing of the XP-79B from May 1944. *Alan Griffith*

The XP-79B pictured during final assembly and prior to painting. This extraordinary looking machine, a very eye-catching aircraft in the author's opinion, had a near straight trailing edge. The 'No-Smoking' sign was particularly important with magnesium alloy in the room! *Northrop via Alan Griffith*

operational; indeed it was felt that rocket propulsion was in all likelihood unsuited for use in an operational aircraft. The biggest problem was to find a way of supporting the pilot's head so that he could withstand the plus 12g accelerations that might be experienced in this aircraft. The Aero Medical Laboratory at Wright Field, the University of Southern California and the contractor worked on the problem and eventually found a solution which would allow the pilot to absorb 12g positive accelerations and yet still be able to talk and to operate the flight controls as normal.

One contribution from Avion concerned the use of vertical fins. As first proposed the XP-79 had no fins, but Avion's calculations indicated that not having this flying control, as Northrop had envisioned, was unacceptable. In-depth studies had been made into factors such as pitch and rolling motions and Avion declared that the situation could be improved by introducing different designs of vertical fin, but when compared to conventional aircraft these weaknesses could never be cured completely. As late as May 1944 Avion was still making assessments for

Nose view which provides further cockpit detail and for the relatively bulky wing root engine nacelles. *Northrop via Alan Griffith*

A view looking down on the near complete prototype which shows the upper fuselage clearly along with detail for the prone position cockpit. *Northrop via Alan Griffith*

having no fin, just a single fin or two fins (which give an indication of the problems the company was having moving the project forward). For a twin finned XP-79B Avion reported an estimated maximum speed of 499mph (803km/h).

Next, during July 1943 it became clear that Aerojet was struggling with the development of the XP-79's rocket motor. Avion advised that the delivery of the first prototype would be postponed from the contracted 30 September back to 15 December 1943, and this was later revised to 15 January 1944. Then in December 1943 the estimated first flight was pushed back once more, again through delays with the rocket motor, to 15 April 1944. In the meantime, during November 1943 the armament mock-up was taken to Wright Field where it was test fired and proved to be "very satisfactory".

The troubles with the Aerojet programme brought a decision in March 1944 to give first priority to the jet-powered XP-79B. Wind tunnel spinning tests for the XP-79B were conducted by NACA Langley in June 1944 and indicated that a normal spin recovery would be satisfactory, and that the XP-79's unconventional configuration would not present any special problems. Also in June 1944 there were reports that in the Avion shop there was "high scrappage, undesirable practices and low morale" and so a Northrop engineer was now placed in charge of the project. As a small inexperienced company, Avion lacked the ability for example to weld and fabricate heavy gauge magnesium, and a lot of material and time had been wasted. This move, together with a final admission from Aerojet that they were unable to cure all of the problems with the rocket, led to the cancellation of the two XP-79 prototypes plus the static test airframe (which were scrapped). From this point only the XP-79B would be completed, in the Northrop factory, and in September 1944 Northrop's subcontract to Avion was cancelled entirely.

The incomplete airframe was moved to Northrop's plant at Hawthorne on 1 December 1944. It is understood that at Avion only the XP-79B's outer wing panels had reached a near complete state, and the aircraft's wheels and other parts and assemblies were scattered around the factory. Work on the cockpit had hardly begun and Northrop's staff had to squeeze this new prototype into its schedule, around all of their other programmes.

The first Westinghouse 19B was shipped to Northrop during the first part of January 1945 and the contractor began engine trials and pre-flight tests on the 13th. There were teething troubles but the second engine arrived on 26 February. After some further problems with the assembly the XP-79B was finally shipped to Muroc Flight Test Base on 12 June 1945, in readiness for its flying programme to commence.

BELOW LEFT The rudder flap (brudder) in the partially open position. *Northrop via Alan Griffith*

BELOW RIGHT One of the wing tip ducts on the XP-79B. *Northrop via Alan Griffith*

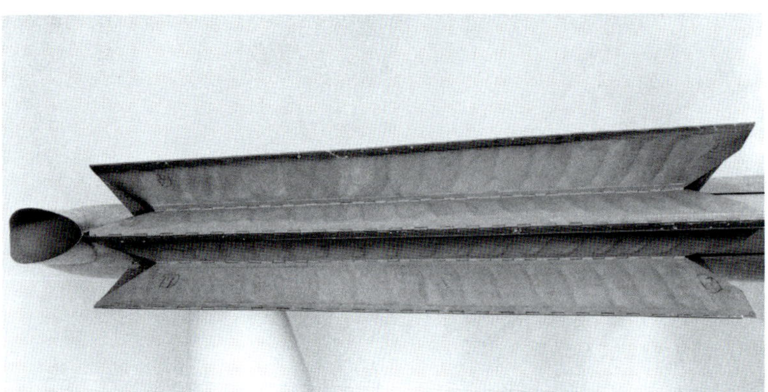

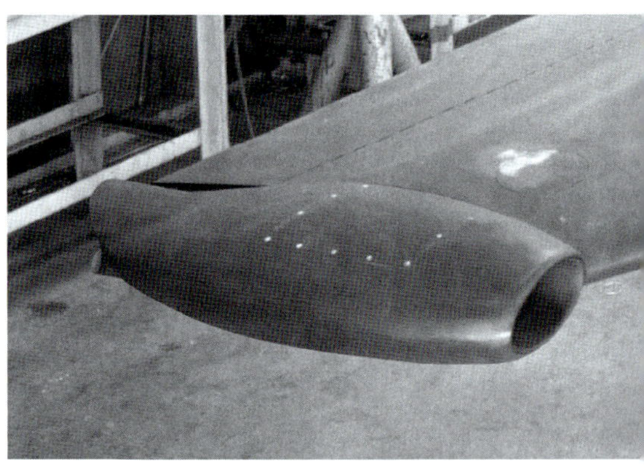

These views from a series of shots taken on the ramp at Hawthorne appear to be the only stills made of the completed XP-79B prototype 43-52437. The aircraft parked right background is Fairchild AT-21 Gunner serial 42-11742. *Northrop via Alan Griffith*

Another view from the 'walk-around' set at Hawthorne, here presenting side angle detail including the quadricycle landing gear. *Northrop via Alan Griffith*

The twin fins and wing trailing edge are well shown in this rear angle photo. All of the XP-79B's trailing edge was used for control surfaces and here the inner and middle surfaces are deflected, but the outboard flaps are closed. *Northrop via Alan Griffith*

Flight test

In May 1944 Northrop's test pilot Harry Crosby had been cleared to make some familiarisation flights in the Bell YP-59A fighter, to enable him to acquire a degree of experience in flying jet propelled aircraft prior to taking the XP-79B aloft. The XP-79B prototype itself, with engines in place, completed its low speed taxi runs at Muroc on 11 July 1945. High speed taxi tests started two days later but, because of tyre failures and problems with the brakes, these lasted into September 1945.

The maiden flight was made on 12 September 1945 but resulted in tragedy as 43-52437 crashed after about 14 minutes of flight, killing Crosby; the aircraft was a total loss after hitting the ground. The Accident Investigation Board concluded that the crash resulted after the pilot appeared unable to get the aircraft out of a roll. During the first part of the flight the XP-79B was apparently very stable, but it went into an unintentional roll after Crosby had made some shallow dives and pull-ups and steep banks to the right and left. The aircraft continued to roll until its axis was vertical and it dove into the ground from an altitude of about 7,000ft (2,134m) whilst still rolling. Crosby was seen to leave the aircraft at an altitude above 2,000ft (610m) but was probably struck by the gyrating XP-79B before opening his parachute, since a ground examination of the chute indicated his rip cord had not been pulled.

In December 1945 the prototype was accepted by the AAF as a crash delivery, and in January 1946 action was taken to terminate the remaining portions of the XP-79 contract. John Northrop described the flight in a talk to the UK's Royal Aeronautical Society in 1947:

> "The take-off for this flight was normal, and for 15 minutes the airplane was flown in a beautiful demonstration. The pilot indicated mounting confidence by executing more and more manoeuvres of a type that would not be expected unless he were thoroughly satisfied with the behaviour of the airplane. After about 15 minutes of flying, the airplane entered what appeared to be a normal slow roll, from which it did not recover. As the rotation about the longitudinal axis continued the nose gradually dropped, and at the time of impact the airplane appeared to be in a steep vertical spin. The pilot endeavoured to leave the ship but the speed was so high that he was unable to clear it successfully. Unfortunately, there was insufficient evidence to fully determine the cause of the disaster."

When the emergency equipment arrived at the crash site the fire fighting personnel, as normal, applied water to the burning wreckage. This was not wise for a magnesium fire because here water will intensify the inferno. Thus, 43-52437 was completely consumed - magnesium burns very fiercely! Northrop's chief aerodynamicist, William Sears, declared that the XP-79B had flown sufficiently well prior to the point when the pilot lost control, and that the unanticipated stall characteristics he experienced were recoverable. But for the AAF this tragic event was enough and the XP-79B programme was now closed.

On 12 September 1945 John Northrop wrote to General H.H. Arnold and his letter included another description:

> "The pilot flew the airplane to an altitude of 8,000ft to 10,000ft [2,438m to 3,048m] above the flying field and for 12 minutes put it through its preliminary paces in a manner that indicated his entire satisfaction with the stability, manoeuvrability and controllability of the ship. This portion of the flight included steep and gradual climbs, medium dives and

Perfect side view of the completed prototype, with a close up of the wing tip rudder bellows which operated instead of conventional rudders, one of numerous advanced features employed on this aircraft. *Northrop via Alan Griffith*

zooms. It also included rolling the ship rapidly from a near vertical right hand bank to a near vertical left hand bank, indicating good aileron control. The ship appeared to observers on the ground to be extremely fast, but unfortunately the recording camera was destroyed and we have no record of how fast it was."

Many published sources have stressed that the P-79 was intended to operate as a Flying Ram, to intentionally collide with enemy aircraft to bring them down. John Northrop did make one reference to this idea in the letter quoted earlier, but no official documents refer to such a role. The concept of the P-79 operating as a Flying Ram appears to have been completely false. The XP-79B was a fascinating design and one wonders what could have been achieved if the prototype had not been lost so early in the programme.

ABOVE The XP-79B's small size is put into perspective by two engineers standing alongside. Note the open access hatch. *Northrop via Alan Griffith*

LEFT The cockpit appears almost to have been moulded around the XP-79B's prone pilot. The wide track nose wheel undercarriage was a very unusual feature. *Northrop via Alan Griffith*

43-52437 loaded onto its trailer ready for transportation to Muroc, a journey of little over 100 miles (161km) by road.
Northrop via Alan Griffith

The burnt out remains of 43-52437 following its tragic crash. The magnesium structure has almost disappeared!
Northrop via Alan Griffith

XP-79B structure

The single seat XP-79B flying wing fighter had a semi-monocoque structure and was built throughout in welded magnesium alloy. It was not purely a flying wing, since two small vertical fins were mounted above the centre line of each engine housing. The moderately swept wing was of cantilever construction with stressed skin covering, and the skinning itself was of very heavy gauge metal to enable the principal loads to be carried by the skin; wing leading edge sweep angle was 27.8°.

Elevators, ailerons, and rudders ('brudders'), all constructed of magnesium, were attached to the trailing edge in that order from the centreline preceding out to the wing tip; both ailerons and elevators were of the sealed balance type. The brudder bellows were housed within wing 'nacelles', which in fact were aeroboost ducts that allowed air to flow into them, this ram-air then passed through a control valve to operate the drag rudder. The resulting drag produced by opening the surfaces on just one of the wing tips would produce a yawing moment or 'rudder effect' to provide the aircraft with directional control. But if the controls on each wing tip were opened together then the resultant drag would act in the same way as speed brakes.

The magnesium structure's heavy gauge was also to provide a degree of armour protection for the integral fuel tanks, because battle damage to the original XP-79 with its Aerojet liquid rocket motor might have resulted in the mixing of the two liquid propellents, and potential serious consequences in terms of explosions and fire. The XP-79B's powerplant was two Westinghouse 19B gas turbines located in large nacelles to each side of the prone pilot's cabin. The unusual fully retractable undercarriage consisted of two main wheels near the centre of gravity and two smaller nose wheels towards the wing leading edge. There was no fuselage, all of the fuel tanks being integral in the wing. A total of 350galUS (1,325lit) of fuel could be carried.

XP-79 data

(Northrop Performance Estimates from Rocket Powered Interceptor Pursuit Aircraft Brochure dated 5 August 1943)

Length:	13ft 2.6in (4.03m)
Wing span:	38ft 0in (11.58m)
Wing area:	278sq.ft (25.85sq.m)
Empty weight:	4,348lb (1,972kg)
Design gross weight:	13,500lb (6,124kg)
Powerplant:	1 x 2,000lb (9kN) thrust Aerojet XCALR-2000A (AS.2) rocket motor plus for take-off 2 x droppable 1,000lb (4.5kN) thrust Aerojet motors
Maximum speed:	518mph (833km/h) at 40,000ft (12,192m)
Time to climb to 40,000ft (12,192m):	7 minutes
Maximum range:	454 miles (730km)
Armament:	4 x 0.50in (12.70mm) machine guns – 2 in each inner wing panel. No bombs
Fuel:	8,400lb (3,810kg) in ratio of 2.75:1 by weight of oxidiser (red fuming nitric acid) to fuel (aniline) = 468galUS (1,772lit) nitric acid and 262galUS (992lit) aniline

XP-79B data

(Northrop Performance Estimates from Jet Powered Interceptor Brochure dated 1 August 1943)

Length:	14ft 0in (4.27m)
Wing span:	38ft 0in (11.58m)
Wing area:	278sq.ft (25.85sq.m)
Empty weight:	5,842lb (2,650kg)
Design gross weight:	8,669lb (3,932kg)
Powerplant:	2 x 1,365lb (6kN) thrust Westinghouse 19B (XJ30-W-1) axial flow turbojets
Maximum speed:	547mph (880km/h) at sea level, 508mph (817km/h) at 25,000ft (7,620m)
Time to climb to 25,000ft (7,620m):	4.72 minutes
Maximum range:	993 miles (1,598km)
Armament:	4 x 0.50in (12.70mm) machine guns – 2 in each inner wing panel (never fitted). No bombs

17 Convair XP-81

The first XP-81 prototype pictured during a test flight. *Convair via Alan Griffith*

The USAAF's experience of daylight bombing in the European theatre, with heavy losses of heavy bombers over Germany, prompted the search for a long range escort fighter. The role was filled by the North American P-51 Mustang, but this experience influenced plans in the Pacific to bomb Japan with the Boeing B-29 - here, with the huge distances involved, escort fighters of even greater range would be required. However, with the eventual capture of islands relatively close to Japan, this requirement disappeared and the only such fighter to be ordered into production was North American's P-82 Twin Mustang (the final piston-engined fighter type produced for the AAF).

44-91000 was in the short term fitted with a Merlin piston engine to enable early flight testing to proceed despite the late delivery of the TG100 turboprop. The large slipper or ferry tank under the wing contained extra fuel. *Convair via Dennis Jenkins*

Convair's XP-81 was also intended to fill this very long range escort role.

In mid-1943 the AAF released a requirement for a single-seat twin-engine, long-range escort fighter having an operating radius of 1,250 miles (2,011km), a top speed of 500mph (805km/h) and a combat ceiling of 37,500ft (11,430m). Convair (newly formed in 1943 by the merger of Consolidated and Vultee) responded with its Model 102 proposal.

Playing the major role in the 102's design were Charles R. 'Jack' Irvine, Convair's chief development engineer, and Frank W. Davis, the assistant development engineer and also the firm's test pilot. They chose a compound powerplant with a turboprop for cruising flight across the Pacific, coupled with a supplementary jet to provide extra power for the take-off, for high speed flight and for combat. Deciding on potentially the best engines proved difficult, particularly for the cruise unit, and the Pratt & Whitney R2800 piston engine was one type to be discarded. Eventually they settled on the General Electric TG100 (later XT31) turboprop and the same manufacturer's I-40 (XJ33) centrifugal-flow turbojet.

The TG100 was the first turboprop developed in America and work on it had begun late in 1941. However, due to competing priorities, the first bench test did not take place until May 1943. Only a modest number of units would be produced and the only other type to fly with the TG100 was the Ryan XF2R Dark Shark (Chapter Twenty-Four). By far the greatest portion of the TG100's power came via its propeller, the jet exhaust providing only about 600lb (2.7kN) of thrust.

Two XP-81 prototypes (serials 44-91000 and 44-91001) and a static test airframe were ordered on 18 January 1944 under contract W33-038-AC-1887, and Project Number MX-480. As an escort fighter designed to accompany bombers on very long-range missions the XP-81's estimated top speed with water injection was 551mph (887km/h) at 10,000ft (3,048m) (this was assuming a 30% increase in power due to water). To begin with the AFF looked upon this pair purely as experimental machines to trial the dual powerplant arrangement, but soon afterwards a further thirteen YP-81 aircraft were ordered under MX-796. However, satisfactory progress in the Pacific campaign meant that these soon became unnecessary and the YP-81s were cancelled in August 1945; the two XP-81s were, however, retained.

Test pilot Frank Davis about to enter the XP-81 cockpit. Note the tinted glass. *Convair via Alan Griffith*

The complete Merlin installation was taken from a P-51 Mustang. *Convair via Dennis Jenkins*

For comparison – 44-91000 photographed from a similar angle showing the difference between the Merlin and TG100 engine installations. *Convair via Gerald H. Balzer*

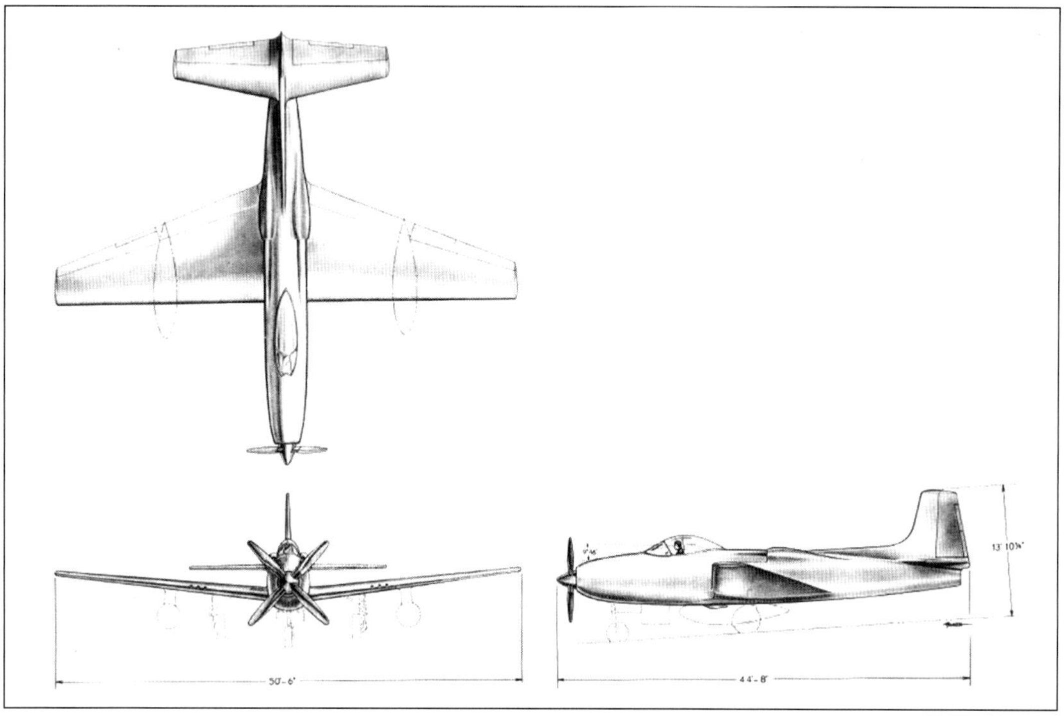

Manufacturer's three-view drawing of the XP-81. *Convair*

Further view of 44-91000 as first flown with a Merlin piston engine installed. The aircraft is pictured at Muroc. *Convair via Alan Griffith*

Flight test

Assembly of the first XP-81 44-91000 began on 20 January 1944. However, in September it became evident that the TG100 would not be ready in time to power it, so a 1,450hp (1,081kW) Packard Merlin V1650-7 piston engine (taken from a North American P-51D Mustang) was installed temporarily. The nose of 44-91000 was suitably modified, including fitting a Lockheed P-38J-type beard radiator intake beneath the propeller spinner, and then the prototype was taken by road to Muroc. The maiden flight took place on 7 February 1945 with the Merlin and the I-40 installed and with Convair test pilot Frank Davis in the cockpit. A summary of the XP-81's flight testing between 7 February and 7 April 1945, all with the Merlin engine, is available in Consolidated-Vultee report DEVF-1469 of 4 June 1945.

Fortunately, the introduction of the Merlin did not require any changes to the airframe's basic structure. This step was just a stop-gap measure to permit the machine to be flown to check its stability and control characteristics, its general operation, and to gain experience with the I-40 jet. XP-81's performance with the Merlin was considerably less than the estimated figures for the TG100 due to the additional weight, reduced horsepower and the aerodynamic penalty of the improvised fitting. In fact the total increase in weight was 954lb (433kg), which included 567lb (257kg) from the engine and 380lb (172kg) of ballast. On top of this was the estimated reduction in power at sea level - 960hp (716kW) for take-off and no less than 1,720hp (1,283kW) at maximum speed/altitude.

Close-up of 44-91000's nose with the TG100 in place. The turboprop's exhaust exited beneath the cockpit. *Convair via Dave Ostrowski*

There were no major problems during the Merlin trials and the majority of flight time was spent improving the I-40 tail pipe installation to maintain safe structural temperatures in that region, to improve the directional stability and control, and to collect performance data. Leakages of oil from the propeller proved to be the greatest hindrance to flight operations but this was overcome. Having a complete shroud of light stainless steel running from the plenum chamber seal to the end of the tail pipe also produced satisfactory results for the jet pipe cooling.

In general, in the air the handling characteristics of the XP-81 were excellent, all control forces were very light and remained so up to the highest speeds yet studied (Mach 0.74). Changes in directional trim due to changes in front engine power and speed had caused some difficulty, which showed up on take-off as a severe tendency to swing to the left due to torque. Wind tunnel tests indicated that this condition would improve with the TG100 installed. However, if this proved insufficient, a further solution would see a vane fitted in the I-40 adjusted to produce a right turning tendency just equal to the left turning tendency produced by the propeller; this vane could be retracted from the jet engine when the undercarriage wheels were retracted.

In order to improve the directional stability a 15in (38.1cm) spanwise addition had been incorporated at the top of the fin and rudder, and a short ventral fin was also added; as a result the directional stability was now satisfactory (the second prototype had this modification from the start, along with an extended ventral fin). Both the lateral and longitudinal stability and control had been satisfactory under all conditions thus far encountered. The XP-81's stalls were flat or with a roll which was easily controllable both with power off and power on. At a gross weight of approximately 18,000lb (8,165kg) the following stalling speeds were obtained:

All up, power off - 106mph (171km/h) IAS
All down, power off - 96mph (154km/h) IAS
All up, rated power - 102mph, (164km/h) IAS
All down, rated power - 93mph (150km/h) IAS

The XP-81 had been flown and landed with either engine operating alone. With both the Merlin and I-40 working together, at a weight of 18,330lb (8,314kg) the maximum rate of climb was 8,600ft/min (2,621m/min) at sea level and the maximum speeds 538mph (866km/h) at sea level and 552mph (888km/h) at 10,000ft (3,048m). The I-40 power available with the Merlin installation was in part reduced by the hot piston exhaust entering directly into the I-40 duct (which would not occur with the TG100 installation).

This three-month programme embraced 46 flights before, on 18 May 1945, 44-91000 was returned to Convair at Downey to have the TG100 installed. Replacing the Merlin with the TG100

The first prototype pictured just after the TG100 had been installed. The fin and rudder were shortened prior to fitting, and the anti-glare panel has not yet been painted on the upper nose. *Convair via Dave Ostrowski*

By 18 January 1946 when this view was made the fin had been extended again. *Convair via Dave Ostrowski*

Also taken on 18 January 1946, the anti-glare panel is now painted on. A small scoop can be seen on the side of the upper nose. *Convair via Dave Ostrowski*

entailed further modifications. These included having the horizontal tail moved 15in (38.1cm) further back, the fin and rudder now reduced in height by 10in (25.4cm), and a 19in (48.3cm) long exhaust nozzle added to the I-40 jet.

Frank Davis covered the XP-81's flight trials with the TG100 in a paper written for *Aeronautical Engineering Review* and published in April 1948. The first flight with the TG100 in place was made at Muroc on 21 December 1945 and testing the first American gas turbine to drive a propeller continued between that date and 19 December 1946. In all 47 flights were completed during this period and there were numerous problems, including starting, control, propeller feathering and vibration. For the most part the solutions developed served as stopgap measures to allow testing to proceed.

Ground trials lasted from 23 June until 18 October 1945. Some were performed on a tilting stand without a propeller, the remainder with the TG100 installed in the XP-81 and both with and without the propeller. Problems with difficult starting came from the considerable inertia of the rotating parts and with the high speed needed to enable the TG100 to sustain itself. The paper noted how "the rotational inertia of the turbine, compressor, and gears was about five times the propeller inertia, when, by comparison, the rotational inertia of the rotating parts of a reciprocating engine was only about one-fifth of propeller inertia."

When taxi runs began a four-blade 12ft 3/8in (3.77m) diameter Aeroproducts propeller had been fitted and certain problems of control were encountered straight away; although inherent with turboprop engines these were affected substantially by the characteristics of the propeller and the propeller governor. The first was the reluctance of the propeller to change pitch and thus to develop thrust when the throttle was advanced. It would take the TG100 about two to three seconds to move from 75% to 100% rpm, but the propeller would then take as long as 20 seconds to alter its pitch to enable full power to be achieved. And, when the throttle was closed during high speed taxi runs a powerful braking affect from the propeller was experienced which occurred quite suddenly around two seconds after the throttle had been closed (i.e. when the propeller had returned to flat

A set of walk-around photographs of the first prototype was taken on 22 January 1946. A little additional paintwork was added for publicity purposes – 'Convair' and 'XP-81' on the fin and 'Consolidated Vultee' on the sides of the nose. The small scoop on the nose has been deleted. *Convair via Dave Ostrowski*

Air-to-air photos provide the opportunity to present underside detail. Five of the flights between numbers 51 to 60 were used for photography and for demonstration and publicity purposes. *Convair via Gerald H. Balzer*

Prominent in this photo is the TG100's exhaust pipe beneath the centre fuselage. *Convair via Alan Griffith*

pitch). So, the pilot had something like a ten second lag when he wished to go forward and then around a two second lag when he needed to stop.

On 21 December 1945, with the XP-81 ready for flight, bad weather was approaching the Muroc Flight Test Base. Heavy rain would make the dry lake bed unusable, so the go-ahead was given to make the maiden turboprop flight despite the existing issues with the TG100. A sortie of just five minutes was completed, again piloted by Frank Davis, during which the turboprop controls were handled extremely carefully. However, a fairly heavy propeller vibration was experienced as soon as the XP-81 left the ground and it continued throughout the entire flight.

A problem on Flight 2 brought home the importance of the propeller drag at flat pitch most forcefully. One of the undercarriage doors would not close fully so the pilot took the XP-81 up to 7,000ft (21,336m) and then, during efforts to close the door, reduced the speed to about 150mph (241km/h). Here the drag increased abruptly, there was buffeting, the controls became extremely sluggish and around 2,500ft (762m) of altitude were lost. Clearly such a condition had to be avoided when approaching to land! It was also apparent that if the TG100 failed then the aircraft could not be landed safely unless the propeller was feathered. The vibration present on the first flight persisted and became worse at higher speeds and power settings (the engine substantially had no shock mounting).

Engine friction was so low that, while the XP-81 was standing on the ground, it could be kept in rotation by finger pressure on the propeller; this was a worry because it was felt that it would be impossible to find a feathered-pitch setting that in the air would result in a motionless propeller. In fact, and a great surprise of all concerned, a position was found just on the second attempt, and the feathered propeller would remain stationary (and without any auxiliary braking) from the stalling speed up to 330mph (531km/h) IAS. For both feathering and unfeathering operations the change in rpm was far slower than was the case for a reciprocating engine, and considerable amounts of power were delivered by or had to be absorbed by the engine. This resulted in longer and more severe effects on the XP-81's handling characteristics than would have been the case with a piston unit.

A total of 21 hours of flying were accomplished with the Aeroproducts propeller, after which it was replaced by a 12ft 6in (3.81m) diameter Hamilton Standard Superhydromatic propeller. Unfortunately, the propeller vibration encountered on the Aeroproducts propeller was repeated with the Hamilton Standard and high air speeds brought the most serious difficulties. At 410mph (660km/h) IAS at 12,100ft (3,688m) large-scale hunting occurred suddenly and without warning. Locking the pitch produced extremely severe oscillation but, fortunately, no failure occurred either in the engine or the airframe. Detail modifications eventually reduced the hunting to a safe value for all level flight speeds.

These experiences led Davis to conclude that using a gas turbine to drive a propeller gave rise "to several serious problems other than those encountered in the turbojet or the reciprocating engine. Furthermore, most of these problems appear to be associated with the propeller and its governing and control system." At the time when these flights were made no propeller specifically designed for gas turbines was available, and using propellers and governors designed specifically for reciprocating engines had in several respects proved unsatisfactory. Testing with the XP-81 had made it clear that considerable development work in the field of turboprop powerplants was still required.

The TG100 itself certainly required some improvement. During the XP-81's flight trials neither the turboprop nor the jet had supplied anything like the predicted levels of power to enable the aircraft to achieve its original estimated performance figures. Instead of the expected 2,300hp (1,715kW) that the TG100 was supposed to provide, the maximum rating came to 1,650hp (1,230kW) which produced a performance little better than that with the Merlin (other sources quote just 1,400hp/1,044kW). And instead of 4,000lb (17.8kN), the I-40 jet had produced just 3,750lb (16.7kN) of thrust. On top of this, such was the unreliability of the TG100 that throughout the flying programme the turboprop had been removed from the aircraft after every five to ten hours of operation to be inspected.

However, in the air the XP-81 itself performed well, with fine handling, light and well balanced controls and with a good rate of climb, but the full programme was curtailed; diving trials, for example, were never completed. And the AAF never reached the point of conducting any of its official performance testing, although both prototypes were accepted by the Service in June 1947.

Records have not been found which confirm the exact date when 44-91001 made its first flight, but it was during February 1947. And there are no detailed flight test records showing what was achieved with the second machine, but it was still flying in April 1947. As noted, this aircraft had the fin modifications, but also introduced NACA-style air intakes instead of straight troughs forward of the I-40's shoulder-mounted intakes.

The first XP-81 completed 94 flights in all (including those with the Merlin) and its flying career came to a close in January 1947. The two prototypes together completed 69 flights with the TG100 installed. Flight testing came to a close on 9 May 1947, the day when the XP-81 programme was officially cancelled.

There were efforts to give the XP-81 better engines. The most detailed was Convair's proposal to replace the TG100 with a more powerful (2,720hp/2,028kW) General Electric TG110 turboprop (official designation XT41) along with a new version of the I-40, a J33-19 which offered a further 250lb (1.1kN) of thrust with water-alcohol injection. These changes would require modifications to the nose, moving the jet intakes forward and placing them lower on the fuselage, a larger tailpipe and, to maintain balance, moving the wing forward by 7in (17.8cm). The gross weight would rise from 19,500lb to 21,188lb (8,845kg to 9,611kg), but the estimated maximum speed would be 544mph (875km/h) compared to the XP-81's (quoted) 510mph (821km/h); rate of climb and range would also improve. This proposal was apparently made in December 1946 (though some published sources suggest that this engine combination was intended for the cancelled YP-81s) but was not taken up.

Neither was a suggestion to fit British engines - a 4,000hp (2,983kW) Armstrong Siddeley Double Mamba turboprop and a 6,250lb (27.8kN) Rolls-Royce Nene jet. These would have involved major airframe changes and an Air Force assessment of September 1950 indicated that almost 70% of the fuselage would need to be changed or modified.

At cancellation Air Material Command's Power Plant Laboratory and Propeller Laboratory were working on the development of propeller controls for the next generation of gas turbine engines. Both laboratories suggested that the now surplus XP-81s might be useful in this effort serving as flying test-beds, so in 1948 they were stored in readiness at Edwards Air Force Base (as Muroc had now been renamed). However, this plan never materialised and on 29 April 1949 the two XP-81s were cleared for salvage. Each airframe was stripped of useful parts and moved to a bombing range at Edwards to serve as photography targets, where they remained until August 1994! Both survived and today the bomb damaged airframe shells are in the hands of

44-91000 shows off its wing shape over the Mojave Desert. *Convair via Alan Griffith*

The considerable size of the I-40 jet engine's air intakes is emphasised in this air-to-air photo taken on 25 January 1946. The pilot was Ellis D. 'Sam' Shannon who in February 1943 had joined Consolidated Vultee to head the manufacturer's newly-formed Flight Research Department. *Convair via Gerald H. Balzer*

The I-40 jet was housed in the rear fuselage with the exhaust exiting beneath the rudder. This photo shows the wing gun positions, although the weapons were never installed. *Convair via Alan Griffith*

Relatively few photos exist of the second XP-81 prototype 44-91001. The main change from the first machine was the addition of a long ventral fin stretching from beneath the cockpit to the end fuselage, although the I-40 intakes were also altered. Test pilot Reuben P. Snodgrass taxis out at Muroc in readiness for one of the final XP-81 test flights, in April 1947. *Convair via Dave Ostrowski*

Both XP-81s also had 15in (38.1cm) extensions made to the fin in the form of a round tip rather than the square arrangement flown at the beginning of 44-91000's career. Here the second prototype poses beneath the rear fuselage of Convair's XB-46 jet bomber prototype serial 45-59582. *Convair via Dave Ostrowski*

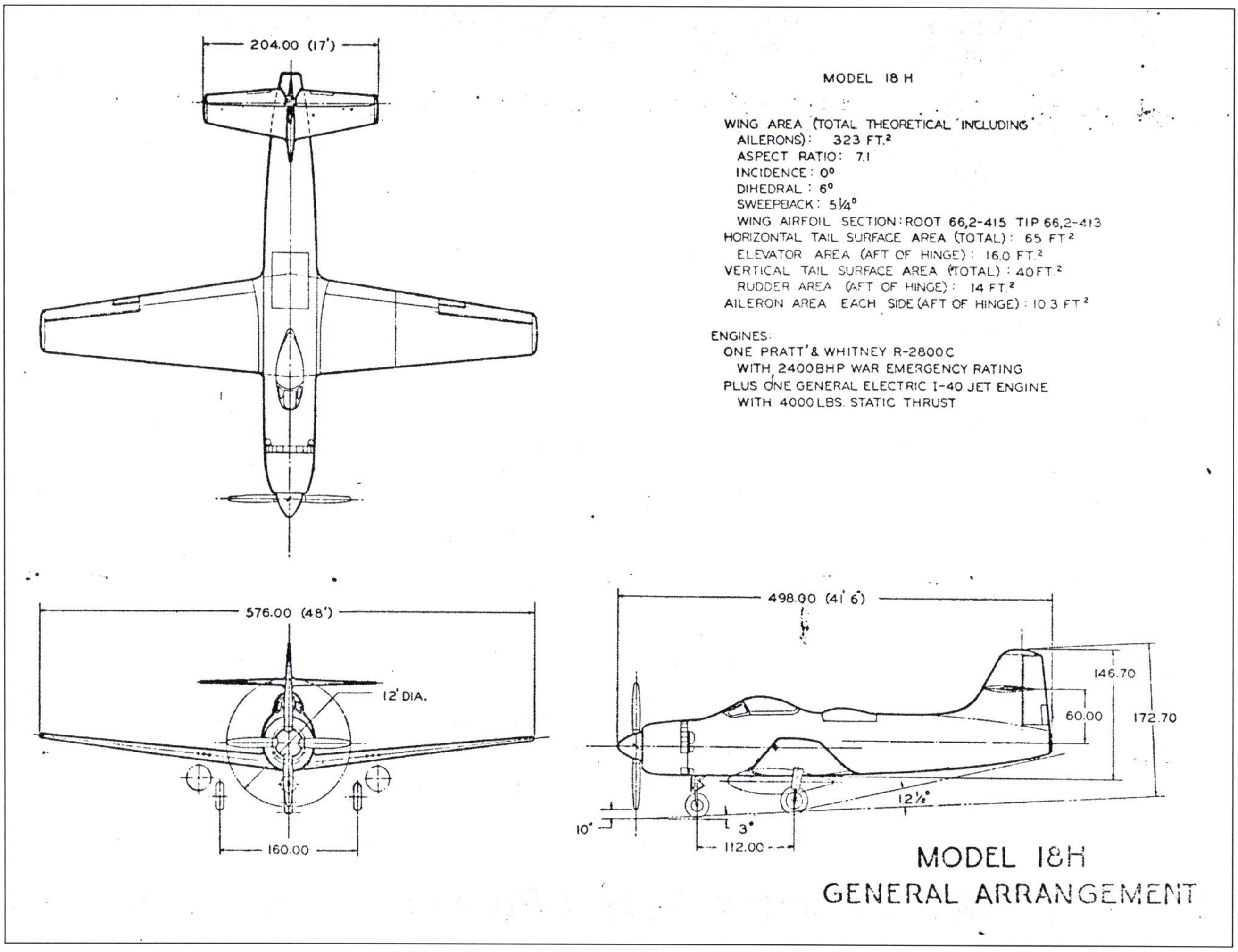

No information seems to be available detailing any rival proposals to the XP-81; indeed it is not known if there were any? However, the McDonnell Model 18H was another mixed powerplant design from the period. McDonnell looked at various designs for an AAF fighter with combined powerplants under its Model 18 label. The 18H had a span of 48ft 0in (14.63m), length 41ft 6in (12.65m) and gross wing area 323sq.ft (30.04sq.m). It was to be powered by a 2,400hp (1,790kW) Pratt & Whitney R2800C piston engine driving a four-blade 12ft (3.66m) diameter propeller and a 4,000lb (17.8kN) thrust I-40 jet. Armament six 0.50in (12.7mm) machine guns, three per wing mounted outside the propeller arc, plus a single bomb carried beneath the fuselage. The drawing is dated 9 September 1944. *Mark Nankivil, St Louis Air & Space Museum*

the USAF Museum at Wright Patterson, in store awaiting some form of restoration.

A memorandum from the UK's Senior Naval Representative at the British Air Commission gives details of discussions about the XP-81 made with the AAF Project Officer at Wright Field on 27 July 1945; these shed a little light on the Service's opinion of Convair's aircraft. The AAF representative revealed that their future designs would include both the pure jet fighter for interception duties and the mixed power plant for fighter escort duties, the XP-81 being the first in the latter class. However, it was not expected that this particular aircraft would reach production since the AAF considered that the weight of the Convair project was too great for it ever to become an effective escort fighter.

There was also the statement "while the Army is interested in mixed power plants we do not feel that the carrying of a turbine jet to give flash performance is an economical feature from the weight standpoint, and drag of the intake for the unit." The memo added that the AAF's requirement for the operation of the turbine was five minutes during combat. This being the case, the AAF was now extremely interested in the use of a monofuel rocket to replace the turboprop since this installation, as envisaged by the Americans, was exceedingly simple, light, and readily accessible. As a first step in the implementation of this type of powerplant the Army had requested Convair to submit a proposal for a new mixed powerplant escort fighter weighing 14,000lb (6,350kg) and to be powered with a TG100 and a monofuel rocket. It is understood that this project had been in the mind of Consolidated before the AAF had approached the firm, and the contractor was now in the process of submitting its proposal to the Army Air Force.

XP-81 structure

The XP-81 was a single-seat all metal fighter prototype of relatively conventional design with a tapered straight cantilever wing and a retractable tricycle undercarriage. A laminar flow aerofoil was used with a very smooth surface made possible by the use of heavy aluminium alloy skin and flush riveting. Age-hardened flush-riveted 24S-RT aluminium alloy was used extensively in the assembly of the semi-monocoque forward fuselage, while the rear fuselage was manufactured in stainless steel. A pressurised cockpit and an ejection seat were fitted.

The unconventional element was the compound powerplant which comprised a TG100 turboprop (propjet was the term used in publications at the time) in the nose turning a four-blade 12ft 3/8in (3.77m) diameter propeller, plus an I-40 turbojet engine positioned behind the pilot. The TG100 was installed much like a conventional reciprocating piston engine but was very closely cowled with air entering through an annular nose scoop; additional thrust was obtained from an exhaust jet directed rearwards beneath the fuselage just under the pilot. Intakes for the I-40 were positioned on the upper fuselage shoulder to the rear of the cockpit and the exhaust passed through a tailpipe below the rudder.

All fuel was carried internally, although provision had been made for fitting droppable 350galUS (1,325lit) underwing tanks; internal fuel totalled 811galUS (3,070lit) all in the fuselage. Groups of three 0.50in (12.7mm) machine guns were to be mounted in the wings (these were never fitted) and consideration was given to replacing these with 20mm cannon. Outboard of the guns a hard point under each wing could take, besides the drop tanks, bombs of up to 1,600lb (1,452kg) weight, depth charges or rockets. Further, stub pylons along the wings were available to carry 5in (12.7cm) HVAR rockets.

XP-81 data

Length:	44ft 8in (13.62m)
Wing span:	50ft 6in (15.39m)
Wing area:	425sq.ft (39.525sq.m)
Empty weight:	12,755lb (5,786kg)
Gross weight:	19,500lb (8,845kg)
Maximum take-off weight:	24,650lb (11,181kg)
Powerplant:	1 x 2,300hp (1,715kW) General Electric XT31-GE-1 (TG100) turboprop and 1 x 4,000lb (16.7kN) Allison J33-GE-5 turbojet
Maximum speed achieved with TG100:	546mph (879km/h) Mach 0.745 on Flight 90 on 4 September 1946
Maximum rate of climb:	8,300ft/min (2,530m/min)
Service ceiling:	49,000ft (14,935m)
Range:	2,500 miles (4,023km)
Armament:	6 x 0.50in (12.70mm) machine guns or 6 x 20mm cannon, 2 x 1,600lb (1,452kg) bombs, 14 x 5in (12.7cm) rockets

18 Bell XP-83

An early American jet fighter prototype to fail to achieve production was the Bell XP-83. Here the designation 'XP-83' is used throughout, though had the aircraft reached production it would have been designated F-83 after the formation of the US Air Force.

The Bell Aircraft Corporation's first jet fighter, and indeed America's first jet aircraft, had been the P-59 Airacomet. One objective for what became the XP-83 was to produce a jet fighter similar in appearance to the P-59 but with an improvement in performance. Some undesirable aerodynamic characteristics experienced in the P-59 were also to be eliminated, the new fighter was to be larger and was to use more powerful engines. Early jet engines were heavy and lacked power and they consumed fuel at a ferocious rate, which limited severely a jet-powered aircraft's range and endurance. As the largest and heaviest jet fighter design to date the XP-83 was intended to be the first of its breed to offer a decent range

The manufacturer's original proposal was called the 'D-16 Stratosphere Fighter' but later became the Model 40. Bell's chief design engineer was Robert J. Woods and on 23 March 1943, after his team had completed considerable background research into the merits of an aircraft powered by two General Electric I-40 engines, he and project engineer Edgar P. Rhodes took the Model 40 documents to Air Material Command at Wright Field. This proposal was the result of a combined effort from the US Army Air Force and Bell, and in AAF eyes the project became 'active' from this date. At Wright Field the project was reviewed by the Engineering Division who now took the decision to switch from an interceptor fighter to a long range escort fighter with more fuel. The Model 40's layout was easily adaptable to the necessary changes, Bell accordingly submitted revised proposals to Wright Field on 3 April and the project was refined during the remainder of 1943.

This view of the first Bell XP-83 prototype serial 44-84990 is well known but remains one of the best images of the type. Relatively few air-to-air photos of the XP-83 appear to have been taken. *Bell Aircraft*

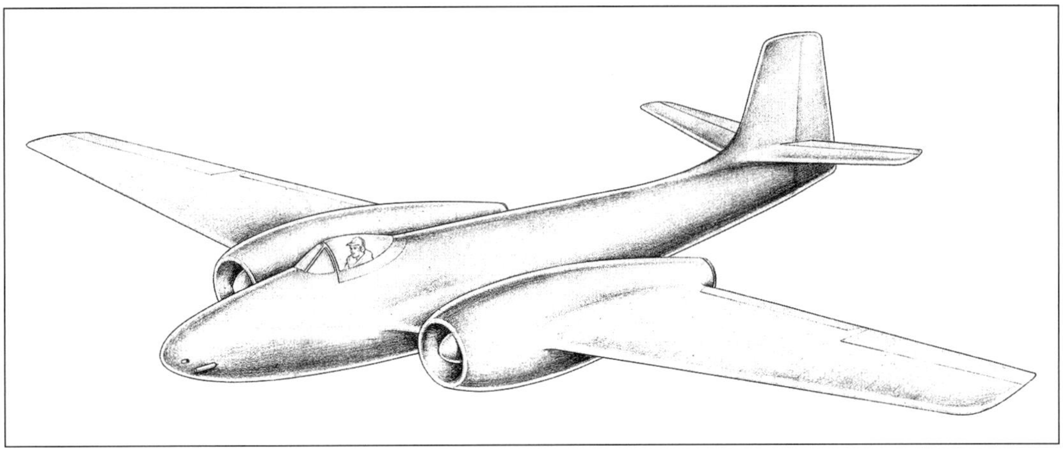

A manufacturer's impression for a design which Bell designated D-16-2, dated 14 February 1944, and which gives an alternative idea of how the new jet fighter might have looked, rather than having the engines positioned beneath the wing roots as in the XP-83 (and the P-59 which preceded it). *Alan Griffith*

On 26 April 1943 Bell was told that, because of combat experience, the design load factors for all fighter aircraft had been reduced from 8 to 7.33. This change enabled the new fighter to carry the extra fuel for long range escort duties with only minor modifications to the structure. However, during early August it became apparent that the structure weight had in fact been increasing beyond the original estimates. It was found that much of the additional weight had come from an inaccurate estimate of the structure required to fit the extensible area landing flaps.

Another change concerned the gun armament. Originally 0.50in (12.7mm) machine guns were selected, but in late August 1943 it was established that .60 calibre (0.60in/15.2mm) guns would be required for future fighter aircraft. Layouts were then prepared for a six gun .60 calibre Model 40 installation and the preliminary studies showed that the best solution would be four guns in the nose with two more in the fuselage sides. This was approved and Bell was told to make the necessary changes to the airframe to permit this arrangement to be introduced. However, when more information on the gun mounting arrangement became available in January 1944 Bell realised that, by extending the fuselage nose by 15in (381mm), it would be possible to have all six guns housed in the nose in the same manner as the .50 calibre format. This presented less of a structural problem and from a firepower standpoint was more desirable, so Bell was told to drop the wing gun layout and to proceed with the six gun nose (the .60 calibre guns were 92ins/2.34m long).

All of this effort had been carried out without a prototype order, but Contract W33-AC-2425 was finally awarded on 11 March 1944 for two XP-83s against Specification MX-511. On 5/6 June 1944 a full-size mock-up was inspected at Bell's Buffalo factory, while later on a static test airframe was tested in Air Materiel Command's laboratory, which structurally was found to be satisfactory.

A new problem, however, concerned the tailplane. By early September 1944 data from NACA Langley Field's wind tunnel testing had indicated that the XP-83 as designed would suffer from directional instability. In response Bell designed a larger fin and rudder with the span increased by 16in (406mm), tests having indicated that this would overcome the problem. However, since the fighter could be flown 'normally' with safety with the original fin and rudder, Bell was told by Air Materiel Command to introduce the larger tailplane only on the second prototype. Modifying the first airframe as well would push back the first flight date and, as it stood, the directional stability was quite adequate for normal flying in this aircraft but not for aerobatics or spin recovery (action was taken to restrict the first XP-83 against entering spins). For the same reason the upgraded gun armament was held back to the second machine.

In late September 1944 Air Materiel Command discovered that the XP-83's airframe weight had risen to an alarming extent. In-depth investigations determined that the increase had been caused by:

a. Using a type of flap which increased the weight far in excess of its aerodynamic benefit.

b. Using existing parts such as landing gear struts to save time and reduce construction costs.

c. A failure by Bell to redesign components once they had been designed, which meant that the manufacturer missed opportunities to reduce weight by redesign.

Subsequent studies established that a redesign could remove around 1,400lb (635kg) of the measured 2,000lb (907kg) of excess weight, so considerations towards abandoning the XP-83 project due to this weight problem were now dropped.

At around the same time new NACA data showed that a redesigned windshield and canopy would provide a 7mph (11km/h) increase in maximum speed. By now, however, the construction of the first XP-83 was at an advanced stage and so once more no effort was made towards incorporating this alteration in the first aircraft, but rather to introduce the redesigned canopy on the second machine along with any other possible weight savings, thereby making this aircraft a clear improvement over XP-83 No. 1.

The first XP-83 44-84990, in snowy conditions at Bell's Buffalo airfield in New York, taxis out for a test sortie early in its career – possibly its maiden flight. Note the aft-sliding cockpit canopy. *Gerald Balzer Collection*

This shot was presumably taken a few moments later as the aircraft prepares to join the main runway. *Gerald Balzer Collection*

44-84990 pictured in flight, again possibly during its maiden sortie on 25 February 1945. *Gerald Balzer Collection*

A set of walk around views of the first XP-83 all taken on the day of its roll-out, 8 February 1945. *All Gerald Balzer Collection*

Side view. Neither XP-83 was ever painted; instead they retained their natural metal finish.

Three-quarter left rear angle, which shows the dihedral tailplane well.

Rear view with jet pipe detail.

Nose angle with the large air intakes and wide-track undercarriage (wheel base 16ft 5.8in/5.02m). The fuselage itself was pretty slim.

LEFT 44-84990's fin and rudder detail. *Gerald Balzer Collection*

BELOW Nose close up of 44-84990, again taken in mid-1945. *Gerald Balzer Collection*

Flight test

The two XP-83 prototypes carried USAAF serial nos 44-84990 and 44-84991, the first was was completed on 8 February 1945 and it made a 45-minute maiden flight from Niagara Airport (next to Niagara Falls) on the 25th of that month. Bell chief test pilot Jack Woolams was in the cockpit and the flight passed satisfactorily until after the fuel from the front fuselage tank had become exhausted. Woolams found that the booster pump for the rear fuselage tank had failed and so he was forced to cut the power back drastically to prevent the engine from stopping. He was able to land safely and the problem was fixed, but then on Flight 2 fuel was seen to be escaping through the vent system and so this too had to be dealt with. In general Woolams found the first XP-83 exhibited satisfactory flight characteristics but the aircraft was underpowered and unstable.

The aileron boost system was connected for the first time for Flight 6 when Woolams attempted to reach high Mach numbers in a shallow dive. However, at about Mach 0.72 severe vibration of the instrument panel was experienced followed immediately by aileron buffeting. To try and cure this the aileron mass balance was increased from 100% to 125% which subsequent test flying showed had raised the critical Mach number from 0.72 to 0.735, but then the same phenomena was encountered again at this higher figure. However, by now any plans to put the XP-83 into production had gone and so no further changes were made to try and increase the critical Mach number.

No difficulty had been encountered with the aileron boost system itself during this flight but the pilot found that the XP-83's "centering characteristics were poor and that there was a marked tendency to over control since the stick forces decreased greatly after the first movement of a fraction of an inch". Modifications made to correct this condition brought no real improvement and indeed the pilot twice reported aileron lock, but on each occasion he was able to overpower the boost system and land safely. This latter situation could never be duplicated on the ground and consequently remained unsolved. Problems were also experienced with closing the landing gear 'flipper' doors, the mechanism that worked them having to be redesigned to prevent the doors from sagging downwards during flight at high speeds.

USAAF flight tests to determine the XP-83's "official performance" began on 9 June 1945 with 44-84990. However, on 10 June they were interrupted by a fire which started after a ruptured fuel line had allowed the fuselage to fill with fuel after landing. Fortunately the XP-83 suffered only slight damage. A second delay came after the pilot had cut off the hydraulic pumps while the engines were running on the ground. The brakes operated hydraulically and 44-84990 now rolled forward into a fire truck, the left wing suffering slight damage. In both cases Bell's engineers were able to repair the aircraft quickly.

The first XP-83 was accepted by the USAAF on 11 October 1945 and the AAF's pilots made few unfavorable comments about the aeroplane. The principal weaknesses were the undesirable characteristics of the aileron boost system, plus the sloshing of fuel back and forth inside the large fuselage tanks which gave an impression of longitudinal instability. A most unusual characteristic was that the XP-83 refused to 'slow down', so its sleek aerodynamic shape coupled with the lack of drag brakes meant that its pilots had to fly very long and flat landing approaches.

| These photos of 44-84990 were taken at the same time in 1946 at Wright Field. *Gerald Balzer Collection*

The first XP-83 is prepared for its ramjet flight trials, which sadly lasted just one sortie before the aircraft was lost. One small ramjet was fitted beneath each wing as shown. In this view the aircraft also has its J33 engine cover removed. *Gerald Balzer Collection*

Close up of the Marquardt RJ30 21in (0.533m) diameter ramjet. *David Smith*

After official testing 44-84990 was returned to Bell, but with no P-83 production programme the aircraft was then reassigned to engine research under the control of Air Material Command's Power Plant Laboratory. A new engineer's 'cockpit' was fitted into the fuselage to the rear of the pilot and an experimental 21in (0.533m) diameter Marquardt RJ30 ramjet engine was attached under each wing on a short pylon. It was hoped that sufficient speed could be reached using J33 jet engine power alone to enable the ramjets to be started up, after which the main engines would be shut down to leave the XP-83 flying purely on ramjet power. The engineer would monitor the behaviour and running of the ramjets and the chosen flight crew for these trials were Bell test pilot Chalmers H Goodlin and Bell flight test engineer Charles L. Fay.

The first flight in this new programme took place on 4 September 1946 but, because of a fuel leak, on ignition the starboard ramjet caught fire and exploded. The wing was damaged and the fire soon spread to and then engulfed the entire wing. With the starboard aileron lost, and the threat of a fuel explosion, Goodlin and Fay bailed out after the pilot had gained sufficient altitude and both parachuted to safety. The first XP-83 was destroyed when it crashed in flames on a farm some 4 miles (6.5km) to the south of Amherst in New York.

XP-83 No. 2's first flight, again from Niagara Airport, was made on 19 October 1945 and the objective of its flying programme was to thoroughly test the 0.60in (15.2mm) gun installation. However, during the very early flights, and because of malfunctions with the weapons themselves, considerable trouble was experienced just in getting the guns to fire. Once these had been overcome, however, a series of three or four flights brought a successful conclusion to the contractor's flight test programme. On 27 June 1946 44-84991 was accepted by Air Material Command at Bell's factory and then ferried to Wright Field for the gun installation's official testing, the aircraft having been assigned to AMC's Armament Laboratory. The trials were conducted throughout 1946 both at Wright Field and at Eglin Field in Florida and were still ongoing in early January 1947, at which stage no criticism of the gun installation had been made. Having completed

ABOVE LEFT View showing the XP-83's cockpit, in this case the second prototype. *US National Archives College Park*

ABOVE RIGHT The six .60 machine gun installation as fitted to 44-84991 and photographed at around the time of the aircraft's first flight in October 1945. *US National Archives College Park*

RIGHT Rarely seen view for the first XP-83 taken from above. This appears to be another of the set of photos taken in snow at Buffalo and shows the slim fuselage beautifully. *Gerald Balzer Collection*

its tenure at Wright Field, the surviving XP-83 was declared surplus in 1948, it was withdrawn from flight status and subsequently scrapped.

In the end the XP-83's performance was judged to be relatively poor and, apart from its range, the type offered no major advantages when compared with other fighter types soon to be available. It appears that there was never any real chance of production which meant that, after wartime success with the P-39 and P-63, the XP-83 proved to be Bell's fighter swansong. The manufacturer would never again fly a new fighter aircraft type.

Structure

The XP-83 had an all metal structure built primarily in aluminum light alloy with a semi-monocoque fuselage. The cantilever laminar flow wing was covered in stressed skin, it had 2° of dihedral and was swept to an angle of 8° at the leading edge. Both tailplane and fin were also of the cantilever type and made in aluminum or magnesium and indeed all of the control surfaces used metal construction. "Extensible area high lift devices" were fitted (i.e. landing flaps) and both the rudder and left hand aileron had trim tabs. The ailerons were of the internal pressure balanced type and the rudder and elevators were balanced by symmetrical leading edge overhangs.

The pilot had a pressurised and air conditioned cockpit and the engines were mounted under the centre wing panel, one on each side of the aircraft, which left the fuselage almost entirely free for fuel and guns. Although designed as a single-seater, for its later ramjet trials the first XP-83 had an engineer's station in the fuselage with an entrance door underneath. There was a tricycle undercarriage with the main gear retracting inboard and the nose gear retracting aft. Internal fuel capacity was 1,150gal(US) (4,353lit) in five tanks – three in the fuselage and one in each wing – and another 300galUS (1,136lit) could be carried in two underwing external tanks, one per wing.

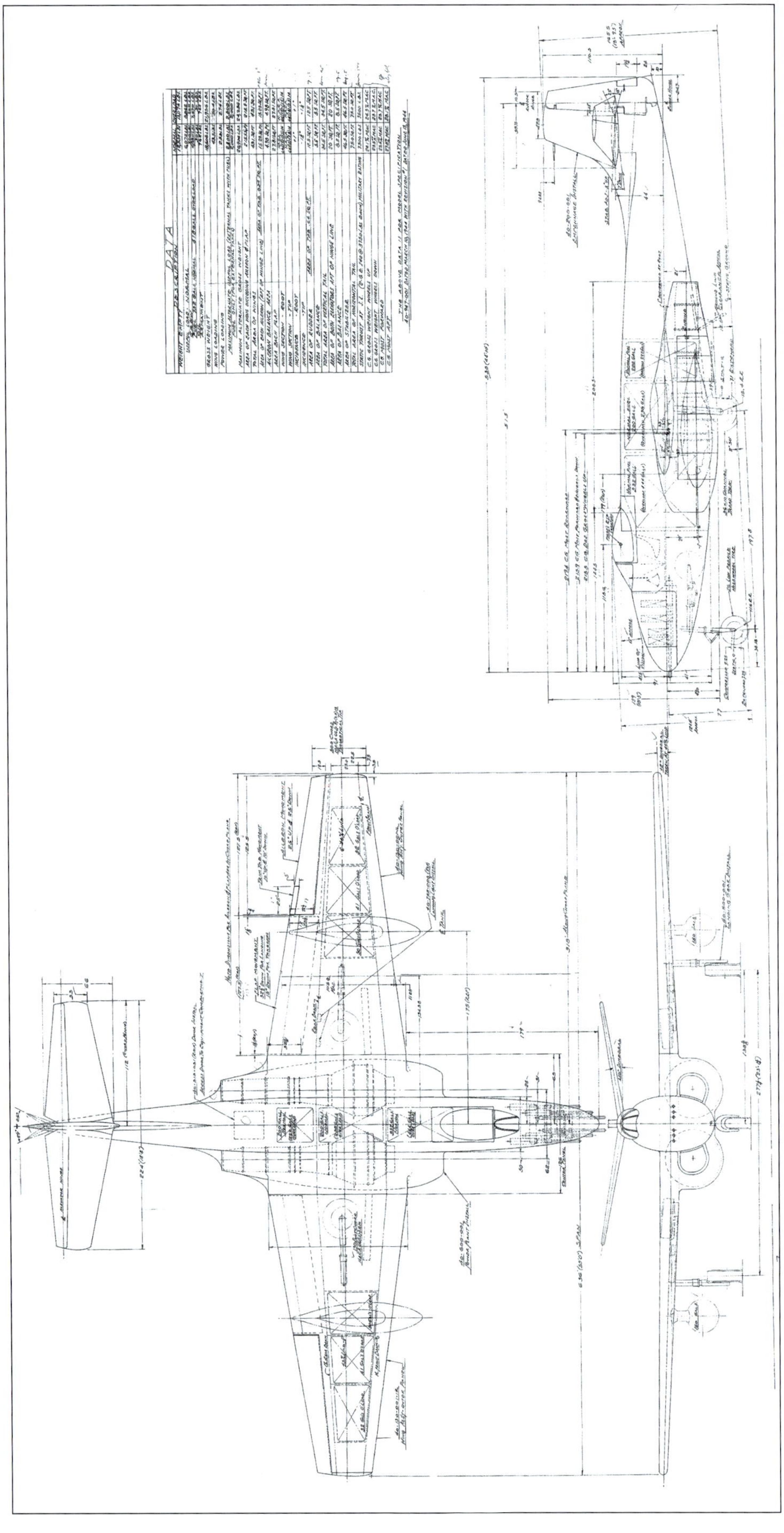

Bell drawing showing the early configuration of the final form of the XP-83, with the short vertical stabilizer. *Alan Griffith*

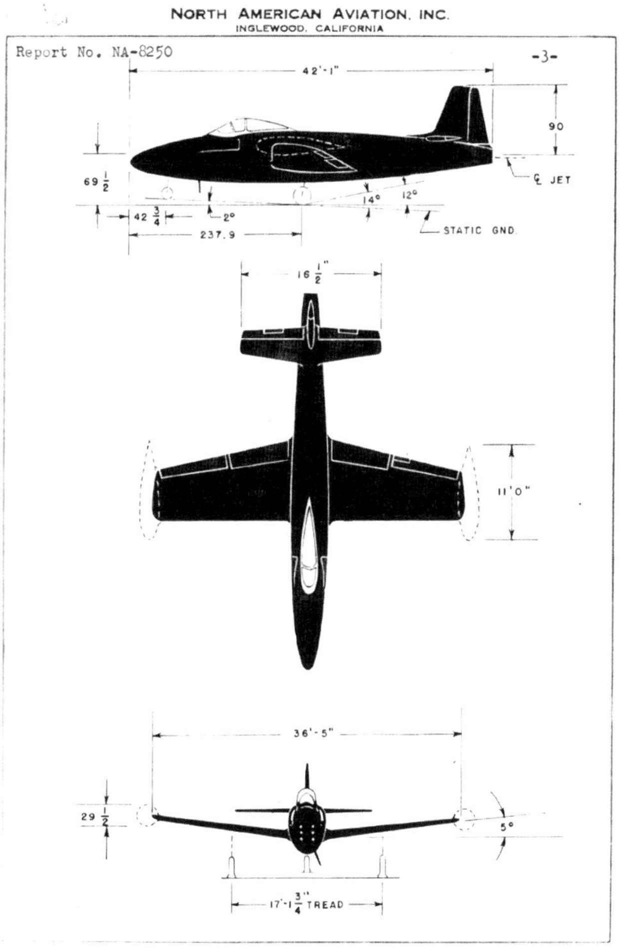

Manufacturer's drawing of the North American NA-129 project. *US National Archives via Alan Griffith*

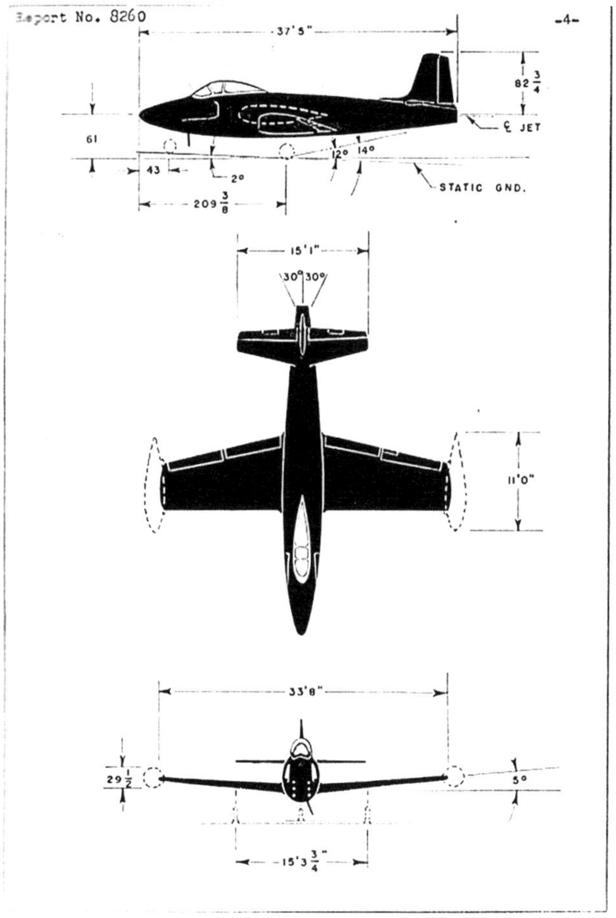

Manufacturer's drawing of the North American NA-131 project. *US National Archives via Alan Griffith*

There are still gaps in the knowledge relating to the very first generation of US jet fighters, and previously unknown designs still appear. This pair have recently come to light, some of the first studies made by North American Aviation for a high-performance single-seat single-engine jet fighter. In timescale they fall a good year behind the XP-83, but in many ways looks quite similar with their straight wings and general configuration. In neither case are details of the engine available, but both were to be armed with six 0.50in (12.7mm) machine guns in the nose and could carry two 160galUS (606lit) external fuel tanks.

The first design was designated NA-129 and the covering brochure was dated 1 August 1944. Manufacturer's estimates – span 36ft 5in (11.10m), length 42ft 1in (12.83m), maximum take-off weight 12,600lb (5,715kg), overload weight (for maximum range) 15,050lb (6,827kg), internal fuel 460galUS (1,741lit). Maximum speed 556mph (895km/h) at 11,000ft (3,353m), maximum rate of climb 4,900ft/min (1,494m/min) at sea level, service ceiling 42,200ft (12,863m), 5.27 minutes to reach 20,000ft (6,096m).

This was followed by the slightly smaller NA-131 of 10 August 1944. The equivalent data figures are - span 33ft 8in (10.26m), length 37ft 5in (11.53m), maximum take-off weight 11,034lb (5,005kg), overload weight 13,480lb (6,115kg), internal fuel 430galUS (1,628lit). Maximum speed 572mph (920km/h) at 8,000ft (2,438m), maximum rate of climb 5,980ft/min (1,823m/min) at sea level, service ceiling 43,700ft (13,320m), 4.3 minutes to reach 20,000ft (6,096m).

Manufacturer's artwork for the North American NA-129. In fact this same illustration appears to have been used for both brochures. *US National Archives via Alan Griffith*

Very rare photo showing the complete second prototype 44-84991. The extended nose and larger tailplane are well shown.
US National Archives via Dennis R. Jenkins

XP-83 data

Length:	First prototype 44ft 10in (13.66m), second prototype 45ft 2in (13.77m)
Wing span: 53ft 0in (16.15m)	
Wing area:	431sq.ft (40.08sq.m)
Gross weight:	24,090lb (10,927kg)
Maximum take-off weight:	27,500lb (12,474kg)
Powerplant:	2 x 3,750lb (16.7kN) thrust General Electric J33-GE-5 (I-40) jets
Maximum recorded speed (44-84990):	522mph (840km/h) at 15,660ft (4,773m)
Cruising speed:	441mph (710km/h) at 15,660ft (4,773m)
Range with external fuel:	1,750 miles (2,816km) at cruise speed
Time to 40,000ft (12,192m) at 23,700lb (10,750kg) weight:	21.4 minutes
Maximum rate of climb (44-84990) at 23,700lb (10,750kg) weight:	7,560ft/min (2,304m/min) at 10,000ft (3,048m)
Service ceiling (44-84990):	42,300ft (12,893m)
Armament:	First prototype 6 x 0.50in (12.7mm) machine guns. Second prototype 6 x 0.60in (15.2mm) machine guns. 2 x 1,000lb (454kg) bombs, one per wing instead of external tanks. Fitting of 4 x 20mm or 1 x 37mm cannon in nose considered.

19 Bell XFL-1

The first US Navy prototype to be reviewed here, the Bell XFL-1 Airabonita, in its appearance looked much like a navalised version of the concurrent Army Air Force's Bell P-39 Airacobra, which was built in some quantity during the war. However, in truth the Navy aircraft was a near all-new design that had a very similar shape to the Army type.

In 1938 the Navy's Bureau of Aeronautics (BuAer) issued Requests for Proposals for both single-engined and twin-engined fighter designs under two new Specifications, SD-112-13 and SD-112-14, the second of which would bring forth the Grumman XF5F-1 described in Chapter Twenty-Three. Bids for SD-112-13 opened on 11 April 1938 and five firms submitted ten designs – Bell, Brewster, Curtiss, Grumman and Vought. The background to the selection of Bell's design was outlined in a review of wartime work undertaken by the BuAer Engineering Division's VF Design Branch (VF = Fighter), as follows.

One of Vought's proposals – Vought Design B – introduced the gull wing and laid down the foundation the winning design, which became the very successful F4U Corsair. But besides Vought, an SD-112-13 contract was also awarded to Bell. The BuAer report noted that "the proposal was similar to an Army project nearing completion [the P-39]. It was felt at BuAer, with the expected advance in the rating of the Allison engine, that this plane would give the Navy a more modern airplane with outstanding performance. With the expected rating of 1,150hp (858kW) at 15,000ft (4,572m) it was felt that an attractive design could be developed around the liquid-cooled engine. A contract was therefore let for the XFL-1 airplane. As 1938 drew to a close it was very strongly felt that the Navy needed the Bell fighter in order to round off its fighter program and have one light weight fighter. This however, depended on the outcome of the Allison engine rating (V1710), for if 1,150hp (858kW) could be attained then a maximum speed of 347mph (558km/h) at 12,000ft (3,658m) could be reached."

The Bell XFL-1 prototype in flight in a picture dated 16 July 1940. *Bell via Gerald H. Balzer*

Photos of the XFL-1 taken on 1 October 1940. The aircraft still has its original shape of fin. *Bell via Gerald H. Balzer*

Another October 1940 view which reveals that the only identity marking on the airframe at this time was 'XFL-1' on the rudder. *Bell via Gerald H. Balzer*

The XFL-1's large canopy with extensive glazing is shown well in another of the walk-around shots taken in October 1940. *Mark Nankivil*

The contract for a single XFL-1 prototype was placed on 8 November 1938, the aircraft received the BuAer Number 1588 (this would be the only example built), and its Allison XV1710-6 engine was the first in-line aeroengine installed in a US Navy fighter for a decade. Designed by Robert Woods as Bell's Model 5, the main changes from the land-based P-39 were the tailwheel undercarriage, a raised cockpit seat position, different fin shape and increased wing area, an arrester hook, and underwing radiators (the fin later had to be enlarged after wind-tunnel testing). Moving the main landing gears up to the forward wing made it necessary to put the XFL-1's radiators beneath the rear of the centre wing, whereas on the P-39 they were in the wing-root. The airframe also had to be re-stressed for flight from carriers. Development work on the XFL-1 prototype was led by project engineer Paul Burr.

BuAer's reviews of its fighter programmes also noted that "there was an attempt to put tricycle landing gear on the XFL-1, but it appeared best to use a P-39 fuselage, modify it, and redesign the remainder of the plane." And from a review of work during the 1940-1941 period "Bell's XFL-1 was awaiting a rebuilt engine from the aircraft factory, and would probably not be flying again until after the first of the year." A similar review during 1941 noted "to date the Fighter Desk had not been able to get any attractive development around the XFL-1 due to the low-powered Allison engine". The aircraft was no longer listed as active in the next Design Branch review, of 7 December 1941.

The official mock-up inspection took place on 19 and 20 December 1938. During the prototype's development at Buffalo the XFL-1's weight went up by 8%, while the delayed delivery of the XV1710 engine and other problems pushed the planned first flight date back considerably, from autumn 1939 to May 1940.

Splendid sequence of air-to-air photos of the XFL-1 taken on 16 July 1940 before even 'XFL-1' had been added to the fin. On show are the original radiator cooling ducts which exhausted through slots near the trailing edge of the upper wing (air having entered via the underwing radiators), the original engine exhausts at the sides of the rear cockpit, inward retracting main undercarriage, and the arrestor hook. *Bell via Gerald H. Balzer*

Colour view also taken on 16 July 1940. The aircraft had been painted overall Navy grey but with the upper wing surfaces in chrome yellow. *Bell via Gerald H. Balzer*

Flight test

Bell test pilot Brian Sparks finally took the XFL-1 on its maiden flight on 13 May 1940, though in actual fact this was an unplanned sortie because the aircraft became airborne towards the end of a high-speed taxi run, a gust of wind pushing the airframe up from the ground. Sparks completed a circuit and landed, but not without some difficulty. And after this the XFL-1's second flight came to an abrupt end in a ditch after the XV1710-6 had cut out during take-off.

Bell's chief test pilot Robert Stanley next flew the XFL-1 on 29 June 1940 but he encountered more trouble. Here yaw oscillations stalled the fin and put the prototype into a spin and Stanley was unable to regain control until the failure of the Plexiglas panel at the canopy apex, which in the process also improved the airflow around the aircraft's rudder to give him more control. Overall the manufacturer's flying trials uncovered plenty of problems, poor handling around all three axes for one, and in particular directionally coupled with rudder reversal. The noted increases in fin area improved this situation, but another trouble was that the air passing through the radiator ducts and exiting over the wing did not provide sufficient cooling. A straight through arrangement was subsequently adopted here.

With about 35 hours of airtime logged from the manufacturer's flight trials, and with the programme now well behind schedule, on 27 February 1941 the XFL-1 was taken to Naval Air Station (NAS) Anacostia in Washington DC for its official trials (flight tests were also to be conducted at the Naval Aircraft Factory in Philadelphia). Here, the prototype recorded maximum speeds of 307mph (494km/h) at sea level and 336mph (541km/h) at 10,000ft (3,048m), a little short of the guaranteed 339mph (545km/h). However, establishing satisfactory levels of control and stability required the addition of a large amount of ballast in the aircraft's nose. Further, troubles with the XFL-1's undercarriage, plus a minimum landing speed that was too high, meant that the prototype also failed its carrier qualification trials; this required Bell to make some modifications once the aircraft had been returned to the manufacturer.

But in fact that was pretty well the end! Having by now seen the clear superiority of Vought's F4U Corsair over the XFL-1, on 12 May 1941 the Navy decided it was not worth taking the latter's development further and so abandoned the project – the would be no production FL-1s. In addition, Navy policy for a long time had been not to take inline liquid-cooled engines aboard carriers, which ensured that many in the Service had disliked the XFL-1 from the start. About a year later the prototype was earmarked for use in destructive armament tests.

XFL-1 structure

The Bell XFL-1 single-seat naval fighter prototype was an all-metal aircraft with a low position wing. The aircraft's supercharged Allison engine was installed in the centre of the fuselage to the rear of and below the pilot and drove a three-blade 10ft 4.5in (3.16m) diameter tractor propeller, via a long shaft. This very streamlined design had a normal fuel load of 126galUS (477lit) and a maximum 200galUS (757lit) and its armament was intended to be twin 0.30in (7.62mm) machine guns in the nose with a further 37mm cannon firing through the propeller hub. However, the 37mm would never be available and it was eventually replaced in the design by a 0.50in (12.7mm) machine gun; in the end only the 0.30in (7.62mm) pieces were fitted, and then just as ballast with no gun ports for them cut into the nose. Production machines would have had wing folding but the XFL-1 did not have this facility. Many of the salient features of the XFL-1 are described in the main text when comparing this prototype to the manufacturer's P-39 AAF fighter.

The XFL-1 pictured in snowy weather at Buffalo. It now has modified side fuselage engine exhausts and straight through underwing radiator ducting. In addition the fin and rudder had been enlarged and the Navy serial number added to the fin. *US Navy via Gerald H. Balzer*

ABOVE This 6 March 1941 photo of the XFL-1 provides good detail for the tailwheel part of the undercarriage. *US Navy via Gerald H. Balzer*

LEFT Close-up view of the XFL-1's forward fuselage and inner wing, including the deployed flaps. *US Navy via Gerald H. Balzer*

The Allison XV1710-6 engine installation. *US Navy via Gerald H. Balzer*

A US Navy photograph from 14 March 1941 showing the XFL-1 flying in landing configuration. *US Navy via Gerald H. Balzer*

Although probably nothing to do with any Navy programme, the XFL-1's association with the P-39 Army fighter suggests that this is the right place to put this Bell proposal for a jet-powered version of the P-39. Sadly, no details or data are available for this project but it has a cannon protruding from the centre nose and machine guns in the upper nose. *Bell via Gerald H. Balzer*

XFL-1 Data

Length:	29ft 9in (9.07m)
Wing span:	35ft 0in (10.67m)
Wing area:	232sq.ft (21.58sq.m)
Empty weight:	5,352lb (2,428kg)
Gross weight:	6,742lb (3,058kg)
Maximum take-off weight:	7,212lb (3,271kg)
Powerplant:	1 x 1,150hp (858kW) Allison XV1710-6 12-cylinder liquid-cooled inline engine
Maximum speed:	307mph (494km/h) at sea level and 336mph (541km/h) at 10,000ft/3,048m (other sources give 281mph/452km/h at sea level and 333mph/536km/h at 12,000ft/3,658m)
Maximum rate of climb:	2,630ft/min (802m/min)
Service ceiling:	30,900ft (9,418m)
Range:	1,127 miles (1,813km)
Armament:	2 x 0.30in (7.62mm) machine guns plus one 0.50in (12.70mm) or one 37mm cannon

20 Boeing XF8B-1

The subject here is the only contribution in the book to come from Boeing, a manufacturer so well known for building large bombers and civil airliners. But the unnamed XF8B-1 was an impressive beast, it was possibly the biggest and the heaviest single-seat, single piston-engine fighter produced in America, and it proved to be the Navy's last fighter powered purely by a reciprocating engine. It became known as the 'five-in-one' fighter, since potentially it could operate either as a fighter or interceptor or as a dive, torpedo or level height bomber.

No competition

Boeing's Model 400 naval fighter was an unsolicited proposal. The manufacturer had been studying the possibilities of a design around the Pratt & Whitney XR4360 two stage engine and on 1 April 1943 it submitted a proposal brochure which described the type as primarily a high performance fighter bomber. This machine would have reasonable manoeuvrability, heavy fire power and in particular long range. Although somewhat large for carrier employment, in the air it was expected to be highly satisfactory as an escort fighter, skip bomber, attack fighter or rocket carrier. It was designed to have six interchangeable 0.50in (12.70mm) or 20mm guns and had features which made it distinctive from other Navy fighter types – counter-rotating propellers and a bomb bay which could accommodate extra fuel as well as bombs.

At this stage the basic aircraft was designed to weigh some 17,000lb (7,711kg) with a top speed of 418mph (673km/h) at 25,000ft (7,620m) and a sea level rate of climb of over 3,000ft/min (914m/min).

Splendid colour photo of the first XF8B-1 57984 after it had received a glossy blue colour scheme in the late summer of 1946. *Boeing via Gerald H. Balzer*

In the long range fighter configuration a 240galUS (908lit) bomb bay tank and two standard external drop tanks would be carried, giving a range in excess of 2,700 miles (4,344km).

On 4 May 1943 Contract NOa(s) 742 was signed for three prototypes designated XF8B-1, with BuAer serial numbers 57984, 57985 and 57986, plus one static test airframe, engineering drawings and spare parts. BuAer design specification SD-349 was used as a guide for the performance requirements, stating a maximum speed of 342mph (550km/h), a minimum speed of not more than 79mph (127km/h), a ceiling of at least 30,000ft (9,144m) and a rate-of-climb at sea level of 3,760ft/min (1,146m/min). Lyle A. Wood became the head engineer working on the XF8B-1, the official airframe mock-up inspection took place between 20 and 24 September and the power plant mock-up inspection from 13 to 15 December 1943. However, a good deal of sub-assembly work on the prototypes had to be undertaken at Boeing's Renton facility, particularly for the wings, and the overall set-up put in place to build these aircraft had to fit around the firm's B-17 and B-29 bomber production programmes, with consequent delays.

Development work was also needed on the new and very large R4360, in fact the biggest displacement aviation piston engine to enter production in America. It was flight tested on Vought Corsair F4U-1 BuAer number 02460, which had been transferred to Pratt & Whitney's Harford plant and fitted with a larger cowling to accommodate the engine. The R4360 was installed from May 1943 and first flown on 12 September with the Corsair now designated F4U-1(WM) - 'WM' for 'Wasp Major'. In this aircraft Pratt & Whitney test pilot A. Lewis MacClain was able to undertake much of the engine's development flying in readiness for service use, dealing for example with aspects such as surging and problems with ignition at heights above 20,000ft (6,096m). Goodyear would take the R4360-powered Corsair a stage further with its F2G Super Corsair (Appendix Two).

On top of this, R4360 experience was forthcoming from Republic Aviation's trials flying with the XP-72 (Chapter Twelve). This was helpful in that the AAF prototype had an Aeroproducts contra-rotating propeller, which was eventually chosen for the XF8B-1 over the rival Curtiss contra-rotating unit. On 30 August 1944 the XP-72's engine had experienced overspeeding when the pilot, Ken Jernstedt, moved the propeller and throttle controls forward at the same time. Despite changes in operating practice this happened again and required further modification.

Close up of Vought Corsair F4U-1 (WM) serial 02460, the R4360 test bed aircraft. *Gerald H. Balzer*

For comparison – the F4U-1(WM) and a standard F4U-1 Corsair placed nose to nose. *Gerald H. Balzer*

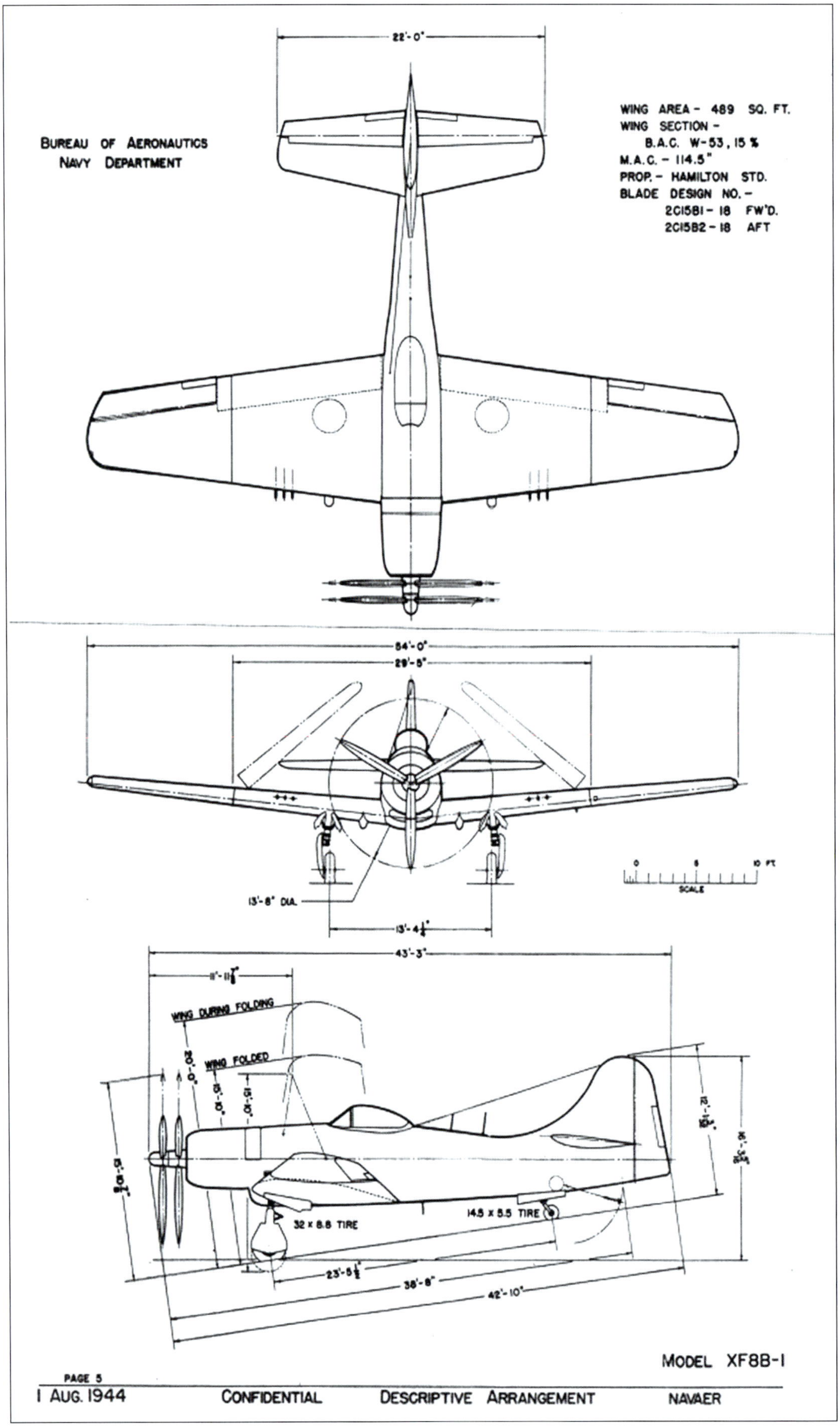

Three-view drawing of the XF8B-1 from the official Standard Aircraft Characteristics Sheet dated 1 August 1944, i.e. a few months before the first flight of the first prototype. *Ryan Crierie*

View of the first prototype as built taken outside the Boeing hanger on 12 October 1944. False windows have been painted on the front of the building as a form of camouflage. *National Archives RG-72*

At a Joint Fighter Conference held at NAS Patuxent River on 16 to 23 October 1944, Don W. Finlay from Boeing stated "We did not put the dual rotation prop on the F8B in any attempt to greatly improve the performance of the airplane. About the only thing we were after was finer handling qualities and elimination of torque particularly for the wave off condition. We believe we can approximately equal the performance of the dual rotation airplane with single rotation propellers and probably in production would plan to use the single rotation prop. We have listened with considerable interest to the stories of planes becoming unstable with dual rotation propellers." In the event none of the prototypes would fly with single-rotation propellers, but BuAer confirmed that any commitment to F8B production hinged on the development of the two stage R4360, the dual counter-rotating propellers, and the XF8B-1 comparing favourably with other fighter types.

Boeing's choice as chief test pilot for the XF8B-1's flying programme was Robert T. Lamson, who had joined the manufacturer in 1942 and, to garner experience, he flew several different single-engined pursuit type aircraft. But by the middle of 1944 the XF8B-1 was not progressing as quickly as had been anticipated, and indeed on completion the first prototype was more than six months behind schedule. In addition, the Navy's original requirement for this type of aircraft to operate with the Fleet in the Pacific was changing. High speed and manoeuvrability, rather than long range, was becoming the most important factor and consideration was now given to converting Boeing's aircraft into an attack-torpedo type.

To this effect, on 10 November 1944 BuAer's VTB (Torpedo Bomber) Design Branch requested an engineering study from Boeing, the modifications for which would include the following:

(a). Remove the two-stage engine and substitute an R4360-4 single stage variable speed single rotation unit.

(b). Remove the dual-rotation and substitute a suitable single rotation propeller for the above engine.

(c). Modify the control surfaces and empennage to provide for the single-rotation propeller.

(d). Move the pilot's cockpit forward.

(e). Incorporate a second seat behind the pilot for a radar/radio operator.

At this time the first XF8B-1 was complete (it began taxi tests on 15 November) and about 80% of the propeller vibration survey had been completed. Discussions regarding the attack version development took place on 26 December (between Lt Cmdr Farrington of BuAer's Military Requirements Division and Edward Wells, Boeing assistant chief engineer, at which time BuAer stated the definite interest of the Navy in this model) and on 24 and 25 January 1945 when representatives of BuAer's VTB Design Branch visited Boeing to view the prototype.

Flight test

The XF8B-1's initial flight finally took place, from Boeing Field, Seattle, on 27 November 1944, when Lamson completed a one hour and three minute sortie. Power plant and performance were both considered very good although the entire trip was flown with the undercarriage down; Lamson reported "the airplane is one that any pilot could fly". Over the next few days prototype 57984 accumulated

The first XF8B-1 conducts high speed taxi runs – note the deployed flaps in one view. Heavy Boeing bombers, primarily B-17s, stand behind. *National Archives RG-72 via Ryan Crierie*

over ten hours of airtime before, on 1 December, the bomb bay doors opened suddenly during a tight turn. The aircraft stayed on the ground until 26 December as Boeing made some modifications, but on 3 January it carried its first passenger, flight engineer Bud Zerega squashed into a second seat behind the pilot.

Lt Cmdr Jack Sutherland, BuAer's project officer on the aircraft, made a preliminary test flight in 57984 on 9 January 1945 and found the handling characteristics excellent and the take-off effortless with no tendency to swing. He described its stability as "remarkable", with longitudinal stability positive in both clean and dirty configurations and directional stability positive in all conditions. However, the aircraft's lateral stability was "weak positive to neutral and undoubtedly influenced by the temporary aileron geared tab installed." (The aileron then installed on the XF8B-1 was a temporary measure with geared balance tabs. This was designed to reduce the tendency for flutter at 275mph/442km/h until Boeing could produce an improved aileron installation.)

The wave-off characteristics were "superior" and the rudder and aileron continued to be effective during the wave-off. Behaviour in the stall was again "excellent" in both clean and dirty states, the elevator force becoming heavier as the stall approached. Level flight could be maintained easily with minimal attention to the controls, and the rate of roll was around 60°/sec at 250mph (402km/h). Finally, and most noticeably, having the contra-rotating propeller had resulted in a complete lack of torque. Sutherland declared that the XF8B-1 should have excellent flying characteristics for carrier operations, it appeared to be an excellent gun platform, and conversion to an attack aircraft appeared practicable.

The pilot retracts the undercarriage of 57984 on an early test flight. Once retracted the main gear was slightly exposed but the protrusion was small. *National Archives RG-72 via Ryan Crierie*

VTB Design Branch staff observed the first XF8B in flight on 24 January 1945 and agreed, in general, that the aircraft appeared to have exceptional performance characteristics. However, unless the need was imperative for an extra man to operate the radar on special missions, the XF8B-1 as currently designed appeared to be an ideal carrier attack aircraft and in combat could be utilised much more effectively than a two-seat version. Plans were prepared to convert the third XF8B-1 prototype into this proposed attack aircraft.

The trials flying was delayed by a crash on 13 February 1945. During a taxi run at high speed

The first prototype receives attention on 27 November 1944, the view providing details of the nose, propeller, air intake, main undercarriage and wing (with no guns fitted). As first flown the prototype was finished in overall natural metal. *National Archives RG-72 via Ryan Crierie*

On 30 January 1945 Bob Lamson flew 57984 with engineer Bud Zerega squashed into the seat behind him. *National Archives RG-72 via Ryan Crierie*

Lamson, with Zerega again in the rear seat, lifted the aircraft off the runway at 120mph (193km/h), but when setting back down the undercarriage retracted and the propeller clipped the concrete. The blades split at their seams and twisted around each other and 57984 slid for 1,000ft (305m) before stopping; Lamson and Zerega were unhurt. The cause of the problem was a faulty microswitch and repairs took nearly three weeks, Boeing taking the opportunity to install new bomb bay doors and undercarriage doors along with a new engine and propeller. Flying resumed on 4 March.

The preliminary evaluation trials with 57984 were officially held at the Naval Air Test Center (NATC) at Patuxent River from 12 March to 4 April 1945, the aircraft having been flown there by Lamson with George Edmonstone. Here no less than 31 Navy and Marine pilots (including one from the Royal Navy) evaluated the prototype, in the process subjecting it to some rough handling. One

The XF8B-1 banks away from the camera aircraft over Washington on 30 January 1945, a pleasing view which gives plenty of underside detail including the beautifully-shaped tapered wing. *National Archives RG-72 via Jared Zichek*

pilot 'performed' an extreme ground loop, while another set the rudder tab 0.6in (15mm) to the left to counter the non-existent torque and as a result reported left wing heaviness! On two occasions 57984 was flown against a Grumman F7F Tigercat piston fighter and a Bell P-59 Airacomet jet fighter, the first time unsuccessfully but on the second, thanks to a more aggressive approach from the pilot Cdr Harrington, with much better results. Harrington also made a dozen consecutive measured take-offs at 20,000lb (9,072kg) weight.

The attack configuration trials were completed satisfactorily, though all of the pilots agreed that the brakes were weak despite being able (just about) to hold the aircraft at take-off power. Nevertheless, the XF8B-1 was clearly an excellent flying machine and it was now released to NAS Anacostia for inspection by more BuAer personnel. Here, another ten pilots sampled the aircraft before, on 9 April, Lamson and Edmonstone flew it back to Seattle.

A VTB Design Branch memo of 19 April 1945 recommended procuring production aircraft with as few changes as possible from the present configuration, except for provision to carry a torpedo. However, on 4 June the Director of Engineering Division wrote to the Director of Military Requirements Division summarising the investigation into using the XF8B-1 as a torpedo aircraft. He stated: "Engineering is unable to make a favourable recommendation for the procurement of the F8B as a torpedo airplane since this involves setting up production of an airplane which has no apparent advantages for this mission." Military Requirements Division followed up stating that there was to be no future procurement of the F8B, so ending Boeing's chances of producing a naval bomber version.

In fact, by early April 1945 the Navy no longer had need for such a large long range fighter. Inasmuch as the second and third airframes were nearly completed, these would be delivered to the Navy, but no further examples of this type were to be constructed. As of January 1946 the contract was being wound up.

View from above with Lamson and Zerega in the cockpit over Seattle. The rear seat was a temporary affair and must have been most uncomfortable for the incumbent. *National Archives RG-72*

Publicity photos described the XF8B-1 as "the most versatile fighter in the world" which could be utilised as a bomber, torpedo plane, attack plane and interceptor. They added that it had "a service ceiling comparable to Boeing's two famous bombers, the B-17 Flying Fortress and the B-29 Superfortress". *National Archives RG-72*

57984 pictured on 23 March 1945 after arriving at Patuxent River. The aircraft now sports an olive-drab anti-glare panel over the nose. *US Navy*

Back at Seattle 57984 was tested with different trim tab settings to try and cure control heaviness, and from 14 July it was in the hangar for the aileron controls to be rebuilt with the five-to-one hydraulic boost system. When it flew again on 22 October 1945 the response at high speed had improved substantially, and by 4 December 57984 had logged over 134 hours of flight time. During 1946 it received a new engine and cockpit canopy and on 8 October the back draft from the first XF8B-1 during a run up was sufficient to blow over a Piper J-3 Cub light aircraft; as such this 'Damaged' was the fighter's only 'Score' during its career.

On 15 October 1946 Lt Frank J. Shaw accepted 57984 on behalf of the Navy and then flew it to Patuxent River. Assigned to Research and Test to begin with, the aircraft was later transferred to Naval Air Material Command (NAMC) at Philadelphia where it was used in the Barrier Development Program. In fact the aircraft was completely wrecked during catapult and arresting trials and it was finally stricken from the Navy inventory for scrap on 31 January 1948.

The second XF8B-1 prototype, 57985, was rolled out complete except for its engine on 31 January 1945. Such was the delay in getting one, however, it did not fly until 27 November (in fact the R4360-10 from 57984 now thoroughly overhauled after the latter's belly landing on 13 February 1945). This aircraft would receive numerous modifications specifically for potential Army Air Force service (below), including a redesigned canopy and air scoop and the introduction of dive flaps (both the second and third prototypes had cleaner airframes than 57984, which raised the critical Mach number and reduced drag).

However, before it could reach the AAF, on 26 December 1945 57985 was being taken through some high-speed manoeuvres when the engine failed. Bob Lamson managed to land at Everett, Washington Municipal Airport, but the aircraft suffered some damage in soft ground. A loose screw had been sucked through the impeller and lodged in a valve opening, which had resulted in a flashback.

Despite being turned down as a Navy bomber, the XF8B-1 was offered to the USAAF as an attack aircraft.

Nose angle view of the first XF8B-1 at Pax River on 23 March 1945. Note the unusual undercarriage doors and what appears to be dummy gun ports in the wings. *US Navy*

Indeed, the Service's interest went back to early 1945 and updated versions of the R4360 were considered, the second giving 3,500hp (2,610kW) military power rating and no less than 3,900hp (2,908kW) war emergency power; the armament would be six 20mm cannon plus a variety of bomb loads. From 13 February 1946 the second prototype began a thorough AAF assessment at Wright Field which lasted until August before being halted by another engine failure. The third and final XF8B-1 prototype, 57986, did not incorporate all of the AAF modifications, in particular the dive flaps, but with the unavailability of the second aircraft, by 23 July 1946 it was at Eglin Field conducting the armament trials originally earmarked for 57985. In spite of this assessment, no XA-designation was allocated to the XF8B-1.

By now the XF8B-1's control and aileron heaviness had been much improved. An AAF Evaluation Report stated that the type's handling characteristics were excellent at low speeds, but the controls tightened up considerably with increases in speed. Above 300mph (483km/h) IAS the aileron forces became excessive but at all speeds the radius of turn was excellent. Longitudinal stability was acceptable but a problem with longitudinal oscillation was considered undesirable for a long range aircraft. The stall warning (a slight buffet 2-3mph/3-5km/h prior to the stall) was marginal and the indicated stall speeds in level flight were 103mph (166km/h) in the clean condition, 105mph (169km/h) wheels down, 85mph (137km/h) with both the wheels and flaps down.

The XF8B-1's control forces were 'reasonable' in all manoeuvres but the ailerons would become increasingly stiff at speeds over 300mph (483km/h) IAS. Normal approach speed was 120mph to 130mph (193km/h to 209km/h) IAS and here the control was excellent; touch down came at 85mph (137km/h) IAS. The loss of 57985 had prevented maximum range and endurance performance flights from being completed, but the longest recorded flight was only five and a half hours, i.e. well under the time needed for a long-range sortie.

For dive bombing the XF8B-1 appeared unsuitable due to longitudinal instability and a fast build-up of speed in the dive; indeed, at a dive angle of 60° the instability would distract the pilot who, at this point, had to concentrate on his bomb run. The recommendation was to add large dive flaps, which of course had been fitted to the incapacitated 57985 at Wright Field. However, for low level bombing, Boeing's aircraft proved much better and its 5° nose down attitude in level flight when flying at 350mph (563km/h), plus the 9° downslope of the cowling, gave the pilot an excellent view out. Up to 3,200lb (1,452kg) of bombs could be carried and as a fighter the XF8B-1 was confirmed as a stable gun platform, but there was a heating problem resulting from the guns being set so close together.

The AAF's Brig Gen Carl A. Brandt recommended that the XF8B-1 "be used only for low-level bombing", not for dive bombing, and stated that "it does not compare favourably with conventional type fighter-bombers, such as the P-47 and P-51 type aircraft." In other words the XF8B-1 was no better than the AAF's current types. In general the AAF's pilots considered that an aircraft as large as the XF8B-1 really should have two engines. The testing of 57986 at Eglin was concluded on 11 December 1946.

The final demonstration of the XF8B-1 for BuAer by Boeing, held at Seattle and using 57986, was conducted between 10 May and 26 June 1946. At this stage the aircraft had neither made a take-off or a landing onboard a carrier nor operated from a catapult. The final demonstration was to show that the XF8B-1 would perform all air manoeuvres in a satisfactory manner, that it had satisfactory handling qualities in level flight at speeds near the stall, and no undesirable characteristics that would make it dangerous or unsuitable for Navy use.

During the demonstration six maximum speed dives were made with pullouts of various load factors at approximately 10,000ft (3,048m). Differing degrees of buffet were experienced and the pilot reported that a damped longitudinal oscillation was set up by changing the elevator trim during the dives. Later during the high altitude performance test the pilot experienced a longitudinal oscillation while flying 'hands off' at 30,000ft (9,144m), full throttle. During spin tests full rudder was required to initiate the spin, and recovery was initiated by full rudder reversal followed by pushing the elevator control forward.

At a trim speed of 180mph (290km/h) indicated the pilot attempted two snap rolls to the right and two to the left after which he reduced the speed to 160mph (257km/h) indicated and attempted one to the left and two to the right. The pilot stated that in all cases the aircraft snap rolled only one-half turn - that is the stalled wing became unstalled when inverted; it was necessary to complete the manoeuvre with an aileron roll and he also reported considerable elevator buffet. Boeing felt that the inability of the XF8B-1 to snap roll was due to its excellent stalling characteristics.

For these tests the normal fighter weight was 17,220lb (7,811kg) and overload 19,523lb (8,856kg). The maximum speed on military rated power at the critical altitude (26,500ft/8,077m) was 432mph (695km/h) – the requirement was 429mph (690km/h) - the minimum speed without power at sea level was 79mph (127km/h) and the sea level rate of climb 3,110ft/min (948m/min). No flights were made specifically to establish the service ceiling, but during these trials the XF8B-1 did reach an altitude of 37,500ft (11,430m).

The second XF8B-1 was accepted by the Navy on 5 November 1946 and, like 57984, was stricken at Philadelphia on 31 January 1948, here after having been assigned to Flight Test and used as a calibration aircraft. 57986 was accepted by the Navy on 1 August 1947 and, after being based at different times at Seattle, San Diego and Philadelphia, it was stricken in Philadelphia on 16 March 1950.

ABOVE The first XF8B-1 appears to have been much the most photographed of the three prototypes. Very few views are available of the second example. *National Archives RG-72 via Gerald H. Balzer*

RIGHT AND BELOW These sequences show 57984 after it re-emerged in 1946 having received a new canopy, a new engine and a coat of glossy blue paint, plus a 'Boeing' logo on the nose. While in Boeing hands these aircraft carried little in the way of military markings. *National Archives RG-72*

In updated form 57984 was used for inflight undercarriage tests, in this case over Mount Rainier. Bob Lamson was again the pilot. *National Archives RG-72*

Excellent general view of one of the XF8B-1 prototypes in its semi-gloss colour scheme. *National Archives RG-72*

The complete lack of identity markings makes it difficult to establish just which prototype is on view here, but it appears to be the third machine prior to delivery to the Navy after having had its spinner painted glossy sea blue. *National Archives RG-72*

A photo taken on 26 June 1946 of the newly completed third prototype 57986. The white 'Boeing' logo on the cowling was removed on transfer to Navy ownership. *National Archives RG-72*

At the same time as losing the logo, 57986 also had a pitot attached to the left wingtip. *National Archives RG-72 via Ryan Crierie*

XF8B-1 structure

Boeing's XF8B-1 was a single seat all-metal (aluminium alloy) cantilever wing fighter-bomber. The wing centre section had a single, continuous, web-type spar with heavy gauge structural skin forward reinforced by stringers; the structure aft of the spar was lighter. The inboard wing section included the bomb bay (since the spar ran through the body and formed the lower part of the forward bomb bay bulkhead) and also the main fuel tanks, guns, main landing gear and large Fowler flaps which, when retracted, formed the lower trailing edge surface.

Flush riveting and aerodynamic smoothing was used on all major frontal surfaces to improve laminar airflow. The wing cross-section was designed with the thickest part further aft than in previous designs so that, with this shape, the wing would cut through the air instead of pushing into it; thus (in theory) a much greater speed could be attained before the 'compressibility effect' became a factor. Control surfaces were large and metal covered and had trim tabs acting as both balance and booster tabs. Dive flaps were provided for emergency pull outs from high speed dives while the rapid acceleration necessary for a wave-off from a carrier landing made it necessary to fit an automatic flap retract feature which would activate at 150mph (241km/h) – this would prevent the surfaces from staying locked when power was applied. The wings could fold and the wing flaps would extend over the fold by 20in (51cm). The main undercarriage would pivot through 90° before retracting rearwards.

Major structural members of the body were two longerons (stretching along the bottom corners of the body from the firewall to the last body bulkhead), channel-type circumferential frames, bulkheads and stressed skin. The Pratt & Whitney R4360-10 with its two-stage supercharger drove a six-blade Aeroproducts dual-rotation propeller 13ft 5.69in (4.16m) in diameter. Besides bombs the rack under each wing could take a 150galUS (568lit) drop tank. In each wing (from the root moving outwards) were three internal tanks holding 100galUS (379lit), 42galUS (159lit) and 50galUS (189lit) respectively, there was a 40galUS (151lit) tank in the forward fuselage, and then a large droppable 270galUS (1,022lit) tank could go in the bomb bay. Provision was made for either six 0.50in (12.70mm) machine guns or six 20mm cannon or any combination of the two, all beyond the propeller arc; if the latter then the 20mm would be installed outboard of the machine guns.

The third XF8B-1 forlorn on the dump awaiting scrapping at the Naval Aircraft Factory (NAF) at Philadelphia in the early 1950s. These views provide good detail of the wing fold mechanism. *Ron Downey*

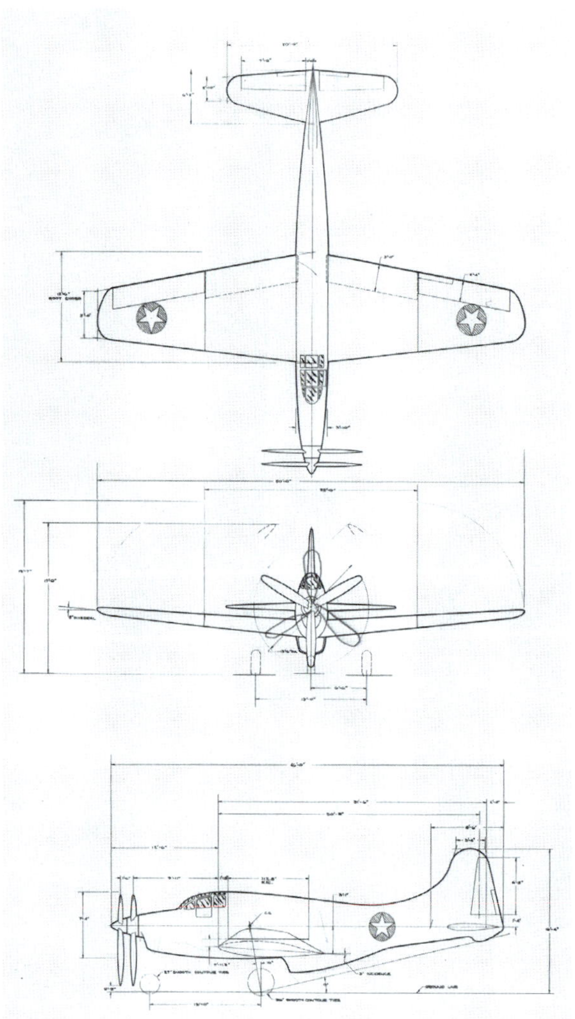

American Secret Projects: Fighters, Bombers and Attack Aircraft 1937-1945 gave details of a series of Boeing projects leading up to the Model 400 XF8B-1. One further design, unknown to the authors at the time of publication, was Boeing's Model 375. The brochure for this preliminary study is dated 30 June 1942.

The Boeing Model 375 would have been a large single seat aircraft designed primarily as a high altitude carrier based fighter, and specifically for operations at 40,000ft (12,192m). The estimated maximum rate of climb at this altitude with military power was over 1,400ft/min (427m/min) and the maximum speeds, also with military power, 450mph (724km/h) at 40,000ft (12,192m) and 436mph (702km/h) at 30,000ft (9,144m). Maximum rate of climb 3,200ft/min (975m/min) at sea level, stalling speed power off 75mph (121km/h).

The engine was to be a 2,300hp (1,715kW) Aviation Manufacturing Corporation (Lycoming) XH2470 (also used by the XP-54 in Chapter Five) equipped with a Turbo Engineering exhaust-driven two stage turbo supercharger. It was placed behind the pilot and drove a six-blade 13ft 6in (4.11m) diameter dual rotating constant speed propeller through an extension shaft and propeller reduction gear. Sufficient fuel for a maximum range of 1,000 miles (1,609km) was carried internally and, for the ferry condition, additional fuel could be carried in the outer wing panels (in integral fuel tanks). The normal fighter condition gross weight was 15,300lb (6,940kg), Model 375's length was 46ft 0in (14.02m) and span 50ft 0in (15.24m). Armament was four 20mm cannon, two in each wing panel, the structure was aluminium alloy semi-monocoque, the movable control surfaces were to be in aluminium with fabric covering, Fowler type flaps would go on the inboard wing panels, and a tricycle landing gear was fitted.

US National Archives RG-341 via Jared Zichek

XF8B-1 data

Length:	43ft 4in (13.21m)
Wing span:	54ft 0in (16.46m)
Folded span:	29ft 4in (8.97m)
Wing area:	489sq.ft (45.48sq.m)
Empty weight:	14,190lb (6,437kg)
Gross weight:	20,508lb (9,302kg)
Maximum take-off weight:	21,691lb (9,839kg)
Powerplant:	1 x 3,000hp (2,237kW) Pratt & Whitney R4360-10 Wasp Major 28-cylinder four-row air-cooled radial piston engine
Maximum speed (Military power):	375mph (603km/h) at sea level, 433mph (697km/h) at 23,200ft (7,071m)
Maximum rate of climb:	3,660ft/min (1,116m/min)
Service ceiling:	At least 37,500ft (11,430m)
Maximum range:	2,300 miles (3,701km)
Armament:	6 x 0.50in (12.70mm) machine guns or 6 x 20mm cannon; 1 x 2,000lb (907kg), 2 x 1,600lb (726kg) or 1,000lb (454kg) or 4 x 500lb (227kg) bombs in bomb bay, 2 x 2,000lb (907kg) or 1,600lb (726kg) or 1,000lb (454kg) or 500lb (227kg) bombs on external underwing racks; 2 x Mk.13-3 torpedoes.

21 Curtiss XF14C-1

Yet another fighter type from Curtiss, the XF14C-1 was on this occasion a prototype designed and prepared for the US Navy, with the intention of operating it from carriers and specifically for high altitude operations.

Early in March 1941 BuAer had plans under study for the design of a fighter around the experimental Lycoming XH2470 liquid-cooled engine which, it was hoped, would provide the Navy with a "full strength full range" fighter in the 450mph (724km/h) class; in general, up to this time, the Navy had bought fighters powered by air cooled radial engines. Eventually Contract 88195 of 30 June 1941 was signed with Curtiss for one prototype fitted with the Lycoming powerplant and designated XF14C-1. The first mock-up assessment was held on 4, 5 and 6 November 1941 at the Curtiss Wright plant in Buffalo and was attended by BuAer's Lt Cdr J. B. Pearson Jr, Head of the VF Design Branch; a second mock-up inspection followed on 12 February 1942. Initially the F14C's armament was to have been four or six 0.50in (12.7mm) machine guns, but eventually a batch of four 20mm cannon became the preferred choice.

During 1942 the Bureau of Aeronautics had three conventional fighter types under consideration, the Grumman F6F Hellcat, Chance Vought F4U Corsair and the Curtiss F14C. However, it was found that the latter programme was not progressing as rapidly or as smoothly as had been expected, and any hopes towards success with this machine, for both the VF Design Branch and the contractor, were diminishing. The problem was that the Lycoming

The Curtiss XF14C-2 prototype serial 03183. Its light colour scheme was at the time unusual. *Curtiss via Gerald H. Balzer*

In a picture dated 7 September 1943, the XF14C-2 shows off its contra-rotating propeller, fairings for the projecting 20mm cannon barrels, and the wide-track undercarriage. *Curtiss via Gerald H. Balzer*

engine was not providing the expected level of power; indeed at critical altitudes in military power it was 300hp (224kW) short of expectations and this reduction, combined with a gradual increase of the normal gross weight of the aircraft, had brought about an appreciable lowering of the prototype's estimated performance. Consequently, there was interest in a possible alternative power unit and the two-stage turbo superchargered Wright R3350 was duly selected.

Accordingly, in January 1942 the contract was amended to add one XF14C-2 prototype, based on the XF14C-1 but incorporating an R3350 two-stage unit fitted with a Birmann turbo (Rudolph Birmann had designed and patented turbochargers from the 1930s). The mock-up for the XF14C-2 was examined officially on 19 March 1942 and, at about the same time that the XF14C-2 section of the programme began its development, further authorisation was given for two XF14C-3s. These would also have the R3350, but in addition they introduced a pressurised cockpit for the high altitude role.

However, the effort to develop the XF14C project still failed to progress as had been hoped and in 1943 it was confirmed that the Lycoming XH2470 could not fulfil its promise. Consequently the XF14C-1 was never completed, work having stopped by the end of 1943 despite the airframe (BuA number 03184) being well advanced in its construction (the Navy had also built a production plant in Toledo in Ohio specifically to undertake F14C-1 production). This aircraft (plus one of the XF14C-3s) was cancelled in December 1943, leaving the turbo-supercharged XF14C-2 and the second pressure cabin XF14C-3 to undergo further development. In the end, however, only the XF14C-2 was completed and flown, and in 1945 the second XF14C-3 still under contract was also cancelled.

Flight test

Development work on the XF14C-2 prototype, Navy serial number 03183, continued albeit very slowly, primarily because other more important large scale war programmes now had priority; for example the R3350 was much needed for the Boeing B-29 bomber, which had been placed on a very high priority. This point is reflected by photographs dated 7 September 1943 which suggest that the prototype

Another 7 September photo, this side angle shot shows off the fighter's stocky and quite ungainly fuselage. The 'Coral Princess' diving girl was painted on both sides of the engine cowling. *Curtiss via Tommy H. Thomason*

ABOVE Near rear view which shows the XF14C-2's tall and quite narrow fin and rudder. *Curtiss via Gerald H. Balzer*

RIGHT For carrier stowage the wings would fold upwards and inwards. *Curtiss via Gerald H. Balzer*

BELOW Nose view which reveals the dihedral on the outer mainplanes. *Curtiss via Gerald H. Balzer*

Another port side view (and another September 1943 photo), though here the aircraft is angled slightly with the nose toward the camera. Note the engine exhaust directly beneath the centre wing, and the open canopy. *Curtiss via Tommy H. Thomason*

was at that time near complete, and yet the XF14C-2 did not make its maiden flight until 4 July 1944. In truth, by this time the Navy no longer needed a special high altitude fighter, although 03183 was formally accepted by the Service on 2 September 1944.

As far as is known to the author, little information appears to have survived relating to the XF14C-2's flight test programme, how it behaved in the air and any descriptions of its characteristics. What is known is that in the air there was considerable vibration from the propellers, accompanied by high levels of noise, and the highest recorded speed (398mph/640km/h) was well down on the predicted maximum. The XF14C-2 was eventually delivered to the Naval Air Material Center (NAMC) in Philadelphia where it was principally used for engine installation trials.

The XF14C programme was finally cancelled early in 1945 after the US Navy had equipped its squadrons with the Grumman Hellcat and Vought Corsair, so a production F14C never had the chance to join these outstanding fighters in the air war over the sea. George Spangenberg of BuAer, the man responsible for the Design Requirements for new naval aircraft, and who also evaluated them from the 1940s onwards, did not like the XF14C-2 at all; in fact he was particularly critical, describing the prototype as "a dog". Said prototype was last observed standing derelict in long grass minus engine cowlings and propeller (and covered with canvas covers), with the wings folded and the guns replaced by plugs. It was presumably scrapped soon after this viewing.

XF14C structure

The stocky single-seat Curtiss XF14C had an all metal airframe and structure, a straight tapered wing of slightly 'inverted gull-wing' form and a tall but relatively small round-topped fin and rudder with a set-back tailplane. Since the contra-rotating propellers had removed the effects and problems of torque, it is assumed that a bigger fin would have been made necessary had a large single-rotation propeller been fitted (which would have produced plenty of torque). A very large cowling enclosed the engine and there was a substantial exhaust pipe beneath the fuselage. Air intakes were positioned in the wing leading edges alongside the wing roots, the cockpit canopy was formed with heavy framing, a retractable tail-wheel type undercarriage was used and the armament was housed in the flat-base centre section wing inside the wing-fold position.

Both versions had fixed internal tankage for 230galUS (871lit) of fuel and would also carry a pair of 75galUS (284lit) external tanks. Each version had a Curtiss CS propeller - the XF14C-1 was to have had a four-blade single-rotation 14ft 2in (4.32m) diameter type, the XF14C-2 received a six-blade dual-rotation 13ft 0in (3.96m) and 13ft 2in (4.01m) diameter type. For the latter installation the rear left-hand three-blade prop had root cuffs or coverings, to reduce (it is understood) the degree of turbulence and thus provide a smoother airflow into the intakes that were situated so close to the spinner.

In this picture the end of the retractable arrester hook is just visible behind the tailwheel, protruding from the bottom of the end fuselage. *Curtiss via Gerald H. Balzer*

Photographs from 24 March 1942 and 15 January 1943 respectively, showing the R3350 installation in the XF14C-2. *Curtiss via Gerald H. Balzer*

It was a very pleasant surprise for the author to find a photo of the XF14C in flight. *Curtiss via Gerald H. Balzer*

XF14C-1 data

Estimates at November 1942	
Length:	38ft 4in (11.68m)
Wing span:	46ft 0in (14.02m)
Folded span:	22ft 6in (6.86m)
Wing area:	375sq.ft (34.875sq.m)
Empty weight:	9,868lb (4,476kg)
Gross weight:	12,691lb (5,757kg)
Maximum take-off weight:	13,868lb (6,291kg)
Powerplant:	1 x 2,200hp (1,641kW) Lycoming XH2470-4 24-cylinder 'H'-shape liquid-cooled inline piston engine
Maximum speed (normal gross weight):	344mph (553km/h) at 3,500ft (1,067m), 374mph (602km/h) at 17,000ft (5,182m)
Sea level rate of climb:	2,810ft/min (856m/min) at sea level
Service ceiling:	30,500ft (9,296m)
Normal range:	1,080 miles (1,738km)
Maximum range (with auxiliary tanks):	1,520 miles (2,446km)
Armament:	4 x 20mm cannon in wings

XF14C-2 data

Length:	37ft 9in (11.51m)
Wing span:	46ft 0in (14.02m)
Folded span:	22ft 6in (6.86m)
Wing area:	375sq.ft (34.875sq.m)
Empty weight:	10,582lb (4,800kg)
Gross weight:	13,405lb (6,081kg)
Maximum take-off weight:	14,582lb (6,614kg)
Powerplant:	1 x 2,300hp (1,715kW) turbo supercharged Wright XR3350-16 Duplex Cyclone 18-cylinder two-row air-cooled radial piston engine
Maximum speed (estimate 11.42):	317mph (510km/h) at sea level,
Maximum speed (best achieved):	398mph (640km/h) at 32,000ft (9,754m)
Sea level rate of climb (estimate 11.42):	2,700ft/min (823m/min)
Service ceiling (estimate 11.42):	39,500ft (12,040m)
Normal range (estimate 11.42):	950 miles (1,529km)
Maximum range (estimate 11.42):	1,355 miles (2,180km)
Armament:	4 x 20mm cannon in wings

22 Curtiss XF15C-1

Another big prototype designed by Curtiss, the XF15C-1 represented a final and complete break from the manufacturer's old P-40 Warhawk line, but this aircraft would be the last fighter type produced by the manufacturer for the Navy. It was intended to operate from combat carriers only and not from the smaller wartime escort carriers.

The adoption of turbojet-powered aircraft for carrier operations in the early days of this new form of power unit presented a problem for the Navy, in that the first generation engines could not provide enough thrust to ensure that an aircraft could get off the deck safely, even if a catapult was used. Combining the jet with a traditional reciprocating engine was seen, at least in the short term, as a solution; now there would be sufficient power to take off. In addition, the first turbojets also consumed fuel very quickly, so shutting the jet down and using piston power only would ensure that the fighter could cruise over long distances; then, when bursts of high speed were required, say for combat, the jet would supply the necessary extra power.

BuAer's VF Desk historical report from February 1946 noted that within the first group of experimental Navy jet fighters there were two combination-jet/piston-powered types, the Curtiss

Superb picture of the second Curtiss XF15C-1 in flight. *Curtiss via Gerald H. Balzer*

The first XF15C-1, serial 01213, had a very short life and, as a result, there are relatively few photographs of the aircraft. However, those that are available include a number of fine air-to-air studies. *Curtiss via Gerald H. Balzer*

XF15C and the Ryan XFR-1. These conformed to the Navy's belief at this time that a pure jet-fighter would not be suitable for carrier based operations and would require supplementary piston power as back up. The FR Fireball first flew in June 1944 and entered service in limited numbers in March 1945, but only one squadron was equipped with the type and it was withdrawn from service in mid-1947. The second project was the much larger and heavier XF15C, which was designed to have a greater radius of action than the Fireball.

Curtiss Wright delivered its proposals for what became the XF15C-1 to VF Design Branch on 1 February 1944. This aircraft was designed to be an all-purpose medium range fighter with a radius of action comparable to that of the Vought F4U Corsair and Grumman F6F Hellcat, and capable of attaining extremely high performance. And it was to be a heavily armed with four or six lightweight 20mm (T-31) cannon which was at the time the most recent development in aircraft armament. Like the Ryan FR, it had a conventional R2300-E single stage piston engine as its main power plant with an additional auxiliary jet unit arranged in tandem. But the jet chosen here differed from any of the others used in US Navy fighters in that it was to be a British de Havilland Halford H-1 unit, selected because of its high power and because it was expected to be available earlier. This combination would furnish the fighter with the necessary power requirements for a carrier-type aircraft.

The H-1B Goblin was to built in the US under license by Allis-Chalmers as the J36 and with this engine the XF15C-1's performance was calculated to be about 485mph (780km/h) at 25,000ft (7,620m) altitude, with a sea level rate of climb in excess of 4,890ft/min (1,490m/min). Indeed, the XF15C promised extremely high performance at all altitudes, from sea level up to 35,000ft (10,668m), and a procurement directive for three prototypes and one static test article was signed on 24 February 1944. On 7 April 1944 contract N0a(s) 3245 was signed to cover the order and BuA serials 01213, 01214 and 01215 was allotted to these aircraft (some publications state that the aircraft was named 'Stingeree'); project engineer at Curtiss was Fred Steele. A mock-up conference was held on 6, 7 and 8 April at the contractor's plant in Buffalo and was followed by the power plant mock-up assessment on 1 May. Three officers from VF Design Branch, Cmdr Tyra, Lt Cdr Sutherland and Lt Gavin, were on the mock-up board.

As an aside, the VF Branch report looked more generally at the pace of development of jet propulsion in the UK as compared to the US. Capt Pearson of VF Design Branch had recognised early in

Excellent view of the underside of the first prototype which shows the short jet pipe for the H-1 engine. No large scale serial identity numbers appear to have been carried by any of the three prototypes, that is at least until the third example reached NATC at Patuxent River. *Curtiss via Tommy Thomason*

Views from similar angles showing the first prototype with its low tail position, and then for the second aircraft after the horizontal surface had been moved to the top of the fin. *Curtiss via Gerald H. Balzer and US National Archives RG-72 via Kevin Morrow*

the war the trend towards the development of jet propelled aircraft and he was anxious that the Navy should have a part in this process. Although the first all jet Navy aircraft, the McDonnell XFD-1 (later the FH Phantom) was under development in 1942, there was "only meagre jet-propulsion information and experience available in the US". England had gone further in the way of getting a useable jet engine and, in order to survey their progress, a group from BuAer's Engineering Division, which included Capt Pearson, visited the UK. It was felt that the scope of English jet development surpassed that of the United States by about 10 to 1.

As a result of the visit of this Naval group, it was recommended that (a) a larger effort be directed toward jet development, (b) the commitment for Allis-Chalmers to manufacture the Halford H-1 in America should be carried out at high priority, (c) further liaison on these problems to take place between organisations in America and Great Britain, in order that full advantage might be taken of the extensive work which had been accomplished in England up to that time, (d) that a representative be attached to the office of the Naval Air Attaché in London, whose full time efforts could be applied toward following and reporting on jet development, and (e) a joint Army-Navy-NACA working committee should be organised to study the whole field of gas turbine applications to aircraft, and to assist in guiding the development of these machines in the United States. In spite of these recommendations the report declared that, at the time of writing (4 February 1946), "the relative scale of effort remained greatly in favour of the British".

Port side photos of the XF15C-1 with differing tail configurations. However, in this case they depict the same aircraft, the second prototype 01214. Note how the extended dorsal fin on the upper rear fuselage is larger for the T-tail. *Curtiss via Gerald H. Balzer and US National Archives RG-72 via Kevin Morrow*

Flight test

Up to this time Curtiss had no prior experience with jet engines and so a Navy attack aircraft, Grumman TBF Avenger serial 24141, was acquired on loan to serve as a test bed. The necessary modifications to this aircraft were carried out during spring 1944 with the J36 housed in a belly nacelle and fed by a pair of air inlets beneath the forward fuselage. Ground tests with the H-1 installed took place during November 1944, with flight trials beginning during December.

By the spring of 1945 the construction of the first prototype 01213 was progressing well, and on 27 February it was possible to complete taxi runs and some short hops. Curtiss test pilot Lloyd Child then made the maiden flight on the 28th but all of this was conducted using the piston engine only (in fact an R2800-22W), without the jet. The Halford unit was late arriving from England but it finally reached Buffalo on 20 March; delivery of the intended R2800-34W was also late.

On 3 May 1945 the first prototype began flying with the experimental H-1 unit installed and initially without any major troubles being experienced, although the aileron rudder forces were somewhat heavy at low speeds and then light at 350mph (563km/h) indicated, and work was also needed on the flight controls. Tragically, on 8 May 1945 the first XF15C-1 crashed at low altitude after suffering fuel starvation (caused by a faulty valve) while approaching to land. This was during trials prior to delivery to the Navy and the pilot, Charles Cox, was killed.

In June 1945 Curtiss had proposed incorporating a T-tail on the second and third airframes, i.e moving the horizontal surface from its original low position to the top of the fin. This new arrangement had the advantage of a 30% increase in spot aboard a carrier and appeared to offer improvements for the aircraft's aerodynamics during the approach, plus improved stability during high speed flight. The following changes were in due course implemented:

1. A new horizontal tail with sealed internally balanced elevators.

2. Tilting the thrust axis downwards by 5°.

3. Replacing the double slotted flaps with NACA 27.5% chord single slotted flaps.

4. Incorporating a down spring or blowback tab in the elevator control system.

5. Off-setting the fin by 2° and using a larger dorsal fin than that originally fitted.

The second prototype 01214 first flew on 9 July 1945, again with Child in the cockpit and now with an Allis-Chalmers-produced J36 engine installed; both airframes two and three were fully equipped for carrier operation, with catapult fittings and tail arrestor hooks. While their performance created a favourable impression, early Service testing at NATC Patuxent River during October, November and December 1945 revealed problems with instability when flying at low speeds for landing. In fact the stability characteristics were found to be so poor that the XF15C-1s were returned to Curtiss for modifications, and it was at this point that the T-tails were fitted and the vertical tail surfaces enlarged; as a result the horizontal tail was now positioned well above the jet exhaust. The third prototype would also be tested and assessed by the Army Air Force.

On 11 October 1946 Curtiss issued a General Flight Test Report covering recent contractor's trials with the second and third prototypes, serials 01214 and 01215. This was a very in-depth document and what follows has been filtered from its pages. This is the only XF15C-1 flight test report known to the author.

Flights were conducted in short batches, for 01214 at times between 14 January and 12 September 1946 (21 flights in all) and then for 01215 between 13 March and 18 September (33 flights); these flights covered the low Mach number only. Various aileron and rudder configurations and

Walk around views of the second XF15C-1. This would have been a very large aircraft to operate from the biggest aircraft carriers of the day. *US National Archives RG-72 via Kevin Morrow*

RIGHT Underside photo of 01214 which shows a plate on the bottom rear fuselage fitted in order to protect the airframe structure from hot exhaust gases. *Curtiss via Gerald H. Balzer*

BELOW Similar view but with the aircraft now flying with undercarriage down. *US National Archives RG-72 via Kevin Morrow*

CofGs were tested, and with the T-tail the take-off weights for these flights were 16,270lb (7,380kg) for 01214 and 16,917lb (7,698kg) for 01215. In fact during the course of the tests numerous alterations were made to all of the control surfaces and to the auxiliary controls. However, thanks to difficulties encountered with engine cooling at military power in high blower at altitude, the flight cooling tests had to be discontinued before any data had been obtained for climbs to service ceiling; indeed, excessive temperatures were encountered at altitude at military power in high blower.

Longitudinal stability, stick fixed, was positive for all configurations tested at low speeds in the 100mph to 150mph (161km/h to 241km/h) range. The lateral stability was positive, stick fixed, for all conditions, and then neutral, stick free, in the carrier approach condition; the directional stability was positive, control

The XF15C-1 flying on jet power only, with the propeller feathered. The recurrent problem of hot gases from the piston engine is reflected by the plating added just to the rear of the exhaust, along with the discolouration further back on the side of the fuselage. *Curtiss via Gerald H. Balzer*

The increased wing root fillet which was tried as part of an effort to improve the fighter's stall characteristics and to produce a more clearly defined stall. Note the wool tufts on the wing and the piston engine exhaust arrangement. *US National Archives RG-72 via Kevin Morrow*

A further attempt to improve the stall characteristics was to take away the aft portion of the wing fillet plus the complete jet engine fairing. *US National Archives RG-72 via Kevin Morrow*

both fixed and free for all configurations. Aileron control and rudder pedal forces were found to be slightly high at large surface deflections only, but the control effectiveness was adequate. No formal performance tests had been conducted with the T-tail and so it was not possible to quote any values for other parts of the performance.

Stall tests were conducted with both 01214 and 01215 respectively, with the former equipped with conventional single slotted flaps, and with double slotted flaps installed on 01215. But no clearly defined stall could be accomplished with either aircraft in any configuration due to severe buffeting which occurred at speeds somewhat above the minimum obtainable, and which made the aircraft very difficult to control. However, in choosing the speed at which the machine became uncontrollable as the stalling speed, it could be said that there appeared to be no appreciable difference attainable with the double slotted flap. The doubtful validity of the chosen stall speed also made it clear that no proper evaluation of the double slotted flap could be obtained until this buffet condition was alleviated. That said, the stalls conducted with both single and double slotted flaps indicated that the XF15C-1 had failed to meet its guaranteed stall requirements. Tuft studies conducted with 01215 in both the clean and landing configurations showed the stall forming at the wing root trailing edge and then progressing normally forward and outboard.

Between 19 September and 8 October 1946 01214 flew six further flights and 01215 another ten. Here the two machines were used to obtain longitudinal stability data, lateral control characteristics information and to determine the critical altitude for normal rated power. Again the longitudinal stability was positive through the complete speed range, stick fixed, in both power approach and landing configurations, at forward or aft centre of gravity locations. The lateral stability, stick fixed, with the basic aileron configuration, was found to be positive through the yaw and speed investigated for both aircraft configurations.

In an attempt to improve the stall characteristics and obtain a more clearly defined stall, the volume of the wing-root fillets was increased. However, the pilot reported no improvement from this alteration, and no data was taken with the small fillets installed. The next step was to completely remove the aft portion of the wing fillet and jet engine fairing (see photographs).

Following contractor flight-testing through the autumn of 1946 the two surviving prototypes went to NATC for evaluation, and were then disposed of during 1947. Having made its last flight in May 1947, 01215 went into store before, many years later, becoming a museum exhibit; the other prototype was scrapped. The sole surviving XF15C-1 is currently on static display at the Hickory Aviation Museum in North Carolina.

The development of jet engines offering greater thrust meant that very soon take-off's from carriers could now be accomplished without the need for the greater complexity of a composite powerplant. As a result, the Navy terminated its contract for the XF15C on 10 October 1946, which ended Curtiss's wartime efforts to build a new production fighter. As the various chapters have shown, the firm had expended a great deal of effort towards this objective and there was one more type to come, the post-war XP-87 jet fighter that falls outside the scope of this book. But that too failed and for Curtiss, as a manufacturer of fighter type aircraft, that was the end.

Further views of 01215 at Patuxent River. *Gerald H. Balzer*

01215 in NATC hands. This picture is full of interest because, apart from the XF15C-1, there are two ex-German Arado Ar 234 jet bombers parked behind, and then behind those a single-engine aircraft with a large contra-rotating propeller. *Gerald H. Balzer*

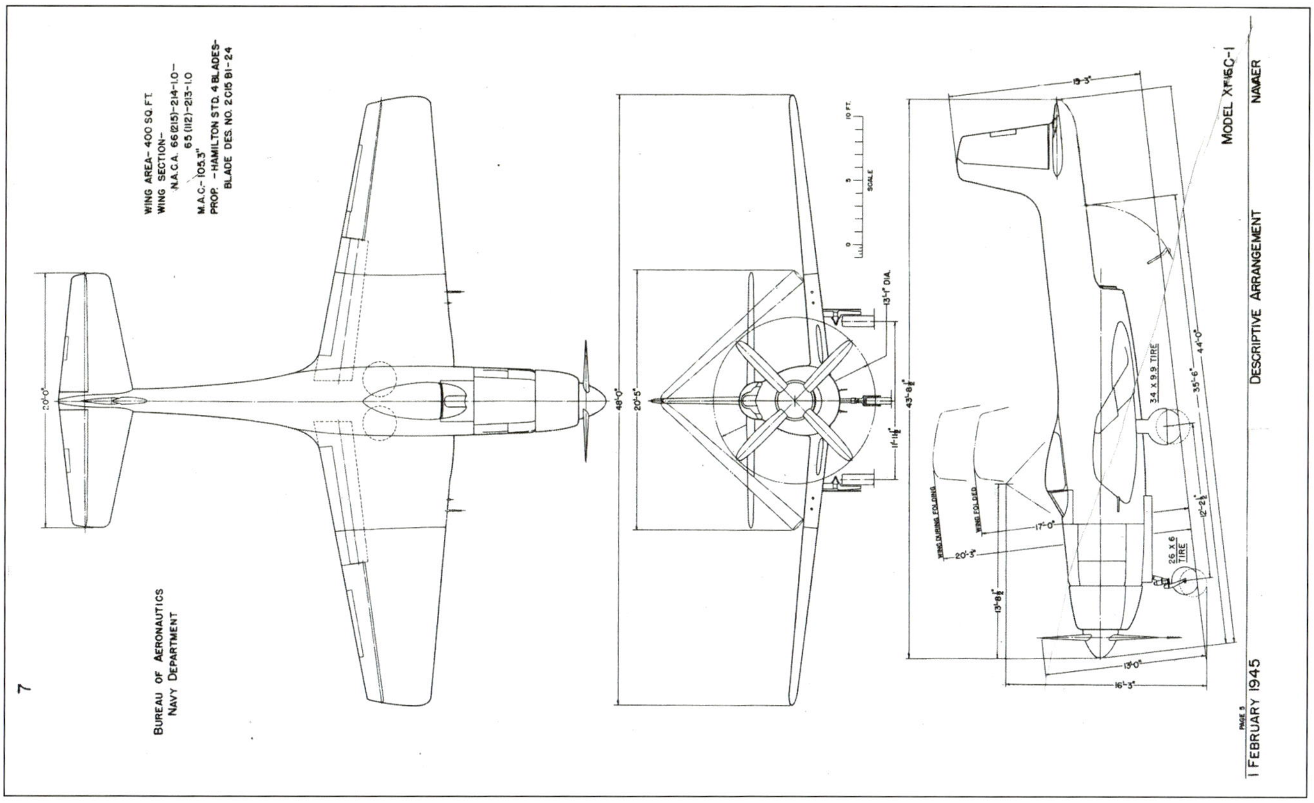

| Original three-view drawing dated 1 February 1945 which shows the XF15C-1 in its original configuration. *Gerald H. Balzer*

| The XF15C-1 in its later configuration with a T-tail. *US National Archives RG-72 via Kevin Morrow*

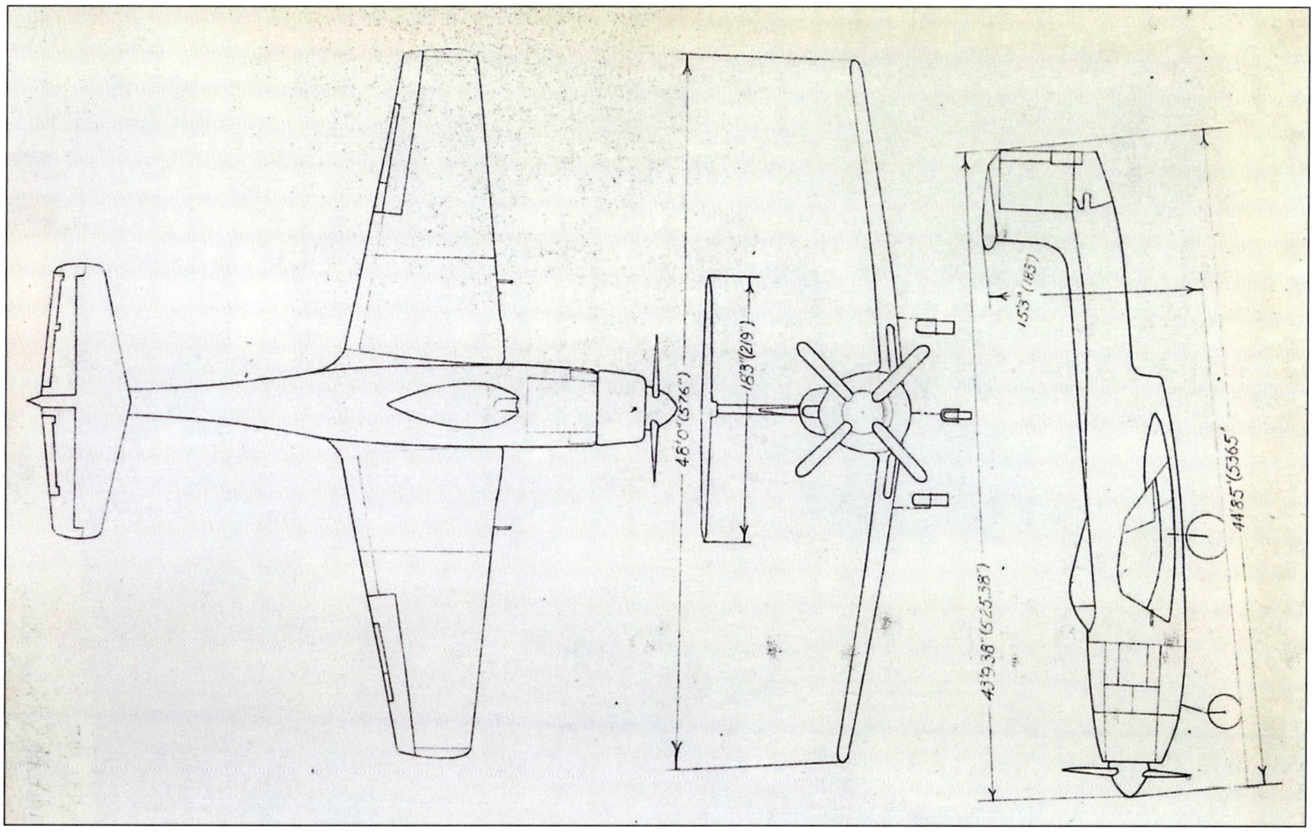

The third XF15C-1 now has more in the way of markings, with '215' painted on the side of the middle fuselage and (but not visible) under the port wing; in addition the large spinner has been removed. *Gerald H. Balzer*

XF15C-1 structure

The Curtiss XF15C-1 was a single-seat all-metal fighter with a low cantilever wing and a tricycle landing gear. The wing had a laminar flow aerofoil and could be folded for stowage aboard carriers. For its time this was an unconventional design with its Allis-Chalmers Halford H-1 jet engine augmenting the conventional Pratt & Whitney R2800-34W as an auxiliary power plant. The piston unit drove a 13ft 1in (3.99m) diameter Hamilton Standard four-blade constant speed propeller while the jet engine was mounted low in the rear fuselage; the latter had wing root intakes and a short tailpipe, with the shallow rear fuselage then being extended as a boom for the tail. Both engines used the same aviation gasoline fuel and the internal fuel capacity came to 376galUS (1,423lit) and the maximum with external tanks 526galUS (1,991lit).

Having abandoned the original low set horizontal tail, after modification the empennage also presented a slight departure from convention in that the horizontal tall was now mounted on top of the vertical fin as a T-tail. The pilot had a bubble canopy and the four 20mm armament was to be installed in the wings outside of the propeller arc. To save weight the airframe made use of the new 75ST aluminium alloy.

XF15C-1 Data (original tailplane)

Length:	43ft 8.5in (13.32m), with T-tail 43ft 9.4in (13.34m)
Wing span:	48ft 0in (14.63m) – unaltered by change to T-tail
Folded span:	20ft 5in (6.23m)
Wing area:	400sq.ft (37.20sq.m)
Empty weight:	12,648lb (5,737kg)
Gross weight:	16,630lb (7,543kg)
Maximum take-off weight:	as fighter 17,691lb (8,025kg), as bomber 18,698lb (8,481kg)
Powerplant:	1 x 2,100hp (1,566kW) Pratt & Whitney R2800-34W radial piston engine and one 2,700lb (12.0kN) Allis-Chalmers/de Havilland (H1-B/J36) Goblin turbojet
Maximum speed (both engines running):	432mph (695km/h) at sea level, 469mph (755km/h) at 25,300ft (7,711m)
Maximum speed (piston engine only):	322mph (518km/h) at sea level,) 373mph (600km/h) at 25,300ft (7,711m
Sea level rate of climb (both engines):	5,020ft/min (1,530m/min)
Service ceiling:	41,000ft (12,497m)
Normal range:	635 miles (1,022km)
Maximum range:	1,385 miles (2,228km)
Armament:	4 x 20mm cannon, 2 x 1,000lb (454kg), 2 x 500lb (227kg), 2 x 250lb (113kg) or 6 x 100lb (45kg) bombs, or 8 x 5in (12.7cm) rocket projectiles.

23 Grumman XF5F-1 Skyrocket

The early sections of Chapter Nineteen referred to the design competitions against Navy Specifications SD-112-13 and SD-112-14, the former resulting in the ordering of fighter prototypes from Chance Vought and Bell. The second competition, for a twin-engined fighter, brought forth the Grumman XF5F-1.

Unusual design

The background to the XF5F-1 starts with an earlier design competition held in 1937 for a small twin-engine fighter in which none of the proposals submitted were considered suitable. The Bureau of Aeronautics then conducted studies of its own to determine what levels of performance could be expected from carrier-based fighters powered by either twin turbosupercharged Pratt & Whitney R1535 Twin Wasp Junior or R1830 Twin Wasp radial engines or a single Allison turbosupercharged V1710 liquid-cooled unit. The two Specifications listed above were the result and the Grumman Model G-34, submitted in April 1938, was favourably acted upon by BuAer as the winner of the SD-112-14 competition.

As first designed the G-34 had a single fin and a fuselage nose that stretched ahead of the wing leading edge, and as part of the research a full size mock-up was tested in NACA's wind tunnels. However, by

The Grumman XF5F-1 Skyrocket prototype seen flying over Long Island. Colour film was at this time a very new facility. *Grumman*

The full scale wind tunnel model of Grumman's first twin-engine Navy fighter. *Grumman via Alan Griffith*

The model in the NACA wind tunnel. The 'humped' rear fuselage blending into the cockpit canopy was later cut down, while the fin and rudder were enlarged. Note that 'guns' have been fitted. *US National Archives RG-72*

The sole XF5F-1 prototype during manufacture with flotation bags deployed (should the aircraft have to ditch in the sea). *Grumman via Angelo Romano*

September 1938 further analysis had resulted in the XF5F-1's nose being cut back so that it terminated at the forward wing spar. This, plus a switch to twin fins and rudders, made the fighter's configuration quite unique and quite exotic in appearance.

The full-scale tunnel model was completed by October 1938; although built primarily in wood it also featured aluminium alloy sheeting and a wood and steel frame. A source of delay was that Grumman had been asked to include two separate types of engine nacelle, with the port side sized to house a Wright R1820 Cyclone and the starboard side a Twin Wasp. The completed full-scale model reached NACA's facility at Hampton Roads in Virginia on 22 October and subsequent tests revealed problems with turbulence around the nacelles and around the aircraft's nose; difficulties with stability also resulted in the horizontal and vertical tail surface areas being increased. It was not until December 1941 that the model was dismantled.

The XF5F-1 was to be powered by two R1535-96 engines developing a total of 1,500hp (1,119kW) at 9,500ft (2,896m), although with the addition of two-stage equipment it was expected that these units would in due course develop this combined horsepower at 17,500ft (5,334m). Having the engines positioned close together, with the two fins now sitting in the propeller slipstream, would make operation for the pilot easier if an engine was lost. The two Hamilton Standard Hydromatic three-blade constant speed propellers were arranged to rotate in opposite directions. Wingspan was 38ft 8in (11.79m) and length 27ft (8.23m).

These photos again show the full-scale tunnel model, but provide good detail of the fighter's basic shape. *NACA*

Black and white photos rarely show the different colours of the Skyrocket's fuselage and wing. Apart from the wing upper surface painted bright Navy Yellow and extending over the leading edges and wingtips, the exterior was silver lacquer over aluminium skin; Navy serial 1442 was then added in black on each fin. From 1941 a standard two-tone Navy scheme was adopted. *Grumman*

A covering specification was written around the design, SD-260 of 5 May 1938, which gave an estimated maximum speed of 290mph (467km/h) at sea level and 350mph (563km/h) at 17,500ft (5,334m), with a service ceiling of 31,500ft (9,601m); the equivalent figures for a bomber version carrying 200lb (90.7kg) of anti-aircraft bombs were 286mph (460km/h), 354mph (570km/h) and 30,000ft (9,144m). Grumman's XF5F-1 design engineer was Richard 'Dick' Hutton and Contract 61586 was issued on 30 June 1938 for a single prototype (BuAer number 1442) as the Service's first twin-engined fighter intended for operations from carriers; indeed, at this time no twin-engined aircraft had ever operated from an American aircraft carrier. The XF5F-1 was eventually named Skyrocket.

Here the port engine of the newly completed prototype is given a ground run. *Grumman via Tommy Thomason*

There were also problems in regard to the XF5F-1's centre of gravity and one modification introduced to help alleviate this situation was to replace the Hydromatic propellers by Curtiss Electric hollow steel propellers, which saved 79lb (35.8kg) in weight. But a choice also had to be made regarding the engines themselves. Pratt & Whitney had dropped its plan to give the experimental 14-cylinder R1535 a two-speed supercharger (an important element of the initial April 1938 proposal), so Grumman had to fit Wright R1820 nine-cylinder radial units instead. These offered more power but against the penalty of greater frontal area and hence drag; only with some reluctance did the Navy agreed to go ahead with this change to prevent delay, and the contract was modified accordingly in November 1938.

Late in the year the Navy's asked Grumman to add anti-aircraft-bomb containers to the XF5F-1's inventory, since its planners now envisaged having the fighter flying above enemy bombers and then releasing small bombs on to them. The resulting requirement included five containers (with doors) in each outer wing panel, each housing two 5.2lb (2.36kg) bombs, plus a pair of 176lb (79.8kg) bombs carried beneath the fuselage.

The full-scale mock-up, featuring nacelles for Wright Cyclones, folding wings for carrier stowage and twin fins, was inspected officially on 23 February 1939. Having the four guns located in front of the pilot, close to the centre-line, received particular praise, but pilot vision to the rear was described as poor. At this time the armament was still two 0.30in (7.62mm) and two 0.50in (12.70mm) machine-guns concentrated in the nose, but with provision for two 23mm Madsen cannon from Dansk Industri Syndikat A/S in Denmark instead of the latter. However, by March it was clear that the cannon would not be available and it was therefore deleted from the requirements.

During the construction and assembly of the prototype a further 750lb (340kg) of equipment was installed by Grumman, above what had been called for in the specification. The fittings included stronger mountings for the potential installation of higher-powered engines and a cut down but strengthened rear fuselage structure to provide a canopy with improved 360° vision. To compensate the additional weight the span was increased to 42ft (12.80m) and the wing area by 16sq.ft (1.49sq.m), which in itself reduced the minimum speed to 69mph (111km/h). Nevertheless, BuAer criticised the failure to meet the original weight specification and in March 1940 Grumman confirmed that the prototype was overweight.

Progress was also hampered by Grumman's other commitments. Delivery to the Navy was initially planned for around 1 July 1939, but orders for its other aircraft types, and priority being given for the manufacturer to develop its single-engine F4F-3 Wildcat fighter, brought significant delays. The XF5F-1 was in fact not completed until March 1940.

Flight test

Grumman test pilot B. A. 'Bud' Gilles took the XF5F-1 prototype 1442 on its maiden flight, from the firm's Bethpage plant near New York, on 1 April 1940, the aircraft having been rolled out late in March. Robert L. Hall then took over the test programme for a period, before in November 1940 Selden 'Connie' Converse completed the manufacturer's flying leading into official demonstrations for the Navy in early 1941.

The first problem was excessively high engine temperatures which necessitated changes to the oil cooler ducting; another was unexpectedly high drag which reduced the maximum speed. Nevertheless, during the first six weeks or so from first flight, 25 sorties were completed and the flying qualities and handling were considered good. A BuAer report noted that at the close of 1940 the XF5F-1 was at the Grumman plant for the correction of various minor deficiencies. This repeated that there had been trouble with the engine developing high oil temperatures, but difficulty had also been experienced with the landing gear housing doors. Pending preliminary demonstration tests at Anacostia, the contractor was now thinking of a development of the fighter with Pratt & Whitney R1830 two stage engines, a tricycle landing gear, more adequate armour protection, and offering an increase in range.

In early March 1941 Grumman compiled a report covering the early preliminary flying and performance assessment undertaken for the Air Corps (AAF from June 1941) which declared that the XF5F-1 had been demonstrated successfully before the Inspector of Naval Aircraft at the contractor's plant at Bethpage. The tests had taken place during January and February and included one hour full power runs, dives, spins and manoeuvres. The following manoeuvres had been performed successfully with the aircraft at normal fighter loading - vertical bank (right and left), loop, aileron roll (right and left) and Immelmann turn (right and left); however, snap rolls (right and left) were attempted but could not be performed.

Two turn spins were made to the right and left on 19 February. The XF5F-1 had a tendency to spin to the left, but recovery was effected in three-quarters of a turn. In order to spin to the right, the nose was brought up until before the stall when the ailerons were fully applied with the spin, along with full rudder and full up elevator. In the right hand spin recovery was effected in a half turn, but the elevator forces built up rapidly requiring the pilot to push with both hands in order to get the stick forward. The rudder forces also showed a tendency to increase rapidly in magnitude as the spin progressed, and the tests showed that the aircraft would spin with the nose well down. The loss of altitude resulting from a complete stall in the XF5F-1

The Skyrocket displays its wing folding. These pictures were taken early in 1940 and the serial number on the fin is incomplete. *Grumman via Mark Aldrich*

The only air-to-air photos taken of the XF5F-1 in its original form may well have been made on the same sortie. In level flight the aircraft flew a little nose-up. *Grumman via Tommy Thomason*

was considered normal, but it was noted that when the aircraft was stalled when landing, the nose had a tendency to drop sharply.

Next, the ability of the prototype to maintain altitude and make turns to the right and left with one engine throttled was demonstrated successfully. The aircraft was flown at at a speed of 175mph (282km/h) indicated and required some rudder force in addition to full rudder tab. Previously, prior to the official demonstration, 1442 had been flown with one propeller fully feathered and had shown that straight and level flight could be maintained with the rudder tabs alone at any speed in excess of 150mph (241km/h) indicated; with the addition of rudder pressure by the pilot, speeds as low as 110mph (177km/h) indicated could be maintained.

The first velocity dive had been made on 22 January, two more followed on 30 January and two more the next day. Finally, the maximum velocity dive was made on 1 February 1941 in which the maximum airspeed obtained was 506mph (814km/h) true. A maximum V-G dive was performed on 11 February and here a maximum acceleration of 6.0g was obtained with a maximum velocity of 485mph (780km/h) true. The pilot's technique in entering all of these dives was the same and he (Converse) considered that the aircraft's stability in the dive was satisfactory.

This preliminary demonstration had indicated that the XF5F-1 would reasonably be expected to meet its contract guarantees, the aircraft seemed normal, but two points were raised:

> 1. The nose dropped sharply when the aircraft was stalled and it was recommended that it should not be stalled near the ground until the pilot had familiarised himself with this characteristic.
>
> 2. The control forces in the spin became rather heavy. Due to the difficulty of entering a spin, and the extreme improbability of inadvertently entering a spin, it was recommended that the XF5F-1 should not be demonstrated beyond two turns of a spin, and it should be placarded against extended spins.

A hand-written note in this report, by Grumman engineer R.T. Cella on 4 March 1941, added that "the indicated speeds attained in the dives are not phenomenally high for a modern high speed fighter. It would seem that the pilot had to be particularly careful in order that he would not exceed the 450mph (724km/h) true speed set up in the revised demonstration requirements. The first maximum velocity recorded 452mph (727km/h) at 12,000ft (3,658m), the sixth recorded (on Flight 60 – 1 February 1941) the maximum achieved, 506mph (814km/h) at 16,000ft (4,877m). The dive weight was 9,993lb (4,533kg) with the weight at take-off 10,113lb (4,587kg).

Rear angle view which shows the very short engine nacelles, enlarged fins and rudders, and the relatively large canopy. The fuselage-wing fillet has still to be introduced. *Grumman*

Well known photos of the XF5F-1. The enclosed tailwheel can be seen in the second shot. *Grumman*

Today the XF5F-1 is still something of a strange-looking beast and this angle reveals the cutback nose, the very low wing and, in contrast, the high position of the tailplane. *Grumman*

Directly after this assessment, the XF5F-1 was delivered to Navy hands at NAS Anacostia in February 1941. The prototype then went back to Bethpage for modifications, the most important of which became, over some period of time, changes to the undercarriage fairings, to the exhaust system, a balanced rudder to improve control, an extended nose (now ahead of the wing leading edge), extended engine nacelles, wing trailing-edge wing/fuselage fillets, and the addition of propeller spinners. It is thought that the first flight in this final form was made in about November 1942 and subsequent trials showed that the problems with high drag and engine cooling were still present. In addition, it was found that the longer nose resulted in a sudden stalling of the wing, which necessitated higher speeds on landing. But the extended nose and engine nacelles, coupled with the introduction of fuselage and wing fillets, increased the maximum speed by some 15-18mph (24-29km/h).

Another feature on which test pilots remarked was how, during climbs at full power, and during

The Skyrocket now fully modified with extended nose and new propeller cowlings. *US National Archives RG-72*

In modified form the prototype almost looked conventional – at least from below! A spin chute and tail fairing were added following Flight 64 made on 11 February 1941. Note the different engine exhaust system from the as-built condition. *Grumman*

high speed runs, the port R1820 engine would consistently run far hotter than the starboard engine, which stayed at its normal operating temperature. A point in the XF5F-1's favour throughout was having propellers which were designed to rotate in opposite directions - this virtually removed the effects of torque generated by each engine on take-off. A further quality, indeed perhaps the best, was an outstanding rate of climb, a figure of 4,000ft/min (1,219m/min) proving to be far superior to the Vought XF4U-1 Corsair prototype's 2,660ft/min (811m/min) and the 2,630ft/min (802m/min) figure for the Bell XFL-1 in Chapter Nineteen; the name Skyrocket appears to have been well chosen!

In mid-1941 the aircraft was back at Anacostia for combat trials, and in September it went to the Naval Aircraft Factory at Philadelphia to permit the Ships Experimental Unit to perform simulated carrier trials with the prototype. Final demonstration flying for the Navy was completed in February 1942, the Commanding Officer at Anacostia, E.P. Moore, declaring that the prototype was 817lb (370kg) overweight. Further modifications were still required to deal with problems such as longitudinal stability during high power climbs. But this no longer mattered because the success of Grumman's F4F Wildcat had helped kill any possibility of production F5Fs being ordered. On 31 March 1942 Grumman advised BuAer that it did not want to put further time and effort into the project, with its technical problems and issues with weight, and the firm considered that the XF5F-1 contract was now closed; the Navy agreed and officially terminated the contract on 4 September 1942.

On 3 February 1942 the XF5F-1 suffered arrester gear failure during an arrested landing at the Naval Aircraft Factory, it ground looped and sustained damage to the starboard wing and aileron, the fin and rudder and to the arrester hook, all of which took four weeks to repair; a similar accident followed on 18 May. When repairs were completed in mid-August 1942, 1442 began familiarisation trials at both NAS Anacostia and at Patuxent River. On 5 June 1943 BuAer officially transferred the XF5F-1 to the Experimental and Development Squadron at Anacostia. Much of the trials work was conducted in support of Grumman's follow-on twin-engine F7F Tigercat fighter programme.

On 11 December 1944, during an approach to land at NAS Floyd Bennett Field, the XF5F-1's undercarriage would not come down and the pilot had to belly land. The resulting damage was enough for the Navy to decide that the aircraft was not worth repairing. Having completed 211 flights and accumulated 155.7 flying hours, it was struck off the active list the very next day. From February 1945 the remains of the airframe were used by airfield crash crews to practice the techniques of rescuing aircrew after forced landings. Despite the XF5F-1 Skyrocket's development problems, the reliability and serviceability of the only example built had led to a very active life lasting nearly five years.

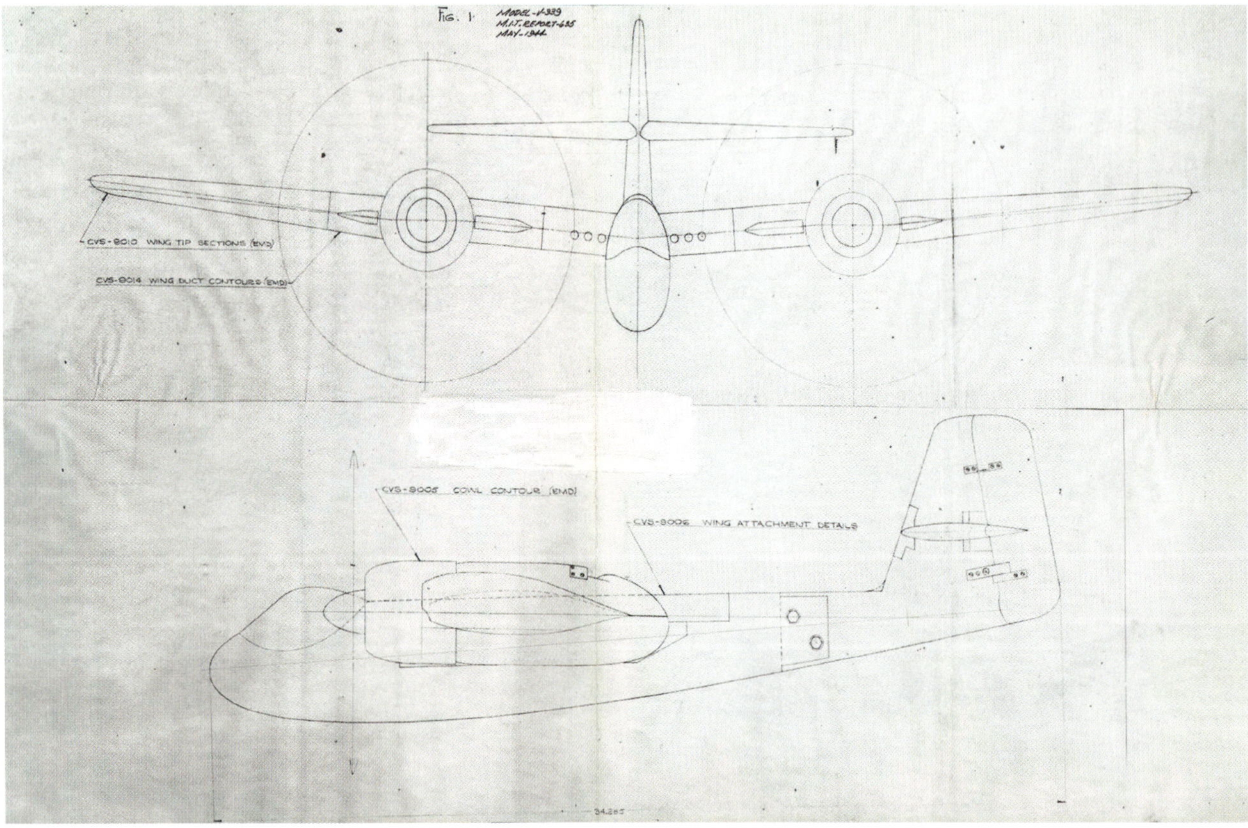

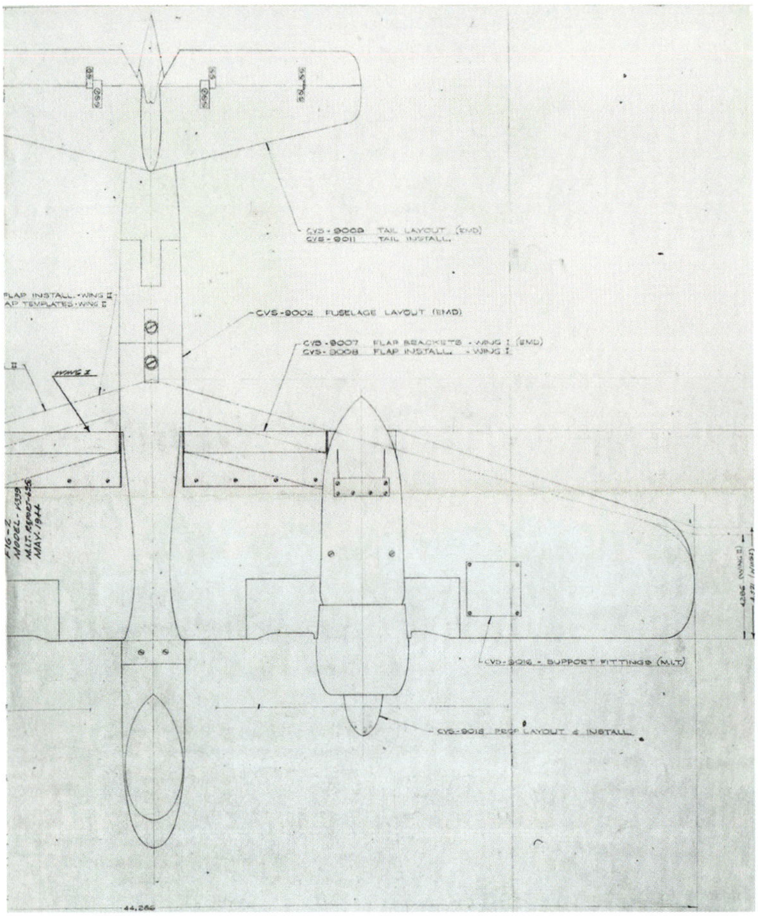

A twin-engine fighter proposal from Chance Vought was the V-339. This came much later in timescale than the XF5F-1, more in keeping with Grumman's later F7F Tigercat, but with such large engine nacelles it makes an interesting comparison to the XF5F-1 of several years earlier. In May 1944 a 1/14th scale model was tested in the Wright Brothers Wind Tunnel at the Massachusetts Institute of Technology, as per this drawing. A conventional twin-engine fighter, the V-339 had a laminar flow-type wing of 19% t/c in the centre and 14% at the tip. There was a slotted flap on the centre panel only and the ailerons stretched along the entire trailing edge from nacelles to tips; the fuselage was narrow in section and two sets of three guns appear to be in the wing roots inboard of the propeller arcs. The model 's wing area was 2.27sq.ft (0.21sq.m) and span 3.69ft (1.125m), which at full scale would have been 51ft 8in (15.75m). Performance data is unavailable. *MIT*

A picture dated 27 April 1943 which shows the prototype in its later Navy scheme with flat sea blue upper surfaces and matt white undersides. Note also the rearward extension of the engine nacelles. *Grumman via Tommy H. Thomason*

XF5F-1 structure

The Grumman XF5F-1 twin engine single seat Navy fighter had an unorthodox configuration for its time. It had a low position all-metal cantilever wing with two outer panels and a centre section. The outer wings could fold upward, just outboard of the engine nacelles, split trailing edge flaps were fitted, and as built, the forward fuselage nose began behind the leading edge (although later the nose extension was extended beyond the wing edge); the XF5F-1 was Grumman's first aircraft fitted with folding wings. The bulky engine nacelles, of welded tube structure, extended forward and a little below the centre section leading edge and the landing gear main wheels retracted into the nacelles. A pair of XR1820-40 and -42 engines drove three-blade 10ft 0in (3.05m) diameter hollow steel propellers rotating in opposite directions. The empennage included twin fins.

Ahead of the windshield the fuselage had a welded steel tube structure, aft of the windshield the fuselage was semi-monocoque aluminium alloy and the pilot was enclosed by a large canopy. The fittings included equipment for catapulting and arresting operations from carriers and a 'taildragger' undercarriage. Provision was made for guns to go in the nose, but no armament was ever installed. Internal fuel came to 178galUS (674lit), with the overload figure with external fuel totalling 277galUS (1,049lit).

XF5F-1 data

Length:	28ft 8.5in (8.75m)
Wing span:	42ft 0in (12.80m)
Folded span:	21ft 2in (6.45m)
Wing area:	303.5sq.ft (28.23sq.m)
Empty weight:	7,990lb (3,624kg)
Normal gross weight:	10,021lb (4,546kg) (as a bomber 10,257lb/4,653kg)
Maximum take-off weight (overload):	10,892lb (4,941kg)
Powerplant:	2 x 1,200hp (895kW) Wright Cyclone GR1820-40/42 (LH/RH) 9-cylinder two-stage supercharged air-cooled radial engines
Maximum speed:	312mph (502km/h) at sea level, 358mph (756km/h) at 17,300ft (5,273m)
Maximum rate of climb:	4,000ft/min (1,219m/min)
Service ceiling:	34,500ft (10,516m)
Range:	1,170 miles (1,883km)
Armament:	4 x 0.50in (12.70mm) machine guns, four 176lb (79.8kg) bombs

24 Ryan XF2R-1 Dark Shark

The Ryan FR Fireball mixed powerplant (piston/jet) naval carrier-based fighter entered service in 1945 but, because of the end of the Pacific war, orders for the type were cut back drastically and only one squadron would be equipped with it. There were efforts to fit different powerplants, the most extreme being the replacement of the piston engine with a turboprop which resulted in the XF2R-1 Dark Shark.

Modified airframes

Various studies were conducted in the hope of improving the Fireball's performance by taking advantage of new engines currently under development. Two versions, one with an an R1820-74W piston engine and updated propeller (as the FR-2), and another with a General Electric I-20 jet instead of the original I-16 (as the FR-3), were not built. But before looking

Restored colour view of the Ryan XF2R-1 Dark Shark in flight. *Ryan via Mark Aldrich*

at the Dark Shark, mention should be made of the FR-4.

The designers of the FR Fireball were Ben T. Salmon and William T. Immenschuh and they were working on a modification of the FR-1, powered by an R1820-74W piston engine and a 3,400lb (15.1kN) thrust Westinghouse J34-WE-22 (24C) jet unit, which the Bureau of Aeronautics designated XFR-4. The jet required a wider and stretched end fuselage, making the aircraft 8in (0.20m) longer. Flush air intakes were positioned on the fuselage sides instead of the Fireball's wing root inlets, and there was a taller fin. Taking away the wing intakes made for a straighter leading edge, while the new inlets remained closed (to cut drag) when the jet was not running; in fact they would open when the pilot triggered the sequence to start the J34.

BuAer serial 39665 was the aircraft fitted out in this form and some sources state that it first flew in November 1944, although this is not confirmed. It was assigned to NACA Ames Aeronautical Laboratory at Moffett Field from 17 February 1945 until 1 June 1947 where it was used to evaluate the flying qualities, stability and control and performance with the more powerful jet in place. In addition, variations in engine tilt, wing dihedral and aileron shape were assessed. Sources have stated that the XFR-4 was 100mph (161km/h) faster than the standard Fireball.

Moving on to the XF2R-1, this modification came from a BuAer requirement to combine a turboprop with a turbojet in the design of a single-seat fighter. The 15th Fireball airframe, BuAer number 39661, was accordingly heavily reworked to take a General Electric XT31 (TG100) turboprop driving a propeller, whilst retaining its J31 (I-16) jet. This changed the fighter's appearance considerably though, from the front spar below the cockpit floor rearwards, it was essentially a Fireball airframe bar an extended dorsal fin fillet (to handle for the increase in torque, both from the heavy propeller and from the turboprop's spinning turbine wheel). Apart from the longer body the aircraft's dimensions were unchanged from the Fireball, though the extra length (2ft 6in/0.762m) did give the illusion of placing the wing farther towards the rear of the aircraft.

Introducing a turboprop brought several advantages, not least that now only one type of fuel need be carried – kerosene. In addition, the Hamilton

Ryan pilot Al Conover takes the XFR-4 on a test flight. *Ryan via Gerald H. Balzer*

The Ryan XFR-4 'prototype' was serial 39665. *Ryan via Gerald H. Balzer*

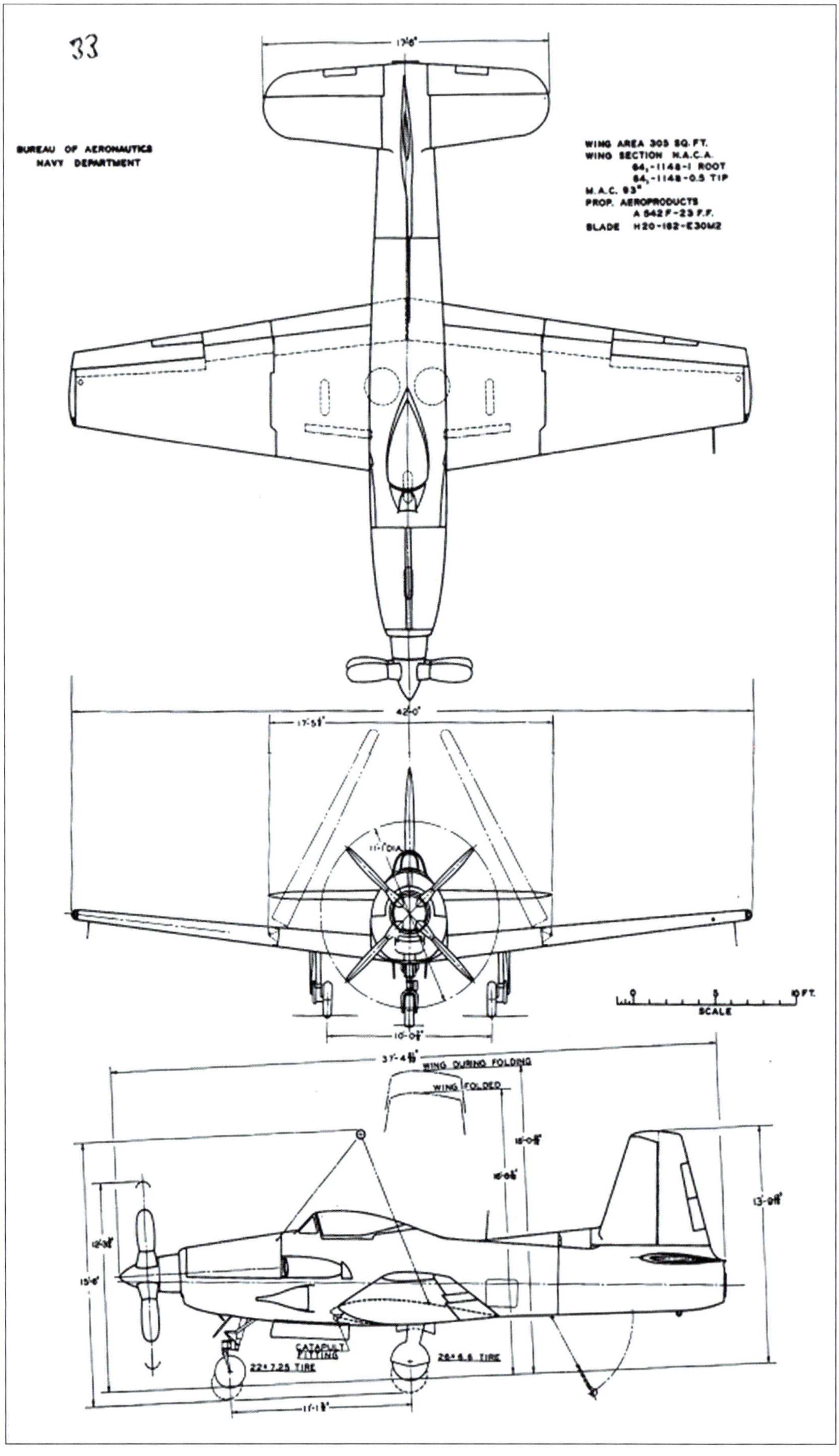

Ryan's XF2R-2 development featured a new tapered wing and a more squared-off fin. This is how the design looked at January 1947. *Ryan Crierie*

Standard propeller could be set to a very flat pitch which would serve as a dive brake when landing (see below), while in flight the power was controlled by propeller pitch and so engine/aircraft acceleration and deceleration became near instantaneous; in the FR-1 the latter was slower because the propeller was turned by a reciprocating engine. The role of the jet in the aft fuselage was to supplement the propeller thrust when bursts of higher speed and/or more rate of climb were required.

In February 1947 the aeronautical press revealed the new type to the public, at the time calling it the 'dark shark Fireball', the name given to the aircraft at Muroc. Contemporary articles also indicate that the XF2R-1 was serving strictly as an experimental flying laboratory to acquire operational experience with this type of powerplant and propeller and the associated accessories. Ryan claimed that the XF2R-1 was the first prop-jet aircraft to make a cross-country flight in the US.

Following on from the XFR-4 above, an XF2R-2 version of the Dark Shark was proposed by Ryan on 16 August 1945 with a J34 jet installed, and indeed this was built in mock-up form before the project was dropped. The arrival of more powerful turbojets was making the mixed power concept redundant, but the XF2R-2's estimated maximum speed was 480mph (772km/h) at 14,500ft (4,420m) and sea level rate of climb 7,300ft/min (2,225m/min). Besides the change in power plants the XF2R-2 was also designed to have increased fuel capacity and redesigned wings, and it was anticipated that cabin pressurisation, a pilot ejection seat and afterburning would be incorporated.

The full size mock-up of the XF2R-2 had NACA flush-type side air intakes instead of the XF2R-1's wing leading edge inlets, plus rocket projectiles under the wings and a canopy of reduced size. *Ryan via Gerald H. Balzer*

Flight test

The Dark Shark's maiden flight was made in November 1946 with Ryan test pilot Alan W. Conover in the cockpit, the prototype becoming the first Navy turboprop aircraft to fly. It demonstrated some impressive performance attributes and in particular an excellent rate of climb. Ryan's Preliminary Demonstration Flight Test Report, prepared for the Navy and dated 21 April 1947, noted that the aircraft was restricted from carrier type landings and its wing fold mechanism and arresting hook had been removed. The subject aircraft was also not equipped with dive recovery flaps and so high speed dives had to be entered with caution.

The Dark Shark receives maintenance in the hanger with its wings in the fully folded position. *Ryan via Mark Aldrich*

ABOVE AND LEFT A large number of staff and considerable equipment was seemingly required for ground testing the Dark Shark. Here the propeller spinner has not yet been painted red. *Ryan via Mark Aldrich*

BELOW 39661 pictured (it is thought) early in its career with Al Conover in the cockpit. The prototype received the same all-over Navy dark blue colour scheme as did the standard FR Fireball, but it did not have a black anti-glare panel ahead of the cockpit. Note the large paddle blades. *Ryan via Mark Aldrich*

During diving trials, on dive number two a maximum Mach number of slightly over 0.73 was obtained and the XF2R-1 had a definite tendency to tuck under, but this was restrained when the pilot applied force. During a dive in which compressibility was encountered, it was generally not recommended to use the trim tab for recovery because of the possibility of exceeding the aircraft's structural limitation as the Mach number became lower. The trim tab did not stall out on the aircraft and therefore it could be used to assist dive recovery if care was taken to retrim as the indicated airspeed was reduced. The trim tab had been used to assist in recovering from dive number two but the stick forces were excessively high. Since the aircraft could be recovered from a 0.7 Mach number dive without the use of trim tab and without excessive stick forces, it was recommended that the XF2R-1 be restricted to a maximum Mach number of 0.7.

The XF2R-1 Dark Shark gets away for another test flight. *Ryan via Gerald H. Balzer*

Views of the sole XF2R-1 on the ground. With its longer body it was a more balanced and elegant design than the Fireball. The large sliding canopy and dorsal fin fillet are well shown. *Ryan via Gerald H. Balzer*

This excellent view of the Dark Shark was taken on 20 January 1947 above the California desert. *Ryan via Gerald H. Balzer*

Dive number three was made with a full 100galUS (378lit) drop tank attached beneath the right wing centre section. Unlike the FR-1 Fireball in the same configuration, the XF2R-1 remained steady in the dive until a speed of 400mph (644km/h) IAS. At this speed lateral and directional stability became affected and the aircraft began to weave, roll and yaw because of the airflow over the tank. This appeared as a high speed Dutch roll and was controllable up to approximately 420mph (676km/h); in the basic FR-1, this manoeuvre appeared at a speed slightly over 335mph (539km/h). Since the stability was affected, it was recommended that this be considered the maximum attainable speed.

The diving trials, with Conover the pilot, had begun with Flight 26 on 10 April to establish the maximum speed in the clean condition. The gross weight at the start of this dive, at 19,850ft (6,050m), was 10,350lb (4,695kg) and the lowest altitude was 10,350ft (3,155m) – the speed at the start of the pull out was 472mph (759km/h). With the drop tank aboard (gross weight now 11,620lb/5,271kg) the maximum speed was 421mph (677km/h). The demonstration flying overall had begun with Flight 20 on 4 April 1947 and the maximum weight during the trials was 11,830lb (5,366kg). The maximum recorded level speed appears to have been 460mph (740km/h) indicated = 462mph (743km/h) true.

Because of the abnormal amount of torque present in the TG100 installation, caution also had to be taken while flying the aircraft slow in the high drag configuration. It was noted that the power approach condition could be dangerous unless the stall warning was heeded and the recovery controls were used decisively. For the stall it was possible to hold the aircraft in a nose high landing attitude until the stall occurred. With a power approach and gear and flaps down the stall occurred at 77mph (124km/h) - the right wing had a tendency to drop until the stall occurred, then the left wing dropped quickly, but this could be controlled by rapid movement of rudder. With the drop tank in place the stall speed was 78mph (126km/h).

The TG100 turboprop's propeller could be fully feathered or reversed to zero blade angle extremely rapidly, the drag of the flatter blade angle serving as an effective air brake. In fact the XF2R-1 was used to help demonstrate this new system of 'braking' an aircraft's speed in the air by flattening the pitch of the propeller during the final landing approach. The increased drag produced a steeper glide angle and markedly reduced the landing roll and this unique air braking system, made possible by the huge Super-Hydromatic propeller, could be used during landings to supplement the drag created by the aircraft's wing flaps. Indeed, so effective was the drag-creating feature of the reversing propeller that Al Conover declared that normal runway landings could be made in a distance no greater than the length of the decks of the large *Midway* class aircraft carriers. Up to now this type of propeller had been used only on multi-engined transport aircraft.

The constant speed, full feathering and reversing propeller had an automatic adjustment coordinated with the throttle to change the blade angle from normal operating pitch, when the power was reduced for landing, to the flatter pitch position which converted it into an effective brake in the air to reduce speed. The propeller arrangement also incorporated a tie-in circuit to the landing gear so that the propeller could immediately be changed to an even flatter angle when contact with the runway was made, thus reducing the landing roll to an absolute minimum. The XF2R-1's propeller had a much greater blade area compared with previous versions of the Fireball, and a diameter of 11ft (3.35m) compared to the FR-1's 9ft 6in (2.90m) three-bladed fitting.

The XF2R-1 Dark Shark, like previous models of the Fireball, was capable of flying on jet engine power alone, and in such flights the propeller was 'feathered' by changing the blade angles so that their chord lay in the direction of flight. In this position they acted as brakes to stop the propeller and turbine wheel from rotating, while at the same time offering the least possible drag.

Although the Dark Shark flew well its TG100 turboprop proved to be quite unreliable and, instead of providing the expected 2,200hp (1,641kW), in general it produced no more than 1,700hp (1,268kW). By the time the prototype had completed what was a protracted test programme at Muroc Dry Lake, the decision had been taken not to place production orders. The only Dark Shark prototype was scrapped, but precisely when is unknown.

XF2R-1 structure

The XF2R-1 Dark Shark was a single place low-wing monoplane powered by two engines. The forward unit was a General Electric TG100 turboprop (prop-jet) with a four-blade 11ft (3.35m) diameter Hamilton Standard Super Hydromatic fully feathering constant

Now banking towards the camera, the Dark Shark reveals its leading-edge wing configuration. *Ryan*

When the aircraft was first made public it was called the 'dark shark Fireball' by the press. *Ryan via Gerald H. Balzer*

The underwing pylons and end fuselage jet exhaust pipe are well shown in this picture taken from slightly beneath 39661. There appear to be no photos of the aircraft fitted with external tanks. *Ryan via Gerald H. Balzer*

Later in its flying career the prototype sported updated national markings with red bars, plus a new red warning stripe around the forward fuselage just ahead of the cockpit. Note the height of the narrow canopy. *Ryan via Gerald H. Balzer*

speed propeller, the hollow-steel paddle blades of which were square-tipped. A streamlined spinner gave something of a shark-nosed shape to the front end. In the rear fuselage was a General Electric I-16 jet engine, as used by the Fireball. About 75% of the turboprop power was absorbed by the propeller, but the remainder of the TG100's energy was converted into around 550lb (2.4kN) of residual thrust by a jet exhaust stream ducted into nozzles exiting on each side of the fuselage. A dorsal extension to the fin was fitted to compensate and different forms of exhaust nozzles were tried.

Ryan's FR Fireball had an all-metal structure with laminar-flow wings and a very smooth flush-riveted skin. Essentially the XF2R-1 reused the main body and flying surfaces of the Fireball (including the upwards folding wing), but ahead of the canopy the change to a turboprop altered the appearance completely. The span was the same but the length was increased to 36ft (10.97m). A tricycle landing gear was used but all of the armament had been taken out. Shackles beneath the wings could take 1,000lb (454kg) bombs or 100galUS (378lit) drop tanks and the prototype did not have catapult attachments or an arrester hook.

XF2R-1 data

Length:	36ft 0in (10.97m)
Wing span:	42ft 0in (12.80m)
Wing area:	305sq.ft (28.365sq.m)
Gross Weight:	11,000lb (4,990kg)
Powerplant:	1 x 2,220hp (1,655kW) + 550lb (2.4kN) thrust General Electric XT31-GE-2 (TG-100) turboprop engine plus 1 x 1,600lb (7.1kN) thrust General Electric J31-GE-3 (I-16) turbojet engine
Maximum speed (estimate – both engines running):	497mph (800km/h) at sea level
Rate of climb:	4,850ft/min (1,478m/min) at sea level
Service ceiling:	39,100ft (11,918m)
Armament:	4 x 0.50in (12.70mm) in wings (not fitted). Production aircraft to carry bombs or unguided rockets under wings.

Photos of the Dark Shark taken late in its career with the red forward fuselage stripe added. *Ryan via Gerald H. Balzer*

XF2R-2 data

(Standard Aircraft Characteristics Sheet 1 January 1947. Performance figures – both engines running.)	
Length:	37.656ft (11.48m)
Wing span:	42ft 0in (12.80m)
Folded span:	17ft 5.5in (5.32m)
Wing area:	305sq.ft (28.365sq.m)
Empty weight:	9,700lb (4,400kg)
Gross weight:	13,043lb (5,916kg)
Maximum take-off weight (as fighter):	14,363lb (6,515kg)
Powerplant:	1 x 2,190hp (1,633kW) + 550lb (2.4kN) thrust General Electric TG100 turboprop engine driving a 4-blade 11.0ft (3.35m) diameter Aeroproducts propeller plus 1 x 3,000lb (13.3kN) thrust Westinghouse J34 (24C-4A) turbojet engine
Maximum speed:	450mph (724km/h) at sea level, 458mph (737km/h) at 20,000ft (6,096m)
Maximum rate of climb:	7,450ft/min (2,271m/min) at sea level
Service ceiling:	52,200ft (15,911m)
Internal fuel:	550galUS (2,081lit)
Armament:	4 x 20mm cannon

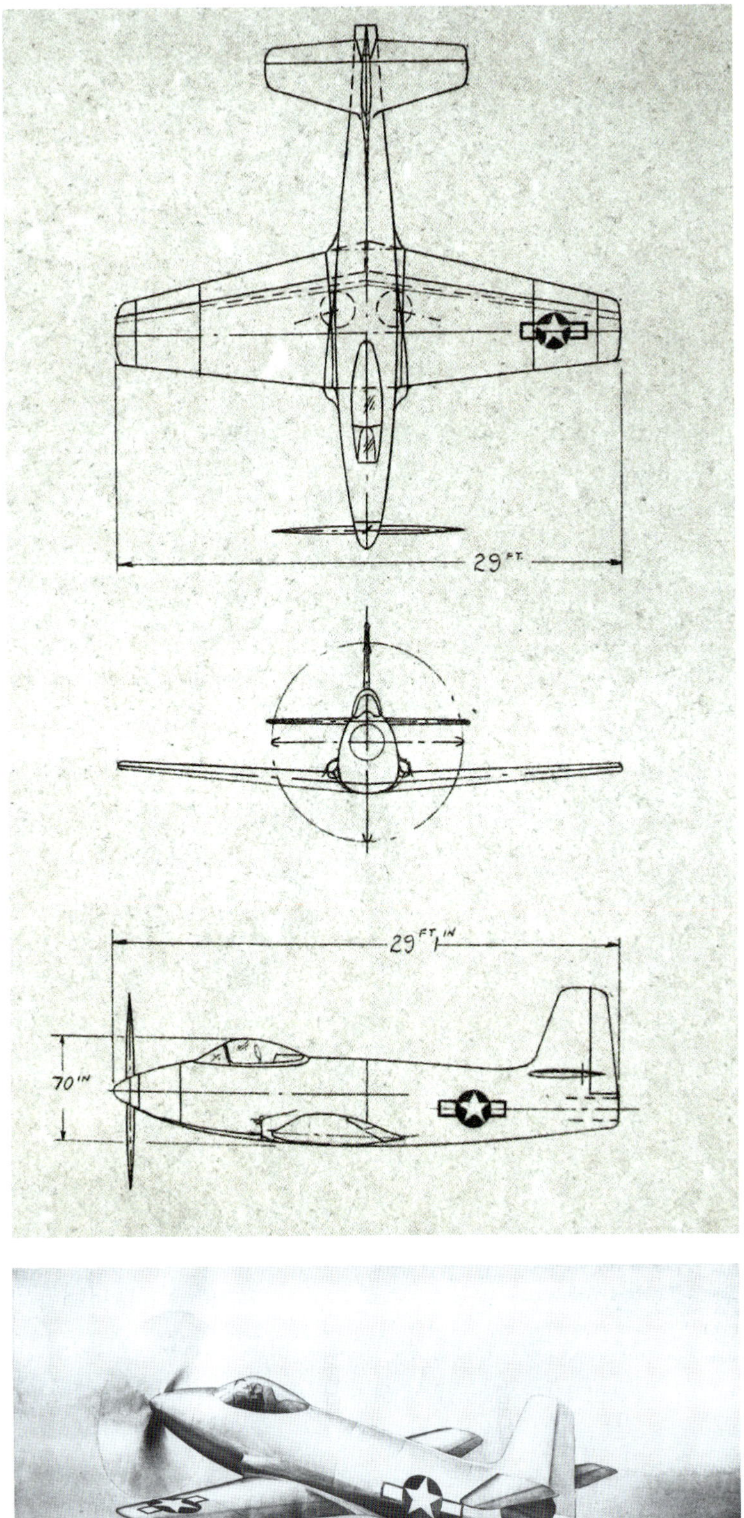

LEFT AND BELOW Two proposed designs from Convair were contemporaries of the Dark Shark. The first was the Model 4502 of May 1945, a single seat design with tapered straight wing, a 2,345hp (1,749kW) General Electric TG100 driving a four-blade 11ft (3.35m) diameter propeller, wing root intakes and a nose-wheel undercarriage. Span 29ft 0in (8.84m), length 29ft 1in (8.865m), wing area 180sq.ft (16.74sq.m), wing thickness:chord ratio 13%, internal fuel 215galUS (814lit) kerosene, external fuel 150galUS (568lit), empty weight 5,904lb (2,678kg), gross weight (full internal fuel) 8,444lb (3,830kg). It would have been armed with four 20mm cannon and two 250lb (113kg) or 500lb (227kg) bombs, ten 5in (12.7cm) or one 13.5in (34.3cm) HVAR rockets. Maximum speed at 130% power (with water injection) 489mph (787km/h) at sea level, 513mph (825km/h) at 12,500ft (3,810m), sea level rate of climb 8,150ft/min (2,484m/min), service ceiling 41,500ft (12,649m); equivalent figures for 100% power 483mph (777km/h), 487mph (784km/h), 6,400ft/min (1,951m/min) and 38,000ft (11,582m). Combat radius 300 miles (483km). *US National Archives RG-72 via Norman Friedman*

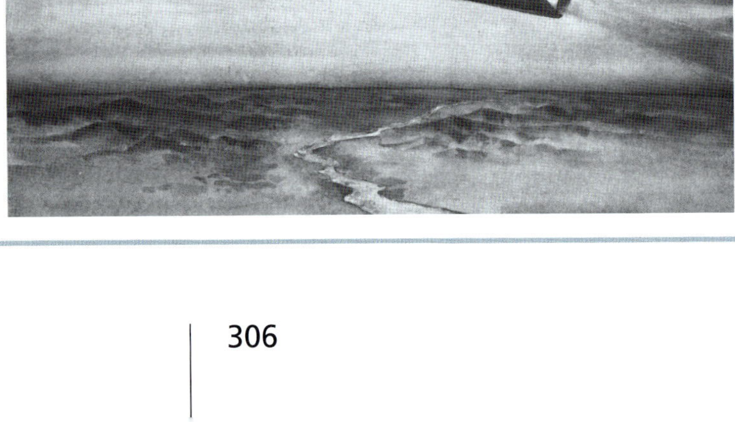

RIGHT This drawing and artwork show a second proposal from Convair which is similar to the firm's XP-81 in Chapter Seventeen. It is dated 10 July 1945 and would have combined a TG100 turboprop and a GE I-40 jet engine. Span 43ft (13.11m), length 41ft 4in (12.60m), gross weight 15,000lb (6,804kg). Estimated maximum speed 545mph (877km/h) at 15,000ft (4,572m), or 567mph (912km/h) at 130% power with water injection, sea level rate of climb 8,200ft/min (2,499m/min) or 10,550ft/min (3,216m/min) with water injection, combat radius 300nm (483km). *US National Archives RG-72 via Norman Friedman*

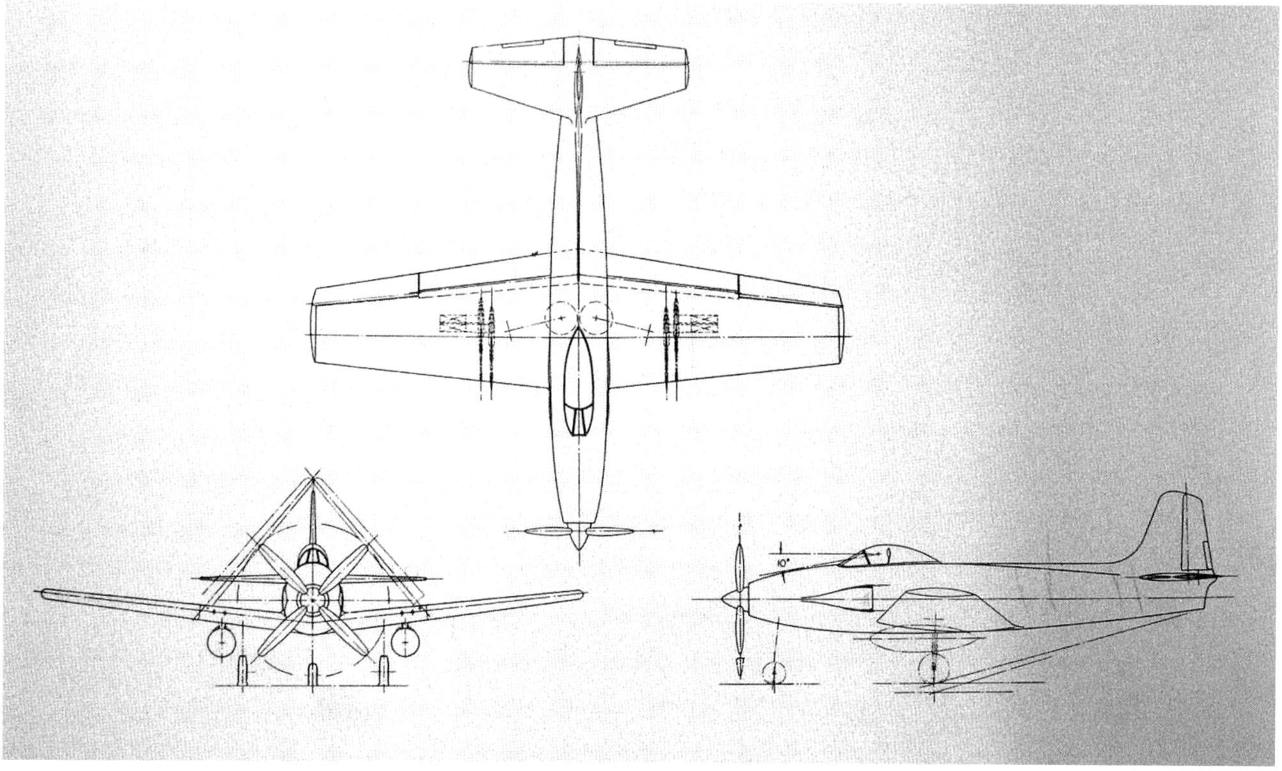
10°

Appendix One

Official USAAF Review of Fighter Projects, November 1942

A USAAF memorandum/letter dated 6 November 1942, written by Colonel F.O. Carroll of the Experimental Engineering Section, gave a view of the then current situation of new fighter development. The document also went on to review new bomber, attack and cargo types, which of course fall outside the parameters of this book, but the most important and revealing sections of the text detailing the fighters covered here is reproduced below. Some fascinating observations were forthcoming.

"The Curtiss XP-60 started out originally as a structural and aerodynamic study of the low drag airfoil on a standard [Curtiss] P-40 airplane. However, the Curtiss Company and Production Engineering began to get interested in production possibilities for this airplane so that it finally wound up as a completely new airplane which was designed to take either the Allison, Continental or the Chrysler engine. As a result of this completely new design, the project, as far as the low drag airfoil was concerned, was considerably delayed. This airplane is now flying and will shortly have the high altitude Merlin engine installed for further flight tests. The development of this airplane did result, however, in the solution of the problem of adequate aileron control coupled with the low drag airfoil, since Curtiss succeeded in applying the sealed gap type of aileron to this airplane, which resulted in unusually good aileron control and low stick forces throughout the flight range; and this development is consequently available to any other manufacturer who decides to use a low drag airfoil in his particular design.

The Curtiss XP-60A, B and C are what might he termed a consolation prize given to Curtiss when the decision was made for Curtiss to go into production on [Republic] P-47 airplanes. Because of the relatively low performance of these three airplanes, the first of which was to have an Allison engine with General Electric turbo, the second an Allison engine with Wright turbo, and the third to be held for the later installation of the Chrysler liquid cooled engine, the Pursuit Projects Unit did not feel that these airplanes had much to offer and recommended cancellation of this contract. However, in view of the fact that the engineering was so far along and the cancellation of the contract would result only in the saving of shop assembly time, the recommendation was never forwarded. Recently, when the pressure was exerted for a fast climbing interceptor as a competitor to the Jap [Mitsubishi] Zero and the Focke-Wulf 190, it was decided to utilize the XP-60C airplane for a quick installation of the two-stage [Pratt & Whitney] R2800 engine. This airplane at a gross weight of 10,400lb [4,717kg], and with war emergency engine ratings, will have a high speed of 430mph [692km/h] at 22,000ft [6,706m], rate of climb 3,450ft/min [1,052m/min] at 20,000ft [6,096m], and a rate of climb of 4,600ft/min [1,402m/min] at sea level. This is another illustration of the need for having a number of strings to one's bow, since this airplane already was well under way when the need for a fast climbing interceptor arose, and offered a convenient vehicle for the two stage R2800 engine. This airplane will be a companion piece to the [North American] P-51B and the [Bell] XP-63 as an immediate answer to the Directorate of Pursuit's urgent plea for fast climbing interceptors.

The Lockheed XP-49 is here listed in the experimental category although it is somewhat of a borderline case, since it is a direct improvement of the standard [Lockheed] P-38 with two Continental engines substituted for the Allison engines. This airplane is due to fly any day, but has been considerably delayed due to the delays and troubles with the Continental development. In view of the improved horsepower of the Allison V1710 engine and the enhanced performance of the XP-38H as a result, the XP-49 has lost a great deal of its original attractiveness and is now seen mainly as a test vehicle to get flight experience on the Continental engine, and to learn some of the problems involved in the installation of this engine in a high performance pursuit type.

The Vultee XP-54s one of the three pure experimental airplanes developed as a result of the

R-40C pursuit competition which was held about three years ago. Although it is hoped the airplane will fly next month, it really has been delayed seriously because of the change from the original design conception of a medium altitude, high speed airplane embodying a low drag airfoil and the ultimate in aerodynamic refinement of a reasonably conventional arrangement, to a high altitude, pressure cabin airplane with a rated altitude of 40,000ft [12,192m]. This change resulted in the complete redesign of the airplane, after a great deal of time and money had been expended in elaborate wind tunnel tests at the NACA of a beautiful all-metal model, and it now is much farther from the immediate desires of the pursuit people for a fast climbing interceptor than it was as originally conceived, in which version it would have had a rate of climb of something over 5,000ft/min [1,524m/min].

The Curtiss-Wright (St. Louis) XP-55 was the second of the R-40C airplanes, which embodied the tail first design in an effort to get the ultimate in aerodynamic cleanliness and high speed performance. Although this airplane has been considerably delayed due to the higher priority production designs in the Curtiss-Wright plant and the interjection of the wood transport into the picture [it is assumed that this referred to the C-76 Caravan first flown in May 1943], it is now to come out in a stripped version with about a 7,000lb [3,175kg] gross weight, wing loading of 34.5lb/sq.ft [168.5kg/sq.m], and power loading of 5.8lb/hp (2.63kg/hp] which should make it unusually attractive from the interceptor point of view. This airplane and the XP-56 are 'naturals' for the later installation of the jet engine or rocket propulsion units, since they have no rear empennage to interfere with such installations.

The Northrop XP-56, the third of the R-40C airplanes, is a truly experimental airplane if ever there was one, since it embodies a tailless arrangement with the low drag airfoil, coupled with the maximum utilization of helium arc-welded magnesium in its primary structure, and with a completely housed blower-cooled R2800 engine driving a pusher dual rotation propeller. This airplane is a major engineering step forward, as is the XP-55, and it is unfortunate that the high priority of Northrop production sub-contract work, the XP-61 night fighter and the XB-35 bomber have delayed the completion of this airplane. In spite of this delay, it is believed that every man hour expended in its design and development will pay liberal dividends.

The Lockheed XP-58 airplane was procured as a result of the foreign sale agreements, and its original conception was as a high altitude, medium range bombardment escort airplane. When Lockheed ran into the compressibility troubles on the P-38 design, they became worried about similar difficulties on the XP-58 and suggested the elimination of the turbo super-charger and its related equipment, and the redesign of this airplane as a low altitude ground support airplane with the 75mm cannon. This was agreed to by this Section, but as a result of the recent conference on pursuit airplanes in Washington and the interjection of the [Beech] XA-38 design, it was felt that this airplane in the high altitude version represented an excellent immediate answer to the Pursuit Directorate's requirements for a bombardment destroyer type of airplane. This type of airplane is not conceived as one which will .have to be employed in terminal velocity dives, and hence the compressibility problems are not so serious. As a result of the Pursuit Board's recommendations, we are now going ahead with the procurement of two of these XP-58 airplanes in their original conception as high altitude airplanes. Here is another excellent illustration of the absolute necessity having a number of strings to one's bow, since this airplane now appears to be just what the pursuit boys want in the way of an immediate bombardment destroyer airplane. It is fortunate that, in spite of numerous attempts on the part of Lockheed and others to drop this airplane, we succeeded in keeping it in the picture where it now appears it will play a most important role.

The Curtiss XP-62 is another airplane which was sold 'from the top down' and for which there was little enthusiasm originally on the part of this Section. This airplane was sold on the basis of twelve .50 caliber guns and a speed of 468mph [753km/h] at 27,000ft [8,230m] with turbo-superchargers and a pressure cabin. The design was later revised to eight 20mm guns, and the speed brought down to about 448mph [721km/h] at 47,000ft [14,326m]. As a result of the sudden frenzy for subjugation of other performance items to rate of climb at the ground, there are a number of people who would like to wash out this airplane, and Curtiss has lost interest in it since the production contract for 200 was cancelled. However, this airplane has given the Curtiss Company an opportunity to solve the problems of a pressure cabin installation coupled with a low drag airfoil and the latest turbo-supercharger. In addition, it is the first attempt to use the [Wright] R3350 engine in a pursuit version coupled with the dual rotation tractor propeller, and from the Experimental Engineering standpoint is an extremely worthwhile project, even though no more than the two experimental models are ever built.

The McDonnell XP-67 is another example of a real experimental model, with the twin engine tractor Continental installation mounting six 37mm guns, which represents the ultimate in aerodynamic refinement of a conventional arrangement with the fuselage and the engine nacelles merging smoothly into the wing itself. With an overload of gasoline, it should have usually good range and may turn out to be another airplane to meet the Pursuit Directorate's desires for a bombardment destroyer airplane.

The Republic XP-69 airplane is the heavy, high altitude fighter type with the Wright [R2160] Tornado engine, which was designed specifically as a pursuit engine. This is the only airplane of its type now under development around the Tornado engine, and although the airplane is approaching dangerously close to 18,000lb [8,165kg] gross weight, it is believed essential that this end of the scale should be adequately explored just as we are trying to explore the other end of the scale of extreme lightness and low horsepower interceptor type in the Bell XF-77. [Note: The XP-69 prototype was never completed and so did not fly.]

The Curtiss-Wright (St. Louis) XP-71 is another case of where this section has apparently stolen a march on the tactical people, since it now appears to be the solution already in hand for their latest desires for a bombardment destroyer airplane. This Section attempted many months ago to get a destroyer type of airplane designed around the 75mm gun, as a result of the astonishingly accurate firing tests which were conducted with the original 75mm installation of the hand loaded gun in the [Douglas] B-18 airplane some years ago. Curtiss-Wright were somewhat lukewarm about the project originally, but finally we succeeded in getting this airplane under contract and apparently that is just what the doctor ordered. Without intending to be unduly repetitious, this is again a beautiful illustration of the importance of having a number of irons in the fire so that one of them will be heated to proper temperature when needed. [Note: The XP-71 was also never completed or flown.]

The General Motors (Fisher Body) XP-75 is an attempt to solve the problems incidental to the installation of the Allison R3420 engine in a pursuit airplane. There is an interesting point that should be mentioned here, and that is that while General Echols was still at Wright Field as Assistant Chief, Materials Division, we tried to interest several of the existing pursuit manufacturers in an airplane mounting the R3420 engine. However, apparently none of them were interested and said in effect that it was not a pursuit engine and would never be of any use as such. However, when Mr Don Berlin left Curtiss and went with Fisher Body Division he made some preliminary studies, and it now appears that this airplane can be built for something between 12,000lb and 12,500lb [5,443kg and 5,670kg] gross weight with an excellent rate of climb at the ground in the two stage version of this engine. Due to Mr Berlin's personal drive, this project is going forward rapidly, utilizing parts of existing airplanes to the maximum extent in order to get the first airplane flying within the deadline date of six months.

The Bell XP-77, the ultimate in a light weight, small interceptor airplane built of non-strategic materials, was really sold from 'the top down' initially. Our own Pursuit Project officers are not too enthusiastic about this airplane at the present time, since there are so many problems involved in the proper development of the Ranger [V770] engine with the Szydlowski-Planiol supercharger to give the required horsepower at 23,000ft or 50,000ft [7,010m or 15,240m] which will be necessary to make the altitude performance of this airplane at all interesting, However, Mr Bob Woods is furnishing a lot of personal drive to this project, and it does offer an answer to General Arnold's frequently voiced desires for a really light weight, simple and cheap interceptor airplane. Even though it results in negative information to indicate that such an airplane cannot be built with the performance and the equipment which the pursuit people insist upon having, it will still be a valuable project and will probably result in an excellent pursuit training airplane, which will be much cheaper and easier to build than the standard tactical pursuit types."

Finally, although falling outside the scope of this book, this memo's observations on the Merlin-powered North American XP-51B Mustang prototype also make interesting reading. It noted:

"The North American XP-51B is a logical development of the XP-51 Mustang which has proved to be so popular with the British. Incidentally, this Section was anxious to go ahead with a similar project nearly a year ago, but at that time it was decided that it was not advisable to put North American into the pursuit production picture. However, when the P-51 original Mustang turned out to be so popular and such a nice flying airplane with a surprisingly good speed at a medium altitude, the British really demanded that this airplane have the Merlin 61 engine installed, in order to improve its altitude performance, and feel that this together with the Spitfire IX will be an adequate answer to the Focke-Wulf 190."

The Merlin-powered Mustang of course went on to become one of the great fighters of World War II, something to which many of the types in this book aspired, but would never get close.

Appendix Two

Standard types as trials and testbed aircraft

This appendix brings together a selection of the standard production fighter types that were adapted and used for aerodynamic and powerplant trials during and just after the war. The list is by no means complete, but it presents some of the more interesting programmes and is sufficient to give an idea of the work that was conducted during the period under review. Also here is the Goodyear F2G which, had the war continued, would most likely have proceeded into full scale production; had that occurred it could not have been included in the book.

The Curtiss XP-42 pictured in flight whilst serving with NACA. The view is reportedly dated 13 April 1945 and the aircraft has the all-moving tailplane fitted. *NACA via Dick Hallion*

Curtiss XP-42

The prototype for what would become the Curtiss P-36 fighter first flew way back in May 1935. In 1939 Curtiss installed a 1,050hp (783kW) Pratt & Whitney R1830-31 Twin Wasp engine in the fourth production P-36A airframe along with a very aerodynamically refined cowling. However, in the air this aircraft, serial 38-4 and designated XP-42, experienced severe problems with overheating and with propeller vibration, and altogether 12 different experimental cowlings were to be assessed before these problems were overcome. The XP-42 was not ordered into production but it was used by both NACA and the Air Corps for further aerodynamic research, in particular to assess the penalties in aerodynamic drag with the installation of an air-cooled radial engine (with its large diameter cowling) compared to the narrower liquid-cooled V-type unit.

The XP-42 joined NACA's Langley Memorial Aeronautical Laboratory in September 1940 and, once the powerplant trials had been concluded, the aircraft had an all-moving horizontal tailplane fitted along with servo tabs. This was the first time that an all-moving tail surface had been trialed in America and would of course benefit the high speed test flying conducted after the war had ended. The fitting was just about the same size as the XP-42's original horizontal tail (but had a greater aspect ratio) and was test flown during 1942, 38-4 making dives to Mach numbers that approached the point where compressibility would appear; the all-moving surface apparently made recovery easier.

This one-off machine was scrapped in July 1947. Had it first flown at a later date then the XP-42 would have had a chapter of its own in this book. The XP-42 had a span of 37ft 3.5in (11.37m), length 30ft 3in (9.22m), wing area 236sq.ft (21.95sq.m), empty weight 4,818lb (2,185kg), gross weight 5,919lb (2,685kg), and maximum take-off weight 6,260lb (2,840kg). Its maximum speed was 344mph (553km/h) at 14,500ft (4,420m).

Contra-rotating propellers

Contra-rotating propellers feature on numerous occasions throughout this volume and, alongside the prototypes covered in separate chapters, two standard production fighter types also had dual-

The experimental Chance Vought F4U-1A pictured at Rentschler Field in East Hartford with a counter rotating Hamilton Standard propeller installed. *Tom Fey*

rotation props fitted, the Republic P-47 Thunderbolt and Vought F4U Corsair.

A high power piston engine driving a single-rotation propeller produces high levels of torque which would always make the aircraft want to 'swing' or yaw to the side on take-off, with consequent handling problems for the pilot. Torque is a lateral displacement created by the rotating propeller[s] and becomes especially prevalent after the throttle has been set at high power ready for take-off. This problem was made worse by the ever increasing power from the newest military piston engines produced during the war.

Contra-props or contra-rotating propellers, or dual-rotation in the US, used the engine's power to drive two propellers positioned one behind the other and rotating in opposite directions about the same axis. This permitted more power to be transmitted for a given propeller radius, it allowed more blades to be used which increased the efficiency, and having propellers rotating in opposite directions effectively cancelled out the torque, making the pilot's workload on take-off more straightforward. By the late war years this was one of the best ways to ensure maximum use was made of these high power engines.

However, the benefits were offset by the contraprop's mechanical complexity and extra weight, the installation could be very noisy and it required more maintenance. Dual-rotation propellers were difficult to design and vibration from the two sets of blades passing one another was a big problem, since the blade pitch usually had to be different for the two sets to match the different airflows entering the fore and aft propellers.

An early American aircraft employed on contra-rotating propeller research was a Douglas B-23 bomber which trialled a Super Hydromatic contraprop in around early 1943. Then a P-47B, serial 41-5942, had an Aeroproducts propeller attached by Republic to its Pratt & Whitney R2800-21 engine also in (most likely) 1943, and apparently in great secrecy. It was flown just once by manufacturer's test pilot C. Hart Miller, the aircraft was found to be seriously destabilised by its contra-props, apparently the increase in speed was minimal (one source suggests just 1mph/1.6km/h),

The Vought XF4U-4 which received a 12ft 7in (3.84m) diameter Aeroproducts six-blade propeller. It flew in this experimental configuration during the period June to August 1945. The picture is dated 17 July 1945. *Bill Spidle, and Ramsay Research Library at New England Air Museum via Tom Fey and Mark Aldrich*

and so the installation was removed from the aircraft the very next day. Previously, during 1942, 41-5942 had been used to test six different four-blade single rotation propellers at Republic's Farmingdale facility. This aircraft was lost in a crash on 2 February 1944.

A Vought F4U-1A Corsair had an experimental Hamilton-Standard Super Hydromatic unit installed during 1944 and was flown at Rentschler Field, where Pratt & Whitney and Hamilton Standard flight tested their new engines and propellers (the identity/serial of this aircraft is unknown). Also in 1944, at the request of BuAer to try to increase the Corsair's top speed, Aeromatic Aircraft Propellers fitted a six-blade (two x three-blade) contra-rotating propeller to an F4U-4 (either serial 49763 or 50301). Unfortunately, the modest gain in performance was offset by the propeller gearboxes lacking sufficient reliability for operations in air-to-air combat, so this propeller was not adopted for production. Finally, XF4U-4 02460 was flown with a six-blade 12ft 7in (3.84m) diameter Aero Products dual-rotation unit between 6 June and 22 August 1945. The object here was a vibration and performance survey on this type of propeller, which weighed 864lb (392kg), and to perform an evaluation against a standard 667lb (303kg) four-blade single-rotation propeller. It was found that at 26,000ft (7,925m) the contra-prop reduced the maximum speed by 10mph (16km/h), and it also affected the rate of climb rate at sea level which fell by 300ft/min (91m/min), so the four-blade single-rotation type was retained.

The development of contra-rotating propellers proved to be a long process and in America was never really taken on board with any real success. In addition to the fighters in several chapters of this book, some attack aircraft and the Convair R3Y Tradewind used such propellers during the 1940 to 1948 time frame. The Fisher XP-75 (Chapter Fourteen) did reach production but it never entered service. Historian Tom Fey explained to the author that the the reason so few types went into production/service was that the marriage of high horsepower engines with contra-rotating propellers was much more complicated than had first been anticipated. Manoeuvring loads on shafts, gearboxes and engine mounts and struts, vibration, the weight penalty, managing reverse pitch and negative torque with contraprops, were all factors that had to be taken into account.

V-Tail

Examples of the Bell P-63 Kingcobra were used for experiments with V-shaped tailplanes. The surfaces on this type of fitting would serve both as rudders and elevators whilst in the process reducing an aircraft's weight and drag, but the effects on the machine's stability and control needed to be examined. It was Bell test pilot and engineer Bob Stanley who instigated this research with Wright Field and it began in August 1943 with a V-tail P-63 model in a NACA Langley wind tunnel. This was followed by P-63A 42-68861 (assigned to Langley from 26 July to 25 November 1943) modified for ground trials only, and then by two examples for flight testing. These had their tails rebuilt with 36° of dihedral and there was a ventral fin to help with directional stability.

The flight test aircraft were P-63A serial 42-69606 and an RP-63G-1 target version 45-57300. Twelve sorties in all were conducted during the spring of 1945, totalling 9.5 hours airtime, and a full programme of tests looked into the adapted aircraft's stability and control and their spinning characteristics. Apart from a degree of deficiency with longitudinal control they apparently performed well, but the modification was not adopted for production.

One of the Bell P-63s which flew with a V-tail. *Gerald H. Balzer*

The sole XP-47F built was serial 41-5938. *Gerald H. Balzer*

These drawings, reproduced by Alan Griffith directly from an original NACA report, show the subtle change in wing shape between the P-47B and XP-47F. *Alan Griffith*

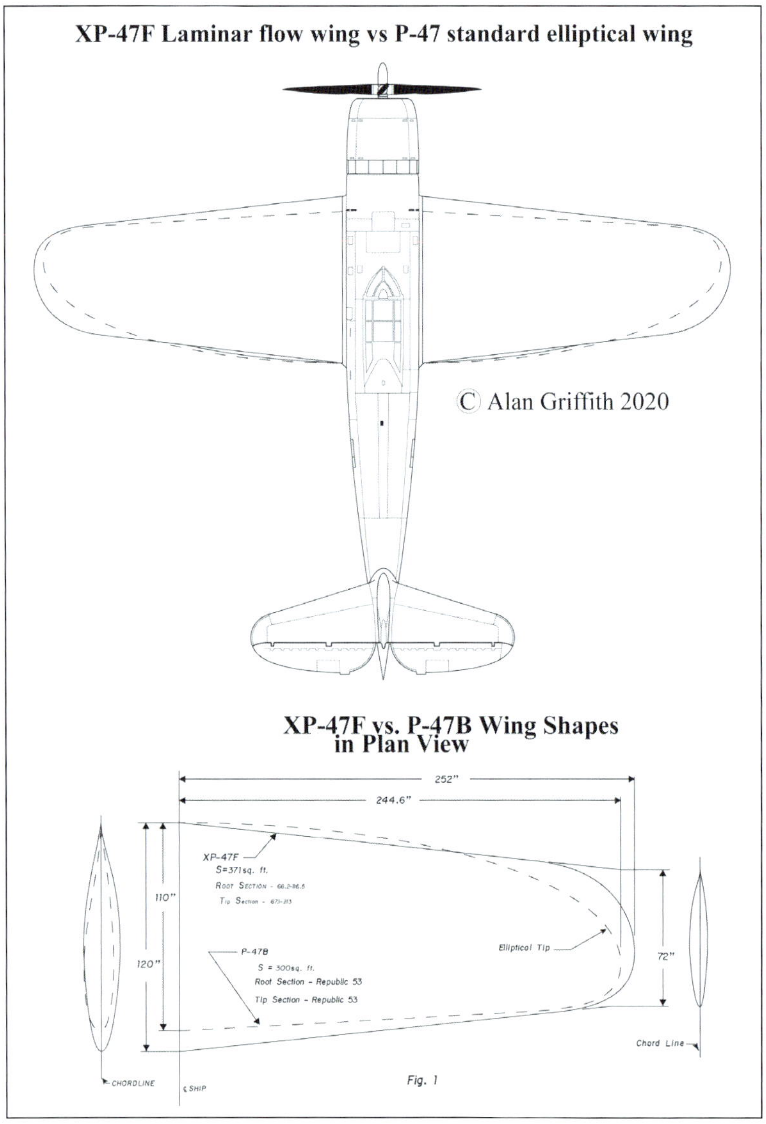

Laminar flow

Laminar flow is defined as the steady motion of a fluid or gas in which the medium can be considered as a series of sheets sliding smoothly over each other and over solid bodies, such as a wing. Essentially World War Two designers had two ways of ensuring that laminar flow could be prolonged over a flying surface. Firstly, a suitable wing section, in fact one with its maximum thickness placed further back than with earlier wing designs. Second, a very smooth and regular surface free of dents, protruding rivet heads, dirt and dust. Unfortunately in practice, with the rough handling aircraft experienced as part of wartime operations, the latter was very difficult to achieve.

On 7 October 1941 plans were drawn up to test two different panels on a P-47 Thunderbolt, the first a complete wing section with no interruption of the covering except for skin splices, the second a panel that would include a section of aileron, gun access doors and a leading edge opening for a gun blast tube. Designation XP-47F and Project MX116 were allocated to the laminar flow wing aircraft and the chosen airframe was serial 41-5938, powered by a Pratt & Whitney R2800-21 engine with four-blade Curtiss Electric propeller.

Switching from a conventional to a low drag wing resulted in the following:

(a). Gross weight increased from 12,500lb (standard P-47B) to 13,250lb (XP-47F) (5,670 to 6,010kg) with armour plate removed for balancing purposes;

(b). Wing area increased from 300sq.ft to 322sq.ft (27.90sq.m to 29.95sq.m);

(c). Semi-span increased from 246in to 252in (625cm to 640cm);

(d). The rear spar was approximately 25% deeper at the hinge fittings than on the production wing.

The laminar wing was designed for an applied load of 8g and a maximum allowable dive speed of 580mph (933km/h) IAS, while the airframe itself was quoted as 6g and 480mph (772km/h) IAS (the P-47B's terminal velocity was given as 553mph/890km/h IAS). It is possible that the first sortie took place in around late July 1942 (but not confirmed) and that Joseph Parker, chief test pilot at Republic, was in the cockpit.

Parker's report, dated 4 August 1942, observed that the XP-47F's indicated take-off speed was approximately 105mph (169km/h) compared to the P-47B's 110mph (177km/h) and the climb seemed slightly flatter. In the air the ailerons were very heavy approaching lock conditions at 350mph (563km/h), and they would overbalance at low speeds and high angles of attack at altitudes in excess of 20,000ft (6,096m). It appeared that in manoeuvres, when the airspeed dropped below 200mph (322km/h), the laminar flow wing's efficiency fell away considerably.

Also, under the present loading conditions the XP-47F became very unstable at low speeds and high angles of attack at high altitudes. The stability increased with speed until 350mph (563km/h), when the ailerons approached the heavy stick force or lock conditions.

On the approach the angle of glide was flatter and the landing speed slower. For landing the indicated air speed was approximately 90mph (145km/h), with the glide at 120mph (193km/h). Parker concluded that the aeroplane was unstable with the present loading and, curiously, the XP-47F's weight was given as 11,990lb (5,439kg) with the P-47B 12,565lb (5,699kg), so here the XP-47F was lighter. A second report, dated 14 September 1942, added that "the high speed of the XP-47F is 411mph (661km/h) at 25,000ft (7,620m) compared to 420mph (676km/h) at 25,000ft for the P-47B."

The XP-47F flew with the NACA Langley Memorial Aeronautical Laboratory in Virginia from 22 February to 23 May 1943, before joining Air Materiel Command at Wright Field. Its general handling characteristics were found to be satisfactory and, with the exception of aileron control, very similar to the P-47B. In due course the balance was reduced which now made the ailerons reasonably satisfactory, though at high speeds they tended to become very stiff. Here the level flight high speed at rated altitude was found to be 8mph (13km/h) less than with the P-47B, of which approximately 4mph (6.5km/h) of this decrement was accounted for by the 22sq.ft (2.05sq.m) increase in wing area. In Materiel Command hands 41-5938 was used to investigate stalling speeds and characteristics, and to measure wing profile drag. The stalling characteristics were excellent, with a sharp straight ahead stall immediately preceded by very heavy tail buffeting. Aileron control was satisfactory to the stall.

In the end the laminar flow wing did not find its way on to production Thunderbolts, while the sole XP-47F suffered a tragic ending. On 14 October 1943 41-5938 flew into the ground at Bacova in Virginia (possibly after a collision) and pilot Malvin L. McAdams Jr. was killed.

Goodyear F2G Super Corsair

Perhaps falling outside the parameters for this appendix, but important to include nonetheless, is the Goodyear F2G Super Corsair. All of the previous versions of the Vought Corsair had been powered by the Pratt & Whitney R2800 radial engine, including the large numbers built under contract by such as Goodyear themselves, right up to the close of the war. But the Super Corsair introduced a Pratt & Whitney R4360 unit and, although today it can be looked upon as non-standard, had the war been prolonged further then this development would have been produced in some numbers.

The Goodyear production version of the original Corsair had been designated FG-1. Three examples of the FG-1A, serials 12992, 13471 and 13472, were the first to have a 3,000hp (2,237kW) Pratt & Whitney R4360-4 installed. This updated form was designated XF2G and the new engine increased the length to 33ft 10in (10.31m). Further extensive modifications to the airframe included the removal of the turtle-deck fuselage behind the cockpit and the introduction of a bubble canopy, all to improve the pilot's view. Entirely a Goodyear-developed project designed for low-altitude operations, the -1 was to be a land-based version and the F2G-2 (with a slightly larger fin and a 'sub-rudder' to counteract the extra torque of the engine on take-off) would be carrier-capable.

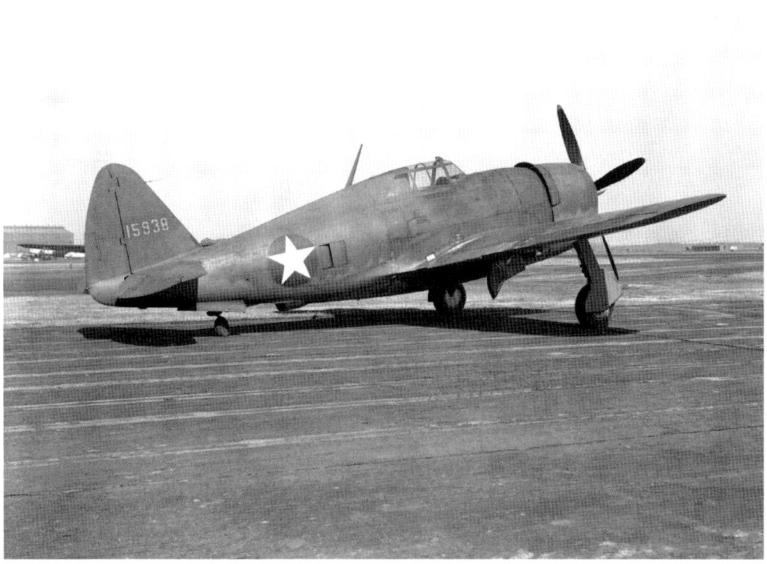

NACA Langley photo of 41-5938. *NACA via Gerald H. Balzer*

Test pilot David Armstrong took XF2G-1 13471 on its first flight on 26 August 1944. Ten XF2Gs were ordered on 22 March 1945 but only five were built (serials 14691 to 14695), and with the close of the war another 418 F2G-1s and 62 F2G-2s were cancelled as no longer required. Flight trials apparently revealed a lack of speed plus weaknesses in lateral control, but serial 14694 was tested at Mustin Field at Philadelphia and at NAS Patuxent River from October 1945 to May 1947. Having been stricken from Navy records on 31 May 1947 this particular aircraft, carrying civil register N91092, took part in the 1947 and 1949 National Air Races. It was later scrapped.

F2G-2 Data: span 41ft 0in (12.50m), folded span 17ft 0.5in (5.19m), length 33ft 10in (10.31m), wing area 314sq.ft (29.02sq.m), empty weight 10,249lb (4,649kg), gross weight 13,346lb (6,054kg), maximum take-off weight 15,422lb (6,995kg), powerplant one 3,000hp (2,237kW) R4360-4 Wasp Major. Maximum speed 399mph (642km/h) at sea level, 431mph (693km/h) at 16,900ft (5,151m), rate of climb 4,400ft/min (1,341m/min), service ceiling 38,800ft (11,826m), range 1,000 miles (1,609km). Armament four 0.50in (12.70mm) machine guns and 3,200lb (1,452kg) bombs.

Views of Goodyear XF2G-1 Super Corsair prototype. Note the bubble canopy. *US National Archives via Ryan Crierie*

Index

AIRCRAFT

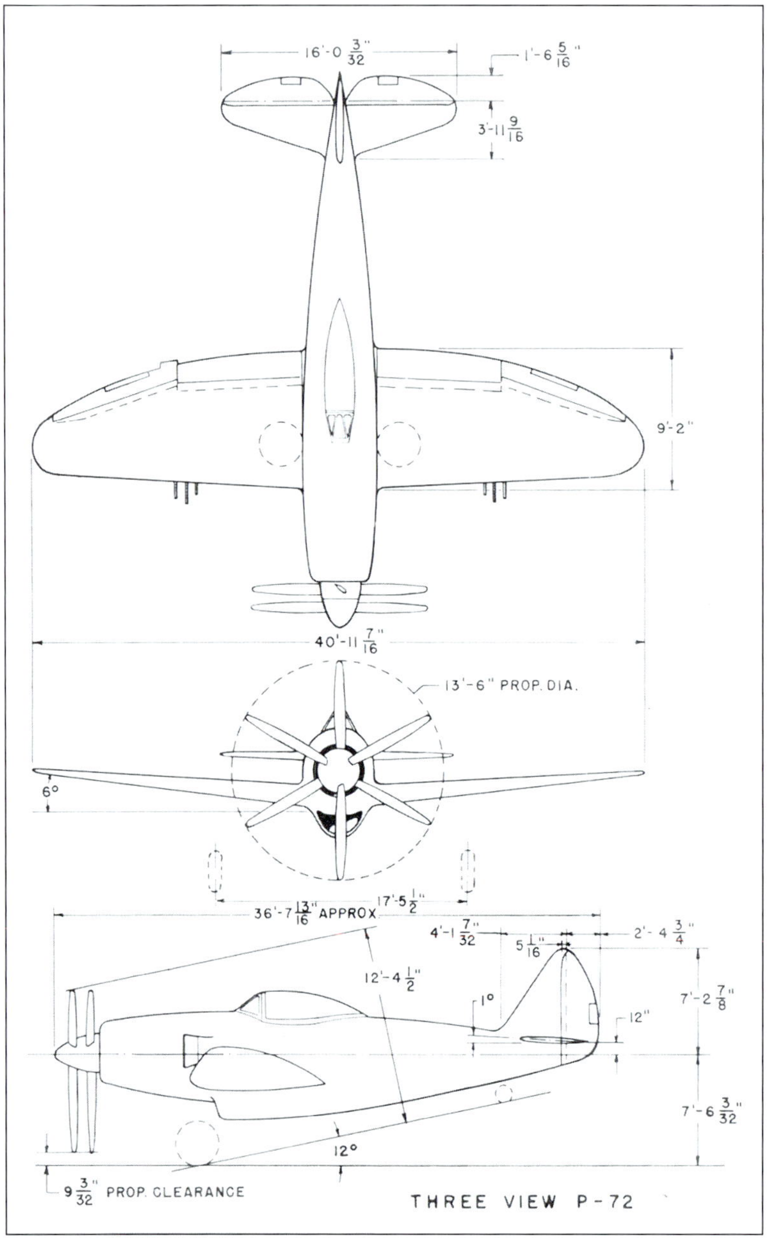

Three-view drawing of the Republic XP-72. *US National Archives RG-342 via Tony Landis*

One of the more well-known views of the XP-72. Fitted with dual-rotation propellers, this was an impressive beast. *US National Archives RG-342 via Tony Landis*